Adirondack Mountain Club

Western Trails

Adirondack
ADK
Mountain Club

First Edition
Forest Preserve Series (4th ed.), Volume 4

Editors, Norm Landis and Bradly A. Pendergraft

Adirondack Mountain Club, Inc.
Lake George, New York

Copyright © 2016 by Adirondack Mountain Club, Inc.
All rights reserved
Cover photograph, the Moose River, by Chris Murray
Other photographs by James Appleyard, Nancie Battaglia, Mark Bowie, James Bullard, Stephanie Graudons, Mark Hemendinger, David Hough, Laurie Grover Humbolt, Joanne Kennedy, John Kettlewell, Norm Landis, Gerry Lemmo, Dick Mooers, Chris Murray, NYS DEC, Richard Nowicki, Jamie Savage, Betsy Tisdale, and Daniel Way
Page maps by Therese S. Brosseau
Overview map by Forest Glen Enterprises; redesigned by Therese S. Brosseau
Hiking boots illustration by Colette Piasecki-Masters
Design by Ann Hough
First edition published 2016, revised 2019

Published by the Adirondack Mountain Club, Inc.
814 Goggins Road, Lake George, NY 12845-4117 ▲ ADK.org
Working for Wilderness

ADK (Adirondack Mountain Club) is the only nonprofit organization dedicated to protecting and advocating for New York State's wild lands and waters while also teaching people how to enjoy natural places responsibly.

Library of Congress Cataloging-in-Publication Data

Names: Landis, Norm, 1949- | Pendergraft, Bradly A., 1953- | Adirondack Mountain Club.
Title: Adirondack Mountain Club Western Trails/ Editors, Norm Landis and Bradly A. Pendergraft.
Other titles: Adirondack Trails: West-Central Region, Adirondack Trails: Northern Region
Description: First Edition. | Lake George, NY: Adirondack Mountain Club, Inc., 2016. | Series: Forest Preserve Series (4th ed.); Volume 4 | Includes index.
Identifiers: LCCN 2015006216| ISBN 9780989607346 (Guidebook only) | ISBN 9780989607353 (Western Trails & map pack)
Subjects: LCSH: Hiking—New York (State)--Adirondack Park—Guidebooks. | Trails—New York (State) —Adirondack Park—Guidebooks. | Adirondack Park (N.Y.) —Guidebooks.
Classification: LCC GV199.42.N652 A3422 2016 | DDC 796.5109747/47--dc23
LC record available at http://lccn.loc.gov/2015006216

ISBN 978-0-9896073-4-6   Printed in the United States of America

25 24 23 22 21 20 19   2 3 4 5 6 7 8 9 10 11 12

Dedication

To outdoor "helpers," those who protect the environment and the people enjoying it: forest rangers, assistants, foresters, and trail and search crews.

—*Norm Landis*

Though my name is on the front cover of this book, it would not have been possible without previous editions of ADK's now-discontinued *Guide to Adirondack Trails: Northern Region*, written by Peter O'Shea. I have only continued to build the tower taller after Peter completed the hard work of digging and laying the foundation of the book on strong Adirondack bedrock. To quote Sir Isaac Newton, "If I have seen further, it is by standing on the shoulders of giants."

Peter is indeed a giant, a good friend, and an outstanding woodsman in the mold of the great Adirondack guides. He helped when asked, but his greatest gift to readers and to me was his extensive research and knowledge of the flora, fauna, history, and geography of the Adirondacks, which are still evident throughout this book.

In the many years I have known Peter, he has been a great advocate, lover, and defender of the Adirondacks. So it is with great pleasure that I dedicate this book to Peter O'Shea, thank Peter, and acknowledge his massive contributions. In fact, this book is as much his as it is mine.

—*Brad Pendergraft*

WE WELCOME YOUR COMMENTS

Use of information in this book is at the sole discretion and risk of the hiker. ADK makes every effort to keep our guidebooks up-to-date; however, trail conditions are always changing.

In addition to reviewing the material in this book, hikers should assess their ability, physical condition, and preparation, as well as likely weather conditions, before a trip. For more information on preparation, equipment, and how to address emergencies, see the introduction.

If you note a discrepancy in this book or wish to forward a suggestion, we welcome your comments. Please cite book title, year of most recent copyright and printing (see copyright page), trail, page number, and date of your observation. Thanks for your help!

Please address your comments to:
Publications
Adirondack Mountain Club
814 Goggins Road
Lake George, NY 12845-4117
518-668-4447
pubs@adk.org

24-HOUR EMERGENCY CONTACTS

In-town and roadside: **911**

Wilderness emergencies in the Adirondacks: DEC dispatch, **518-891-0235**

Wilderness emergencies elsewhere: **518-408-5850**, or toll-free **877-457-5680**

(See page 25 for more information)

Contents

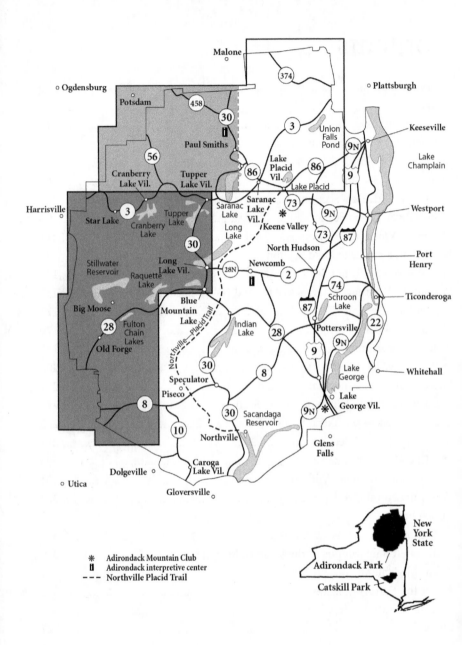

Malone

374

○ Ogdensburg

○ Plattsburgh

Potsdam

458

30

Paul Smiths

3

Union Falls Pond

Keeseville ●

9N

56

Tupper Lake Vil.

86

Lake Placid Vil.

86

Lake Champlain

Cranberry Lake Vil.

Saranac Lake

Saranac Lake Vil.

Lake Placid

9

Harrisville ○

3

Tupper Lake

Long Lake

73

9N

Westport ○

Star Lake

Cranberry Lake

✳

Keene Valley

73

87

Stillwater Reservoir

30

Raquette Lake

North Hudson

Port Henry ○

Big Moose

Long Lake Vil.

28N

Newcomb

2

87

74

Schroon Lake

22

Ticonderoga ○

28

Fulton Chain Lakes

Blue Mountain Lake

Indian Lake

28

Pottersville

9

Old Forge

8

30

Speculator

Piseco

9N

Lake George

Whitehall ○

8

10

30

Sacandaga Reservoir

9N

✳

Lake George Vil.

Northville

Glens Falls

Dolgeville ○

Caroga Lake Vil.

○ Utica

Gloversville ○

✳ Adirondack Mountain Club
ℹ Adirondack interpretive center
--- Northville Placid Trail

New York State

Adirondack Park

Catskill Park

Preface

Adirondack Mountain Club Western Trails, the fourth of six volumes in ADK's Forest Preserve Series, includes most of the area covered in ADK's former Northern region and West-Central region guidebooks, and some trails from the former Southern region guidebook. The region covered in this book is defined by the Adirondack Park boundary to the west, north, and south, and the villages of Paul Smiths, Tupper Lake, and Long Lake to the east. Rivers, flatlands, and mountains are found throughout the region, as well as numerous ponds and lakes.

This guide corresponds to National Geographic Trails Illustrated Map 745: Old Forge/Oswegatchie and the western side of National Geographic Trails Illustrated Map 746: Saranac/Paul Smiths. Both are large-format, two-sided, folding, waterproof maps created in partnership with the Adirondack Mountain Club.

Although the boundaries of the old guidebooks have changed, the area covered in this book remains the wildest part of the Adirondacks. Many have argued it is the wildest area in the eastern United States. Those seeking seclusion and an escape from the masses can find it here. The state's purchase of forest property formerly held by logging companies has greatly increased the percentage of public land holdings in the Adirondacks. This has resulted in an amazing number of new trails and canoeing opportunities. There are long trails to challenge the strongest hikers and short engaging hikes for the entire family.

The trails in the southern portion of this region (south side of T.I. Map 745 and a few trails on the north side) had been contained in ADK's West-Central guide. In the Independence River Wild Forest, the long-planned removal of the "East Bridge," accomplished in 2014, coincided with the Department of Environmental Conservation's decision to stop maintaining several trails in the area and the rerouting of a couple of others.

There are several parts of the Ha-De-Ron-Dah Wilderness Area and Black River Wild Forest where loops can be hiked. These allow for long hikes with little duplication. This section offers miles and miles of wilderness. It is possible to map out a multiday trip from trailheads off Number Four Road in Lewis County through the Independence River Wild Forest, crossing into the Ha-De-Ron-Dah Wilderness, then taking short on-road sections (out of the woods for less than an hour) either through Thendara or across NY 28 between Browns Tract and Nelson Lake into the Black River Wild Forest, to North Lake Road or Nobleboro in Herkimer County.

One of the most exciting additions to this guide is the

Lake Lila. Joanne Kennedy

William C. Whitney Wilderness Area and NY 30 Section, which includes both great hikes to remote lakes on old logging trails and great canoeing. Large and varied loops can be made by canoe and carry trails through Lows Lake, Lake Lila, Little Tupper Lake, and smaller lakes of the region.

The Paul Smiths Section includes some trails at Paul Smith's College, noted for its forestry and hotel management programs, and the site of the Visitor Interpretive Center (VIC). The VIC offers a great introduction to the area, with short family-friendly trails and more challenging hikes such as Jenkins Mt. Nearby St. Regis Mt. provides a strenuous hike with rewarding views and a soon-to-be-restored fire tower.

Grass River–White Hill Wild Forest Section describes many of the most beautiful and little known waterfalls in the Adirondacks. They are now open to the public after state purchase of land and easements from Champion International Corporation and Forestland Group in the Tooley Pond Tract. A wonder-filled day can be spent hopping from waterfall to waterfall on short trails off Tooley Pond Road.

Cranberry Lake–Wanakena Section has new trails and covers many of the trails formerly closed after the July 1995 derecho in the area of Star Lake–Cranberry Lake and Five Ponds Wilderness. These are back in service, many thanks to the help of volunteers. A new fifty-mile challenge, called the Cranberry Lake 50, has been developed based on new and old trails around Cranberry Lake. These trails are listed individually in Cranberry Lake–Wanakena Section and have also been placed in a new Cranberry Lake 50 Section. Here they are listed in order, proceeding in a counterclockwise direction starting at the Peavine Swamp Trail. Now in addition to climbing the forty-six major peaks in the Adirondacks or hiking the Northville-Placid Trail, hikers can tackle the challenge of the Cranberry Lake 50. The trails of this loop are much gentler than those of the High Peaks. They have something for everyone, and when the loop is completed hikers can join the Cranberry Lake 50 registry online and order an embroidered patch. In addition to hiking, some of the sections are open to bikes. Much of the circuit can be skied and sections of the trail can be accessed by canoe across Cranberry Lake.

The *Western Trails* region includes many short family-friendly hikes, such as Arab Mt., Coney Mt., and Goodman Mt. The last two mountains have new trails, while the Arab Mt. trail has been hardened with stone and wooden steps. All three provide the reward of an excellent view after a short hike. The Goodman Mt. trail was dedicated to Andrew Goodman, a civil rights worker murdered in 1964 while working to register voters in Mississippi. This trail not only provides a great hike, but also a valuable history lesson.

Trails described in this volume are located in the following management units:
- Wilderness Areas: Five Ponds, Ha-De-Ron-Dah, Pepperbox, Pigeon Lake, Round Lake, West Canada Lake, and William C. Whitney
- Wild Forest Areas: Aldrich Pond, Black River, Cranberry Lake, DeBar Mountain, Ferris Lake, Fulton Chain, Grass River, Independence River, Moose River Plains, Saranac Lakes, Sargent Ponds, Watsons East Triangle, and White Hill
- Canoe Area: St. Regis
- Primitive Area: Eastern Five Ponds Access (one trail)
- State Forests: Independence River, Otter Creek

There are many more new trails in this guide, and as you hike, canoe, ski, and travel on these trails, enjoy and take care of them, remembering that they are not only your trails, but also belong to our children.

—*Norm Landis*
Rome, New York
November 2016

—*Brad Pendergraft*
Parishville, New York
November 2016

Northville–Placid Trail. Joanne Kennedy

Introduction

The Adirondack Mountain Club Forest Preserve Series

The Forest Preserve Series of guides to Adirondack and Catskill trails covers hiking opportunities on the approximately 2.6 million acres of Forest Preserve (public) land within the Adirondack Park and close to 300,000 acres in the Catskill Park. The Adirondack Mountain Club (ADK) published its first guidebook, covering the High Peaks and parts of the Northville–Placid Trail, in 1934. In the early 1980s, coinciding with the decade-long centennial celebration of the enactment of the Forest Preserve legislation in 1885, ADK set out to achieve its goal of completing a series of guides that would cover the two parks. This series now includes the following guidebooks:

1 Adirondack Mountain Club High Peaks Trails
2 Adirondack Mountain Club Eastern Trails
3 Adirondack Mountain Club Central Trails
4 Adirondack Mountain Club Western Trails
5 Adirondack Mountain Club Northville–Placid Trail
6 Adirondack Mountain Club Catskill Trails

The public lands that constitute the Forest Preserve are unique among all other wild public lands in the United States because they enjoy constitutional protection against sale or development. The story of this unique protection begins in the 1800s and continues today as groups such as ADK strive to guard it. This responsibility also rests with members of the public, who are expected not to degrade the Forest Preserve in any way while enjoying its wonders. The Forest Preserve Series of trail guides seeks not only to show hikers, skiers, and snowshoers where to enjoy their activities, but also to offer guidelines whereby users can minimize their impact on the land.

THE ADIRONDACKS

The Adirondack region of northern New York is unique in many ways. It contains the only mountains in the eastern United States that are not geologically Appalachian. In the late 1800s it was the first forested area in the nation to benefit from enlightened conservation measures. At roughly the same time it was also the most prestigious resort area in the country. In the twentieth century, the Adirondacks became the only place in the Western Hemisphere to host two winter Olympiads. In the 1970s the region was the first of significant size in the nation to be subjected to comprehensive land-use controls. The Adirondack Forest Preserve (see below) is part of the only wild lands preserve in the nation whose fate lies in the hands of the voters of the entire state in which it is located.

Geologically, the Adirondacks are a southern appendage of the Canadian Shield. In the United States the Shield bedrock, which is over one billion years old, mostly lies concealed under younger rock, but it is well exposed in a few regions. Upward doming of the Adirondack mass in the past few million years—a process that is still going on, resulting in the mountains rising a few millimeters every century—is responsible for erosional stripping of the younger rock cover. The stream-carved topography has been extensively modified by the sculpting of glaciers, which, on at least four widely separated occasions during the Ice Age, completely covered the mountains.

Ecologically, the Adirondacks are part of a vegetation transition zone. The northern portion is largely a coniferous boreal forest. (Its name comes from the Greek god Boreas, owner of the north wind, whose name can be found on a mountain peak and series of ponds in the High Peaks region.) The southern zone is a deciduous forest, exemplified by beech-maple stands, intermingling to present a pleasing array of forest tree species. Different vegetation zones are also encountered as one ascends the higher mountains in the Adirondacks; the tops of the highest peaks are truly Arctic, with mosses and lichens that are common hundreds of miles to the north.

A rugged and heavily forested region, the Adirondacks were generally not hospitable to Native Americans, who used the region principally for hunting. Remnants of ancient campgrounds have been found in some locations. The native legacy survives principally in place names.

The first European to see the Adirondacks was likely the French explorer Jacques Cartier, who on his first trip up the St. Lawrence River in 1535 stood on top of Mont Royal (now within the city of Montreal) and discerned high ground to the south. Closer looks were had by Samuel de Champlain and Henry Hudson, who came from the north and south, respectively, within a few weeks of each other in 1609.

For the next two centuries the Champlain Valley to the east of the Adirondacks was a battleground. Iroquois, Algonquin, French, British, and eventually American fighters struggled for control over the valley, and with it, supremacy over the continent. Settlers slowly filled the St. Lawrence Valley to the north, the Mohawk Valley to the south, and somewhat later, the Black River Valley to the west. Meanwhile the vast, rolling forests of the interior slumbered in virtual isolation, disturbed only by an occasional hunter, timber cruiser, or wanderer.

With the coming of the nineteenth century, people discovered the Adirondacks. Virtually unknown as late as the 1830s (the source of the Nile River was located before the source of the Hudson), by 1850 the Adirondacks made New York the leading timber-producing state in the nation. This distinction did not last for long, though, as the supply of timber was quickly brought close to extinction. Meanwhile, mineral resources, particularly iron, were being exploited.

After the Civil War, people began to look toward the Adirondacks for recreation. At the same time, resource conservation and wilderness preservation ideas began to take hold, sometimes conflicting with the newfound recreational interests. Conservation and preservation concepts were given legal standing in 1885, when the New York State legislature created the Adirondack Forest Preserve and directed that "the lands now or hereafter constituting the Forest Preserve shall be forever kept as wild forest lands." This action marked the first time a state government had set aside a significant piece of wilderness for reasons other than its scenic uniqueness.

In 1892, the legislature created the Adirondack State Park, consisting of Adirondack Forest Preserve land plus all privately owned land within a somewhat arbitrary boundary surrounding the Adirondacks, known as the "blue line" because it was drawn in blue on a large state map when it was first established. In 1894, in response to continuing abuses of the Forest Preserve law, the state's voters approved the inclusion of the "forever wild" portion of that law in the constitution of New York State, thus creating the only preserve in the nation that has constitutional protection. Today the Forest Preserve (the lands owned by the people of the State of New York) includes 2.6 million acres within the 6-million-acre Adirondack Park, the largest park in the nation outside of Alaska.

After World War I, tourism gradually took over as the primary industry in the Adirondacks. The growth of the second-home industry spurred implementation of land use plans and an Adirondack Park Agency to manage them. Although the plans and the agency have remained controversial, they indicate the need to address the issues facing the Adirondacks boldly and innovatively.

STATE LAND UNITS AND CLASSIFICATIONS

Since 1972, most Forest Preserve lands in the Adirondacks have been classified as either Wilderness, Primitive, or Wild Forest, depending on the size of the unit and the types of use thought to be desirable for that unit. The largest and most remote units are generally Wilderness, with only foot travel permitted and minimum facilities, such as lean-tos.

Primitive areas are similar, but with a nonconforming "structure" such as a fire tower, road, or private inholding. Wild Forest areas are generally smaller but potentially more intensively used, with snowmobiles and mountain bikes permitted on designated trails. Management of each unit is prescribed in a unit management plan (UMP), which determines what facilities, such as trails or shelters, will be built and maintained as well as any special regulations needed to manage each unit effectively.

USING THIS GUIDEBOOK

Like all volumes in the ADK Forest Preserve Series of guides to Adirondack and Catskill trails, this book is intended to be both a reference tool for planning trips and a field guide to carry on the trail. All introductory material should be read carefully; it contains important information regarding current camping and hiking regulations as well as numerous suggestions for safe and proper travel by foot.

The guide is divided into geographic sections. The introduction to each gives

Legend

– – – – – – – –	Trail
= = = = = = =	Woods road with vehicular access
▶	Lean-to
▲	Summit
⋏	State campground
■	Outpost or lodge
♠⊠	Fire tower
P	Parking
—⑧—	State or local highway
—⟨9⟩—	U. S. highway
—(87)—	Interstate highway
+—+—+—+—+	Railroad
	Private land
	Stream or river
	Lake or pond
⚘ ⚘ ⚘	Wetland

hikers an idea of the opportunities available in that area as well as information on facilities and regulations common to that section. Each section introduction also provides recommended hikes in the "short," "moderate," and "harder" categories. Many of these recommended hikes incorporate lesser-used trails in an attempt to make hikers aware of the many beautiful and seldom-visited places aside from the most popular hiking, climbing, and camping areas.

MAPS

Every guidebook is this series matches trail information provided on National Geographic Trails Illustrated maps

---

SO WHAT IF IT'S NOT MAINTAINED?

Hikers in the Adirondacks should note the nuances of route terminology.

A formal, DEC-marked trail and a bushwhack form the bookends of hiking possibilities in the Adirondacks—with lots of range in between. Unmaintained trails, unmarked trails, "trailless" routes, and herd paths have two things in common: they lack official DEC signs and markers, and they may necessitate advanced orientation skills.

Unmarked paths can range from reasonably well-trodden, well-defined routes with cairns to a whisper of a track with no discernible tread. A hiker's experience with one kind of unmarked path doesn't necessarily assist him or her on another.

Hikers should carry a map and compass and know how to use them. They shouldn't let past experience inspire false confidence or tempt them to forgo packing a map and compass.

---

to the Adirondack and Catskill Parks. These large-format, two-sided, folding, waterproof maps were created in partnership with ADK. Together the guides and maps are vital hiking tools, the latter also serving as road maps within the Adirondack and Catskill Parks. The following list identifies each map and the Forest Preserve Series guide to which it corresponds. All are available from ADK.

ADK Guide	Trails Illustrated Map	Additional Information
High Peaks Trails	742 Lake Placid/High Peaks	
	746 Saranac/Paul Smiths	E side covers N High Peaks
Eastern Trails	743 Lake George/Great Sacandaga	
Central Trails	744 Northville/Raquette Lake	
Western Trails	745 Old Forge/Oswegatchie	
	746 Saranac/Paul Smiths	W side covers NW portion of Western region
Northville-Placid Trail	736 Northville-Placid Trail	
Catskill Trails	755 Catskill Park	

These maps are letter-number coded, with letters running up and down the

MOBILE PHONES

Mobile phones can't always be relied upon in case of an emergency in the backcountry. Despite many highly publicized stories, their use is limited by terrain, distance from communication towers, battery life, and other factors.

Those who carry them should, out of consideration for their fellow hikers, use them only when necessary—and should have alternative plans for handling emergencies in case they do not operate.

If you must use your mobile phone in an emergency, it is sometimes possible to obtain better range and reception by moving to a higher elevation and/or an area where you are not blocked by steep cliffs or other obstructions.

right and left borders, and numbers running horizontally along the top and bottom. Each trail's coordinate appears with the corresponding description in this book (sample coordinate: A4), and each trail is numbered on the map and in the book. These numbers are not used on signs on the trails.

A few hike descriptions are supported by maps located within the text. See the map legend on p. 14 for symbols used on the page maps.

All of the maps discussed in the preceding are available from ADK, as is ADK's pocket-size, waterproof topographic map, *Trails of the Adirondack High Peaks,* which corresponds to the series' first volume, *High Peaks Trails.*

Other maps, guidebooks, and information also can be obtained from ADK's Member Services Center in Lake George and the High Peaks Information Center on ADK's Heart Lake Property near Lake Placid.

ABBREVIATIONS AND CONVENTIONS

In each of the books in the Forest Preserve Series, *R* and *L*, with periods omitted, are used for right and left. The R and L banks of a stream are determined by looking downstream. Likewise, the R fork of a stream is on the R when one faces downstream. *N, S, E,* and *W,* again without periods, are used for north, south, east, and west. Compass bearings are given in degrees. *N* is 0 degrees, *E* is 90 degrees, *S* is 180 degrees, and *W* is 270 degrees.

The following abbreviations are used in the text:
ADK   Adirondack Mountain Club
APA   Adirondack Park Agency
ATV   all-terrain vehicle
DEC   New York State Department of Environmental Conservation
GPS   Global Positioning System
PBM   permanent benchmark
USGS United States Geological Survey
4WD   four-wheel-drive vehicle
ft   foot or feet
jct.   junction
km   kilometer or kilometers
m   meter or meters

mi	mile or miles
yd	yard or yards

TRAIL SIGNS AND MARKERS

Marked and maintained DEC trails for Adirondack hikers, cross-country skiers, snowshoers, and snowmobilers tend to have signs posted at trailheads and major trail junctions. Trail signs usually give the distance to named locations on the trail.

Trail markers are plastic disks placed on trees or posts along the trails and on the signs at trailheads and junctions. The color and type of marker used on a trail is included in the descriptions in this book. (Painted blazes on trees generally indicate property boundaries and should not be confused with trail markers.)

With normal alertness to one's surroundings and exceptions made for lightly traveled trails, most marked trails are easy to follow. Although this guidebook does mention particularly tricky turns or trails that might pose special difficulties, each hiker must remain alert at all times for changes of direction. Group leaders have a particular responsibility not to let inexperienced members of their party travel by themselves. A trail that seems obvious to a more experienced person may not be that way at all to an inexperienced member of the group.

GPS

Many hikers use GPS navigation devices and mobile phones equipped with GPS to find trailheads and navigate the backcountry. Be sure to practice these skills before needing them in a remote area. Keep in mind that GPS reception in some areas may be limited owing to surrounding steep terrain and heavy forest cover. And, like all electronic devices, an unintended dip in an icy stream or a lack of fresh batteries can put your equipment out of commission for the rest of your trip.

Prudent hikers will not rely solely on electronic gear. Always carry a map, a guidebook, and a compass, and know how to use them.

National Geographic Trails Illustrated maps are designed to be compatible with GPS. The maps include latitude and longitude markings, as well as UTM grids.

One should never remove any sign or marker. Hikers noticing damaged or missing signs should report this to the DEC.

All trails described in this guide are on public land or public rights-of-way that cross private land. The continued goodwill of public-spirited landowners is directly dependent upon the manner in which the public uses this land. The "posted" signs occasionally found on rights-of-way serve to remind hikers that they are on private land over which the owner has granted permission for hikers to pass. In most cases, leaving the trail, camping, fishing, and hunting are not permitted on these lands. Hikers should respect the owner's wishes.

DISTANCE AND TIME

Trails in this guidebook have been measured with a professional surveyor's wheel and in some cases using GPS devices. Distances are expressed to the nearest tenth of a mile. Shorter distances are expressed as yards, and the number of yards has usually been derived from a wheel measurement in the field.

NOTE: Where there is disagreement between a sign and the guide's stated distance, the latter can be assumed to be correct. DEC has been informed of these discrepancies.

The start of each section of this guide includes a list of trails in the region, the mileage unique to the trail, and the page on which the trail description begins. All mileages given in the trail description are cumulative, the beginning of the trail being the 0.0 mile point. A distance summary is given at the end of each description, with a total distance expressed in kilometers as well as miles. If a trail has climbed significantly over its course, its total ascent in feet and meters is provided.

To the inexperienced hiker, distances are likely to seem longer on the trail, depending on the weight of the pack, the time of day, and the frequency and degree of ascents and descents. He or she will quickly learn that there is a significant difference between "sidewalk miles" and "trail miles."

No attempt has been made to estimate travel time for these trails. A conservative rule to follow in estimating time is to allow an hour for every one and one-half miles, plus one half-hour for each one thousand feet of ascent, letting experience indicate how close the individual hiker is to this standard. Most day hikers will probably go a little faster than this, but backpackers will probably find they go somewhat slower. Some quickening of pace usually occurs when descending, though this may not be true on steep descents.

DAY HIKING and WILDERNESS CAMPING

It is not the purpose of this series to teach one how to hike or camp. The information below should, however, serve to make hikers aware of the differences and peculiarities of New York's backcountry while giving strong emphasis to currently recommended procedures for reducing environmental damage—particularly in heavily used areas. Users who intend to hike or camp for the first time are urged to consult a current book on the subject, attend one of the many workshops or training sessions available, or at least join a group led by someone with experience.

Except for Johns Brook Lodge, 3.5 miles up the Marcy Trail from Keene Valley (*Adirondack Mountain Club High Peaks Trails*), there are no huts in the Adirondacks or Catskills for public use, such as are common in the White Mountains of New Hampshire. There are many lean-tos at convenient locations along trails and also many possibilities for tenting. The regulations regarding tenting and the use of lean-tos are simple and unrestrictive compared to those of other popular backpacking areas in the United States and Canada. It is important that every backpacker know and obey the restrictions that do exist because they are designed to promote the long-term enjoyment and protection of the resource.

The following are some of the most important Forest Preserve regulations, many of which pertain to day hikers as well. Complete regulations and recent

LEAVE NO TRACE

ADK supports the seven principles of the Leave No Trace program:

1. Plan Ahead and Prepare
Know the regulations and special considerations for the area you'll visit.
Prepare for extreme weather, hazards, and emergencies.
Travel in groups of less than ten people to minimize impacts.

2. Travel and Camp on Durable Surfaces
Hike in the middle of the trail; stay off of vegetation.
Camp in designated sites where possible.
In other areas, don't camp within 150 feet of water or a trail.

3. Dispose of Waste Properly
Pack out all trash (including toilet paper), leftover food, and litter.
Use existing privies, or dig a cathole five to six inches deep,
then cover the hole.
Wash yourself and dishes at least 150 feet from water.

4. Leave What You Find
Leave rocks, plants, and other natural objects as you find them.
Let photos, drawings, or journals help to capture your memories.
Do not build structures or furniture or dig trenches.

5. Minimize Campfire Impacts
Use a portable stove to avoid the lasting impact of a campfire. Where fires are
permitted, use existing fire rings and only collect downed wood. Burn all fires
to ash, put out campfires completely, then hide traces of fire.

6. Respect Wildlife
Observe wildlife from a distance.
Avoid wildlife during mating, nesting, and other sensitive times.
Control pets at all times, and clean up after them.

7. Be Considerate of Other Visitors
Respect other visitors and protect the quality of their experience.
Let natural sounds prevail; avoid loud sounds and voices.
Be courteous and yield to other users on the trail.

For further information on Leave No Trace principles,
log on to www.lnt.org.

updates can be found at the DEC website (www.dec.ny.gov).

• Except where marked by a "Camp Here" disk, camping is prohibited within 150 feet of roads, trails, lakes, ponds, streams, or other bodies of water.

• Groups of ten or more persons camping (nine in the High Peaks Region) *or* groups of any size staying more than three days in one place require a permit from the New York State Forest Ranger responsible for the area.

• Lean-tos are available in many areas on a first-come, first-served basis. Lean-tos cannot be used exclusively and must be shared with other campers.

• Use pit privies provided near popular camping areas and trailheads. If none are available, dispose of human waste by digging a hole six to eight inches deep at least 150 feet from water or campsites. Cover with leaves and soil.

• Do not use soap to wash yourself, clothing, or dishes within 150 feet of water.

• Fires should be built in existing fire pits or fireplaces if provided. Use only dead and down wood for fires. Cutting standing trees is prohibited. Extinguish all fires with water and stir ashes until they are cold to the touch. Do not build fires in areas marked by a "No Fires" disk or sign. Camp stoves are safer, more efficient, and cleaner.

• At all times, only emergency fires are permitted above 4000 feet in the Adirondacks and 3500 feet in the Catskills.

• Carry out what you carry in. Use Leave No Trace practices (see p. 19).

• Keep your pet under control. Restrain it on a leash when others approach. Collect and bury droppings away from water, trails, and campsites. Keep your pet away from drinking water sources.

• Observe and enjoy wildlife and plants, but leave them undisturbed.

• Removing plants, rocks, fossils, or artifacts from state land without a permit is illegal.

• Do not feed any wild animals.

• Store food properly to keep it away from animals—particularly bears.

• No camping is permitted above 4000 feet (1219 meters) at any time of the year in the Adirondacks.

• Except in an emergency or between December 21 and March 21, camping is prohibited above an elevation of 3500 feet in the Catskills.

LEAN-TOS

Lean-tos are available on a first-come, first-served basis up to the capacity of the shelter—usually about eight persons. Thus a small party cannot claim exclusive use of a shelter and must allow late arrivals equal use. Most lean-tos have a fireplace in front (sometimes with a primitive grill) and sanitary facilities. Most are located near some source of water, but each camper must use his or her own judgment as to whether or not the water supply needs purification before drinking. Carving or writing one's initials in a shelter is in very poor taste. Please try to keep these rustic shelters in good condition and appearance.

Because reservations cannot be made for any of these shelters, hikers often carry a tent or other alternate shelter. Many shelters away from the standard routes, however, are seldom used, and a small party can often find a shelter open in the more remote areas.

The following regulations apply specifically to lean-tos, in addition to the general camping regulations listed above:
- No plastic may be used to close off the front of a shelter.
- No nails or other permanent fastener may be used to affix a tarp in a lean-to, but it is permissible to use rope to tie canvas or nylon tarps across the front.
- No tent may be pitched inside a lean-to.

GROUPS

Any group of ten or more persons or smaller groups intending to camp at one location three nights or longer must obtain a permit before camping on state land. A permit is also required for group events, including day hikes, involving more than twenty people. This system is designed to prevent overuse of certain critical sites and also to encourage groups to split into smaller parties.

Permits can be obtained from the New York State Forest Ranger closest to the actual starting point of one's proposed trip. The local forest ranger can be contacted by writing directly; if in doubt about whom to contact, send a letter to the DEC Lands and Forests Division Office address for the county in which your trip will take place. They will forward the letter to the proper ranger. Be sure to write early enough to allow a response before your trip date.

BEAR CANISTERS

Bears in many parts of the Adirondacks have figured out the long-popular campers' technique of hanging food from a rope strung between two trees. Thus the DEC recommends—in some cases requires—the use of bear-resistant, food-storage canisters.
- Bear canisters are required in the Eastern High Peaks Wilderness Area April 1 through November 30.
- The canisters can be obtained from many outdoor retailers, borrowed from many ADK chapters, or rented or purchased at ADK's Heart Lake or Lake George facilities. The canisters also protect food from many smaller forest creatures.
- The DEC's current management goal with respect to bears is to educate campers about proper food storage. Bears unable to get food from campers will, it is hoped, return to their natural diet. Thus campers play an important role in helping to restore the natural balance between bears and humans. Losing one's food to a bear should be recognized as a critical failure in achieving this goal.

One can also make the initial contact with the forest ranger by telephone (see p. 22). Note that forest rangers' schedules during the busy summer season are often unpredictable. Forest rangers are listed in the white pages of local phone books under "New York, State of; Environmental Conservation, Department of; Forest Ranger." Bear in mind when calling that most rangers operate out of their private homes; observe the normal courtesy used when calling a private residence. Contact by letter is much preferred. Camping with a large group requires careful planning with a lead time of several weeks to ensure a happy, safe outing.

DEC CONTACT INFORMATION FOR PLANNING

Region 5
Ray Brook, general information: 518-897-1200
Rangers: 518-897-1300
Environmental conservation officers: 518-897-1326
Northville: 518-863-4545

Region 6
Herkimer: 315-866-6330
Lowville: 315-376-3521
Potsdam: 315-265-3090

FOREST SAFETY

The routes described in this guidebook vary from wide, well-marked DEC trails to narrow, unmarked footpaths that have become established through long use. With normal alertness and careful preparation the hiker should have few problems in land navigation. Nevertheless, careful map study and route planning are fundamental necessities. Hikers should never expect immediate help should an emergency occur. This is particularly true in winter, when fewer people are on the trails and weather is a more significant factor.

In addition to a map, all hikers should carry a compass and know at least the basics of its use. In some descriptions, the Forest Preserve Series uses compass bearings to differentiate trails at a junction or to indicate the direction of travel above timberline. More important, a compass can be an indispensable aid in the event that you lose your way.

Winter trips, especially, must be carefully planned. Travel over ice on ski and snowshoe trips must be done with caution. The possibility of freezing rain, snow, and cold temperatures should be considered from early September until late May. True winter conditions can commence as early as November and last well into April, particularly at higher altitudes. It is highly recommended that hikers travel in parties of at least four people, be outfitted properly, rest when the need arises, and drink plenty of water. Leave trip plans with someone at home and then keep to your itinerary.

DRINKING WATER

For many years, hikers could trust almost any water source in the backcountry to be pure and safe to drink. Unfortunately, as in many other mountain areas, some water sources have become contaminated with a parasite known as *Giardia lamblia*.

This intestinal parasite causes a disease known as giardiasis—often called "beaver fever." It can be spread by any warm-blooded mammal when infected feces wash into the water; beavers are prime agents in transferring this parasite because they spend so much time in and near water. Hikers themselves have also become primary agents in spreading this disease because some individuals appear to be unaffected carriers of the disease, and other recently infected individuals may inadvertently spread the parasite before their symptoms become apparent.

Prevention: Follow the guidelines for the disposal of human excrement as stated above. Equally important, make sure that every member of your group is aware of the problem and follows the guidelines as well. The health of a fellow hiker may depend on your consideration.

Water Treatment: No water source can be guaranteed to be safe. Boil all water for two to three minutes, utilize an iodine-based chemical purifier (available at camping supply stores and some drug and department stores), or use a commercial filter designed specifically for giardiasis prevention. If after returning from a trip you experience recurrent intestinal problems, consult your physician and explain your potential problem.

Ann Hough

HUNTING SEASONS

Unlike the national park system, public lands within the Adirondack and Catskill state parks are open to sport hunting. There are separate rules and seasons for each type of hunting (small game, waterfowl, and big game), but it is the big-game season (i.e., deer and bear) that is most likely to concern hikers.

Try to avoid the opening and closing day of regular deer season. For safety, wear a bright-colored outer garment; orange is recommended. Avoid heavily hunted areas during big-game seasons. Because it is difficult to carry a deer or bear carcass long distances or over steep terrain, hikers will find few hunters more than a mile from a roadway or in rugged mountain country. Lower slopes of beech, maple, and hemlock have much more hunting pressure than cripplebush, spruce, and balsam fir on upper slopes. Motorized vehicles are not allowed in areas designated as Wilderness, so hike there; most areas designated as Wild Forest have woods roads where vehicles can be used, so avoid these areas, which are likely to be favored by hunters.

ADK does not promote hunting as one of its organized activities, but it does recognize that sport hunting, when carried out in compliance with the game laws administered by the DEC, is a legitimate sporting activity.

Big-game seasons in the Adirondacks are usually as follows:
• Early Bear Season (some wildlife management units only): The first Saturday after the second Monday in September through the day immediately preceding early muzzle-loading season.
• Early Bowhunting Season (bear): The first Saturday after the second Monday in September through the day immediately preceding the regular season.
• Early Bowhunting Season (deer): September 27 through the Friday immediately preceding the regular season.

• Early Muzzle-loading Season (deer and bear): Seven consecutive days beginning the first Saturday after Columbus Day.
• Regular Season (deer and bear): Forty-four consecutive days beginning the second Saturday after Columbus Day.
• Late Bow and Muzzleloading Season (deer; some wildlife management units only): Seven consecutive days immediately following the regular season.

On occasion, special situations require DEC to modify the usual dates of hunting seasons. See DEC's website (www.dec.ny.gov) for updates.

BEAR SAFETY

Most wildlife in the Adirondacks and Catskills are little more than a minor nuisance around the campsite. Generally, the larger the animal the more timid it is in the presence of humans. The exception is the bear, which can be emboldened by the aroma of food and quickly habituate to human food sources.

The following tips will reduce the likelihood of an encounter with a bear.
• Never keep food in your tent or lean-to.
• Use bear-resistant canisters. DEC requires their use by campers in the Eastern High Peaks Wilderness Area between April 1 and November 30.
• In other areas, use a canister or hang food at least fifteen feet off the ground from a rope strung between two trees that are at least fifteen feet apart and one hundred feet from the campsite. (Hangs using a single branch and one tree have a high failure rate.) Using dark-colored rope tied off five or more feet above the ground makes it less likely that a foraging bear will see the line or find it while sniffing along the ground.
• Wrap aromatic foods well.
• Plan carefully to keep trash and leftovers to a minimum. Wrap in sealed containers such as large Ziploc bags, and hang or place in canister.
• Hang your pack, along with clothing worn during cooking.
• Keep a garbage-free fire pit, preferably away from your camping area.
• Should a bear appear, do not provoke it by throwing objects or approaching it. Bang pots, blow a whistle, shout, or otherwise try to drive it off with sharp noises. Should this fail, leave the scene.
• Report bear encounters to a forest ranger.

RABIES ALERT

Rabies infestation has been moving north through New York State. Although it is most often associated with raccoons, any warm-blooded mammal can be a carrier.

Although direct contact with a rabid animal in the forest is not likely, some precautions are advisable:
• Do not feed or pet any wild animals, under any circumstances.
• Particularly avoid any wild animals that seem to be behaving strangely.
• If bitten by a wild animal, seek medical attention immediately.

EMERGENCY PROCEDURES

All backcountry emergency assistance, including help from the local ranger, is dispatched from the following hotlines. Make sure the person going for help has these telephone numbers as well as a complete written description of the type and exact location of the accident. A location marked on the map or UTM grid coordinates can be very helpful. If possible, leave a call-back number in the event those responding to the incident require additional information.

- **For all backcountry emergencies in the Adirondacks,** call the DEC 24-hour hotline: 518-891-0235.
- **For backcountry emergencies elsewhere,** call 518-408-5850; or toll-free, 877-457-5680; or 911.

Calling one of the DEC numbers is preferable to calling 911. At the DEC emergency number, the caller is usually able to speak directly with someone knowledgeable about the area where the accident has occurred. Mobile phone callers are especially prone to problems because the call may be picked up by a distant tower in a neighboring jurisdiction (or even a different state) with the message then having to be relayed through several agencies.

BUG-BORNE DISEASES

Although not unique to the Adirondacks and Catskills, two pests found in these areas have the potential to carry diseases. Mosquitoes can transmit viral encephalitis (inflammation of the brain) and deer ticks can spread Lyme disease and other diseases. These are issues of particular concern in the Catskills.

In both instances, protection is advisable. Wear long pants and long-sleeved shirts and apply an insect repellent with the recommended percentage of N, N-diethyl-meta-toluamide (commonly known as DEET); treating clothing with a permethrin product is a well-established and safe preventive measure. On returning home, thoroughly inspect yourself, and wash yourself and your clothing immediately. Seek immediate attention if any early symptoms (rash, headache, fever) arise.

Independence River below Gleason Falls. Richard Nowicki

Independence River Section

The land in this section does not have high relief; in fact, it is among the flattest areas in the entire Adirondack Park. Although the trails have plenty of minor ups and downs, there are no peaks to scale. Trails in this section generally do not go to one particular hill or lake, but take the hiker on a meandering course through forests, past pretty ponds, and along fast-running water.

There are also a number of horse trails, which are popular with cross-country skiers.

Those traveling through Lowville may want to visit the Lowville Demonstration Area NE of town on the W side of NY 812. (Parking can be found next to a fire tower just S of the DEC offices.) A nature trail there helps visitors learn how to identify trees. There is also a fishing access site for the disabled across the road on the Black River.

The trails of this section are accessible from various roads leading off Erie Canal Rd. (N–S along the Blue Line) or from Number Four Rd.–Stillwater Rd. between Lowville and Stillwater. In general, available highway maps do not show the necessary rural roads along the Blue Line. A Lewis County highway map is an aid for people intending to hike in this section. These are $3 each (verify cost at 315-376-5350) with a check to Lewis County Highway Dept., 7660 State St., Lowville, NY 13367. The map shows state, county, and town roads, but not private roads, such as the continuation from the end of a town road on a "road" (single lane with bedrock outcroppings and sharp turns) to the Stony Lake trailhead, for example (see Fish Trail, trail 13). Another example is the drivable portion of the snowmobile trail of Steam Mill Rd. at Brantingham to Drunkard Creek trailhead (see Pine Lake Trail, trail 54). The county map does show the change between Erie Canal Rd. in the town of Watson to Chases Lake Rd. in the town of Greig, and the strange swing NE of Beach Mill Rd. for the Beach Mill Pond (and Gleasmans Falls) trailhead (Beach Mill Pond Trail, trail 2).

A few suggested hikes for this section are listed below.

SHORT HIKES
Payne Lake Horse Trail: 1.8 mi (2.9 km) round-trip. Interesting pine hills and sandy flats above and beyond Payne Lake. See trail 4.

Panther Pond: 2.6 mi (4.2 km) round-trip. Panther Pond and lean-to are an excellent setting for a quiet summer day of lounging. See trail 18.

Sunday Lake: 0.8 mi (1.3 km) round-trip. Nice lake. Easy walk except for some rutted spots in the old road. See trail 19.

MODERATE HIKE

Gleasmans Falls: 5.8 mi (9.3 km) round-trip on Beach Mill Pond Trail (trail 2). Five and 10 ft thundering falls in a narrow gorge, with views straight down, if you wish. Be sure to step out for a look on the boulder-strewn riverbed below the falls at the crossing of Second Creek.

1 Halfmoon Lake

Trails Illustrated Map 745: R2

Halfmoon Lake was once the site of a private camp. Traces of the home site and other improvements are still visible. Halfmoon Lake is small and surrounded by white pines. The stream crossing requires worrisome wading or good athletic ability.

▶Trailhead: From Lowville, turn E on River Rd. and go 4.1 mi to Watson. Turn L on Number Four Rd., and go 8.9 mi to a small dirt road on the R (S) with posted land on either side (1 mi past the Adirondack Park boundary). The road is not marked and is easy to miss. The placement of the posted signs creates the impression that the road is also posted; it is not.

From the E, it is 4.5 mi from the Stillwater Rd.–Number Four Rd. jct. Turn S on the dirt road, and pass some private dirt roads on the R. Go 1.4 mi to a Y jct., turn R, and go another 0.1 mi. Park in the small unmarked space on the R. There are no trail markers.◄

From the trailhead (0.0 mi), the old road goes slightly downhill to a bulldozed barrier at Burnt Creek. The washed-out bridge beyond left a hole in the trail only partly covered by boulders; it will probably require wading. There are no plans to replace the bridge. After the creek crossing, a small climb uphill is followed by level terrain through white pines. There's another crossing at Tuttle Creek.

After the second creek, the route turns farther E and meets the outlet of Halfmoon Lake at 0.9 mi. Proceeding around the shore, the route ends on a peninsula at 1 mi at the site of a former summer home. This spot is beautiful and peaceful.

❄ Trail in winter: Suitable for snowshoeing or backcountry skiing, but the creek crossing can be treacherous if not fully crusted over. Winter parking is along Number Four Rd.

ⵜ Distances: Number Four Rd. to trailhead, by car, 1.5 mi; from trailhead to Halfmoon Lake, 1 mi (1.6 km).

2 Beach Mill Pond Trail

Trails Illustrated Map 745: Q3

The trail starts near the outlet of a wetland that was once Beach Mill Pond. The dam and mill are long gone. This route connects the Blue Line region with the interior of the Independence River Wild Forest, but is more notable for the fact that it passes Gleasmans Falls on the Independence River. The falls are of modest height, but pass through a narrow gorge, with the trail offering views from 50 ft straight above. They are well worth the trip.

►Trailhead: From Lowville, turn E on River Rd. and go 4.1 mi to Watson. Turn L on Number Four Rd. Go 2.7 mi and turn R on Loson Rd., going 0.4 mi to McPhilmy Rd. Turn R. Proceed 2.5 mi, crossing Erie Canal Rd. and continuing on a dirt road to unmarked Beach Mill Rd. (dirt), L. Turn L and go 3 mi on Beach Mill Rd., keeping L at a split in the road where Cleveland Lake Rd. goes R, to the barrier and trailhead parking.◄

From the parking lot (0.0 mi), the yellow-marked trail turns S, descends the creek bank, and crosses the creek headed E. After a trail register, the old road climbs very gently NE toward the remains of Beach Mill Pond, then turns farther E and ascends to easy hilltop walking. Watch for a marvelous white pine beside the trail in these uplands.

A gradual turn to the SE eventually leads back to low lands and the Independence River at 2.5 mi, at the point where Second Creek reaches the river. The wide, boulder-strewn riverbed to the R is worth a side trip for the view up toward the falls.

Not long after the trail crosses Second Creek, the falls can be heard ahead. The trail reaches solid rock and approaches the gorge at an informal campsite at 2.9 mi, then follows in and out along the cliffs above, finally approaching the top of the highest falls (10 ft) at 3.1 mi. Beyond the falls, the trail is almost unused, but is generally well marked. The trail is mostly easy, though an exception occurs soon after the falls.

At 3.4 mi, the route approaches the riverbank, but bypasses this wetland by turning L and skirting a beaver pond. It turns E to go alongside an embankment that dams yet another beaver pond above. The high bank seems out of place and human-made, but is no doubt natural. The trail goes below the short beaver dam at its E end and crosses the creek. It may take a little searching to recognize the trail. Continue L (E) on the trail through another short wetland.

Once out of the area of beaver activity, the trail goes E for a short way, then turns N to skirt a private parcel of land. The route is obscure; watch carefully for the yellow trail markers.

The route goes N for 0.4 mi, then turns E into another large beaver pond. Cross on the 200 ft long beaver dam, then go L for about 50 ft to regain the trail. The next 0.4 mi E is decently marked, but the footpath is obscure and on uneven ground (with thin soil that barely covers an enormous field of boulders). The route crosses a creek on a fine bridge at 5.3 mi and turns S on the hillside beyond. Be careful to follow the yellow-marked route S and not the well-worn unmarked trail that goes R onto private land at about the same location.

Continuing S along the hillside, the path curves E as it approaches Third Creek, then turns S to cross it. After another small hill, the route finally approaches the Independence River after joining with an old road to the private land just bypassed (turn L when you reach this road). This road crosses the river at a fording place, while the trail goes L and continues along the N bank for another 0.4 mi.

Finally, at 7.1 mi, the trail reaches a jct. at the Independence River West Bridge. Across the river, Fish Trail (trail 13) goes 1.7 mi to Stony Lake Rd., roughly accessible by car. Using Mt. Tom and Silvermine Trails (trails 14 and 50), Partridgeville Rd. out of Brantingham can be crossed to make connections (via trail 51, for example) to Ha-de-ron-dah Wilderness Area. (See Brantingham and Old Forge–Thendara Sections.) Eastward and then northward, Panther Pond–Independence River Trail (trail 18) goes to a trailhead at Smith Rd. in 5 mi.

❀ Trail in winter: Suitable for snowshoeing and backcountry skiing, but Beach Mill Rd. is not plowed in winter. This adds 3 mi to the trip from Erie Canal Rd. Snowmobiles use Beach Mill Rd.

🐾 Distances: Beach Mill Rd. trailhead to Gleasmans Falls, 2.9 mi; to Independence River West Bridge, 7.1 mi (11.4 km); to Smith Rd. trailhead, 12.1 mi; to Stony Lake Rd. trailhead, 8.8 mi (14.1 km).

3 Beach Mill Horse Trail

Trails Illustrated Map 745: R2

This trail goes through semi-open pine plains with sandy soil. Its major attraction is the pleasant, easy walking and the interesting plant life that survives on rather infertile sandy soil. It is short enough to allow an easy loop trip, including the soft, sandy road-walk back to the car.

▶Trailhead: From Lowville, turn E on River Rd. Proceed 4.1 mi to Watson. Turn L on Number Four Rd., go 2.7 mi, and turn R on Loson Rd. Proceed 0.4 mi to McPhilmy Rd., then turn R. After 2.5 mi, cross Erie Canal Rd. and continue on a dirt road to unmarked Beach Mill Rd.(dirt), L. Turning L, go 2 mi on Beach Mill Rd. to the first trailhead or 2.5 mi to the second trailhead, both on the L side. ◀

Starting from the W trailhead (0.0 mi), the blue-marked horse trail goes almost straight N from the road, turns E at 0.4 mi, turns S at 1 mi, and reaches the second trailhead at 1.2 mi. The terrain is remarkably level and pleasant going.

❄ Trail in winter: Suitable for snowshoeing or skiing, but snowmobiles may be active. Beach Mill Rd. is not plowed in winter.

🏵 Distances: Trailhead to trailhead, 1.2 mi (1.9 km).

4 Payne Lake Horse Trail

Trails Illustrated Map 745: Q2

Payne Lake is quiet and scenic, with sandy soil and surrounding evergreens. The high sand bank on the N side of the lake gives the trail some elevation, with one small scenic vista.

▶Trailheads: To reach the N end, from Lowville, turn E on River Rd., go 4.1 mi to Watson, and turn L on Number Four Rd. Proceed 2.7 mi and turn R on Loson Rd., going 0.4 mi to McPhilmy Rd. Turn R. Go 2.5 mi, crossing Erie Canal Rd. and continuing on a dirt road to unmarked Beach Mill Rd., L (also dirt). Turn L and go 2 mi on Beach Mill Rd. to the trailhead on the R.

To reach the S end, proceed from Lowville as above to unmarked Beach Mill Rd., L (dirt). Turn L and go 1 mi on Beach Mill Rd. to Cleveland Lake Rd. Turn R and go 0.6 mi to an unmarked fork in the road. The trail is on the L at the fork. It is a blue-marked horse trail. ◀

Starting at the N trailhead (0.0 mi), the blue-marked horse trail goes through open scrub, briefly joins an old road, and finally plunges into white pine forest at 0.5 mi. The trail climbs briefly to reach a long, narrow ridge above Payne Lake. The pines almost mask the lake, allowing just a hint of a view. The vista is somewhat better at a rail and bench found near the W end of the lake at 0.7 mi. From here, the trail slowly descends through an open forest of large pines to Cleveland Rd. near the W end of the lake at 0.9 mi.

❄ Trail in winter: Suitable for snowshoeing or skiing, but snowmobiles may be active. Beach Mill Rd. is not plowed in the winter.

ᴹ Distances: N trailhead to Payne Lake ridge, 0.5 mi; to S trailhead, 0.9 mi (1.4 km).

5 Cleveland Lake Horse Trail

Trails Illustrated Map 745: Q2

▶Trailheads: To reach the N trailhead, turn E from Lowville on River Rd., go 4.1 mi to Watson, and turn L on Number Four Rd. Proceed 2.7 mi and turn R on Loson Rd., going 0.4 mi to McPhilmy Rd. Turn R. Go 2.5 mi, crossing Erie Canal Rd. and continuing on a dirt road to unmarked Beach Mill Rd., L (also dirt). Turn L, go 2.5 mi on Beach Mill Rd. to the trail on the R.

To reach the S trailhead, proceed as above to unmarked Beach Mill Rd., L (dirt). Turn L and go 1 mi on Beach Mill Rd. to Cleveland Lake Rd. Turn R and go 0.6 mi to an unmarked fork in the road. Take the R fork and continue for 0.5 mi. The trail is on the L, just inside private land. The prudent course is to park about 0.1 mi W along the road, on state land.◀

The blue-marked horse trail crosses almost level terrain covered with pines for 0.8 mi. The S half passes through private land; be sure to stay on the trail.

❄ Trail in winter: Suitable for snowshoeing or skiing, but snowmobiles may be active. Beach Mill Rd. is not plowed in winter.

ᴹ Distance: 0.8 mi (1.3 km).

6 Frost Pocket Horse Trail

Trails Illustrated Map 745: Q2

▶Trailheads: To reach the N trailhead, from Lowville, turn E on River Rd., go 4.1 mi to Watson, and turn L on Number Four Rd. Proceed 2.7 mi and turn R on Loson Rd., going 0.4 mi to McPhilmy Rd. Turn R. Go 2.5 mi, crossing Erie Canal Rd. and continuing on a dirt road to unmarked Beach Mill Rd., L (also dirt). Turn L and go 1 mi on Beach Mill Rd. to Cleveland Lake Rd. Turn R and go 0.6 mi to an unmarked fork in the road. The trail is on the R at the fork.

To reach the S trailhead, proceed from Lowville as above to McPhilmy Rd. Turn R. Go 2.9 mi, crossing Erie Canal Rd. and continuing on a dirt road past unmarked Beach Mill Rd., L (also dirt), to a minor unmarked road, L. The trail is on the L just after the road. (Proceeding Trail also starts at this trailhead and connects in 0.7 mi to Old Number Four Horse Trail, trail 7.)◀

Like all trails in this region, the path of this blue-marked horse trail is through pine forest with pleasant sandy soil and little change in elevation.

❄ Trail in winter: Suitable for snowshoeing or skiing, but snowmobiles may be active. Beach Mill Rd. is not plowed in winter.

ᴹ Distance: 1.3 mi (2.1 km).

7 Old Number Four Horse Trail

▶Trailheads: To reach the N trailhead, turn E from Lowville on River Rd., go 4.1 mi to Watson, and turn L on Number Four Rd. Proceed 2.7 mi and turn R on Loson Rd., going 0.4 mi to McPhilmy Rd. Turn R. Go 2.5 mi, crossing Erie Canal Rd. and continuing on a dirt road to unmarked Beach Mill Rd., L (also dirt). Turn L and go 1 mi on Beach Mill Rd. to Cleveland Lake Rd. Turn R and go 0.6 mi to an unmarked fork in the road. Take the R fork and continue for 0.3 mi. The trail is on the R.

To reach the S trailhead from Lowville, turn E on River Rd., go 4.1 mi to Watson, and turn L on Number Four Rd. Go 2.7 mi, turn R on Loson Rd., and go 0.4 mi to McPhilmy Rd. Turn R. Go 3.5 mi, crossing Erie Canal Rd. and continuing on a dirt road to paved Bailey Rd. on the L. Turn L and go 0.6 mi to the trailhead on the L.◀

This old jeep road (a blue-marked horse trail) offers easy going through level but somewhat varied terrain. At the S end, another old road goes SW. Called the Proceeding Trail, it connects to Frost Pocket Horse Trail (trail 6). These connections close a loop, allowing one to park at Payne Lake and take a pleasant 3.3 mi circuit starting on Frost Pocket Horse Trail and returning W to Payne Lake from the N trailhead of Old Number Four Horse Trail. Elbow Horse Trail (trail 8) connects to this trail 0.4 mi from the S trailhead. It is worth the side trip to go 0.2 mi to the Elbow on the Independence River. The banks are undercut by the river. Do not stand on the very edge; the bank could easily collapse, sending one plunging down the steep slope to the river.

✻ Trail in winter: Suitable for snowshoeing or skiing, but snowmobiles may be active.

🚶 Distance: 1.1 mi (1.8 km).

8 Elbow Horse Trail

▶Trailhead: From Lowville, turn E on River Rd. Go 4.1 mi to Watson and turn L on Number Four Rd. Proceed 2.7 mi and turn R on Loson Rd., going 0.4 mi to McPhilmy Rd. Turn R. Go 3.5 mi, crossing Erie Canal Rd. and continuing on a dirt road to paved Bailey Rd. on the L. Turn L and go 1.1 mi to the trailhead (a two-track road) on the L.◀

This short blue-marked horse trail connects Bailey Rd. on the S to Old Number Four Horse Trail (trail 7) on the N. Its chief attraction is the Elbow, an oxbow on the meandering Independence River. The trail approaches the high bank, giving a good view. The banks are undercut by the river. Do not stand on the very edge; the bank could collapse, sending one plunging down the steep slope to the river.

✻ Trail in winter: Suitable for snowshoeing or skiing, but snowmobiles may be active.

🐾 Distances: Trailhead to the Elbow, 0.2 mi; to Old Number Four Horse Trail (trail 7), 0.4 mi (0.6 km).

9 Dragline–Evies Pond–Gumdrop Horse Trail

Trails Illustrated Map 745: Q2

This path is labeled by the DEC as four short trails: Dragline, Evies Pond, Fish Pond, and Gumdrop Trails. Each uses pieces of old roads that start on private land. Although the route described does not go to any of the named ponds, one can easily make side trips on the old roads to reach these ponds. Chase Creek Horse Trail (trail 11) connects to the present route 0.3 mi from the N trailhead.

▶Trailheads: To reach the N trailhead, turn E from Lowville on River Rd., go 4.1 mi to Watson, and turn L on Number Four Rd. Proceed 2.7 mi and turn R on Loson Rd., going 0.4 mi to McPhilmy Rd. Turn R. Go 3.5 mi, crossing Erie Canal Rd. and continuing on a dirt road to paved Bailey Rd. on the L. Turn L and go 1.4 mi to the bridge over the Independence River. The trailhead is on the R just across the bridge. Park back from the bridge on the W side or at the old gravel pit on the E side; the rest of the land E of the bridge is private.

To reach the middle trailhead, follow Lovers Lane Rd., 1 mi W of the S trailhead.

To reach the S trailhead, turn E from Lowville on River Rd., go 4.1 mi to Watson, and turn L on Number Four Rd. Proceed 2.7 mi, turn R on Loson Rd., and go 0.4 mi to McPhilmy Rd. Turn R and go 2.3 mi to Erie Canal Rd. Turn R and go 1.9 mi to Stony Lake Rd. Turn L and go 2.7 mi to the trailhead on the L.◀

Starting from the N trailhead (0.0 mi), the blue-marked horse trail goes along the riverbank for 0.2 mi until it passes private land, then turns L (E) to meet Chase Creek Horse Trail (trail 11) at 0.3 mi and Evies Pond Trail at 0.7 mi. The road L at the corner leads to private land. Turning R, the route passes the end of Evies Pond, then zigzags. At 0.8 mi, a road leads L for 0.3 mi to a turnaround (the middle trailhead) on the beautiful ridge between Evies Pond and Long Pond. Continuing S on Evies Pond Rd., the trail soon turns E to Fish Pond Rd. That road continues to the N shore of Fish Pond, but the trail leaves it at 1.3 mi to go S around Mahan Pond and on to the S trailhead on Stony Lake Rd. (1.9 mi).

❄ Trail in winter: Suitable for snowshoeing or skiing, but snowmobiles may be active.

🐾 Distances: N trailhead to Chase Creek Horse Trail jct., 0.3 mi; to Evies Pond side road, 0.8 mi; to Fish Pond jct., 1.3 mi; to S trailhead, 1.9 mi (3 km).

10 Hinchings Pond Horse Trail

Trails Illustrated Map 745: Q2

▶Trailheads: To reach the N trailhead, turn E from Lowville on River Rd., go 4.1 mi to Watson, and turn L on Number Four Rd. Proceed 2.7 mi and turn R on

Loson Rd., going 0.4 mi to McPhilmy Rd. Turn R and go 2.3 mi to Erie Canal Rd., then turn R and go 1.9 mi to Stony Lake Rd. Turn L and go 2.7 mi to the trailhead on the R.

To reach the S trailhead, proceed from Lowville as above to Erie Canal Rd. Turn R. Proceed 2.3 mi to Sand Pond Rd. Turn L and go 1.2 mi (passing a private road to Chase Lake) to a fork in the road. Take the narrow L fork (Bull Pond Rd.). Proceed another 1.5 mi, crossing a section of private land and continuing to another jct. (The better road to the R leads to private land.) Fletcher Horse Trail (trail 44B) comes in on the R at this jct. Continue straight ahead a short distance to the end. The trail turns L off the end of the road. ◀

The blue-marked horse trail leads through scrub and pine plain, with two creek crossings. There is no convenient circuit route. One must return by the same route to the starting point.

✳ Trail in winter: Suitable for snowshoeing or skiing, but snowmobiles may be active.

🐾 Distance: 1.1 mi (1.8 km).

11 Chase Creek Horse Trail

Trails Illustrated Map 745: Q2

This trail leads from the Confusion Flats parking lot and across Stony Lake Rd. (the N trailhead), to end on Dragline–Evies Pond–Gumdrop Horse Trail (trail 9). It passes Parsons Pond and makes one creek crossing in the S section, while the N section is more varied, with ups and downs and no water to wade. This is a pleasantly interesting route to Evies Pond, but is not the shortest way to get there (see trail 9).

▶ Trailheads: To reach the N trailhead, turn E from Lowville on River Rd., go 4.1 mi to Watson, and turn L on Number Four Rd. Proceed 2.7 mi and turn R on Loson Rd., going 0.4 mi to McPhilmy Rd. Turn R and go 2.3 mi to Erie Canal Rd., then turn R and go 1.9 mi to Stony Lake Rd. Turn L and go 1.6 mi to trailheads on both sides of the road.

To reach the S trailhead, from Lowville proceed as above to Erie Canal Rd. Turn R. Proceed 2.3 mi to Sand Pond Rd. Turn L and go 0.8 mi to the Confusion Flats parking area on the R. The trail starts across the road from Confusion Flats Rd. ◀

Starting at the S trailhead (0.0 mi), this red-marked horse trail heads NE through level scrub pine, crossing a dirt road from Chase Lake at 0.6 mi. Turning N, the trail passes Parsons Pond at 0.7 mi. After a few ups and downs, the path is even until it approaches Chase Creek. The creek must be waded at 1.5 mi. The trail regains 40 ft of elevation to meet the N trailhead at Stony Lake Rd. (1.6 mi). The N section has considerably more ups and downs and a 50 ft notch to cross at 2 mi. It joins trail 9 at 2.5 mi. To the L, it is another 0.3 mi to the Bailey Rd. trailhead.

✳ Trail in winter: Suitable for snowshoeing or skiing, but snowmobiles may be active.

🐾 Distances: S trailhead to Chase Creek, 1.5 mi; to N trailhead, 1.6 mi; to trail 2G, 2.5 mi (4 km).

12 Independence River and Shady Horse Trails

Trails Illustrated Map 745: P1

This is an especially pleasant trail. It drops 270 ft on fairly gentle slopes to reach the meandering Independence River. Of course, what goes down must come up, and the ascent is equally interesting.

▶Trailheads: To reach the N trailhead, turn E from Lowville on River Rd., go 4.1 mi to Watson, and turn L on Number Four Rd. Proceed 2.7 mi and turn R on Loson Rd., going 0.4 mi to McPhilmy Rd. Turn R and go 2.3 mi to Erie Canal Rd. Turn R. Proceed 2.3 mi to Sand Pond Rd. The trail is 0.4 mi farther down Erie Canal Rd. on the R, but the best foot access is a two-track dirt road just 300 ft S of the Sand Pond Rd. jct. This horse trail is blue-marked at both ends and yellow in the middle.

To reach the W trailhead, go 2 mi S from Sand Pond Rd. (N trailhead). Turn R on Donnatburg Rd. and go to the end at a closed bridge over the river. An old road goes N for 0.1 mi to meet the trail.

To reach the S trailhead, go 0.5 mi farther S on Erie Canal Rd. from the N trailhead.◀

Starting on the two-track road near the N trailhead (0.0 mi), it is only 250 ft to a jct. where the official trail comes in from the L. Continuing on the old road, the descent begins at 0.2 mi. The old road levels out near a bend in the cascading river at 0.6 mi. The next bend of the river is much more peaceful. The old road follows the riverbank, then takes a sharp L at 1.1 mi. At this corner, the old road continues 0.1 mi down the river to the W trailhead off Donnatburg Rd.

After the turn, the trail ascends an old road, then leaves it to wiggle gently upward, sometimes along property lines and sometimes through rounded notches. After a final spurt of somewhat steeper climbing, the path reaches Shady Trail at 1.8 mi. Up the ridge to the R, it is 0.3 mi on the blue-marked trail to the S trailhead. To the L, the blue-marked Shady Trail follows easy ground to a jct. with the yellow trail from farther up the road. Shady Trail turns R and crosses the trail heading to the horse Assembly Area. Continuing ahead (N) on that trail, the jct. with the two-track road is at 2.6 mi. The N trailhead is 250 ft to the R.

❀ Trail in winter: Suitable for snowshoeing or skiing, but snowmobiles may be active

🐾 Distances: Two-track road near N trailhead to start of descent, 0.2 mi; to bottom, 0.6 mi; to S trailhead, 2.2 mi (3.5 km).

Independence River. John Kettlewell

13 Fish Trail

Trails Illustrated Map 745: Q3

From the N, Fish Trail can be combined with trails 14, 50, and 51 or 52 to reach the Ha-De-Ron-Dah Wilderness Area. There is also a trailhead on the S end of the trail on state land that is accessible over a private road by rugged vehicles. The trail is heavily used by ATVs.

▶Trailhead: One end of this trail is found at the West Bridge over the Independence River, reachable from Beach Mill Pond Trail (trail 2) or Panther Pond–Independence River Trail (trail 18). Although this trail is probably more often used as an interior trail, there is a trailhead on its S end, E of Stony Lake. From Lowville, turn E on River Rd., go 4.1 mi to Watson, and turn L on Number Four Rd. Proceed 2.7 mi, turn R on Loson Rd., and go 0.4 mi to McPhilmy Rd. Turn R and go 2.3 mi to Erie Canal Rd., then turn R and go 1.9 mi to Stony Lake Rd. (gravel). Turn L (NE). (Beyond this jct. on Erie Canal Rd. is North Shore Rd., and the outlet of Chase Lake is just beyond that.) Head E on Stony Lake Rd., entering the Adirondack Park at 0.2 mi. Stony Lake Rd. is paved for 0.7 mi, then drops to one lane, passes Chase Creek Horse Trail (trail 11) at 1.6 mi, passes N of Upper Chase Lake on a short stretch of paving, and then again on dirt passes the Gumdrop (L) and Hinchings Pond (R) horse trails (trails 9 and 10) at 2.7 mi. From here on, the "road," with sharp bends and occasional bedrock outcroppings, is passable by passenger car, but is not for fainthearted drivers.

Private land starts at 5.4 mi from Erie Canal Rd. There is sufficient space for three cars on the R, next to a DEC sign announcing that the next 0.9 mi is a public easement across private land. Hikers may walk the road for another 0.9 mi, but those who have pickups or 4WD vehicles can drive past cabins—cautiously, as some are immediately adjacent to the road—to the state land boundary at 6.3 mi. There is a parking lot 200 ft beyond the boundary sign. Those last 200 ft are very muddy and rough. (The impassable road continues as Mt. Tom Trail, trail 14.) ◀

Assuming that most hikers will avoid the rough road to the Stony Lake trailhead, the following description is S from the West Bridge to the grassy parking lot.

From the West Bridge (0.0 mi), the yellow-marked trail—a dirt road—enters a clearing and turns R (W). It parallels the river for a way, reaching a jct. at 0.2 mi. The route R (NW) goes to an informal campsite overlooking the river and a fording place used to supply a private camp across the river.

The trail turns L (S) on the generally level woods road, bypassing road-width mudholes from time to time. At 0.8 mi it reaches the end of a beaver meadow/pond L; at 0.9 mi the wetland is also on the R. At 1 mi the beaver ponds connect on top of the road. Wading will likely be required, as the clumps of vegetation on the sides appear to be bog plants that sink when stepped on.

At 1.3 mi there is an arrow as the trail moves from the road onto a lightly used footpath L, which crosses a bridge below the main beaver pond (and above another) at 1.4 mi. Passing through ferns, the trail goes over a small rise, bends R, and reaches the grassy parking lot at the Stony Lake trailhead at 1.7 mi. From there it is 6.3 mi R to Erie Canal Rd. The truck road L is Mt. Tom Trail (trail 14).

❈ Trail in winter: Suitable for snowshoeing or backcountry skiing, but the trail is 6.3 mi from the plowed Erie Canal Rd.

🏃 Distances: West Bridge to jct., 0.2 mi; to crossing at beaver ponds, 1 mi; to foot trail, 1.3 mi; to Stony Lake trailhead, 1.7 mi (2.7 km).

14 Mt. Tom Trail

Trails Illustrated Map 745: Q4

This trail does not go to nearby Mt. Tom, but acquired its name because it crosses lands owned by the Mt. Tom Club. This is the shortest route to Balsam Flats, and at one time was known as Balsam Flats Rd. The state has a trail easement on this private land for hiking, snowmobiling, and horse travel, but bicycles are forbidden. Travelers must remain on the trail when passing through the private land.

▶Trailhead: See trail 13.◀

From the Stony Lake Rd. trailhead (0.0 mi), the rocky old road heads E with snowmobile markers, rising rather steeply about 185 ft over a small hill. Shortly after crossing the next creek beyond this hill, the trail reaches private land (stay on the trail) at 0.9 mi. After the next creek crossing, at 1.5 mi, the route ascends gently 260 ft over a more significant hill. At 2.2 mi, a private road enters R; the trail continues ahead, bending L.

As the path levels out at the top, the trail is again on state land at 2.7 mi. Here a 2014 reroute takes it R (S) 1.1 mi to a jct. at 3.8 mi with Balsam Flats Rd. (a snowmobile road, closed to passenger vehicles). To the R, Balsam Flats Rd. leads in approximately 2.8 mi to a jct. with Silvermine Trail (trail 50), also rerouted in 2014.

(The old trail 14, now unmaintained, continues roughly straight [E] for 0.6 mi, descending to a jct. with an [unmaintained] section of the Silvermine Trail [trail 50]. Ahead, it is 0.2 mi to an access point on the Independence River.)

❄ Trail in winter: Snowmobile trail. Suitable for snowshoers and intermediate skiers, but 5 mi or more from the nearest plowed road (Chases Lake).

🎿 Distances: Trailhead to private land, 0.9 mi; to state land, 2.7 mi; to Silvermine Trail (trail 50), 3.8 mi (6.1 km).

15 Francis Lake (unmaintained)

Trails Illustrated Map 745: R4

Francis Lake is close to Stillwater Rd. and has two good sites for picnicking (no facilities), both of them on paths that are not the main trail, which goes to the other (S) end of the lake (see below, "W Access" and "E Access"). There are two private holdings on the lake.

▶Trailhead: From the jct. of Number Four Rd. and Stillwater Rd. at Number Four settlement, go 0.9 mi W on Number Four Rd. Turn L (S) on Smith Rd. and proceed 1.5 mi. Park in a former gravel pit on the L (E). The trail is an old road starting at the R rear of the gravel pit. Because this is an unofficial trail, there are no markers.◀

From the gravel pit (0.0 mi), the route is an unmarked old road, easy to follow, leading NE through open woods. At 0.5 mi, the SW end of the lake is visible through open forest L.

The old road soon passes within 50 ft of a tiny inlet of the lake, then curves away and becomes more overgrown. It is probably not of interest to hikers past this point. The lake edge on this S side is somewhat boggy and the forest floor is too uneven for camping. Camping is reported to be easier on a point of land farther around the lake to the E.

Two other paths lead to points on the NE end of Francis Lake:

For the W access, from the jct. of Number Four Rd. and Stillwater Rd. at Number Four settlement, go 0.6 mi E on Stillwater Rd. There is parking on the R (S) for one car at a turn-in for a barricaded former private road. The route, for foot traffic only, follows this road past the barricade for 500 ft along the outlet stream, then turns L and goes another 300 ft to the cleared site of a former summer home. This site is on a point of land, with nice views and a pleasant open area suitable for camping.

For the E access, go 0.3 mi farther E on Stillwater Rd. Park off the road on the S side just before a bend, and slightly beyond a barricaded former access road on the R (S). The route goes between two wooden posts at the roadside and reaches the lake in a few paces. This route has been hardened to allow wheelchair access. A floating dock is available during summer for canoe, kayak, and car-top boat launching. No trailers are allowed. To the R, on a slight hill, a beautiful grove of large white pines has been somewhat degraded by attempts to build fires on the forest floor; that practice could prove disastrous for these fine old trees. A very short road section just E of this access is also on state land for the first 0.1 mi, and is worth the short walk to get the view.

❊ Trail in winter: Suitable for snowshoers and skiers.

🏃 Distance: Gravel pit to closest approach to lake, 0.5 mi (0.8 km).

16 Bills Pond Trail (unmaintained)

Trails Illustrated Map 745: R4

▶Trailhead: On Number Four Rd., go 0.9 mi W of the jct. with Stillwater Rd. at Number Four settlement. Turn L (S) on Smith Rd., identified by a DEC trailhead sign. Drive S past the location of the former Number Four fire tower at 0.1 mi (R). Continuing S, the parking spot is at the end of the drivable road, 3.8 mi from Number Four Rd. ◀

From the back end of the parking area (0.0 mi), the old Bills Pond Rd. heads NE. Although unmarked, the trail on this road shows some use, and the road is obvious. (Trail 18 starts on a good road to the R [S], past a roadblock.)

Beyond the parking lot, the old road continues its gentle climb, weaving a bit, but aiming generally NE. Near the top, at a jct. at about 0.6 mi, the route turns onto a faint road L (N)—the Bills Pond Rd. It shows no obvious use, and has not been cleared for several years. (Beyond this jct., the main road starts down, with a noticeable hillside up to the L, and enters a clearing. If you enter the clearing, you've gone too far.) Attempt to follow this faint road through blowdown. It continues N to Bills Pond, keeping about 50 ft above a notch (L).

As the pond comes into view at 0.8 mi, the old road turns R and parallel the pond, arriving at a wetland at the E end. The hiker should leave the old road when the pond first comes into view and head for the pond. There are no trails. If you go L to the outlet, and cross on the beaver dam, you can reach an open rock slab at water's edge on the N side for a nice stopping place and a good view of the pond.

❊ Trail in winter: Suitable for snowshoeing or backcountry skiing. Smith Rd. is not plowed, however. Distance to the pond in winter is 4.6 mi from Number Four Rd.

🏃 Distances: Trailhead to jct., 0.6 mi; to Bills Pond, 0.8 mi (1.3 km).

17 East Bridge Trail (unmaintained)

Trails Illustrated Map 745: R4

This trail, also known as Independence River Trail and Panther Pond Loop, goes to the Independence River at the site of the former East Bridge. The bridge was removed in 2014, and the trail is no longer maintained. This is an interior trail, although the N end is only 0.3 mi from the Smith Rd. trailhead for the Panther

Pond–Independence River Trail (trail 18). The description begins at the S end. The trail is marked as a snowmobile trail.

▶Locator: The N end of the trail is on the Panther Pond–Independence River Trail (trail 18), 0.3 mi S of the trailhead on Smith Rd. On the S, this unmaintained trail connects with an unmaintained section of the Mt. Tom Trail (trail 14). ◀

From the jct. on the old (unmaintained) section of the Mt. Tom Trail (0.0 mi), the East Bridge Trail heads N, dropping to the site where the East Bridge was once located at 0.4 mi. There is an informal campsite R, upstream about 20 yd. Wading is required to cross the river, and caution is advised if the water is high.

Rising slightly on a brief stretch of muddy ground, the trail bends L (W) and goes along the river, sometimes out of sight and sometimes near, eventually turning R (N) away from the river at 1.1 mi. There are ups and downs as the trail heads generally N until crossing Fourth Creek on a bridge at 2.6 mi., then passing another abandoned trail on L. Bending NE, it passes a number of mudholes, and at 3.7 mi clings to the edge next to a cliff rising L. The trail passes a beaver pond R for nearly 75 yd, passes more mudholes, and reaches a jct. at 4 mi. (Trail R is the Emmet Hill Rd. Snowmobile Trail, trail 10, which heads NE 1.7 mi to the drivable McCarty Rd. (trail 23), 2.9 mi S of Stillwater Rd.)

Bending L at the jct., the trail heads generally NW with minor ups and downs, crossing a small beaver dam at 4.2 mi and a mudhole at 4.7 mi on a section of otherwise decent road-width. It reaches a jct. at 7 mi. (Trail R is an old section of the North Crossover Snowmobile Trail, trail 9; the trail was rerouted in 2014 owing to flooding.) The wide trail bends L (W), generally on a gravel truck road over a rise and down to end at a jct. at 7.5 mi. The trail R goes 0.3 mi N to the Smith Rd. trailhead. The yellow-marked Panther Pond–Independence River Trail L (trail 18) goes 1 mi to the Panther Pond lean-to.

❋ Trail in winter: Snowmobile trail. Otherwise, suitable for snowshoeing and backcountry skiing, but remote. The winter trailhead may be at Number Four Rd.

🐾 Distances: Jct. with former Mt. Tom Trail (old trail 14) to Independence River, 0.4 mi; to bend N away from river, 1.1; to Fourth Creek bridge, 2.6 mi; to jct. with Emmet Hill Rd. Snowmobile Trail (trail 22), 4 mi; to register on Panther Pond–Independence River Trail (trail 18), 7.5 mi (12 km).

18 Panther Pond–Independence River Trail

Trails Illustrated Map 745: Q4

Panther Pond and its lean-to are reason enough to make this trip, but the pleasant additional hike to the Independence River is also worth the effort. Smith Rd. twists SE through hardwood forest, past the private gate to Trout Pond, and ends at a barricade by Pine Creek. Foot and snowmobile trails extend from here in many directions, such as the unmarked one straight ahead (E), which goes to Bills Pond (trail 16). The yellow foot trail R goes S to Panther Pond lean-to, then over a hill with an open rock ridge (no view), and joins with snowmobile trails leading S to the Independence River.

▶Trailhead: On Number Four Rd., go E 16.2 mi from CR 26 in Lowville or go 1 mi W from the jct. with Stillwater Rd. at Number Four settlement. Turn S on Smith Rd., identified by a DEC trailhead sign opposite a "Number 4 Business District" sign. Pass the Trout Lake private gate R at 2.1 mi, continuing to the end of the drivable road, 3.8 mi from Number Four Rd. ◀

Heading S past the barricade (0.0 mi), the trail follows an old road over Pine Creek and continues on this road past an unmarked fork at L. The trail reaches a jct. with North Crossover Snowmobile Trail (trail 21), R, at 0.2 mi, and a trail register at 0.3 mi. There is a fork at the register. To the L is East Bridge Trail (trail 17, which is no longer maintained).

Continuing ahead on the R fork, the yellow-marked Panther Pond Trail goes 90 yd on an old woods road, then turns L into the woods and along a hillside on a footpath. Watch for that turnoff as the wider path continues ahead with snowmobile markers. The trail goes through a couple of low sections with corduroy, then up a hill and around a magnificent white pine at 1.25 mi, and reaches the lean-to and Panther Pond at 1.3 mi. This setting is beautiful, perfect for a lazy summer day.

Going L around the pond, the yellow trail continues near the shore, past a beaver pond on the L, and finally leaves Panther Pond at some notable cliffs on the L side at 1.9 mi. The trail follows along Third Creek for a way, then goes into the woods and across Snake Creek. The trail continues away from this creek, past a swampy region, and then ascends a ragged little hill with open rock along the summit ridge starting at 2.7 mi and continuing to beyond 2.8 mi. The open regions are not large enough for distant views, but the openings are pleasant, with many white pines in the area. This hill has a gently descending ridge on the S side, with the trail following the ridge nearly to the bottom.

When the flats of a vlei feeding Third Creek come into view, the trail descends a short way. Watch for a turn L where another trail, now abandoned, goes ahead at 4.2 mi. The route follows an old woods road through easy terrain, with an occasional wet spot. At 4.4 mi, a noisy cascading creek signals a gentle turn to the R. The trail follows this creek (Fourth Creek) for several minutes, until reaching the Independence River. Here it turns R and follows the bank of this busy river to end at the West Bridge at 5 mi. Beach Mill Pond Trail (trail 2) continues W along the N bank of the river, past Gleasmans Falls, to a trailhead on Beach Mill Rd. Across the bridge is Fish Trail (trail 13).

❋ Trail in winter: The trailhead is at Number Four Rd. This is snowmobile territory. Easy for snowshoes, generally easy for skis, but the trip can be a long one with trail-breaking in deep snow. The section just S of Panther Pond is for experienced skiers.

🐾 Distances: Trailhead to Panther Pond and lean-to, 1.3 mi; to Fourth Creek, 4.4 mi; to West Bridge on the Independence River, 5 mi (8 km).

19 Sunday Lake

Trails Illustrated Map 745: S5

▶Trailhead: From the jct. at Stillwater, go W on Stillwater Rd. 4 mi to McCarty Rd. (3.5 mi E of Number Four Rd.). Turn S onto McCarty Rd. Go 0.4 mi to a road L (E). Park here and walk. The road looks good, but it gets very difficult in a short distance, suitable only for high-center vehicles. There are no trail markers, but the route is unmistakable. ◀

From McCarty Rd. (0.0 mi), head E 0.4 mi to the shore of Sunday Lake at an informal campsite. It is a very pretty lake.

❄ Trail in winter: Suitable for snowshoe or ski access to Sunday Lake. McCarty Rd. is not plowed.

⚐ Distances: McCarty Rd. to Sunday Lake, 0.4 mi (0.6 km). Winter access from Stillwater Rd., 0.8 mi (1.3 km).

20 Sunday Lake Link Trail

Trails Illustrated Map 745: S5

Trails 20–22 all start from the drivable McCarty Rd. and Snowmobile Trail (trail 23) and are convenient for further exploration in the region, possibly by mountain bike. This 0.6 mi trail, which is marked with DEC snowmobile markers, allows snowmobiles and hikers a connection between trails 23 and 24.

▶Locator: The W trailhead is on the L at 0.3 mi on McCarty Rd. and Snowmobile Trail (trail 23). The E trailhead is on the R at 0.1 mi on Basket Factory Rd. and Snowmobile Trail (trail 24). ◀

21 North Crossover Snowmobile Trail

Trails Illustrated Map 745: R4

Like trail 20, this trail starts from the drivable McCarty Rd. and Snowmobile Trail (trail 23). It connects Panther Pond–Independence River Trail (trail 18) and McCarty Rd. and Snowmobile Trail (trail 11), S of Stillwater Rd. The W end is 0.2 mi S of the trail 18 parking area on Smith Rd. It is an easy-to-follow route, 2.9 mi long and marked with DEC snowmobile markers. It is perhaps usable for extended loop travel. About one-third of the trail (on the W end) was rerouted in 2014 to bypass flooded areas. The trail crosses the Lewis-Herkimer county line, but no sign indicates the boundary.

22 Emmet Hill Rd. Snowmobile Trail (unmaintained)

Trails Illustrated Map 745: R4

This trail connects East Bridge Trail (trail 17) and McCarty Rd. and Snowmobile Trail (trail 23) S of Stillwater Rd. and S of the North Crossover Snowmobile Trail (trail 21), and thus can be used for a loop, possibly by bicycle. This is an old road past a log cabin, now tumbled down, located on a pond in Fifth Creek, 1.5 mi from the E end. The cabin belonged to Emmet Hill, former forest ranger at Stillwater.

McCarty Rd. and this trail might be usable for a shorter trail access to the Independence River. The trail is marked with DEC snowmobile markers and yellow foot trail markers. It shows damage from ATVs, but is mostly easy grades. A beaver pond can be crossed on a dam at the Herkimer-Lewis county line 1.6 mi from the E end.

🚶🚶 Distance: McCary Rd. to jct. with East Bridge Trail (trail 17), 1.7 mi (2.7 km).

23 McCarty Rd. and Snowmobile Trail

Trails Illustrated Map 745: R5

This old road connects with Stillwater Rd. 3.5 mi E of its intersection with Number Four Rd. (4 mi W of Stillwater). It leads S past Sunday Lake Link Trail (trail 20) at 0.3 mi, Sunday Lake Rd. and Trail (trail 19) at 0.4 mi, North Crossover Snowmobile Trail (trail 21) at 1.9 mi, and Emmet Hill Rd. Trail (trail 22) at 2.9 mi, and ends at a private land boundary at 5 mi (8 km).

The road is easily drivable for the first 4 mi, but the last mile is in poor shape. A pickup or 4WD vehicle would be best used here. The road is a snowmobile trail, but markers are not likely to be seen. The state has acquired a recreational easement on a block of private land 0.2 mi E of the end of the road. Sportsmen can park off the road before the gate and bushwhack to reach the easement area, which includes Blue, Hitchcock, Grass, and Moose Ponds.

24 Basket Factory Rd. and Snowmobile Trail

Trails Illustrated Map 745: S5

Basket Factory Rd. connects with Stillwater Rd. 4 mi E of the jct. with Number Four Rd. and 3.5 mi W of the jct. at Stillwater. It is a good gravel road extending 3.3 mi to a turnaround. Trail 20 connects on the R at 0.1 mi. The trail going L at the end-of-road turnaround leads 0.4 mi to private land. At 2.3 mi from Stillwater Rd., a two-track road forks R and goes down a short distance to an unofficial campsite at Sunday Creek. There is a small bridge over the creek, and an old, unofficial trail continues S.

25 Stillwater Mt.

Trails Illustrated Map 745: S6

This short hike along a steady, pleasant uphill grade leads to a 47 ft fire tower that was erected in 1919. The fire tower has been restored (2016). The first lookout on this site was a tower made of timbers, built in 1912. The trail is in the Big Moose Easement and in keeping with the terms of the conservation easement, the part of the trail that crosses land owned by Lyme Timber Company is closed from the second Tuesday in October through December 20.

▶Trailhead: There are two approaches. From the E, access to the trailhead is from NY 28 on Big Moose Rd. The turn onto Big Moose Rd. is well signed in Eagle Bay on NY 28 near Inlet. Follow Big Moose Rd. to Big Moose Station at 7.9 mi. and the end of the paved road. The unpaved road continues for 8 mi to the trailhead. During mud season it is best to check with the Town of Webb Highway Department for road conditions (315-369-3412). The trailhead is on the L. From the W, in Lowville, access to the trailhead follows Number Four Rd. at its junction with NY 12. At 22 mi turn R onto Stillwater Rd. (end of pavement) and continue 6 mi to the junction with Big Moose Rd. Turn R onto Big Moose Rd. (Straight ahead takes you to a boat launch, store, restaurant, and hotel.) Trailhead parking will be at 1.9 mi on the R.

The parking area is a level cut into a low slope that holds approximately 7–8 cars. ◀

At the rear of the parking area (0.0 mi) look for a short set of wooden stairs, followed soon after by a bridge crossing a small stream. From here, the trail goes gently uphill, mostly traversing the slope from R to L. At 0.5 mi the trail takes a more direct uphill direction and intersects a logging road that looks as if it has seen some recent wheeled activity. Continue straight at this intersection; do not turn either way onto the logging road.

The trail is now on lands owned by Lyme Timber Company, which has granted public right-of-way except for the second Tuesday in October through December 20, when the trail is closed. Please respect the rights of the property owner.

Just past the logging road intersection the trail levels at an old clearing that is being taken over by small pioneering tree species. At 0.7 mi two red signs indicating private property and an old logging path appear on the L. Go straight. The trail is obvious and not hard to follow. At 0.8 mi, after going mostly straight, the trail offers a few subtle turns, first to the R and then to the L, and at 0.9 mi the base of the fire tower comes into view. Summit elevation is 2264 ft (690 m).

✼ Trail in winter (see date constraints above): The relatively short distance and easy grade make the trail good for snowshoers. This could also be an interesting ski trip for competent skiers with the proper equipment who are comfortable skiing on varied terrain.

♨ Distances: Trailhead to beginning of Lyme Timber Company lands, 0.5 mi; to summit, 0.9 mi (1.4 km). Summit elevation, 2264 ft (690 m). Elevation change, 564 ft (172 m). 🪶

View of Fourth Lake. Chris Murray

Big Moose Section

This network affords a variety of circuit and through hikes that visit one or more wild lakes and ponds: Cascade Lake, Chain Ponds, Windfall Pond, Queer Lake, Mays Pond, Chub Lake, Constable Pond, Pigeon Lake, and Otter Pond. There are several ascents to viewpoints: Billys Bald Spot, West Mt., Cork Mt., Onondaga Mt., Eagle Cliff, and Bald (Rondaxe) Mt.

Several of the trails located on the eastern edge of the area covered in this section are close to or cross into the area covered in *Adirondack Mountain Club Central Trails*. These are described in the Western-Central Overlap Section of this guidebook, as well as in *Central Trails* and include trails to Rocky Mt., Black Bear Mt., and Constable Pond. Among these, Rocky Mt. Trail is notable because of its shortness and the quality of the scenery.

The trails of this section are reached from Big Moose Rd. between the communities of Eagle Bay and Big Moose, all within 9 mi of the jct. of NY 28 and Big Moose Rd. in Eagle Bay. Many of the trails form a network extending E and NE of Big Moose Rd. and originating at trailheads on that road and on Higby Rd. S of Big Moose Lake. Together with the trails reached by boat, they lie in the Pigeon Lake Wilderness Area of the Forest Preserve. These are foot trails only; bicycles are not allowed in Wilderness Areas.

TRAILS REACHED BY BOAT

Three DEC trails to lakes, and a side trail to a stream, are accessible only by boat going to the E end of Big Moose Lake. Each of the four trails ends at a lean-to. See boat launch information for trail 30 and descriptions for trails 30, 31, and 32.

A few suggested hikes for this section are listed below.

SHORT HIKES

Moss Lake Circuit: 2.5 mi (4 km) loop. Easy walking through woods around the lake, with access routes to the lake on the N side. See trail 39.

Eagle Cliff: 0.6 mi (1 km) round-trip. Climbs to a good view of Fourth Lake and Eagle Bay. See trail 43.

MODERATE HIKES

Cascade Lake: 6 mi (9.6 km) round-trip. Gentle grades past waterfalls and nice picnic areas as well as a great ski. See trail 38.

HARDER HIKES

Queer Lake Loop: 8.7 mi (13.9 km) round-trip. Visit Constable Pond, Chub Lake, and Queer Lake using the Constable Pond–West Mt. trailhead and trails

33, 35, and *Central Trails* trail 72 (described in this book in Western-Central Overlap Section).

26 Razorback Pond

Trails Illustrated Map 745: R8

▶Trailhead: From Eagle Bay, drive 7.3 mi NW on Big Moose Rd. to the hamlet of Big Moose. Just before the railroad crossing, turn R onto Twitchell Rd. (paved for the first mile) and drive 2 mi to a parking lot on the lake at the end of the road. The lake is 1.5 mi long and has private camps around it. There is a boat landing at the parking area.◀

The path starts L (W) at the edge of Twitchell Lake (0.0 mi), crossing the gravel boat handling area. It follows an old logging road with yellow markers and is wet and muddy in places.

At 0.3 mi, it turns L at a fork; the R fork goes to a private camp on the lake. At 0.4 mi, Beaver River–Twitchell Trail (trail 128) starts on the hillside R. At 0.8 mi, as it enters private land, the trail curves R and starts to climb. Shortly beyond the curve, an obscure unmarked trail goes L 150 ft to Silver Lake. This is a private lake, with limited access except at this trail point.

Continuing on past the jct., the path follows the old road, climbing and skirting the E side of the lake. As the route turns W, it leaves the old road and starts climbing the hillside N of the lake. After bumping over another hillside, the trail heads N on level ground. It crosses an inlet of Razorback Pond at 1.7 mi, leaves private land, and meets the Pigeon Lake Wilderness Area at the NE corner of the pond. Climbing a hillside partway, and staying back in the thick woods, the trail follows along the pond to its midpoint, then turns S and ends at a small camping area at the edge of Razorback Pond, 2 mi from the trailhead.

❀ Trail in winter: Easily skied as far as Silver Lake. The hillside section just beyond Silver Lake is best left to experienced skiers. Easy snowshoeing.

🐾 Distances: Twitchell Lake to Silver Lake, 0.8 mi; to Razorback Pond, 2 mi (3.2 km).

27 Snake Pond Trail

Trails Illustrated Map 745: R8

This short trail extends NW down from Twitchell Rd. to Twitchell Creek, adjacent to Snake Pond, for a round-trip hike of 1.4 mi. It passes impressive timber and attractive conifers. It descends 200 ft, although it may seem like more, in just over two-thirds of a mile. Its main attraction seems to be access to the water.

▶Trailhead: From Eagle Bay, drive 7.3 mi NW on Big Moose Rd. to the hamlet of Big Moose. Just before the railroad crossing, turn R onto Twitchell Rd. and drive 1.1 mi to where the trail starts on the L after the Post camp. Parking is on the wide shoulder.◀

From the road (0.0 mi), the blue-marked trail descends gradually to a register, bends L for nearly 300 yd, and then turns R. It heads generally NW the rest of the way. A dense stand of small balsam and spruce surrounds the trail, with mature spruce towering above, at 0.5 mi.

The trail ends at 0.7 mi at Twitchell Creek, fringed by a brushy wetland and conifers, including balsam and tamarack. The creek, the outlet of Twitchell Lake, runs W and then N to the Stillwater Reservoir in the Beaver River–Black River watershed.

On the other side of the creek is a narrow point of land separating it from the conifer-lined, mucky-bottomed Snake Pond. Conifers obscure a view of the pond. It is possible to ford the creek and cross the point of land to reach the pond, but a path downstream a few steps from the end of the trail offers an alternative route that doesn't require fording. The path leads 85 yd across mostly dry land and a couple of mossy wet areas back to a point on the boggy Twitchell Creek streamside where a view of the pond, perhaps including a loon, is possible.

❀ Trail in winter: Of no obvious interest, but done easily with snowshoes.

🐾 Distances: Trailhead to Twitchell Creek, 0.7 mi (1.1 km).

28 Billys Bald Spot–Squash Pond Trail

Trails Illustrated Map 745: R8

This trail climbs 340 ft from Martin Rd. on the N shore of western Big Moose

Lake to Billys Bald Spot, where there is a view over the lake, and continues to Squash Pond to the W. This is a private trail on private land, but for many years the owners have permitted the public to use the trail.

▶Trailhead: From NY 28 in Eagle Bay, drive 5.6 mi NW on Big Moose Rd. Turn R on Martin Rd. (no road sign) and follow it parallel to the N shore of Big Moose Lake for 0.6 mi, to where the trail starts at some gravel over a culvert on the L, opposite Camp Vetti. Park along the road; do not block driveways. In addition to yellow and orange metal markers, there is also flagging.◀

From the road (0.0 mi), the trail, worn into the hillside, immediately ascends. Within yards it angles R (nearly N) and upward (despite a large log that might divert hikers L) for 0.1 mi. It then bends L, rising farther W to reach Billys Bald Spot near the top at 0.4 mi. The last two-thirds of the trip is up the slope at an angle, with the uphill side on the R. At the site of a privately built lean-to covered with names, an open ledge at the edge of a steep slope offers a nice view over much of Big Moose Lake, more than 3 mi long. Forested hills are seen beyond the lake.

The trail continues slightly upward NW from the W back corner of the lean-to (avoid path descending to the side), marked by flagging and orange metal disks. It proceeds over a hill above the viewpoint, reaching 2250 ft and passing impressive red spruce, among other tall trees. It descends to approach a stream at 0.9 mi, turns R, and reaches the end of Squash Pond at a beaver dam at 1 mi. There are a couple of islands, one of which may be reached via blowdown, but otherwise the pond has a mostly boggy shoreline.

❈ Trail in winter: Steep hill suitable for vigorous snowshoeing, although roadside parking could be difficult.

🐾 Distances: Martin Rd. to viewpoint, 0.4 mi; to Squash Pond, 1 mi (1.6 km). Ascent to viewpoint, 340 ft (104 m).

29 Safford Pond Trail

Trails Illustrated Map 745: Q8

This is both a DEC blue-marked hiking trail (on the N half) and a DEC-marked snowmobile trail. It leads from Big Moose Rd. near the W end of Big Moose Lake SW past West Pond, Safford Pond, and Goose Pond to the second trailhead just N of Lake Rondaxe. The S half is marked only as a snowmobile trail, but is a good hiking trail except for a 50 yd spot below a beaver dam. High water coming up the trail may limit side trip access to Goose Pond. The hike, including side trips, totals 6.4 mi, while the driving distance is 12.7 mi between trailheads.

▶Trailheads: To reach the N trailhead from NY 28 in Eagle Bay, drive 5.5 mi on Big Moose Rd. to the Orvis Schoolhouse trailhead parking lot on the L. This is about 100 ft from the jct. where Big Moose Rd. goes L and Martin Rd. (unmarked) goes R to the N shore of Big Moose Lake.

To reach the trailhead on the S end from the Tourist Information Center in

Old Forge, drive 4.4 mi NE on NY 28. Turn L (W) on Rondaxe Rd. Go 1.4 mi to a crossover jct. between two parallel roads. Turn R, then immediately L, continuing NW parallel to the previous route. This is the bed of the old Raquette Lake Railroad. Go 0.5 mi farther to a bridge, and turn R at the next corner (North Rondaxe Rd.). Go 0.7 mi to the snowmobile trail on the L. Park on the N edge of the road near the trailhead.◀

At the N end (0.0 mi), this route is broad, easy, and mostly used for access to West Pond. A short red-marked side trail at 0.4 mi leads 70 yd to a waterfall among huge rocks on the outlet of West Pond. Water is sometimes hidden behind the rocks. This side trail goes L just as the trail turns R and begins a short, steep climb.

Some 100 yd beyond this jct., a red-marked side trail goes L (S and E) 300 yd to a clearing on the W shore of West Pond next to its outlet. The pond is very scenic, although much of the shoreline is boggy.

From the jct. with the West Pond side trail, Safford Pond Trail (R) continues with ups and downs, crossing some snowmobile bridges. At 2.3 mi, a blue-marked side trail goes R (SW) 190 yd to an informal campsite on the inlet to Safford Pond. It lies in a spruce-fir setting. Downstream a short way, the stream enters a large open wetland at the end of Safford Pond. This side trail can be somewhat obscure.

The main trail continues to another jct. at 2.4 mi, where the main route continues L as a snowmobile trail. The jct. may be noticeable only by the trail signs high on the trees. Going R (S), toward the pond, the blue trail goes through scrub evergreens, crosses a wetland with many tamaracks, reenters woods, and climbs over a ridge. Turning L for 100 yd, this trail ends in a small spot near the pond where campfires have been made. This is 2.7 mi from the trailhead, and 0.3 mi from the jct.

The clearing is set in pines and tamaracks and has a pebbly beach. To the R lies the bog-lined N arm and inlet of the pond. The pond is nicely surrounded by spruce, white pine, and fir. Too narrow and right on the shoreline, this is not a suitable place to camp, but it is a nice place to stop for a rest. Viburnum undergrowth is especially dense and tall near Safford Pond, then seems to get shorter and shorter as one goes S.

Continuing from the jct., the snowmobile trail goes SE and then S. It turns SW while crossing a marsh and creek, eventually turning SE again to approach Goose Pond at 3.7 mi. The pond is visible in the distance (the sign says 0.1 mi), but high water comes within about 15 yd of the main trail. Slide Off Mt. is across the pond.

Continuing S, the main trail, now generally level and smooth, reaches a wide wetland at 4.5 mi on old corduroy road and a misplaced bridge that may look like an island. The trail then swings around the base of a hill and heads E toward the road, passing on the L a snowmobile trail that leads to private land at Dart Lake. The trail is smooth and easy to the North Rondaxe Rd. trailhead at 5.2 mi.

❃ Trail in winter: The S half is suitable for beginning skiers at least as far as

Goose Pond, and easy-intermediate skiing to Safford Pond. The N half is better left to the intermediate to expert skier.

𝕄 Distances: N trailhead to West Pond, 0.7 mi; to Safford Pond campsite, 2.5 mi; to Safford Pond, 2.7 mi; to Goose Pond, 3.7 mi; to S trailhead, 5.2 mi (8.3 km). From the S trailhead to Goose Pond, 1.5 mi; to Safford Pond, 3.1 mi (5 km).

30 Gull Lakes

Trails Illustrated Map 745: S9

The two small Gull Lakes (Gull Ponds) lie N of the E end of Big Moose Lake. The trail passes Lower Gull Lake and ends at a lean-to on Upper Gull Lake, where there is good swimming. The trail is accessible only by boat on Big Moose Lake.

▶Locator: There is a launching site (without ramp) near the E end of Moose Lake at the bay on the SE shore. This is reached by driving almost to the end of Higby Rd. (which goes NE off Big Moose Rd. S of the lake, 3.7 mi from NY 28 at Eagle Bay) and then turning R at the fork and proceeding less than 0.2 mi to the bay. The parking area is maintained by the Town of Webb.

Canoes and motorboats may be rented and launched at Dunn's Boat Service, located on Big Moose Rd. on the S shore at the W end of Big Moose Lake 5.2 mi from NY 28 at Eagle Bay. Parking is available. This adds 2 mi or more each way to the boat distance, and includes the larger, W part of Big Moose Lake, which can be especially choppy on windy days.

The trailhead is roughly 35 degrees magnetic from the launch site at the end of Higby Rd. Go by boat about 1.1 mi to the marshy inlet at the NE end of Big Moose Lake. Continue NE along the N side of the inlet for 0.4 mi. Past a stream L emptying into the inlet, about 150 yd beyond, is a landing with a sign for the Gull Lake Lean-to. ◀

From the lake (0.0 mi), the trail heads NE, gradually gaining ground to approach the Gull Lakes outlet stream. It parallels the stream to the S shore of Lower Gull Lake, 208 ft higher than the inlet. After crossing the outlet, the marked trail turns W and becomes narrow and muddy around the lower lake between cliffs L and the lake R, then heads N to the lean-to on the S shore of Upper Gull Lake (1.2 mi). There is a Herkimer-Hamilton county line marker about 15 ft from the trail on the L, just 20 yd before the lean-to.

❊ Trail in winter: May be suitable for snowshoeing or backcountry skiing from Higby Rd. over the ice, when Big Moose Lake is frozen solid. Watch for bad ice at the narrows on the long arm known as "the Inlet."

𝕄 Distances: Landing to lean-to, 1.2 mi (1.9 km).

31 Sister Lake (and Andys Creek)

Trails Illustrated Map 745: S10

Lower Sister Lake, remote and pristine, lies NE of Big Moose Lake and is connected by a narrow waterway with Upper Sister Lake on the NE. Bushwhacking to the Upper Lake from the trail's end is reported to be very messy. This trail is accessible only by boat on Big Moose Lake.

▶Locator: Refer to the Gull Lakes trail (trail 30) for launching site information, but note that the E end of the inlet where this trailhead is becomes very shallow, so getting through to the stream may be possible only with a canoe or kayak.

Travel by boat to the NE corner of Big Moose Lake (NW of East Bay, heading roughly 35 degrees magnetic), about 1.1 mi from the launch site at the end of Higby Rd. Proceed NE and E to the shallow end of a marshy waterway (called "the Inlet") at about 2.3 mi, where a canoe or kayak would be best for finding your way into the stream. Proceed about one-third of a mile up a winding stream, staying L, to a landing about 2.6 mi from Higby Rd. It is 2.3 mi from the Higby Rd. launch to the landing, and 5 mi from the W end of Big Moose Lake to the landing.◀

The trail begins (0.0 mi) with an elevated bog bridge of nearly 70 yd, then is on mostly dry land with few markers. At 0.2 mi, a spur leads L to Andys Creek lean-to.

(This blue-marked trail goes N from the main trail and crosses Andys Creek at 0.2 mi [0.4 mi from the landing] on an impressive bridge with six steps up to the top of a crib. The steps allow the bridge to line up with the higher bank on the other side, and decrease the danger of it being swept away like its predecessors. The trail then turns NE to the lean-to at 0.3 mi [0.5 mi from the landing]. The stream, which flows S to the Inlet, has attractive rapids near the lean-to. The round-trip hiking distance from the boat landing to the lean-to and back is 1 mi.)

From the Andys Creek spur jct., the main Sister Lake trail goes NE, first along the level for nearly 1 mi, then ascending nearly 200 ft. The trail contours around a sharp hill, turns R (E) as it approaches Lower Sister Lake, and continues on the contour to reach the lean-to at 3.3 mi. The lean-to has a fine location on a point along the E shore of Lower Sister Lake. There is a nice ledge at the shoreline and a beach nearby.

❄ Trail in winter: It is 2.3 mi from Higby Rd. over the ice, when Big Moose Lake is frozen solid, to the start of the trail. Watch for bad ice at the narrows on the Inlet, and get off the lake on either side at the end to avoid the thin ice on the marsh at the inlet creek.

Distances: Landing to Andys Creek Lean-to via spur, 0.5 mi; landing to Lower Sister Lake Lean-to, 3.3 mi (5.3 km).

32 Russian Lake

Trails Illustrated Map 745: R9

▶Locator: This trail is accessible only by boat on Big Moose Lake. Refer to Gull Lakes (trail 30) for launching site information.

Go by boat to the end of East Bay on Big Moose Lake. From the Higby Rd.

boat launch, this is reached by following the shore R. At the end of East Bay there is a dock on the L (N) side. It is 1.3 mi from the Higby Rd. launch to the landing, and 3.5 mi from the W end of Big Moose Lake to the landing. ◄

From the dock (0.0 mi), the trail goes slightly N of E to a lean-to, which is nicely located by a ledge at the edge of Russian Lake, at 0.7 mi.

❄ Trail in winter: Smooth 1.3 mi trip over Big Moose Lake from Higby Rd. when the lake is frozen solid. Watch for thin ice when approaching the shore on East Bay.

❧ Distances: Landing to lean-to, 0.7 mi (1.1 km).

33 Hermitage Trail

Trails Illustrated Map 745: R9

The trail is named after a private camp located near the end of the trail. It provides some pleasant walking, although the S end tends to be rough and wet. The route has moderate ups and downs and in part goes through a mixed forest with large specimens of yellow birch.

►Locator: The N end of this interior trail is on Constable Pond–West Mt. Trail (see Western-Central Overlap Section, *Central Trails* trail 72), 0.5 mi from the trailhead. The S end is on Queer Lake Trail (trail 35), 2.2 mi from its trailhead. ◄

From the jct. with Constable Pond–West Mt. Trail (0.0 mi), the red-marked route goes SE. At 0.1 mi, a private trail comes in on the L at an acute angle and at 0.3 mi the wetland of the Mays Pond outlet appears on the L.

At 1 mi the route forks R. It crosses an intermittent stream in a wetland at 1.2 mi and ascends to a jct. at 1.3 mi. Here, 1.8 mi from the Higby Rd. trailhead, the Hermitage Trail ends at the yellow-marked Queer Lake Trail (trail 35). To the R, the latter trail goes WSW 2.2 mi to Big Moose Rd. via Windfall Pond. Avoid the path going immediately L at this jct.; it goes to a private camp. Straight ahead, Queer Lake Trail goes 1.3 mi to the lean-to on Queer Lake via a final side trail.

❄ Trail in winter: Easy backcountry skiing or snowshoeing.

❧ Distances: Jct. with Constable Pond–West Mt. Trail to jct. with Queer Lake Trail (trail 35), 1.3 mi (2.1 km). Higby Rd. to Queer Lake Lean-to (a likely use for this trail), 3.1 mi (5 km).

34 Mays Pond Trail

Trails Illustrated Map 745: R10

►Locator: The N end of this interior trail is on Constable Pond–West Mt. Trail (see Western-Central Overlap Section, *Central Trails* trail 72), 1.3 mi from its Higby Rd. trailhead. The S end is on Queer Lake Trail (trail 35), 2.6 mi from its trailhead. ◄

From its N end on Constable Pond–West Mt. Trail (0.0 mi), the yellow-marked path ascends gradually through a tall forest, levels off, and descends 100 ft past lofty red spruce to Mays Pond. At 0.4 mi, where the trail forks L, a short R fork drops down to the edge of the pond near the E end of its N shore. The towering white pines around this pond add to its beauty.

The yellow trail continues beyond the side trail and along the NE shore of Mays Pond, past majestic pines and through dense spruce. The trail crosses an inlet to the pond at 0.6 mi and then goes up somewhat steeply almost 300 ft. At 1.1 mi the trail reaches height of land and crosses the divide between the Moose-Black River and Raquette River watersheds. Finally, there is a descent.

At the bottom, at 1.3 mi, the trail ends on the yellow-marked Queer Lake Trail (trail 35). This point is 2.6 mi from the Higby Rd. trailhead. To the L on the yellow trail, it is 0.5 mi to the Queer Lake Lean-to. A loop trip to Queer Lake lean-to and return by the Hermitage Trail (trail 33) equals 6.2 mi.

❄ Trail in winter: Easy snowshoeing. Owing to steepness, this trail is for good backcountry skiers only.

⚏ Distances: Jct. with Constable Pond–West Mt. Trail to jct. with Queer Lake Trail (trail 35), 1.3 mi (2.1 km). Higby Rd. to Queer Lake Lean-to (a likely use for this trail), 3.1 mi (4.8 km). Return to start via Hermitage Trail (trail 22), 6.2 mi (including Queer Lake Lean-to).

35 Queer Lake Trail

Trails Illustrated Map 745: R9

▶Trailhead: From NY 28 in Eagle Bay, drive 3.2 mi N on Big Moose Rd. and turn R into the parking area for the Windfall Pond trailhead. The other end of the trail is on Constable Pond–West Mt. Trail (see Western-Central Overlap Section, *Central Trails* trail 72). ◀

From the register (0.0 mi), the yellow-marked trail goes E on the S side of a stream in an easy stretch. At 0.1 mi it forks L and crosses the stream on a bridge. (The path straight ahead leads in a few yards to an informal campsite by the stream.)

The trail goes E on the N side of the stream. At 0.7 mi, the trail recrosses the stream on a bridge with a flume on the R. It climbs SE along Windfall Pond's outlet, reaching a jct. at 1.1 mi, just W of the pond. The blue-marked Chain Ponds Trail (trail 36) goes R here; the yellow trail turns L toward Queer Lake. The trail promptly crosses the outlet of Windfall Pond after which, with an informal campsite on the R under the hemlocks, a side trail goes R a few yards to the edge of Windfall Pond. This is a small body of water partly lined by fallen trees.

Continuing ENE along the N side of the pond and beyond, the route goes through stands of towering hardwoods and along a slope that drops off L. At 1.9 mi there is a short, moderately steep descent, partly on bedrock outcropping. In an area of tall timber, the red-marked Hermitage Trail (trail 33) connects on the L at 2.2 mi. The yellow-marked Queer Lake Trail turns R (SE), climbs a ridge, and in 200 yd turns N and descends moderately. This bypass up and down the hillside avoids a crossing of private land at the Hermitage.

After a brook crossing at the bottom, another jct. appears at 2.4 mi. An unmarked trail leads L (W) 60 yd to the Hermitage, a private camp. The marked trail goes R at this jct. and travels ENE along the level, crossing a wetland at 2.5 mi. At 2.7 mi, the blue-marked Chain Ponds Trail (trail 36) rejoins on the R; 13 yd beyond, the yellow trail turns L (NW). (A side trail goes straight ahead, reaching the muddy edge of the NW bay of Queer Lake at 2.7 mi. There is an informal campsite set in the spruce with a view of the enclosed bay and a red-marked spur trail to a suggested campsite.)

From the jct., the yellow trail crosses a wetland at the corner of the bay, climbs steeply, and parallels the N shore of the bay. At 3 mi the yellow-marked Mays Pond Trail (trail 34) comes in from the L (N).

Following the lakeshore, the trail passes a red-marked spur R to the Queer Lake Lean-to at 3.3 mi. (This side trail goes S and SE to the beginning of the peninsula projecting from Queer Lake's N shore. It then crosses the narrow wetland on split logs at the base of the peninsula, follows the edge of the lake's NW bay a short way, and crosses the peninsula at its narrowest section to reach the lean-to 0.2 mi from the main trail. The spur route here is lent primeval charm by tall hemlocks, white pines, and red spruce. The lean-to is nicely situated on the NW shore of the main body of Queer Lake, with some large rocks at the water's edge. The distance from the trailhead on Big Moose Rd. is 3.5 mi. There is an unmarked path from the log planks at the base of the peninsula to its tip, ending at a large boulder on the tip after a massive blowdown.)

From the lean-to spur jct., the yellow trail continues E along a hillside, turns N at 4.7 mi, and crosses the divide between the Raquette River and Moose-Black River watersheds. Descending, the trail weaves a bit, then reaches a brook with beaver activity at 5 mi. At 5.2 mi, Chub Lake is partly visible through the trees on the R, the trail passing above its S shore. The path crosses an inlet at 5.4 mi on a plank bridge in a spruce-fringed wetland, with the pond visible on the R.

The trail reaches a jct. at 5.6 mi, where it turns L toward Constable Pond. (A yellow-marked side trail to Chub Lake continues straight [NE] and then turns E for 0.2 mi to the NW shore of conifer-lined Chub Lake. There is an attractive informal camping area under a stand of spruce, as well as a nice rock ledge at the shoreline extending underwater.)

From the jct. with the side trail, Queer Lake Trail continues NW through stands of spruce, and with further small ups and downs, to end at 6 mi at the blue-marked Constable Pond–West Mt. Trail (see Western-Central Overlap Section, *Central Trails* trail 72) on the SE shore of Constable Pond. To the L, it is 2.6 mi to the Higby Rd. trailhead. To the R, it is 5.5 mi to West Mt. and 10.5 mi to the Uncas Rd. trailhead (see *Central Trails* trail 71).

❃ Trail in winter: For intermediate backcountry skiers. Easy snowshoeing.

🐾 Distances: Big Moose Rd. to Windfall Pond and Chain Ponds Trail (trail 25) jct., 1.1 mi; to Hermitage Trail (trail 22) jct., 2.2 mi; to jct. Chain Ponds Trail E end, 2.7 mi; to Queer Lake, 2.7 mi; to Mays Pond Trail (trail 34) jct., 3 mi; to Queer Lake Lean-to spur, 3.3 mi; to turn N, 4.7 mi; to Chub Lake, 5.2 mi; to jct. Constable Pond–West Mt. Trail, 6 mi (9.6 km).

36 Chain Ponds Trail

Trails Illustrated Map 745: Q9

This overall V-shaped trail starts from the yellow-marked Queer Lake Trail (trail 35) at Windfall Pond, goes SE to a jct. with the red-marked Cascade Lake Link Trail (trail 26), and then proceeds N past Chain Ponds to rejoin Queer Lake Trail just W of Queer Lake, forming a triangle with Queer Lake Trail. The trail has considerable ascents and descents. It passes areas of rugged rock formations and cliffs. The E section tends to be narrow and overgrown. For scenery, this is the more interesting route from the road to the Queer Lake area.

▶Locator: Chain Ponds Trail joins Queer Lake Trail (trail 35) on both ends, by Windfall Pond at 1.1 mi from Big Moose Rd. (W end) and at 2.7 mi near the W bay of Queer Lake (E end). The trail also meets Cascade Lake Link Trail (trail 26), and thus is accessible from the Cascade Lake (trail 38) trailhead.◀

From Windfall Pond (0.0 mi), the blue-marked Chain Ponds Trail heads SE. After a few yards, a short side trail goes L to the edge of small Windfall Pond. Passing S of the pond, the main trail ascends SE through stately hardwoods. At 0.4 mi a faint path leads R a short way to the edge of a boggy pond.

The trail makes a further ascent at 0.5 mi near an imposing rock wall on the L with rock going up through the treetops and out of sight, and then descends, going through ferns and muddy spots. At 1 mi, an interesting area of cliffs, crevasses, caves, and large boulders begins on the L. At a jct. at 1.4 mi, the blue trail turns L (N) toward Chain Ponds, and the red Cascade Lake Link Trail (trail 37) comes in from the R.

Continuing N, the blue-marked trail crosses the outlet of Chain Ponds at 1.8 mi. To the L is the S section of Chain Ponds lined by fallen timber, and to the R a wetland through which the outlet runs. Chain Ponds is one body of water divided into three sections by two necks of land. It has a predominantly wetland shoreline with some dead standing timber. A side trail at 1.9 mi goes L to the end of the pond.

The trail goes N above the E side of the S section of Chain Ponds and through a mixed hardwood-coniferous forest, then ascends, Chain Ponds being no longer visible. It then starts to drop with a glimpse of the N end of the ponds at 2.5 mi. At 2.8 mi, it ends at the yellow-marked Queer Lake Trail (trail 35). To the L on the yellow trail it is 1.6 mi to Windfall Pond and the other end of Chain Ponds Trail, and 2.7 mi to the trailhead on Big Moose Rd. To the R, the NW bay of Queer Lake is almost at hand.

❊ Trail in winter: For good skiers only, owing to the hills. Easy snowshoeing.

🐾 Distances: W jct. with Queer Lake Trail (trail 35) to Cascade Lake Link

Trail (trail 37), 1.4 mi; to Chain Ponds, 1.8 mi; to E jct. with Queer Lake Trail near Queer Lake, 2.7 mi (4.3 km).

37 Cascade Lake Link Trail

Trails Illustrated Map 745: Q9

This route goes N from the Cascade Lake trail (trail 38) at a point just W of the lake to the blue-marked Chain Ponds Trail (trail 36). It ascends 275 ft and crosses the divide between the Moose-Black River and Raquette River watersheds, providing a link between Cascade Lake on the S and Windfall Pond, Chain Ponds, and Queer Lake on the N. It allows for longer trips from lake to lake within the Pigeon Lake Wilderness Area.

▶Locator: This is an interior trail linking the Cascade Lake trail (1.4 mi from the Cascade trailhead) with Chain Ponds Trail, leading to the rest of the Wilderness Area trails.◀

From the jct. with Cascade Lake Trail (trail 38) just W of Cascade Lake (0.0 mi), the red-marked trail goes W on level ground, skirting a hill. At 0.2 mi, the trail turns N and climbs a ridge. It begins to level off at 0.5 mi, but further small ascents follow. It bends NE and then curves back N through a couple of gullies to meet the blue-marked Chain Ponds Trail (trail 36) on the level at a high point at 1.1 mi.

To the L are Windfall Pond via Chain Ponds Trail and the Big Moose Rd. trailhead via Queer Lake Trail (trail 35). To the R, Chain Ponds Trail leads to Chain Ponds, Queer Lake, and other trails of the Pigeon Lake Wilderness Area.

❇ Trail in winter: For good wilderness skiers only, owing to the fairly steep ascents and descents. Easy snowshoeing.

🐾 Distances: Jct. with the Cascade Lake trail (trail 38) to Chain Ponds Trail (trail 36), 1.1 mi (1.8 km).

38 Cascade Lake

Trails Illustrated Map 745: Q10

This is a 6 mi ski-touring circuit and hiking trail from Big Moose Rd. E to Cascade Lake, then around the lake and back to the road over the initial route. The high points of the trip are a camping area halfway along the N side, and the falls at the E end of the lake.

This description covers the trail as a circuit hike clockwise around the lake, but the hiker headed for the falls should use the S shore trail, because it is much drier than the trail segment past the E end beyond the falls. Trail connections on the W end of the lake allow for a trip to the interior of the Pigeon Lake Wilderness Area, a loop trip to trailheads farther W on Big Moose Rd., or access to the lake by hikers from the Big Moose Lake area.

Cascade Lake Camp, now the camping area, was a summer camp for girls, with a clientele of fifty girls and a stable of twenty-five horses in 1947. The camp's original building was previously the summer home of Charles Snyder, an attorney who bought the land when Dr. William Seward Webb first subdivided his vast holdings.

▶Trailhead: From NY 28 in Eagle Bay, drive NW on Big Moose Rd. for 1.2 mi (avoiding an old trailhead on a dangerous S curve at 0.8 mi), and park in the DEC parking lot on the R. There are DEC yellow ski trail markers around the lake. This is also a designated horse trail.◀

From the back R corner of the parking lot (0.0 mi), the trail goes 0.4 mi SE to join an old woods road, which it follows with yellow ski markers (there may also be red hiking trail markers) NE through a hardwood forest. The rocky road goes gradually up and down, passing the Herkimer-Hamilton county line (marker R) soon before reaching a Y jct. at 1.1 mi. Here the S section of the circuit around Cascade Lake diverges. Hikers headed for the falls should turn R here, and follow a good route—possibly a little wet just before the end—E to the falls at 2.9 mi.

Continuing on the clockwise route, the trail turns L and descends to level ground as it approaches the outlet. At 1.3 mi, a field on the R, lying just W of the lake, is the site of a nineteenth-century lumber camp. Those hauling a canoe can enter this clearing and look for an opening through trees about 30 yd L from the back R corner for access to the end of the lake, just over 0.1 mi from the trail. In another 150 yd a bridge crosses the lake's outlet with a wetland on the L.

At 1.4 mi, the red-marked Cascade Lake Link Trail (trail 37) goes L (N) to the blue-marked Chain Ponds Trail (trail 36). Straight ahead on a broad, pleasant route E on the N side of Cascade Lake, the route passes an informal campsite on the R. At 1.9 mi, an inviting open area R is an obvious and pleasant site for camping. This rounded point of land has grass, white pines, a beach, and a sandy lake bottom. This was the site of the summer camp for girls. Returning from here makes a pleasant hike of 3.8 mi round-trip.

Beyond the open area, this wide road passes other open areas that were sports fields for the camp, including a tennis court R at 2.1 mi. Beyond them, the trail passes side paths R to campsites near the lake, then descends to a wet, muddy section and across the marshy end of the lake. It then climbs gradually to a 90-degree turn R (may be tricky for skiers coming down from the falls). Drier terrain follows. The trail crosses a stream at 3 mi, within earshot of the falls. This is Cascade Lake's main inlet, and approximately 25 yd farther up is the high, narrow waterfall that gives the lake its name.

After the waterfall, the route turns W and goes parallel to the lakeshore, but at some distance, so the lake is not visible. The old road passes a safe (without a door or any money in it) L, climbs a hillside above the lake, then follows along the contours to reach a jct. that completes the circuit of the lake at 4.9 mi. Ahead, it is 1.1 mi to the trailhead, for a total distance of 6 mi.

❄ Trail in winter: This is a DEC ski route, gentle and suitable for novice skiers, with one 90-degree turn on a gentle slope NW of the falls of any concern. Before the snow is thick enough, the creeks and wetlands on the E end of the lake may be messy for novices. Ski the route counterclockwise, starting on the S trail. If the creek crossing is messy, you can still see the falls and then turn back.

 Distances: Trailhead to loop jct., 1.1 mi; to falls by S route, 2.9 mi; to campsite on N side, 1.9 mi; to falls by N route, 3 mi; to return to trailhead after complete circuit, 6 mi (9.6 km).

39 Moss Lake Circuit

Trails Illustrated Map 745: Q9

Moss Lake (a later simplification of Morse Lake), on the SW side of Big Moose Rd., was for fifty years the site of a girls' camp. The State of New York acquired the property in 1973, and whatever structures remained were removed. The area now has no facilities other than privies at campsites, some reachable only by water, and the trail, which makes a circuit of the lake. There is a descriptive photo board at the trailhead showing many aspects of the former camp. After the state acquired the land, the camp was, for a time, occupied by Mohawk settlers, whose confrontation with New York State was very much in the news at the time.

The trail has DEC yellow markers of both the hiking and ski-touring variety, and it provides an easy and attractive hike along a mostly level woods road. This is also a designated horse trail.

Bubb Lake Trail (trail 40) joins the Circuit trail near the SE corner of Moss Lake, so all or part of each trail may be covered in one hike.

▶Trailheads: Drive 2.1 mi NW on Big Moose Rd. from its beginning at Eagle Bay and park in the area outlined by posts on the L. A small shelter contains two registers, one for those choosing a campsite (by sliding a site number over into the "Occupied" column) and one for those visiting for the day. Drive 0.1 mi NW up the road for another trailhead with disabled access. Paths have been hardened for access to the lake and one or more campsites.

There is also a winter trailhead on the L at a curve in the road 1.7 mi from Eagle Bay. A 100 yd woods road leads from that trailhead to a jct. with the trail. ◀

From the trail register at the main parking lot (0.0 mi), turn L (SE) on a dirt road to start the circuit of the lake. (Turning R, one would hike the Circuit trail in the opposite or counterclockwise direction.) For a view of the lake, walk straight ahead (SW) from the entrance for 135 yd to the shore of the lake at a beach. An island in the lake, a bluff on its W side, and white pines and beaches along the lakefront add to the attraction of the scene.

Hiking SE on the dirt road at the start of the circuit, some campsite openings can be seen to the R; these lead to sites of former camp buildings and to the lakeshore. After crossing the edge of a bare clearing (where raspberries can be found in season), the route becomes a pleasant woods road, dropping through a gully at 0.3 mi. At 0.4 mi another woods road leads L (ENE) 100 yd to a parking area at a curve in Big Moose Rd. This can be used as a winter trailhead for skiing

Moss Lake outlet. Chris Murray

on the Circuit trail.

At 0.5 mi there is a bridge over Moss Lake's main inlet (Cascade Lake's outlet). At 0.7 mi, with the lake visible through the trees, Bubb Lake Trail (trail 40) comes in from the L (S) with yellow markers. It is 0.7 mi along that trail to the NE end of Bubb Lake, a route that may also be skied in winter. That route continues on past the Vista Trail (trail 41) to NY 28.

The Circuit trail continues W along the woods road on the S side of Moss Lake, and at 1.2 mi crosses a bridge over the beginning of the lake's outlet. Here there is a view of the lake's S bay, one of the clearest views of the lake to be had from this trail. Tall white pines grace the shoreline here.

The trail passes through tall red spruce, hemlock, and yellow birch, and at 1.5 mi it descends almost to the edge of the SW end of the lake. From here NE along the W shore, one has views through the trees of the lake and of a 500 ft hill beyond it on the SE.

At 1.7 mi, a tree nearly three feet in diameter grows on top of a rock, its roots running several feet down the sides. An open area with ferns is traversed, followed at 2 mi by the first of several openings on the R leading to sites of former buildings, the lake shore, and another one of the campsites.

At 2.2 mi a cleared area off to the R, a campground framed with white pines, has abandoned stone steps going down to a beach at a N corner of the lake. The trail turns R at 2.4 mi. (The route ahead goes to a parking lot for the disabled on nearby Big Moose Rd.) The starting point of the Circuit trail is at 2.5 mi.

❉ Trail in winter: Easy skiing. Access can be from a winter parking place 0.4 mi E of the summer trailhead if the latter is not cleared.

♨ Distances: From trailhead clockwise to winter trailhead access, 0.4 mi; to Bubb Lake Trail (trail 40), 0.7 mi; to outlet, 1.2 mi; to beach, 2.2 mi; return to trailhead, 2.5 mi (4 km).

40 Bubb Lake Trail

Trails Illustrated Map 745: Q9

From NY 28, the route goes over the shoulder of Onondaga Mt., skirts Sis Lake and Bubb Lake on nearly level ground, and joins Moss Lake Circuit (trail 39). This is a scenic forest route. A round-trip of Bubb Lake Trail plus the circuit around Moss Lake would make a hike of 7.1 mi. A through hike to the Moss Lake trailhead on Big Moose Rd. would be 4.1 mi, taking the longer segment of the circuit trail around the lake's W side, or 3 mi taking the shorter part on the lake's E side.

Early settlers at Big Moose Lake used this route to reach Big Moose from Fourth Lake. After reaching Bubb Lake, they paddled to the inlet, portaged to Moss Lake, paddled to the N shore, portaged to Dart Lake, paddled across, and portaged to Big Moose Lake.

▶Trailhead: From the jct. of NY 28 and Big Moose Rd. in Eagle Bay, drive 1.4 mi W on NY 28 and park on the L (S) side of the road opposite the trailhead, which may not have a sign. The N trailhead is on Moss Lake Circuit (trail 39).◀

From NY 28 (0.0 mi), the yellow-marked trail ascends 150 ft NW on an eroded section. At 0.2 mi, the Vista Trail (trail 41) ascends L, while Bubb Lake Trail continues ahead. The broad trail levels out, but becomes muddier in places. At 0.4 mi a side trail forks R and goes 55 yd to Bubb Lake's S end. From here one can see most of this pleasant body of water.

Bubb Lake Trail continues W, and at 0.7 mi it forks R. After 40 yd, a side trail forks L and goes 65 yd through conifers to the SE corner of Sis Lake. This pond-size lake has rocks along much of its shoreline.

The main trail continues R, going N along the E side of Sis Lake, on a smooth footway through a splendid stand of hemlocks. The trail then crosses a bridge over the stream between Bubb and Sis Lakes at 0.9 mi. Both lakes are visible from here, but a full view of Sis Lake can be had by going a short way L to its rock-lined shore.

The trail continues parallel to the NW side of Bubb Lake past some stately hardwoods. Beyond them, the trail nears the lake in an attractive area of hemlocks. At 1.6 mi, it reaches the shore at the lake's narrowed NE end where there is a good view up the lake, with Onondaga Mt. rising from the far side. Soon the trail leaves Bubb Lake, bending L and heading NE. At 1.8 mi it crosses a bridge over the Bubb Lake outlet. On the downstream side is a dam with a spillway, built as a fish barrier.

The trail becomes broader and ends at 2.3 mi at Moss Lake Circuit (trail 39). The shortest route to Big Moose Rd. is to the R, but both directions end finally at the same trailhead (see trail 39).

❊ Trail in winter: Easy skiing, mostly level.

⚎ Distances: Trailhead to Vista Trail (trail 41), 0.2 mi; to Bubb Lake, 0.5 mi; to Bubb and Sis Lake stream, 0.9 mi; to Moss Lake Circuit (trail 39), 2.3 mi (3.7 km); to Big Moose Rd., 3 mi (4.8 km).

41 Vista Trail

Trails Illustrated Map 745: P8

This is a through trail with three trailheads. It has some nice views from several selected points along the way. It can be accessed from either end, or by using the Mountain Pond trailhead listed below to reach Cork Mt.

Vista Trail is a more strenuous hike than most in the region, with a good deal of climbing (some of it steep), and many ups and downs, especially along Onondaga Mt. The trail passes through some handsome forest with notable hemlock stands in the SW section. The NE section of Onondaga Mt. offers some good views over Fourth Lake and elsewhere.

Onondaga Mt., a ridge extending 2.3 mi along Fourth Lake from just SE of Mountain Pond to SE of Bubb Lake, does not have an official or generally known name, but it is apparent from David H. Beetle's book, *Up Old Forge Way*, that this is what it has been called in the past.

The trail is described from W to E. Shorter trips can be had by traveling from Rondaxe Rd. to the Mountain Pond trailhead, or from the Mountain Pond trailhead to the Bubb Lake trailhead.

▶Trailheads: To reach the W trailhead, from the Tourist Information Center in Old Forge, drive 4.4 mi NE on NY 28 and turn L (NW) on Rondaxe Rd. After 0.2 mi, park in the DEC parking area on the L, which also serves Bald (Rondaxe) Mt. (trail 42) and is likely to be overflowing on autumn weekends. The trailhead is on the other side of the road (NE).

To reach the center trailhead, go 5.5 mi from the Old Forge Tourist Information Center (3.4 mi from Big Moose Rd. in Eagle Bay). Turn L (NW) across from Daiker's Brookside Motel, and L again onto a dirt road. The trailhead is on the R, 0.2 mi from NY 28.

To reach the Bubb Lake trailhead on NY 28, go 1.4 mi W of Big Moose Rd. in Eagle Bay. Park on the L (S) side of the road, opposite the trailhead, which may not have a sign. ◀

Starting at the W trailhead on Rondaxe Rd. (0.0 mi), the blue-marked trail drops through a tall forest with a mix of conifers and broadleaf trees. At 0.2 mi, a red-marked spur trail goes L for 85 yd to Fly Pond, which is flanked by Rondaxe Rd. and a muddy wetland. The route reaches the SW end of the larger and more attractive Cary Lake at 0.4 mi, then goes N along the pond's W side on the lower slope of Bottle Mt., through a nice section of tall hemlocks.

Skirting the wetland at the N end of the pond, the trail reaches a dirt road at

0.7 mi and turns R on the road (no signs or markers). This road, used as a snow-mobile and bicycle trail, goes L to Lake Rondaxe and R to NY 28, following the route of the old Raquette Lake Railroad, which operated from 1900 to 1933, as indicated on a sign next to the turnoff; the sign also cites the railroad as the first to use oil-burning steam locomotives. The Mountain Pond trailhead is farther down this road.

After 160 yd along the road, crossing a wetland of Cary Lake, the trail turns L, again without a sign. Briefly following a muddy stretch along the wetland, the trail makes a 300 ft ascent N and E to the crest of Cork Mt. The climb, which uses switchbacks, has both moderate and steep grades on a picturesque slope of open forest with impressive hemlocks.

At 1.3 mi, a little below the crest, a red-marked spur trail goes L and climbs to the top of Cork Mt., where there is a partial view. (This spur trail climbs steeply N to Cork Mt.'s closed-in summit at 2280 ft elevation, a 0.3 mi round-trip off the main route. The red-marked L fork at 0.1 mi goes to the summit. The R fork descends a short distance to a partial view of hills to the NE. Cork Mt. is so named because, from the Lake Rondaxe area on the NW, it supposedly looks like the cork of the bottle; a reference to Bottle Mt., to the SW.)

Continuing from 1.3 mi, the blue-marked Vista Trail crosses over a saddle and descends E to Mountain Pond (elevation 2005 ft). The trail skirts the S end of the pond, and at 1.6 mi a short side path leads L to the shore of the pond. To the R of this path is an attractive area for camping under hemlock trees on the E side of the pond.

The blue trail climbs SE a short distance through mud to the gap between Cork and Onondaga Mts., where it passes an informal campsite and at 1.9 mi reaches a jct. Straight ahead is the red-marked Mountain Pond Trail, which descends very steeply to a dirt road connecting with NY 28, dropping about 250 ft in a quarter mile.

The blue Vista Trail turns L at this jct. This is the beginning of a more rugged section going ENE along the entire crest of Onondaga Mt., with many ascents and descents, some steep. There are some attractive views along the way, narrow sections of crestline, tall hardwoods, stands of spruce, and areas of ferns and bedrock. Immediately after the jct., the route is somewhat obscure.

The trail climbs 300 ft up the W flank of Onondaga Mt. to the mountain's highest point (2340 ft). At 2.3 mi there is a pretty view from the edge of a steep slope over a major section of Fourth Lake, with hills and mountains beyond. At 2.6 mi there is another view of the larger E section of Fourth Lake.

At 2.8 mi the trail descends to a notch that separates the W and E segments of Onondaga Mt., and then makes a gradual ascent. After reaching another notch at 3.1 mi, the trail climbs to follow the first of several sections of narrow crest. At 3.5 mi there are limited views SE and E over parts of Fourth Lake.

The descent of the E end of the ridge starts at 3.7 mi. A red-marked spur trail climbs steeply L a short way to a fine open view N over Bubb and Moss Lakes. The trail becomes steeper and reaches Becker's Outlook, with a limited view over hills to the NE, including Blue Mt. It makes a final steep descent to end at 4.2 mi on Bubb Lake Trail (trail 40). To the L, the path reaches the S end of Bubb Lake in 0.3 mi, and continues on to Moss Lake. Going R, one descends SE for 0.2 mi to the Bubb Lake trailhead on NY 28.

❄ Trail in winter: Steep sections. Suitable for hardy snowshoers.

🏃 Distances: Rondaxe Rd. to Fly Pond, 0.2 mi; to Cary Lake, 0.4 mi; to old Raquette Lake Railroad bed, 0.7 mi; to Cork Mt. spur, 1.3 mi; to Mountain Pond, 1.6 mi; to Mountain Pond trail jct., 1.9 mi (to Mountain Pond trailhead, 2.2 mi); to Bubb Lake Trail (trail 29), 4.2 mi (6.7 km); to Bubb Lake trailhead, 4.4 mi (7 km). Highest elevation, 2340 ft (713 m).

42 Bald (Rondaxe) Mt.

Trails Illustrated Map 745: P8

This short trail climbs through woods and then through progressively more open rock to a fire tower with great views at the open summit of Bald Mt. The steel fire tower, originally built in 1917, has been restored through the efforts of the Friends of Bald Mt. The cab is open year round (see www.masterpieces.com/bald.htm).

▶Trailhead: From the Tourist Information Center in Old Forge, drive 4.4 mi NE on NY 28, turn L (NW) on Rondaxe Rd. After 0.2 mi, park in the large area on the L. Or, from the village of Eagle Bay at the jct. of NY 28 and Big Moose Rd., drive 4.5 mi W and SW on NY 28 and then turn R on Rondaxe Rd. There are trail signs and a register at the trailhead.◀

From the register (0.0 mi), the well-trodden red-marked trail ascends SW mostly along moderate grades, although there are some steep pitches. (Some say it's hard on the knees coming down.) As one climbs, the deciduous forest soon gives way to an attractive spruce-fir forest. A large part of the ascent is on bedrock. Starting at 0.4 mi, fine views are to be had of Second, Third, and Fourth Lakes from the edge of cliffs on the L (SE). The final 600 ft to the fire tower on the summit at 0.9 mi is mostly along the rock spine with many viewing places.

The open views from the summit embrace First through Fourth Lakes of the Fulton Chain on the S and E, part of Little Moose Lake on the S beyond First and Second Lakes, Blue Mt. (3759 ft) in the distance to the ENE, and other mountains to the E. Climbing the fire tower to the cabin makes the view more extensive, and on very clear days one may see several of the High Peaks on the NE horizon L of Blue Mt., including Mt. Marcy, the highest of the Adirondack peaks (5344 ft), 55 mi away. SW of the fire tower, 375 ft along the rock crest, is another fine vantage point or two and a balanced rock of sorts: a boulder standing on a sloping ledge near the drop-off. Here the trail ends at 1 mi.

❄ Trail in winter: Snowshoe climb. Skis only for the expert. Crampons may be needed on the icy summit. Extra care needed on the open rock slopes.

🏃 Distances: Trailhead to tower, 0.9 mi; to end of trail, 1 mi (1.6 km). Ascent, 390 ft (119 m). Summit elevation, 2350 ft (716 m).

Bald Mountain. Nancie Battaglia

43 Eagle Cliff

This is an ascent nearly 200 ft from the village of Eagle Bay to the top of Eagle Cliff with its open view of Fourth Lake. The round-trip hike is only 0.6 mi. Access to the trail is on private land and the trail is privately maintained. There is no water. Stay on the well-worn path and respect the private property.

Note that the nearby trails to Rocky Mt. and Black Bear Mt. (*Central Trails* trails 73, 74, and 76) are described in Western-Central Overlap Section of this guidebook, as well as in *Central Trails.*)

▶Trailhead: In Eagle Bay go to the intersection of NY 28 and Big Moose Rd. Park on the roadside near the intersection without blocking driveways. The trail starts on the R off Big Moose Rd. going up Ledge Rd. (gravel).◀

From Big Moose Rd. (0.0 mi), the route goes E for 35 yd on Ledge Rd., passing one residence that faces Big Moose Rd. Look for an Eagle Cliff sign L on a dirt footpath. There are no markers, but the footpath is well worn.

After the L turn before the next dooryard, the trail goes between the cottages, bends a little R, climbs steeply N for a short distance, then climbs E along the edge of a steep slope to a rock outcropping at 0.2 mi with a view S of the nearby bay of Fourth Lake. A metal survey marker is embedded in the rock, signaling the boundary between Herkimer and Hamilton Counties.

The route continues NE along the outcropping to reach the top of Eagle Cliff at 0.3 mi, an elevation of 2000 ft. From the edge of the cliffs Fourth Lake can be seen, lying 300 ft below with Eagle Bay nearest at hand.

❊ Trail in winter: Suitable for snowshoes only. The trail reaches open, sloping rock above the cliff, which could be treacherous if icy, even with crampons.

❈ Distance: Trailhead to Eagle Cliff, 0.3 mi (0.5 km). Ascent, 200 ft (61 m). ❧

Along the trail to Otter Lake. Mark Hemendinger

Brantingham Section

The community of Brantingham Lake is not located on a through road, but it is a center for summer activity, with resorts, a marina, a golf course, many stately summer homes, fine dining, two tiny general stores, and a motel. As with the area covered in the Independence River Section, access roads to the area are local and complicated. A Lewis County highway map shows town roads that may not appear on state maps, as well as state and county highways. They are $3 each (verify cost at 315-376-5350) with a check to the Lewis County Highway Dept. at 7660 State St., Lowville, NY 13367.

The hiking trails of this section are intimately linked to the two major roads passing through it. Brantingham Rd. enters from the highway network to the W and continues E to merge into Steam Mill Rd., a principal trailhead route going 5.7 mi E. The old steam-driven lumber mill is long gone, although timbers cut at this mill and used in the roadway were found preserved under the road and still in good condition when it was reconstructed in the mid-1970s.

Partridgeville Rd. crosses Brantingham Rd. going N, then curves E around the lake. After passing the site of the former village of Partridgeville NE of the lake, it continues E to trailheads at the former Dolgeville, and goes beyond that all the way to Big Otter Lake (as a snowmobile and hiking trail). Dolgeville was also known as Botchfordville. It once had a live-in community with sawmills and tanneries.

In winter, the more distant trails are not decently accessible on foot for day trips, but they are used by snowmobilers. Many of the closer trails, such as Catspaw Lake Rd. (Blueberry Trail) and Centennial Ski Trail, then become more attractive.

The area also includes the Otter Creek Horse Trail System (DEC has a map); those trails are also open to hikers, mountain bikers, and cross-country skiers—the mix not being the problem DEC had anticipated. Bicyclists especially should use caution, particularly at bends or corners, to avoid spooking horses.

A few suggested hikes for this section are listed below.

SHORT HIKE
Catspaw Lake: 3 mi (4.8 km) round-trip. A 4WD road goes around the N side of the lake, with access at the NE and NW corners. The lake is very nice, and the walk pleasant. See trail 45.

MODERATE HIKES
Pine Lake: 5.8 mi (9.3 km) round-trip. This very remote wilderness lake and lean-to is accessible via a good trail on an old road, now the Pine Lake Trail (trail 54).

Big Otter Lake: 9.4 mi (15 km) round-trip. An old jeep road leads to a fine camping spot on the NW side of the lake (see trail 51).

44 Confusion Flats

Trails Illustrated Map 745: P2

Confusion Flats is a vast region of big sand dunes and scrub vegetation, mixed with scrubby pines. It is covered with old two-track roads. Some are passable by car (passenger car on the main routes, but 4WD is better). These roads are principally horse and snowmobile trails, while a few (shown on the map as roads) are marked for motor vehicle use. Motorists, including ATV drivers, may not use those paths not specifically marked for vehicular use. Hikers are welcome to use all trails.

Among the many attractions of this region, Pitcher Pond and Little Otter Lake are especially pretty evergreen-ringed lakes. Some trails cross Otter Creek and connect to trails in the Brantingham area. Other trails on the N go as far as Beach Mill Rd., near the trailhead at Beach Mill Pond.

Trails in this region are linked for continuous horse and snowmobile travel. All of them provide opportunity for a pleasant walk in the woods. The trails listed below have particular appeal for the hiker because of ponds, streams, or longer distances.

There are nice campsites in the Otter Creek State Forest at the southern trail-head. Camping is by advance permit only; call the Lowville office of the DEC at 315-376-3521.

▶Trailheads: To reach the N trailhead from Chases Lake Rd. S of Chase Lake (E of Lowville), go E on Sand Pond Rd. There is a large parking lot at the jct. with Confusion Flats Rd. Take Confusion Flats Rd. S.

To reach the S trailhead, from Pine Grove Rd. N of Grieg, go E on Eatonville Rd. Van Arnam Rd. connects on the R at 1.2 mi. Eatonville Rd. then goes down-hill to Otter Creek at 1.4 mi. The bridge over the creek marks the start of Otter Creek Truck Trail, a DEC road. This 1.5 mi road ending at private land gives access to some of the southernmost trails of Confusion Flats.◀

44A Branaugh Trail

Trails Illustrated Map 745: P2

Sand Pond, E of Chase Lake, is not entirely private. There is a slice of state land on the E side, with a nice sand beach. Starting from the N trailhead (see Confusion Flats, trail 44), go E on Sand Pond Rd. for 0.5 mi to a parking area on the R, next to a gate. Walk around the vehicle barrier and go 0.3 mi (0.5 km) on the old road, which turns R into a field at the head of the beach. The area to the N and E of the lake is state land.

44B Fletcher Horse Trail

Trails Illustrated Map 745: P2

Starting from the N trailhead (see Confusion Flats, trail 44), use Confusion Flats Rd. to reach Florence Pond Rd. Turn L. Go 0.7 mi and park nearby. Starting from the jct., Fletcher Trail goes N, then E through the scrub pines. The trail turns N at 1 mi and skirts Little Otter Lake, then turns E onto a peninsula with a beautiful view of the lake. The route leaves the peninsula headed W for 0.3 mi, then turns N around Airport Pond and continues to Bull Rd. at 1.3 mi (2.1 km).

44C Little Otter Lake Rd.

Trails Illustrated Map 745: P2

Starting from the N trailhead (see Confusion Flats, trail 44), use Confusion Flats Rd. to reach Florence Pond Rd. Turn L. At 0.7 mi, Fletcher Horse Trail (trail 44B) enters from an old road on the L and leaves on a path straight ahead. Turn R and go another 0.2 mi to an unmarked Y jct. Take the L fork if you have 4WD; otherwise, park and walk the route. The rutted old road winds through scrub pine, first passing a footpath that connects to Fletcher Horse Trail, then a short path down to the lake, and finally ends at 1 mi (1.6 km) just above the middle of the lake's S shore.

44D Florence Pond Rd. and Horse Trail

Trails Illustrated Map 745: P2

Starting from the N trailhead (see Confusion Flats, trail 44), use Confusion Flats Rd. to reach Florence Pond Rd. Turn L. At 0.7 mi, Fletcher Horse Trail (trail 44B) enters from an old road on the L and leaves on a path straight ahead. Turn R and go another 0.2 mi to an unmarked Y jct. (The L fork is trail 44C.) Turn R and continue another 0.5 mi to Little Otter Creek. Parking is suggested, as the road becomes ever less drivable.

The road here (0.0 mi) is pleasantly walkable (though it becomes inaccessible to cars at 1.3 mi from Little Otter Creek). The old road then goes down somewhat steeply to reach Crooked Creek, 1.5 mi (2.4 km) from Little Otter Creek. Crooked Creek Horse Trail (trail 48) joins on the other side (Crooked Creek must be waded).

There is an alternate route on the L at 0.2 mi from Little Otter Creek. It heads E for 0.5 mi to cross an open ridge between two lower wet areas, then turns S to meet the main route at 0.9 mi from Little Otter Creek.

44E Pitcher Pond Horse Trail

Trails Illustrated Map 745: P2

Starting from the N trailhead (see Confusion Flats, trail 44), use Confusion Flats Rd. for 2.5 mi. Park at the jct. with Shortcut Rd. and Erie Canal Horse Trail (trail 44F) L.

Take Erie Canal Horse Trail for 0.2 mi to the jct. with Pitcher Pond Horse Trail (L). The trail drifts through sand flats for 1 mi (1.6 km), then descends gently to the S bank of Pitcher Pond. It continues around the pond to meet Pitcher Pond Rd. on the N side.

44F Erie Canal Horse Trail

Trails Illustrated Map 745: O2

Starting from the N trailhead (see Confusion Flats, trail 44), use Confusion Flats Rd. for 2.5 mi. Park at the jct. with Shortcut Rd. and Erie Canal Horse Trail (L).

Starting from the S trailhead (see Confusion Flats, trail 44), take Van Arnam Rd. E 2.2 mi to the jct. with Catspaw Lake Rd., a dirt road on the L. That road splits in a Y jct. Take the R fork. Go 0.3 mi to Erie Canal Trail on the L.

The trail is a pleasant, easygoing 1 mi (1.6 km) trip across Otter Creek.

44G Streamside Horse Trail

Trails Illustrated Map 745: O1

From the S trailhead (see Confusion Flats, trail 44), go 1.4 mi from Otter Creek to Mike's Rd. on the R. Turn onto Mike's Rd. and go 0.9 mi to the jct. with Ridgeview (or Ridge Top) Trail on the R. This is the end of the officially drivable road. Continue on foot.

The old road ends 0.4 mi from the parking point, but the trail turns R and continues along the high, steep bank of Otter Creek. At 0.7 mi, the route turns N and descends to meet Valley Trail and the bottom end of Ridge Top Trail (two short trails that go E to join Streamside Trail). By Ridge Top Trail, it is 0.4 mi back to the starting point.

Streamside Trail continues along low ground near the creek, then climbs back up to meet Mike's Rd. From there, the start of the trail is 0.4 mi to the R on Mike's Rd. It is 1.7 mi (2.7 km) around the full loop.

David Hough

45 Blueberry Trail

Trails Illustrated Map 745: O2

▶Trailhead: See trail 47.◀

This snowmobile trail meets Partridgeville Rd. just E of Shingle Mill Falls Trail (0.0 mi), but hikers have little need to use that short section. Go down the Shingle Mill Falls Trail and turn L (W) onto Blueberry Trail. This goes to Otter Creek, around a very high esker, and meets Catspaw Lake Rd. at 1.5 mi. It is another 1 mi from there to Partridgeville Rd. The best part of the trail is the section near Catspaw Lake.

The start of the Catspaw Lake Rd. is 0.9 mi N on Partridgeville Rd. from its jct. with Brantingham Rd. It is a simple two-track road, almost unnoticeable on the L. At 1 mi on this old road, trail 45 joins on the R. Catspaw Lake is on the L at the bottom, and is interesting in its own right.

❄ Trail in winter: Snowmobile trail and good ski trail.

🐾 Distance: Trailhead to Catspaw Lake Rd., 1.5 mi (2.4 km).

46 Glenfield Railroad Trail

Trails Illustrated Map 745: O2

▶Trailhead: See trail 47.◀

The route, used by snowmobilers in winter, starts slightly E of Shingle Mill Falls Trail (trail 47), on the opposite side of the road. It goes S to meet the bed of an old lumber railroad, then heads NE to rejoin Partridgeville Rd. at the edge of a private land block, 2.4 mi from the first trailhead. It is not worth coming a long way for, but is a pleasant level hike for those staying in Brantingham.

❄ Trail in winter: Snowmobile trail.

🐾 Distance: Trailhead to trailhead, 2.4 mi (3.8 km).

47 Shingle Mill Falls

Trails Illustrated Map 745: P2

Shingle Mill Falls is a broad, wide, 10 ft high drop in Otter Creek, with some auxiliary falls above and below. Access is easy, and the falls are pretty. A large pool at the bend below the falls looks inviting for swimming.

▶Trailhead: From the crossroads on Brantingham Rd. in Brantingham, go N on Partridgeville Rd., curving to the NE. At 1.6 mi there is a jct. Partridgeville Rd. turns L. At 2.7 mi on the L is a slight grassy region, suitable for parking, next to Shingle Mill Falls Rd. (no markings). Check the distance carefully; there are many turnoffs in the area. This two-track dirt road goes nearly to Shingle Mill Falls. It may be improved in the future, allowing easy access right to the falls. Otherwise, the ruts make it advisable to park passenger cars at the grassy spot next to the paved road.◀

From Partridgeville Rd. (0.0 mi), follow the two-track road N. At 0.2 mi is a jct. where Blueberry Trail (trail 45) crosses. That trail is marked for both snowmobile and horse use. At 0.5 mi there is a sort of parking lot. Shortly beyond, the route reaches the water on open rock slabs just above the falls. Don't bother with the good footpath going L just before the falls; it leads nowhere. Walk along the rocks just back from the water to reach the area below the falls.

❀ Trail in winter: Easy showshoe or ski, but short.

🐎 Distance: Partridgeville Rd. to end of road and falls, 0.5 mi (0.8 km).

48 Crooked Creek Horse Trail

Trails Illustrated Map 745: P2

This horse trail connects Partridgeville Rd. with Confusion Flats. It is an easy and pleasant trail, but does involve wading Otter Creek at the start and Crooked Creek at the other end (if continuing on into Confusion Flats).

▶Trailhead: From the crossroads on Brantingham Rd. in Brantingham, go N on Partridgeville Rd., curving to the NE. At 1.6 mi there is a jct. Partridgeville Rd. turns L. At 2.7 mi on the L is a slightly overgrown grassy parking spot next to the two-track Shingle Mill Falls trail (trail 47). The next trail, at 2.8 mi on the L, is Blueberry Trail (trail 45). Beyond that, the two-track road on the L at 3 mi is Crooked Creek Trail. Park along the road as best you can.◀

From Partridgeville Rd. (0.0 mi), the old road descends a short distance to Otter Creek, where the stream must be waded. It then goes through pleasant open woods N, then curves W and goes down to cross Crooked Creek (wading, no bridge) to meet Florence Pond Rd. and Horse Trail (trail 44D) at 0.7 mi.

❀ Trail in winter: Snowmobile trail, suitable for skiing and snowshoeing if the two creeks are crossable.

🐎 Distance: Trailhead to Crooked Creek, 0.7 mi (1.1 km).

49 Centennial Ski Trail

Trails Illustrated Map 745: O3

This trail is a through route from Partridgeville Rd. to Steam Mill Rd. An extra trail section in the middle allows one to ski or hike a loop trip through interesting country. The through route is called the Centennial Scoot and the loop trip uses a section known as the Bear Ridge Run.

▶Trailheads: To reach the N trailhead, from the crossroads in Brantingham, go N on Partridgeville Rd. At 1.6 mi there is a jct. Partridgeville Rd. turns L. This part of the road was formerly known as Dolgeville Rd., but is now the continuation of Partridgeville Rd. At 4.6 mi, a gravel road goes L. Trailhead parking is on the R, almost opposite this gravel road.

To reach the S trailhead, go E on Brantingham Rd. at the intersection with Partridgeville Rd., passing the golf course. At 0.9 mi from the intersection, where the pavement turns L, continue straight ahead on gravel Steam Mill Rd. At 2.3 mi from the Partridgeville Rd. intersection, the trailhead is on the L (N). This trailhead is 0.4 mi from the end of the plowed road in winter.◀

From Partridgeville Rd. (0.0 mi), the yellow-marked trail goes SE past a trail register and curves S as it passes over some ups and downs. A mild climb leads to a jct. at 0.5 mi on a hilltop overlooking a pond to the L (E). The trail L is Bear Ridge Run (see below).

Continuing ahead (R), the Centennial Scoot goes W following easy terrain above Brantingham Inlet Creek, then turns S across a smooth hilltop. After a gentle descent, at 1.7 mi (1.2 mi after the first jct. with Bear Ridge Run), the two trails meet again. Ahead, the trail leads over gentle terrain to the Steam Mill Rd. trailhead at 3.2 mi.

Back at the jct. at 0.5 mi from Partridgeville Rd., the trail to the L (S) is the Bear Ridge Run, which curves around the pond on a long ridge. This route is very interesting, but definitely not for beginning skiers. It even has "caution, steep hill" signs. It has significant ups and downs. Next to an open area R, the trail drops to a T jct. at 1.2 mi from Partridgeville Rd. The trail L is abandoned and should be avoided. Turning R, the route is gentler than the first part. It continues across an open area, then through evergreens with red hiking trail markers.

At 2.2 mi, after crossing a bridge, Bear Run Trail reaches the other jct. with the Centennial Scoot. To the L (W), it is 1.5 mi to Steam Mill Rd. The route R (N) leads gently up and over a broad hill to a jct. at 3.4 mi marking the completion of a loop. It then heads L (N) downhill to reach Partridgeville Rd. at 3.9 mi.

✻ Trail in winter: Cross-country ski trail. See caution in third paragraph of description.

🐾 Distances: Partridgeville Rd. to jct. of Bear Ridge Run and Centennial Scoot, 0.5 mi; to second jct. of two routes via Centennial Scoot, 1.7 mi; to Steam Mill Rd. using Centennial Scoot, 3.2 mi (5.1 km). Road-to-road distance using Bear Ridge Run, 3.7 mi (5.9 km). Round-trip using both trails, 7 mi (11.2 km).

50 Silvermine Trail

This trail from the Brantingham area had a major reroute in 2014. The old northern section, which connects to an old section (now unmaintained) of the Mt. Tom Trail (trail 14), approaches but does not quite reach the Independence River.

The trail is mostly gentle, wide, and dry. It connects to Balsam Flats Rd., which allows for a connection with the 2014 reroute of the Mt. Tom Trail (trail 14) and through trips across the backcountry. (Note that through trips require cars at two trailheads.) Access is possible by other trails (trails 2, 13) from Stony Lake and from Beach Mill Rd. Of these, Beach Mill Rd. offers good smooth access for automobiles. The last little way off the E end of Stony Lake Rd. is decidedly rough. (See Independence River Section.) The trail retains its name even though it no longer reaches Silvermine.

▶Trailhead: From the crossroads in Brantingham, turn L (N) onto Partridgeville Rd. At 1.6 mi, there is a jct. Partridgeville Rd. turns L. This part of the road was formerly known as Dolgeville Rd., but is now the continuation of Partridgeville Rd. At 7.5 mi, park in the trailhead parking lot on the R, just before a bridge over Otter Creek. This is upstream of the former Dolgeville (Botchfordville), which had sawmills and tannery operations.◀

From the parking lot (0.0 mi), cross the bridge on Partridgeville Rd. over Otter Creek, then turn L onto the trail with red snowmobile markers. At first the wide old road goes N, then E to bypass a section of private lands. The trail was significantly rerouted in 2014, and at 1.4 mi the trail leaves the former route and turns L (NW). At 3.3 mi it ends at the gravel Balsam Flats Rd.

(The eastern end of Mt. Tom Trail [trail 14; also rerouted in 2014] is approximately 2.8 mi to the R [NE] on Balsam Flats Rd. The trail meets Balsam Flats Rd. on the L. Balsam Flats Rd. continues beyond the jct. with Mt. Tom Trail to reach private land near the Lewis-Herkimer county line.)

(The old Silvermine Trail, which continues NE beyond the turn at 1.4 mi, is passable though unmaintained. It leads initially through open hardwoods before beaver ponds send the trail to higher ground, where there is more undergrowth. At 3.6 mi the route drops to cross Crooked Creek at the site of the old Silvermine Dam. It crosses on a bridge, turns R, and follows around a hill. It reaches another lowland beaver meadow to the R, then heads uphill, continuing the NE trend. At 5.2 mi, a slight footpath leads R a few paces to the foundation of an old cabin, the first sign of Balsam Flats ahead. At 5.8 mi, the trail turns L on a dirt road [R leads to private land in 100 ft], then soon crosses a good but restricted access gravel road [R again leads to private land] and heads diagonally L downhill. There is an access point to the Independence River at 7.2 mi. The trail then leaves the river briefly to end at an old section[now unmaintained] of the Mt. Tom Trail, trail 14, at 7.4 mi. The Mt. Tom Trail crosses private land to reach a trailhead at Stony Lake.)

❋ Trail in winter: Snowmobile trail, lightly used. Gentle, easy going.

🏃 Distances: Partridgeville Rd. trailhead to Balsam Flats Rd., 3.3 mi (5.3 km). To jct. with Mt. Tom Trail (trail 14) via Balsam Flats Rd., 6.1 mi (9.8 km).

51 Big Otter Lake West Trail

Trails Illustrated Map 745: P4

This trail is actually an old road, still technically open, with numerous large mud-holes. It is marked and used as a snowmobile trail, but is also hiked. It is the shortest route from a trailhead to Big Otter Lake.

DEC has proposed reopening this road to automobile traffic as far as Big Otter Lake, with a parking lot at the end. Budget constraints, among other things, make this unlikely for some years to come. Reopening would allow transport of canoes, kayaks, and car-top boats to the lake. The parking lot exists, but even ATVs leave the road to go around some spots.

Note that near the end of the lake, where trails 67 and 69 meet, there are some erroneous signs. Some overstate the distance to Steam Mill Rd., measuring to a former trailhead before the Drunkard Creek trailhead was made, and others make reference to the parking lot at the end of the lake, which is virtually impossible to reach, apparently anticipating the road improvement.

▶Trailhead: See trail 50.◀

Beginning at the bridge by the parking lot (0.0 mi), the route goes through a small block of private land, past summer homes, and then enters state land on a rocky but easy old road. At 0.5 mi, there is a wet creek crossing, the first of several. Farther on, a 50 ft washout has left the route under water.

At 3 mi on the R there is a trail to a footbridge referred to as Otter Creek Trail. It is not maintained by the state but serves as a cutover to Pine Lake Trail (trail 54).

Continuing E, at 3.6 mi Big Otter Lake West Trail goes straight ahead. (To the R, through the "parking lot," a trail soon crosses Otter Creek on a two-section bridge no longer usable by snowmobiles and joins the blue-marked Big Otter Lake East foot trail from Thendara [trail 56]. The red and snowmobile trails continue SW on the S side of Otter Creek toward Pine Lake [see trail 54].)

From the jct. at 3.6 mi, Big Otter Lake West Trail continues E, crossing the Lewis-Herkimer county line at a post at 3.7 mi. The route is unmarked for a way, but older snowmobile trail markers show up eventually. The road has numerous wet spots, with wet bypasses, but the woods are open and detours are easy.

At 4.5 mi, a shallow and swampy part of Big Otter Lake comes into view. Two clearings on the trail at 4.6 and 4.7 mi are apparently the sites of an old resort hotel in use around 1900. An informal campsite in the second clearing is well located near shore, with a beautiful view of the lake from a sand beach.

Continuing along the lake, the route passes a tiny sand beach, then climbs, providing nice views out over the lake. At the end of Big Otter Lake at 5.3 mi, the trail passes through a muddy, boggy area. On the other side, now aiming SW, the route leads past a large hemlock and a gigantic white pine to another stream crossing, probably requiring wading. A steep bank on the other side inhibits crossing upstream.

Beyond, the route enters the Ha-De-Ron-Dah Wilderness Area and ends at an elaborate unofficial campsite on a point of land at 5.4 mi. The setting is very nice, and the lake views are excellent. A road once continued N from here, but it is long gone, and the private land a short distance up the creek is posted.

❄ Trail in winter: Snowmobile trail to jct. with trail 54; otherwise suitable for backcountry skiing and snowshoeing. Loop trips for parties of strong skiers are possible using Otter Creek–Pine Lake Trail (trail 52) for a return.

🐾 Distances: Trailhead parking to last houses, 0.4 mi; to jct. with Otter Creek cutoff trail, 3 mi; to jct. with Big Otter Lake East Trail (trail 56), 3.7 mi (to Herreshoff Rd. trailhead at Thendara, 11.6 mi); to old hotel site, 4.7 mi; to E end of Big Otter Lake, 5.4 mi (8.6 km).

52 Otter Creek–Pine Lake Trail

Trails Illustrated Map 745: O4

▶Trailhead: See trail 63.◀

Starting at the back of the parking lot on Partridgeville Rd. (0.0 mi), the trail, marked with snowmobile markers, goes S up a hillside. It bends R at the top and goes W to join the old Pine Lake Rd. at 0.5 mi, where that old road leaves private land gated nearby to the R. Continuing L on the old road, the mostly dry trail heads SE along the hilltop to Hubbards Jct. at 0.9 mi. The trail R (S) is Pico Mt. Trail (trail 53), leading in 2.4 mi to the trail jct. at Spring Hill.

The route ahead (SE) continues over the hill and down the side of a slight ridge, with numerous mudholes and ATV tracks. It continues on to a jct. with the red-marked Pine Lake Trail (trail 54) at 2.8 mi. To the R, it is 2.4 mi to the Spring Hill jct. and 4 mi to the Drunkard Creek trailhead on Steam Mill Rd. To the L, it is 0.1 mi to the Pine Lake Lean-to spur (the lean-to being about 200 ft N) and 2 mi to Big Otter Lake.

❄ Trail in winter: Snowmobile trail. Otherwise suitable for skiing and snowshoeing.

🐾 Distances: Otter Creek trailhead to Hubbards Jct. and Pico Mt. Trail (trail 53), 0.9 mi; to Pine Lake Trail, 2.8 (4.5 km).

53 Pico Mt. Trail

Trails Illustrated Map 745: O4

▶Locator: The N end of this interior trail can be accessed from the Otter Creek–Pine Lake Trail (trail 52) 0.9 mi from Partridgeville Rd. The S end can be accessed from Pine Lake Trail (trail 67) 1.6 mi from the Drunkard Creek trailhead at the E end of Steam Mill Rd. ◀

Starting at the jct. with Otter Creek–Pine Lake Trail (trail 52) at Hubbards Jct. (0.0 mi), the route, marked with snowmobile trail markers, follows an old road S, going gently downhill. The old road is generally wide and pleasant.

After crossing Fish Creek on a bridge at 1 mi, the route continues S to 1.1 mi, then turns nearly E and begins to climb a gentle slope. After reaching a broad ridge, the route turns S again and finishes the climb. Near the top at 2.1 mi, the trail crosses to the SE side of the hill (unofficially named Pico Mt.) and starts angling down. The bottom is only a short distance down, with a small, easy creek crossing. The trail starts up again on a wet slope.

In a short distance, the trail ends at a jct. on Spring Hill at 2.4 mi. Ahead, up the hillside on the Mudhole Trail (trail 55), it is 1.2 mi to Pine Creek near the Mudhole. To the L on Pine Lake Trail (trail 54), it is 2.5 mi to the Pine Lake Lean-to. To the R on Pine Lake Trail it is 1.6 mi to the Drunkard Creek trailhead.

❃ Trail in winter: Snowmobile trail. Otherwise suitable for skiing and snowshoeing.

❀ Distances: Hubbards Jct. on Otter Creek–Pine Lake Trail (trail 52) to Fish Creek bridge, 1 mi; to jct. at Spring Hill, 2.4 mi (3.8 km).

54 Pine Lake Trail

Trails Illustrated Map 745: O3

This trail, part of which is a snowmobile trail, extends from Steam Mill Rd. at Drunkard Creek trailhead to Big Otter Lake, passing Pine Lake on the way. Several connecting trails along the path allow for many varied routes. Pine Lake camping is at a lean-to.

▶Trailhead: From the jct. with Partridgeville Rd. in Brantingham, go E on Brantingham Rd., continuing straight past the golf course. In 0.9 mi, where the pavement turns L, continue ahead on a gravel road (Steam Mill Rd.). The road crosses Poison Creek at 3.1 mi, the approximate site of the old steam-driven lumber mill. At 5.4 mi, by Drunkard Creek, the road ends at a barricade and parking lot. The trail is marked with DEC red and snowmobile markers.◀

Starting at the Drunkard Creek parking lot (0.0 mi), the old road crosses the creek, bends R, and climbs gently to a trail register at 0.1 mi. Bending L, the old road curves to the NE under open canopy and climbs gently. It crosses several bridges before reaching a four-way jct. on Spring Hill at 1.6 mi. To the L (N), Pico Mt. Trail (trail 53) proceeds over a shoulder of Pico Mt. toward Hubbards Jct. and Otter Creek. To the R (S), Mudhole Trail (trail 55) goes toward the Mudhole. The snowmobile trail turns L onto Pico Mt. Trail.

Continuing ahead (NE) on a foot trail, the route curves over a slight hill and descends to the outlet creek of Eight-Foot Swamp at 2.6 mi. The bank is steep. On the E side, the trail goes steeply up to the top of an S-shaped esker and passes along nearly its entire length, about 0.2 mi. The steep-sided esker seems just like a man-made earth dam. At its E end, the trail turns down the side and continues

Richard Nowicki

through heavy undergrowth on a ridge above Pine Creek.

At 2.8 mi, the trail overlooks a beaver dam, R, apparently the end of Pine Lake, which extends NE for nearly 1.3 mi. At 3.8 mi, a couple of walkways assist in crossing a wet area, although hikers may have to wade to get to them as the water covers the steps up to the walkways. At 3.9 mi, there is a side trail R to an overlook, and an opening through brush that drops to a picnic spot next to the lake.

At 4 mi, the route joins the old Pine Lake Rd. To the L (NW), the road forms the route of the yellow-marked Otter Creek–Pine Lake Trail (trail 52). Turning R (E), the red Pine Lake Trail continues on the old road and at 4.1 mi passes a spur trail, which leads N about 200 ft to a lean-to. At a jct. at 4.3 mi, the blue-marked trail R (S) is Lost Lake Trail (trail 57). At about 4.5 mi, there is a fine view of East Pine Pond to the S.

The trail continues NE, then curves around a hill, heading N. Where the trail turns R (E) at 5.7 mi, an unmarked connecting trail continues N on an old road. This is the Otter Creek Trail, leading in a short distance to Otter Creek and then to a jct. with Big Otter Lake West Trail (trail 51). This is a shortcut route for continuing W toward the trailhead on Partridgeville Rd. The footbridge is not maintained by the state.

Pine Lake Trail continues E on the old road to a jct. with the blue-marked Big Otter Lake East Trail (trail 56) at 6 mi. That trail goes E through the Ha-De-Ron-Dah Wilderness Area to the Herreshoff Rd. trailhead at Thendara. To the L (N), Pine Lake Trail continues over a two-section bridge, blocked to snowmobilers, over Otter Creek just W of Big Otter Lake. It joins Big Otter Lake West Trail (trail 51) at 6.1 mi. To the L, that trail leads W to a trailhead on Partridgeville Rd. To the R, the trail leads to campsites on Big Otter Lake (see trail 56).

❄ Trail in winter: Suitable for backcountry skiing or snowshoeing, but Steam Mill Rd. is not plowed in winter, adding about 4.5 mi to the distance. The unplowed road and the trail as far as Spring Hill are also used by snowmobiles. The section from Spring Hill to Pine Lake is rougher, with a few short, steep banks at Eight-Foot Swamp outlet.

🥾 Distances: Drunkard Creek trailhead to Spring Hill jct., 1.6 mi; to Pine Lake, 2.8 mi; to Otter Creek–Pine Lake Trail, 4 mi; to Lost Lake Trail (trail 57), 4.3 mi; to Otter Creek Cutover Trail, 5.7 mi; to Big Otter Lake East Trail (trail 56), 6 mi; to Big Otter Lake West Trail (trail 51), 6.1 mi (9.8 km); to campsite on N side of Big Otter Lake, 7.1 mi (11.4 km).

55 Mudhole Trail

Trails Illustrated Map 745: O4

▶Locator: This is an interior trail that heads S from the jct. of Pico Mt. and Pine Lake Trails (trails 53 and 54).◀

From the jct. at Spring Hill (0.0 mi), the trail goes S gently over a hill, rising about 60 ft and then descending about 100 ft to reach Pine Creek. The short spur trail to the Mudhole leads through grass and bushes to a swampy crossing of a small creek 1 ft wide. Just beyond is a boat launching site on Pine Creek, which is deep, slow, and wide in this area. There is a large boulder at the water's edge just beyond, from which a better view can be had.

An extensive open wetland, the Mudhole can be seen on the N and NE. Mudhole Pond is out of sight beyond the trees to the NE, and would not be easy to reach without a boat.

❄ Trail in winter: Former snowmobile trail.

🥾 Distances: Spring Hill jct. to Pine Creek near the Mudhole, 1.2 mi (1.9 km).

Browns Tract. Mark Bowie

Old Forge–Thendara Section

 The village of Old Forge fronts on Forge Pond at the foot of the Fulton Chain of Lakes. Although the iron mining in this area never got very far, a romantic image of the old iron forge persists. In the center of town, a trip-hammer wheel from the "old forge" is still on display. This would have been powered by a water wheel to lift and drop a large forging hammer that repeatedly smashed red-hot but brittle cast iron until it was mixed well enough to be a low-grade workable steel.

The smaller hamlet of Thendara is adjacent to Old Forge on the SW, both communities being in the Town of Webb (honoring Dr. William Seward Webb, builder of the nearby railroad and owner at one time of much land in the area). Thendara was actually the first community in the region, but Old Forge was at the head of lake navigation and soon became the center of activity.

The main hiking trail network in the area lies W and SW of the two communities in the Ha-De-Ron-Dah Wilderness Area on the NW side of NY 28. (Bicycles are not allowed in Wilderness Areas.) Ha-De-Ron-Dah is an attempt at a more accurate phonetic spelling of the native pronunciation of "Adirondack." On the S and SW there is a trail system around Nicks Lake extending to Remsen Falls and Nelson Lake in the Black River Wild Forest. These trails include long circuit routes that lend themselves to backpacking. Leading to remote ponds and lakes, they do not have long climbs or reach viewpoints over the surrounding terrain. Moderate grades prevail. This section is one of relatively low hills, and there are considerable open spaces, the result of forest fires around the turn of the twentieth century.

Note that the distances given for the trails are not always from a trailhead, but indicate length of the trail named. Most of these trails connect points in the interior.

The trails in John Brown Tract Easement are also included in this section. This area is south of the Ha-De-Ron-Dah Wilderness Area, extending along NY 28 from the Moose River on the S to Gull Lake (near Minnehaha) in the N. The W boundary for most of the way is the Lewis-Herkimer county line, about 1.7 mi W of the highway at Gull Lake.

A 1990 agreement between a paper company and New York State named and opened this smaller piece of the original John Brown Tract to public access for recreational use. The public may enter the tract for recreational use and camping, keeping in mind that the paper company may close part of it for timber harvesting. The DEC will eventually install three trails. At present, two trails are in place: the southern end of Browns Tract Trail and JBT Gull Lake Trail. Motorized vehicles and bicycles are not permitted. Snowmobiles are allowed only on a trail close to and paralleling NY 28.

For a view of the lower lakes of the Fulton Chain (First through Fourth Lakes), one may walk up the ski slopes of McCauley Mt. just SE of Old Forge, or take the chairlift, which operates in summer and early fall in addition to the ski season. It is a 500 ft ascent to the 2320 ft summit. The ascent of Bald (Rondaxe) Mt. (trail 42) just N of Old Forge gives a similarly good view of the lakes. See Big Moose Section for this trail.

A few suggested hikes for this section are listed below.

SHORT HIKE
Lock and Dam: 2 mi (3.2 km) round-trip (or 3 mi round-trip from railroad station at Thendara). Easy walking on an old woods road with only one brief hill, providing views of the Middle Branch of the Moose River along the start and at the end. See trail 66.

MODERATE HIKES
Nicks Lake Circuit: 4.7 mi (7.5 km) round-trip. Beautiful evergreens, one-mile-long woods lake. A day-use fee is charged at the trailhead campground (free access with additional 2 mi round-trip from trail 66). See trail 67.

Middle Settlement Lake via Scusa Trail: 6.4 mi (10.2 km) round-trip. Generally easy going to a beautiful clean lake in a wilderness setting with lean-to. See trails 65, 63, 62, and 60.

Middle Branch Lake from Thendara railroad station: 13.4 mi (21.4 km) loop. Nice two-day backpack with a stay at a scenic lake via Browns Tract, Cedar Pond, Middle Branch Lake and Big Otter Lake East Trails, and NY 28 and Herreshoff Rd. See trails 63, 61, 59, and 56.

HARDER HIKES
Big Otter and Pine Lakes Loop: 24.9 mi (39.8 km) round-trip. Small pieces of several trails and two lean-tos make a good loop trip for two or three days. Start at Herreshoff Rd. trailhead, go to East Pond, Big Otter Lake, Pine Lake, Lost Lake, Middle Settlement Lake, Middle Branch Lake, and return by Big Otter Lake East Trail. See trails 56, 58, 54, 57, 60, and 59.

Remsen Falls, Nelson Lake, Jones Mt. Loops: 18.1 mi round-trip. Smooth trail (snowmobile trails in winter). Overnight at lean-to by Remsen Falls on the Moose River. See trails 66 and 67.

Trail Described	Total Miles (one way)	Page
56 Big Otter Lake East Trail	7.9 (12.6 km)	85
57 Lost Lake Trail	4.0 (6.4 km)	87
58 East Pond–Lost Creek Trail	6.7 (10.7 km)	88
59 Middle Branch Lake Trail	1.7 (2.7 km)	90

Principal Destination	*Miles*		*Trails Used*
(Distances from trailhead using most convenient trails)			
East Pond	4.4	(7.0 km)	56, 58
Middle Settlement Lake	3.2	(5.1 km)	65, 63, 62, 60
Remsen Falls	6.9	(11.0 km)	66

56 Big Otter Lake East Trail

Trails Illustrated Map 745: O6

This is a truck trail built by the Civilian Conservation Corps in the 1930s. In addition to being a hiking trail, it is a DEC-designated ski touring trail. It extends from the trailhead N of the hamlet of Thendara W to the SW end of Big Otter Lake, the last 0.4 mi of the route being a footpath. The trail is broad, with a good number of moderate ascents and descents, and it goes through a second-growth hardwood forest. It is generally easy walking.

East Pond–Lost Creek Trail (trail 58), Middle Branch Lake Trail (trail 59), and Pine Lake Trail (trail 54) all start or end at Big Otter Lake East Trail; these four trails lend themselves especially to circuit hikes.

▶Trailhead: Heading N on NY 28, upon rounding the bend at the railroad station at Thendara, turn L (N) on the dirt Herreshoff Rd. (formerly Tower Rd.) before going under the railroad underpass. If southbound, from the Old Forge Tourist Information Center drive SW on NY 28 for 2 mi; just after the railroad underpass in Thendara turn R onto Herreshoff Rd. Drive N 0.4 mi on the unpaved road and park by the gate at its end. This is also a designated horse trail on the woods road portion. ◀

From the gate (0.0 mi), the blue-marked trail starts N, but in 70 yd it leaves the snowmobile/bicycle trail and turns L (W) on a broad, smooth woods road in a second- or third-growth forest. At 0.4 mi a barrier marks the beginning of the Ha-De-Ron-Dah Wilderness Area, where bicycles are prohibited. A 300 yd traverse of an open wetland of Indian Brook begins at 1 mi, with part of an esker (stratified sediments deposited by the melting continental ice sheet) on the R looking like an elongated pile of fill.

The yellow-marked East Pond–Lost Creek Trail (trail 58) goes R at 1.5 mi. From a clearing at height of land at about 2.2 mi—apparently a former truck turnaround—the red-marked Moose River Mt. Trail angles L. (This trail makes a gradual but steady climb of about 300 ft, bending R shortly before the end at 0.6 mi at the site of a fire tower removed in 1977. Views are limited. The trail allows a ski glide all the way back to East Pond–Lost Creek Trail [trail 58] jct. The mountain is sometimes referred to as Petes Mt. in honor of long-time fire observer Pete Walters, who was there in the 1920s and '30s.)

At 4.9 mi, the yellow-marked Middle Branch Lake Trail (trail 59) goes L (S). (The Middle Branch Lake Lean-to is reached in 1 mi via a spur trail R off trail 59.) At 6 mi, the trail enters an extensive open area, including a wetland fringed by tamarack and spruce that flows N into the South Inlet to Big Otter Lake. The route is flooded for approximately 200 yd because of beaver damming. Wading on the firm road surface through shallow water may be a better option than searching for grass clumps along the edge, which is unlikely to keep you dry anyway.

At 6.6 mi the red-marked East Pond–Lost Creek Trail (trail 58) comes in from the R (NE). Beyond this jct. the woods road narrows somewhat. In approximately 175 yd it passes by the wetland of the Big Otter Lake inlet on the R with a large boulder beside the trail.

The woods road (truck trail) ends at 7.5 mi; a little before this a woods road goes R for a short distance to the edge of the narrow W section of Big Otter Lake. From here a distant view may be had of the broader part of the lake to the NE.

Big Otter Lake East Trail continues ahead as a blue-marked footpath. At 7.9 mi, the footpath ends at a woods road on the boundary of the Wilderness Area. This is Pine Lake Trail (trail 54), marked red for hikers and snowmobilers. To the L, it goes to Pine Lake and beyond. Going R for 50 yd, one reaches a two-section bridge over the beginning of Otter Creek, the outlet of Big Otter Lake, which flows W to the Black River. The bridge is closed to snowmobilers but can be used by hikers. Here are the remains of a dam once used for log drives down Otter Creek. The narrow, boggy W end of Big Otter Lake is on the R.

The red markers continue beyond the bridge a very short way, ending at 8 mi from the beginning of Big Otter Lake East Trail. This point is a jct. with Big Otter Lake West Trail (trail 51). The snowmobile markers continue to this jeep road and then go L on it toward Partridgeville Rd. To the R, Big Otter Lake West Trail goes NE along the W side of Big Otter Lake to some fine camping sites.

❄ Trail in winter: Easy snowshoeing or backcountry skiing. Listed by the DEC as suitable for skiing. A switch-key ski or hike—where two groups start from opposite ends and exchange vehicle keys midway, driving to a pre-arranged meeting point afterwards to swap back vehicles—is possible from Herreshoff Rd. to Partridgeville Rd. (trail 51), although the trailheads are far apart.

🐾 Distances: Herreshoff Rd. trailhead to East Pond–Lost Creek Trail (trail 58) jct., 1.5 mi; to Moose River Mt. Trail, 2.2 mi; to Middle Branch Lake Trail (trail 59) jct., 4.9 mi; to East Pond–Lost Creek Trail (trail 58) jct., 6.6 mi; to Pine Lake Trail (trail 54) and Otter Creek, 7.9 mi (12.6 km). Continuations: to Big Otter Lake West Trail (trail 51), 8 mi (12.8 km); to Big Otter Lake campsite on trail 64, 9 mi; to Pine Lake lean-to via Pine Lake Trail (trail 54), 9.8 mi (15.7 km).

57 Lost Lake Trail

Trails Illustrated Map 745: O4

This trail goes from Pine Lake and East Pine Pond SE to Lost Lake and then E to the SW end of Middle Settlement Lake. It connects Pine Lake Trail (trail 54) with Middle Settlement Lake Trail (trail 60). It is a narrow trail, with much encroachment. In some years, Lost Lake may not be much more than a boggy pond, but when the beavers are active, the pond is especially scenic. The trail also goes through wetlands of some interest. The route is described from the Pine Lake end, assuming a circuit hike is being made from that direction. Pine Lake Trail is described in the Brantingham Section, and can also be reached from Big Otter Lake East Trail (trail 56).

▶Locator: This trail is deep in the interior. It runs from near Pine Lake on Pine Lake Trail (trail 54), 3.1 mi from Partridgeville Rd. via Otter Creek–Pine Lake Trail (trail 52), and ends at a jct. with Middle Settlement Lake Trail (trail 60) 0.6 mi W of the lean-to and 3.8 mi from NY 28 via Scusa Access Trail (trail 65).◀

Starting at the red-marked Pine Lake Trail (trail 54) at the NE corner of Pine Lake (0.0 mi), the blue-marked Lost Lake Trail goes S between Pine Lake and East Pine Pond, with good views of East Pine and some views of Pine. At 0.4 mi it enters an open area in which there are expanses of wetland, open water, and stands of balsam fir and tamarack trees.

The outlet of East Pine Pond flows under a long boardwalk bridge, then the trail goes over a ridge and through a wet area. At 0.7 mi the trail enters a young forest. Fields of ferns stretch as far as one can see. It's a sight to behold. They do try to cover the trail but it is well marked.

The trail enters a second open area at 1.2 mi, encompassing Middle Branch Creek and its wetland. After a small footbridge over a tributary, a long bridge crosses the creek at 1.4 mi. At the end of this bridge the trail climbs a short steep pitch and continues to a section where it disappears in marshy growth heading across a gully.

The trail reenters the forest and starts passing through some tall timber. There are a number of ups and downs as an outlet of Lost Lake is crossed, and the N end of that lake is reached at 2.5 mi, with a view of the boggy shoreline and dead standing timber. Beavers have dammed the adjacent outlet. The trail passes along part of the pond for approximately 0.3 mi, with a view of steep bedrock banks on its far side.

For the rest of the route the trail is rougher. The Lewis and Herkimer County boundary lines cross, marked by a sign. Near the trail's end, rugged rock outcroppings and boulders lend interest to the scene. At the jct. with the yellow-marked Middle Settlement Lake Trail (trail 60) at 4 mi, impressive cliffs stand on the L. Going L (NE) on the yellow trail, it is 0.6 mi to the lean-to on Middle Settlement Lake and 3.8 mi to NY 28 via trails 64, 63, and 65. Going R on the yellow-marked trail 60, it is 1.7 mi S to Browns Tract Trail (trail 63), and another 2.2 mi to NY 28 via the W end of trail 63.

❋ Trail in winter: Suitable for snowshoers and possibly expert skiers, but interior trail not recommended for day trips.

🐾 Distances: Pine Lake to Lost Lake, 2.5 mi; to Middle Settlement Lake Trail (trail 60), 4 mi (6.4 km).

58 East Pond–Lost Creek Trail

Trails Illustrated Map 745: P5

This loop provides access to the N portion of Ha-De-Ron-Dah Wilderness Area from Big Otter Lake East Trail (trail 56). Signs have been posted in this area stating that it is on limited maintenance to provide a wilderness experience. The trail extends from mile 1.5 on Big Otter Lake East Trail NNW past Little Simon Pond and East Pond. (A round-trip hike to East Pond from the Herreshoff Rd. trailhead of the Big Otter Lake East Trail would be 8.8 mi.) Near East Pond, a red side trail goes NE to Blackfoot Pond and the remnants of a mica mine. The trail continues W past East Pond to Lost Creek, then turns SW to rejoin Big Otter Lake East Trail S of Big Otter Lake. The trail goes through wetlands, and parts of it, especially the last half mile before the Big Otter Lake inlet, are overgrown or muddy.

▶Locator: The trail is a loop N of Big Otter Lake East Trail (trail 56), starting on the R (N) 1.5 mi from the Herreshoff Rd. trailhead, with the other end also on Big Otter East Trail (trail 56), 6.6 mi from Herreshoff Rd. trailhead.◀

The trail turns R (N) at 1.5 mi on Big Otter Lake East Trail (0.0 mi). At 0.3 mi, East Pond Trail uses the remains of a half-log walkway to cross an open, brushy, and grassy area that includes a branch of South Inlet Creek and its wetland. Here the trail is especially overgrown; sometimes what's left of the walkway is nearly obscured.

At 0.7 mi, the route crosses another branch of South Inlet Creek on a sturdy split-log bridge. At 1.1 mi, the trail turns L (NW) and passes fields of ferns and stands of spruce, which give some variety to the forest. At 1.6 mi the trail traverses another extensive open area of scrubby growth lined by tamarack and spruce, then crosses a stream several yards downstream from a beaver dam, turning L and down along the stream.

Just before 2 mi, the trail reaches some of the massive blowdown around Simon Ponds, then crosses the outlet of Little Simon Pond which curves out of sight to the NE. The pond here is shallow, with water lilies and a wetland fringe.

After the trail crosses the outlet it continues by the W side of Little Simon Pond, with a further view of part of it. After crossing an inlet, the route provides a glimpse of Simon Pond L and climbs more than 150 ft through tall hardwoods, including some large yellow birches. It then descends through more stately growth to a trail jct. at 2.6 mi overlooking an inlet to East Pond. Here the trail goes L (W) toward Lost Creek.

East Pond Spur

To reach East Pond, a spur trail continues ahead 0.3 mi N and NW, ending at 2.9 mi, or 4.4 mi from the Thendara trailhead. Less than 0.1 mi before the end, a red-marked trail goes R (NE) to Blackfoot Pond (see description below). The East Pond side trail passes an informal campsite on the R before reaching the site of a former lean-to. This site has grown in and would no longer be suitable as a camp-site, even if it weren't so close to the water. A trail leads a few yards to the pond itself with a rock step into the water; the shoreline has a good deal of dead stand-ing timber but is graced with occasional towering white pines and red spruce.

Blackfoot Pond Spur

From the jct. near East Pond, the red-marked Blackfoot Pond Trail heads NE to Blackfoot Pond and the remains of a mica mine W of the pond, a round-trip dis-tance of 2 mi. The first part of the trail is in tall hardwoods. At 0.7 mi, the path reaches the SW end of the W segment of Blackfoot Pond, fringed by a wetland (easy to miss). The only view of the pond from the trail is here. The trail contin-ues on the W side of the pond but at some distance from it, and is encumbered in places by mud and partly obscured by ferns. It ends at 1 mi, where a clearing (an old cabin site) has been filled with blowdown, with the unimpressive rem-nants of a mica mine on the L about a hundred yards before the end.

The mine is more accurately described as a prospecting hole. Mica was used for windows in wood- and coal-burning stoves, but the sheets had to be large to be useful. No doubt this "mine," like many others, proved to have so few large sheets that it wasn't worth the trouble to get them out.

At the jct. with the East Pond and Blackfoot Pond spurs at 2.6 mi, the main trail turns W with blue markers. At 3.2 mi the wide outlet of East Pond and its wetland appear R. At 4.7 mi, the blue-marked section of trail ends at the red-marked section near Lost Creek. To the R is the Lost Creek spur trail (not to be confused with Lost Lake Trail, trail 57).

Lost Creek Spur

From the jct., the red-marked Lost Creek spur trail heads NE. In 50 yd it crosses the East Pond outlet and climbs a steep bank. It goes N on an old road to Lost Creek. Blowdown is encountered along the way. At 0.5 mi, the red markers end at Lost Creek on the L. This is an attractive, broad stream on bedrock with tea- or copper-colored water. This phenomenon occurs in other streams and ponds of the region and is caused principally by tannic acid leached from conifer needles.

Resumption of Main Trail

From the jct. at 4.7 mi, East Pond–Lost Creek Trail goes L (SW) with red markers past majestic sugar maple and yellow birch with occasional tall spruce and hemlock. At 5.8 mi, Big Otter Lake comes into view through the trees to the R. This is the only view of the lake from this trail.

The last part of the trail is dense as it leads through a semi-wetland fern-spruce environment. At 6.6 mi the route reaches the broad South Inlet of Big Otter Lake with metal sticking up from a rock in the middle, apparently from a former bridge. The trail goes upstream L along the bank for 100 yd to cross the inlet on a bridge. At 6.7 mi, the trail ends at a jct. with the blue-marked Big Otter Lake East Trail (trail 56). To the R (NW) it is 1.3 mi to the W end of Big Otter Lake. To the L (SE) it is 6.6 mi to the Herreshoff Rd. (Thendara) trailhead (14.8 mi round-trip from parking lot).

❉ Trail in winter: Suitable for snowshoers and possibly expert skiers, but interior trail not recommended for day trips.

🐾 Distances: Big Otter Lake East Trail (trail 56) to Little Simon Pond, 2 mi; to East Pond/Blackfoot Pond spur, 2.6 mi (to East Pond, 2.9 mi; to old mica mine and Blackfoot Pond, 3.8 mi); to Lost Creek spur, 4.7 mi; to second jct. with Big Otter Lake East Trail, 6.7 mi (10.7 km).

59 Middle Branch Lake Trail

Trails Illustrated Map 745: O5

This trail goes from the end of the red-marked Cedar Pond Trail (trail 61), roughly N to Big Otter Lake East Trail (trail 56). It passes E of Middle Branch Lake, with a red-marked side trail to the lake.

▶Locator: The S end is at Cedar Pond clearing, 3.1 mi from NY 28, using Scusa Access Trail (trail 65), Browns Tract Trail (trail 63), and Cedar Pond Trail (trail 61). The N end is at Big Otter Lake East Trail (trail 56) 4.9 mi W of the Herreshoff Rd. trailhead. The trail is described from S to N.◀

From the trail jct. at a boulder beside a clearing at the end of Cedar Pond Trail (trail 61), this is one of two yellow-marked trails. The other (L) is Middle Settlement Lake Trail (trail 60). Taking the R (E) fork (0.0 mi), Middle Branch Lake Trail heads N. There is an ascent of more than 100 ft over a ridge with a corresponding descent on the other side. This is followed by the more gradual crossing of a wider ridge, passing rock outcroppings before 0.6 mi.

Another brief rise precedes a drop to a jct. at 1 mi. Here, a red-marked spur trail goes L (W) down a gully and then up along a ridge for 0.3 mi, passing a glacial boulder and ending at a lean-to on a point of land on the E side of Middle Branch Lake. This is a nice location at the edge of an attractive lake with several rocky access points for swimming. The main trail continues on through moderate terrain to Big Otter Lake East Trail (trail 56) at 1.7 mi.

The most direct access to Middle Branch Lake is Scusa Access Trail (trail 65) from NY 28, 0.6 mi; R on Browns Tract Trail (trail 63), 0.2 mi; L on Cedar Pond Trail (trail 61), 2.2 mi; R on Middle Branch Lake Trail (trail 59), 1 mi; L on red spur trail, 0.3 mi. Total distance: 4.3 mi.

Middle Branch Lake in the Ha-De-Ron-Dah Wilderness Area. James Appleyard

✳ Trail in winter: Suitable for snowshoers and expert skiers.

🐾 Distances: Cedar Pond clearing to lean-to spur trail, 1 mi (to lean-to on Middle Branch Lake, 1.3 mi); to Big Otter Lake East Trail (trail 56), 1.7 mi (2.7 km).

60 Middle Settlement Lake Trail

Trails Illustrated Map 745: O5

This trail meets Middle Branch Lake Trail (trail 59) and Cedar Pond Trail (trail 61) at a clearing and boulder. From that jct. it goes L (SW) to Middle Settlement Lake and then S to Browns Tract Trail (trail 63). It passes a field of giant boulders, has a short side trail to a cliff top, and goes by the most prized campsite of the Ha-De-Ron-Dah Wilderness Area, a beautifully located lean-to on Middle Settlement Lake.

Two blue-marked trails connect in the middle of this yellow trail, Middle Settlement Lake Access Trail on the SE and Lost Lake Trail on the W (trails 62 and 57). The yellow and blue trails are best used as parts of circuit hikes. For easiest access to Middle Settlement Lake, see Middle Settlement Lake Access Trail (trail 62).

▶Locator: The E end is at Cedar Pond clearing, 3.1 mi from NY 28 using Scusa Access, Browns Tract, and Cedar Pond Trails (trails 65, 63, and 61), or 6.6 mi from Herreshoff Rd. using Big Otter Lake East and Middle Branch Lake Trails (trails 56 and 59). The W end is on Browns Tract Trail (trail 63), 2.2 mi from NY 28 at its W end. The trail is described from E to W.◀

Behind a boulder at the N edge of the Cedar Pond clearing, Middle Settlement Lake Trail is the L of two yellow-marked trails (0.0 mi). It goes WSW, paralleling a wetland and the outlet of Cedar Pond. At 0.5 mi it crosses the outlet. Crossing requires wading or finding downed trees. The trail crosses a small swamp before starting uphill on dry ground at 0.8 mi. At 1 mi, over the hill, a giant boulder sits on the L, broken off from the high cliff on the R.

The blue-blazed Middle Settlement Lake Access Trail (trail 62) comes in from Browns Tract Trail (trail 63) on the L (SE) at 1.1 mi. The trail then passes great boulders, some stacked forming a room-sized shelter. Some yards after the jct. with Browns Tract Trail, the trail crosses an inlet to the lake, skirts a wetland at the NE end of Middle Settlement Lake, then passes along the lake itself.

(Just after the trail rounds the corner where the inlet enters the lake, about 75 yd from the jct., a somewhat obscure red-marked side trail goes R, where most visitors are enjoying the view of the lake L. This side trail, called the Vista Trail, climbs NE about 150 ft to the top of a cliff with a view of the nearby hills and a partially blocked view of the lake. The round-trip from the yellow trail is 0.4 mi.)

The yellow trail follows the shore of Middle Settlement Lake and reaches the lean-to on the W side at 1.6 mi. This is a delightful location on a clean-cut rocky section of shoreline. It's an inviting spot to swim. There are few conifers lining the lake, but loons add to its pristine character.

Beyond the lean-to, the trail passes two marked informal campsites then descends to cross the lake's outlet at 1.8 mi either on one of the beaver dams or following flagging a little downstream to cross on rocks. The trail continues past what could be termed the "back bay" L, the SW end of Middle Settlement Lake. After going along the top of a hill, the trail drops down along an inlet and is muddy for a short stretch.

At 2.2 mi, near impressive cliffs on the R, the route reaches a jct. with the blue-marked Lost Lake Trail (57). The Middle Settlement Lake Trail (signs may refer to this section as Stony Creek Trail) continues L, curving around the S end of a beaver pond. It follows the shore NE, turns R, and ascends through stately hardwoods. After crossing the ridge summit, the route curves R (SW), descends gradually along the hillside, then starts downhill.

At 3.3 mi, the trail reaches a branch of Stony Creek and turns L to cross it. Continuing on the other side, Middle Settlement Lake Trail joins Browns Tract Trail (trail 63) at 5 mi. The route R (S) on Browns Tract Trail continues to Copper Lake Rd., a private road on public land, which leads on both ends to private land. A state trail goes down the road, however, into John Hancock Timber Group woods to a trailhead near NY 28 in another 2.3 mi. To the L (NE), Browns Tract Trail leads 3.5 mi to NY 28 via Scusa Access Trail (trail 65).

✳ Trail in winter: Suitable for backcountry skiing or snowshoeing.

🎿 Distances: Cedar Pond clearing to Middle Settlement Lake Access Trail (trail 62), 1.1 mi; to Middle Settlement Lake lean-to, 1.6 mi; to Lost Lake Trail (trail 57), 2.2 mi; to Stony Creek branch, 3.3 mi; to Browns Tract Trail (trail 63), 5 mi (8 km).

61 Cedar Pond Trail

Trails Illustrated Map 745: O5

This trail goes from Browns Tract Trail (trail 63) NW to the Cedar Pond clearing (a former lean-to site). It does not visit a pond, but it has a spur trail to Grass Pond and ends at a jct. with the trails to Middle Branch Lake and Middle Settlement Lake (trails 59 and 60). It is best hiked as part of a circuit route. The trail crosses many brooks, most of these easily.

▶Locator: The S end is on Browns Tract Trail 0.2 mi E of Scusa Access Trail (trail 65) and 1.3 mi W of the Okara Lakes trailhead. The N end is in a clearing at the jct. of Middle Settlement Lake (trail 60, L) and Middle Branch Lake (trail 59, R) Trails, both yellow-marked.◀

The red-marked trail heads NW from Browns Tract Trail (0.0 mi), first up, then bending briefly L, and then R. It skirts a small hill, continuing to a trail jct. at 0.4 mi. (The yellow-marked spur R goes 0.5 mi to Grass Pond. It gradually descends to an informal campsite in the woods at a trail sign and then R through wetland to a point near the pond's outlet. Shallow water, mud flats, and water lilies can be found.)

From the Grass Pond spur jct., the main trail continues NW. At 0.9 mi it crosses Grass Pond outlet stream, follows a contour, and then descends. At about 1.5 mi the waters of bog-fringed Cedar Pond show through the trees on the L. The trail reaches a clearing at 2.2 mi, ending at a jct. with two yellow-marked trails. Middle Branch Lake Trail (trail 59) goes R (roughly N) and reaches that lake and lean-to via a side trail in 1.3 mi. The similarly marked Middle Settlement Lake Trail (trail 60) behind the boulder goes L (SW) and reaches that lake's lean-to in 1.6 mi.

❋ Trail in winter: Suitable for backcountry skiing or snowshoeing.

❀ Distances: Browns Tract Trail (trail 63) to spur to Grass Pond, 0.4 mi (to Grass Pond, 0.9 mi); to Grass Pond outlet, 0.9 mi; to Cedar Pond clearing, 2.2 mi (3.5 km).

62 Middle Settlement Lake Access Trail

Trails Illustrated Map 745: O5

This connecting trail goes NW from Browns Tract Trail (trail 63) to Middle Settlement Lake Trail (trail 60) at a point just NE of that lake. The lake and lean-to are among the nicest places to stay in the Ha-De-Ron-Dah Wilderness Area.

▶Locator: The S end is on Browns Tract Trail (trail 63), 0.9 mi W of the jct. with Scusa Access Trail (trail 65) from NY 28. The N end is at the W end of Middle Settlement Lake at a jct. with Middle Settlement Lake Trail (trail 60). The trail is described from S to N.◀

From Browns Tract Trail (0.0 mi), the blue-marked trail heads N. At 0.2 mi it crosses a small stream and at 0.4 mi a larger creek on rocks. There is an open wetland on the R. This is a creek that flows E through the wetlands and then into Grass Pond outlet. There follows a gradual ascent of 160 ft (steep for skiers) and a steeper descent of about the same vertical distance to the trail's end at the yellow-marked Middle Settlement Lake Trail (trail 60).

This connecting trail provides the shortest access to the Middle Settlement Lake lean-to. Starting from NY 28, one proceeds 0.6 mi on Scusa Access Trail (trail 65), then L on Browns Tract Trail (trail 63) for 0.9 mi, R on Middle Settlement Lake Access Trail (blue) for 1.2 mi, and finally L on Middle Settlement Lake Trail (trail 60) for 0.5 mi to the lean-to, for a total distance of 3.2 mi.

❋ Trail in winter: Suitable for backcountry skiing or snowshoeing. Listed by DEC as an intermediate-level ski trail.

❀ Distances: Browns Tract Trail (trail 63) to Middle Settlement Lake Trail (trail 60), 1.2 mi (1.9 km).

63 Browns Tract Trail

Trails Illustrated Map 745: N5

This trail roughly parallels NY 28 from Thendara SW to Copper Lake Rd., mostly following the route of the old Browns Tract Rd. established in 1811. Most of the way it's broad and easy hiking, although in some places where the trail is notched into hillsides it tends to be wet, and going around Okara Lakes it's a footpath where the old road is on private property. The trail visits no lakes or ponds, but connects with three trails that lead into the Ha-De-Ron-Dah Wilderness Area. The trail is used primarily in sections for loop trips and for access from Thendara to the other trails. There is no convenient parking at the Thendara trailhead, which is 0.9 mi from the railroad station.

▶Trailheads: There are three trailheads that give direct access to this trail, as well as Scusa Access Trail (trail 65).

To reach the Thendara trailhead, permission to park at the Thendara railroad station might be granted. If so, walk 0.5 mi SW on NY 28 from the station, then turn R on Quarry Ave. and just yards later L (W) on Browns Tract Rd. At 0.2 mi from NY 28 the road becomes unpaved, and in another 0.2 mi it simply becomes the trail at 0.9 mi from the railroad station. There is no suitable place to park in the area.

To reach the Okara Lakes trailhead (in the middle section of the trail), drive 2 mi SW on NY 28 from the Thendara railroad station and look for the "state land access" sign. This is 6.9 mi NE of the Moose River bridge on NY 28. Turn N onto the gravel road. At 0.2 mi along this old highway, turn R onto Okara Rd. Go 0.2 mi and park on the L at a sharp L turn in the road. A sign here shows the yellow-marked Browns Tract Trail on the R with a register.

To reach the S trailhead, drive 5.9 mi S from the railroad station in Thendara (3 mi N of the Moose River bridge) on NY 28. Turn W into a gravel parking area. It's 0.1 mi N of the Nelson Lake trailhead on the E side of the road. In the parking area turn R (N) in the first parking lot and follow the gravel road for another 0.5 mi to a designated parking area. ◀

From the Thendara trailhead (0.0 mi), the yellow-marked trail rises more than 60 ft from NY 28. The climb continues along a road-width path nearly 100 ft higher before generally following the contour line for a while. Sounds from and occasional views of NY 28 appear L while heading SW along the route of the old Browns Tract Rd. At 0.5 mi avoid an old road L; the trail continues straight.

At just under 1 mi a Wilderness Area sign on the R has "Cold Hill" scratched onto it. There are small ups and downs until at 1.2 mi a structure can be glimpsed. At 1.3 mi, with houses nearby, the trail bends R, fords a stream, and goes slightly uphill off the old road. Shortly, it drops back down the hill to the Okara Lakes trailhead at 1.4 mi.

From the register, the trail forks L back uphill into the woods, leaving the old Browns Tract Rd. route for the next 1.3 mi. Any trails L are access trails from private land and should be avoided. The trail is close to private property markers.

After some ups and downs, the trail crosses the end of a wetland at 1.7 mi and reaches a flooded area at 1.8 mi, with crossing possible on a beaver dam R. At just over 2 mi the trail crests an esker in open woods. It then stays R of property line markers toward a hillside until a jct. at 2.7 mi. The red-marked Cedar Pond

Trail (trail 61) heads uphill R and Browns Tract Trail continues L across a walkway of more than 90 ft. At 2.8 mi, the trail turns R, rejoining the old Browns Tract Rd. Eastbound hikers should take care to turn at this well-signed point to avoid private land.

At 2.9 mi, the red-marked Scusa Access Trail (trail 65) comes in on the L from NY 28. The trail W from here is easy walking, mostly a slight decline. At 3.3 mi there is a cut through a hillside. The route crosses a stream and rises through a notch in the opposite hillside. At 3.8 mi, the blue-marked Middle Settlement Lake Access Trail (trail 62) goes R (NW) to that lake.

After a couple of streams (no bridges), at 4 mi a meadow marks the crossing of Middle Settlement Creek. Just beyond this crossing is a clearing where the Middle Settlement House once stood, accommodating nineteenth-century travelers going to and from the Old Forge area. Here, also, Abbey Rd. came in from the W to join the Browns Tract Rd. The trail follows the open wetland of Middle Settlement Creek below on the L, sometimes going a little uphill from the roadway to stay dry, and passes some large black cherry trees in an otherwise second-growth hardwood forest.

At 5.5 mi the trail drops noticeably and at 5.8 mi Middle Settlement Lake Trail (trail 60), referred to on state signs as Stony Creek Trail, also yellow-marked, is on the R. After crossing a wetland that includes two brooks, the trail reaches the dirt Copper Lake Rd., 6 mi from the Thendara trailhead. Both ends of Copper Lake Rd. are on private posted land.

The trail turns L (SE) and continues on the road. To avoid private land, watch for the sharp R (S) turn away from the road where the trail goes gently uphill. It then drops the rest of the way. This section is crisscrossed by a number of old logging roads, so care must be taken to watch for markers while navigating around the ruts.

The trail gradually curves E and starts gently downhill. A trail register is located at 7.4 mi, where the trail turns R on an old road. A barricade and parking lot mark the trail's end at 7.5 mi (0.5 mi from NY 28 on a gravel road that may not be plowed in winter).

❀ Trail in winter: Suitable for snowshoeing or backcountry skiing.

🐾 Distances: Thendara trailhead to Okara Lakes trailhead, 1.4 mi; to Cedar Pond Trail (trail 61), 2.7 mi; to Scusa Access Trail (trail 65), 2.9 mi; to Middle Settlement Lake Access Trail (trail 62), 3.8 mi; to Middle Settlement Lake (Stony Creek) Trail (trail 60), 5.8 mi; to Copper Lake Rd., 6 mi; to S trailhead, 7.5 mi (12 km).

64 JBT Gull Lake

Trails Illustrated Map 745: N5

Gull Lake is a very scenic aspect of the John Brown Tract. It is one of several Gull lakes in the region.

▶Trailhead: On NY 28 a state sign on the L (N), 3 mi NE of the Moose River, indicates a driveway for this trailhead and the S trailhead for Browns Tract Trail (trail 63). If headed S, it's on the R (N) 5.9 mi SW of the railroad station in Thendara. Turn W into a gravel parking area and turn L for Gull Lake parking. Access to Browns Tract Trail is by a gravel road R.◀

From the L (S) end of the parking lot (0.0 mi), go S a few steps, turn R (W) into the woods, and in 100 ft stop at the trail register. Just beyond, the red-marked trail joins an old truck road L, going up a couple of steep slopes before leaving the truck trail for a footpath R at 0.2 mi. The path seems to be wide enough for hauling a canoe.

The trail rises a little more for a total of about 90 ft from the trailhead, then drops several feet as the lake becomes visible on the L at 0.4 mi. At 0.5 mi, the trail ends at the rocky shore of the lake. The lake, with an island, is camera ready.

❄ Trail in winter: Suitable for snowshoeing and for experienced skiers. The trailhead will probably not be plowed.

🎿 Distances: Trailhead to lake, 0.5 mi (0.8 km).

65 Scusa Access Trail

Trails Illustrated Map 745: O6

This trail allows access to several lakes, notably Middle Settlement and Middle Branch, both with lean-tos, in conjunction with Browns Tract Trail (trail 63), which links with other trails.

▶Trailhead: Park in a large parking loop on the S side of NY 28, 3.1 mi SW of the Thendara railroad station and 5.8 mi NE of the Moose River bridge. A state land access sign is just NE of the parking loop on the N side of the road, with a bridge over the ditch.◀

The trail leaves the parking loop (0.0 mi) and passes a register and map board. About 50 yd from the loop, it turns L and ascends SW steeply 120 ft. It turns R and drops L across a bridge. After climbing the other bank the trail slopes down until a short rise just before the jct. with the yellow-marked Browns Tract Trail (trail 63) at 0.6 mi. Going L on Browns Tract Trail, it is 0.9 mi to the jct. with the blue-marked Middle Settlement Lake Access Trail (trail 62). Going R on Browns Tract Trail, it is 0.2 mi to the jct. with the red-marked Cedar Pond Trail (trail 61) after a sharp bend L to stay on state land.

❄ Trail in winter: Suitable for snowshoeing or backcountry skiing. Skiers may have to walk the hill at the start of the trail, just over 0.1 mi.

🎿 Distances: Trailhead to Browns Tract Trail (trail 63), 0.6 mi (1 km).

66 Remsen Falls–Nelson Lake, Jones Mt. Loops

Three sections of trail make two adjacent loops, in the form of a squished-down figure eight, in the Black River Wild Forest. Either loop can be taken separately, or a longer (21.7 mi) trip can be done by hiking the outer sections of both loops. A multi-day trip could be planned using two lean-tos (if available; always carry a tarp or tent in case they are full) and a state campground. The trails are between the Middle Branch of the Moose River on the N and W and the South Branch of the Moose River on the S. Because it's designated Wild Forest, bicycles are allowed.

Nelson Lake Trail goes all the way from Bisby Rd. to the Middle Branch of the Moose River near the NY 28 trailhead described below (although some old signs include part of this with the Jones Mt. Trail). The loop N is the Jones Mt. Trail and the loop S is Remsen Falls Trail. A popular section of trail is the more easterly one leading to Remsen Falls Lean-to, although a shorter trip is possible to Nelson Lake using the NY 28 trailhead. Combining the two loops together, the Nelson Lake section passes down the middle through hardwood regrowth forest. This network can be reached via a common section of trail accessed either by the Bisby Rd. trailhead, through Nicks Lake Public Campground (a fee is charged), or from NY 28 S of Thendara.

▶Trailheads: To reach the E trailhead on Bisby Rd., follow the Nicks Lake Public Campground signs from the jct. with NY 28 in Old Forge, finally turning L on Bisby Rd. Almost immediately on the R is a trailhead for the Humphery Hill, Lock and Dam Loop with snowmobile markers, and 0.1 mi farther on the R is the hiking trailhead, parking space, and trail register (1.2 mi from NY 28).

The W trailhead is on NY 28, 2.9 mi NE of the Moose River bridge and 6 mi SW of the railroad station at Thendara. A yellow-marked trail goes down an old truck road, reaching tracks of the Adirondack Scenic Railroad at 0.3 mi (0.3 mi S of a railroad bridge over the river). From there it is less than 0.1 mi to the river's edge, with rough water L and calmer water R below some islands, across from the jct. of the Nelson Lake and Jones Mt. Trails. Some canoe across. Hikers can also take an unmarked path upstream along the shore. Just N of the railroad bridge a red-marked trail goes several yards N alongside the railroad, then bends R (E) uphill, coming down in roughly 0.5 mi to a jct. with Jones Mt. Trail. ◀

From the Bisby Rd. trailhead (0.0 mi), the blue-marked trail goes S on a broad woods road. At 0.3 mi, the old road straight ahead leads to Nicks Lake, but the trail route turns R. At 1 mi, the Nicks Lake Circuit trail (trail 67) joins on the L. Hikers on that route use this common section of trail, marked both in blue and in yellow, to access either Nelson Lake Trail or Remsen Falls Trail.

The next jct., at 1.7 mi, requires a major decision. To the L is Remsen Falls Trail. Straight ahead the Nelson Lake Trail continues 0.6 mi to the start of Jones Mt. Trail.

Remsen Falls Trail

After a L turn at the jct., 1.7 mi from Bisby Rd., this trail heads S and E along the contours, just out of sight of Nicks Lake. It then turns S and climbs the hill just S of Nicks Lake. At the high point, 2.6 mi, a trail to the L, Nicks Lake Circuit (trail 67), leads downhill 0.8 mi to the beach at Nicks Lake Campground.

Remsen Falls Trail continues S, descending nearer to Nicks Creek, then ascending again to twist through the forest on the rim of the hill above and out of sight of the creek. At 5 mi, a side trail R once led 0.3 mi to little, undistinguished Bloodsucker Pond.

The route continues along the hillside above Nicks Creek. It crosses the outlet stream of Bloodsucker Pond and reaches the Remsen Falls Lean-to on the Moose River at 6.9 mi. Remsen Falls is nicely framed in the view directly up the river from the lean-to. The falls, only a few feet high, are created by a natural rock barrier across the river.

To reach the Remsen Falls Spur Trail, which connects to Woodhull Mt. trail (trail 76), wade across above the falls at the place where the old road crossed. Some hikers prefer to wade across at the lean-to. In either case, it can be dangerous when the water is high. This river gets very deep 24 hours after a rainstorm.

Continuing on past the lean-to, the trail is always in the woods, but seldom more than 200 ft from the river. At the confluence of the South Branch and Middle Branch of the Moose River, the trail turns N and follows the Middle Branch, often just out of sight of the river. The water is sometimes calm and sometimes swift.

At 11 mi, a level area makes an inviting place to stop. The river is quiet here, but still swift. It is hard to believe that this beautiful, remote location is just across the river from the railroad tracks (on which excursion trains operate), not far from NY 28.

At 11.2 mi, after leaving the river, the route joins an old woods road, turning R (E). The old road follows the valley of a creek, eventually leaving it and climbing NE past informal camping access to Nelson Lake on the L. It joins Nelson Lake Trail on level ground at 12.9 mi. The route R leads back to the trailhead (18.5 mi total). The route L leads to Nelson Lake, the South Branch of the Moose River, the NY 28 trailhead, and the W end of Jones Mt. Trail.

Nelson Lake Trail

Continuing from the trail jct. 1.7 mi from the Bisby Rd. trailhead, this route, marked with blue and snowmobile markers, leads SW, going uphill. After gentle climbing, the trail levels off. At 2.3 mi, a snowmobile sign marks the start of Jones Mt. Trail R.

Nelson Lake Trail continues straight ahead through hardwoods, deadwood, and beaver country. At 5.2 mi there is a trail jct. Remsen Falls Trail is to the L and Nelson Lake Trail continues ahead. Nelson Lake can be accessed from either. One may take Remsen Falls Trail L, continuing SW to the S side of Nelson Lake, where there are several informal campsites and access to the shore of this 0.7 mi long lake.

Continuing ahead on Nelson Lake Trail from the jct., one may descend a hill and approach the N side of Nelson Lake. At 5.5 mi (0.3 mi from the jct.), there is an unmarked trail to picnic spots along the E shore of the lake. The trail continues around the N end of the lake, crossing an inlet that provides nice views. Then it bends SW around the lake. After that, a spur trail on the L (S) leads to a lean-to (moved here from Bear Creek near Keene Valley by Lean2Rescue). Nearby is also a picnic spot among birches at a sandy edge of the lake. This turnoff is 0.7 mi from the South Branch of the Moose River (note access from NY 28, above). From that jct., Nelson Lake Trail continues W, ending at the river at 6.9 mi.

Jones Mt. Trail

Starting from the jct. at 2.3 mi W of Bisby Rd. on Nelson Lake Trail, this snowmobile route leads R (NW) on an old woods road. The trail crosses some minor wetlands, easily negotiated, turning gradually to the SW. It drops at 1.1 mi but rises again at 1.3 mi, although the total elevation change over the trail is less than 200 ft.

The Middle Branch of the Moose River comes into view on the R at 2.3 mi. After passing close to the river, the trail climbs away from the water, then approaches it again at 2.9 mi. The hamlet of Minnehaha is just across the river, but out of sight.

The route climbs L, turning away from the river just before 3 mi to pass through a notch just W of Jones Mt. The red-marked trail from the railroad bridge that is described in the NY 28 trailhead description comes in at this section of the trail. The trail then descends to the river, ending at 3.9 mi, at the water's edge in a level field. There was once a bridge across the river here, but now no trace remains. This is about 0.5 mi across from the NY 28 trailhead.

❈ Trail in winter: Suitable for snowshoeing or backcountry skiing. If you can get across the river, use of a portion of Nelson Lake Trail with the Jones Mt. Trail would be less than 10 mi. Shared with snowmobiles.

🐾 Distances: Bisby Rd. trailhead to Nicks Lake Circuit (trail 67), 1 mi; to jct., 1.7 mi; to Remsen Falls, 6.9 mi; Remsen Falls, Nelson Lake Loop, 18.5 mi (29.6 km); Middle Branch of Moose River via Nelson Lake Trail, 6.9 mi (with less than 0.5 mi more across the river to NY 28 trailhead); Nelson Lake Trail and back via Jones Mt. Trail, 13.1 mi (21 km).

67 Nicks Lake Circuit

Trails Illustrated Map 745: O7

Nicks Lake, S of Thendara, has beautiful stands of conifers on its shores and is surprisingly wild for a lake that has a public campground reachable by a paved road. By combining trails and a campground road you may hike a 4.7 mi circuit of this mile-long lake, starting at the campground where a day-use fee is charged. This is Nicks Lake Circuit.

A longer access to the circuit, where no fee is involved, is via a woods road going S from the Bisby Rd. trailhead of the Remsen Falls–Nelson Lake, Jones Mt. Loop (trail 66), adding 2 mi round-trip to the route. That trail uses part of Nicks Lake Circuit. There are ups and downs around the lake, especially some ridges on the NE end of the lake, but the elevation variation is only about 100 ft all the way around.

▶Trailhead: From Old Forge, turn SE from NY 28 by the school at the Nicks Lake campground sign and drive 1.7 mi, following campground signs and finally going E on Bisby Rd. Then turn R (SW) onto the campsite entrance road, paying a day-use fee at the registration booth.

For the circuit hike, two trailheads are in the campground. The one that is more convenient for the additional activities of swimming and picnicking is in the beach area near the lake's SE end, reached by driving SW through the campground to the parking area at the road's end. For the other trailhead, take the first R after the registration booth onto Loop A road, drive 0.2 mi, and park on the R. The trailhead is another 50 yd down the road, where a side trail begins. ◀

From the beachfront trailhead (0.0 mi), a clockwise route around the lake starts at the far end of the beach with a sign. The yellow-marked trail crosses a bridge over the lake's inlet, goes along a boardwalk over a wetland, and continues on a well-worn footpath along the S side of the lake through a handsome stand of spruce and hemlock.

At 0.7 mi there is a red-marked spur trail L to a fish barrier dam on Nicks Creek, the lake's outlet. (This spur is less than 0.3 mi, round-trip.) In another 100 yd a bridge carries the trail over Nicks Creek. The trail leads uphill on a woods road to a jct. at 0.8 mi with another woods road, part of the blue-marked Remsen Falls Trail. To the L it is 4.3 mi to the Remsen Falls Lean-to. Continuing R on this yellow trail, the Nicks Lake Circuit goes N and W on the W side of the lake, but out of sight of it. The woods road passes through a second-growth hardwood forest.

At 1.7 mi, the trail L goes to Nelson Lake, while the Nicks Lake Circuit goes R on the yellow- and blue-marked woods road. The trail heads N and then E, still out of sight of the lake. Much of the route here is grassy, and it goes through an open section as well as more second-growth forest.

At a jct. at 2.5 mi, the blue trail continues ahead to a trailhead on Bisby Rd., 1 mi away. This is the trail that can be used to avoid the fee at the campground or when the campground is closed for the winter. The Nicks Lake Circuit turns R (E) on a broad trail, with yellow markers, on the N side of the lake. At 2.7 mi a broad path goes R 100 yd to the edge of the lake where there is a picnic spot. From here one looks S down this handsome lake to the narrows at its midsection.

At 2.8 mi, the Nicks Lake Circuit forks R onto a footpath, initially wet in places. At 3 mi an unmarked woods road crosses the trail and goes to the edge

Wood sorrel in the Moose River Plains. Richard Nowicki

of the lake. This marks the boundary of the public campground and is the most direct access to the Nicks Lake Circuit from the Bisby Rd. trailhead on the N. From here on, the trail is more attractive and interesting, passing through stands of spruce, hemlock, and white pine along the lake, with views of the latter.

At 3.1 mi, the trail crosses an inlet stream on a bridge and ascends to traverse an area of splendid white pines with nice views of the lake. At a map board at 3.2 mi, yellow markers go L on a side trail to a trailhead in the public campground (on Loop A road), while the Circuit Trail continues on the yellow markers. It follows around a cove at the NE corner of the lake. This is an especially beautiful section, with handsome conifers and narrow beaches going up and over a ridge on a peninsula.

The Nicks Lake Circuit continues down the E side of the lake, passing several campsites on the L. At 4.1 mi the trail leaves the lakeside to reach a paved road on Loop E road. There is no trailhead parking here. The Circuit goes R along the campground road, keeping R at junctions, and reaches the beach parking area. The trailhead and register, where Nicks Lake Circuit started, is across the beach, at 4.7 mi.

❄ Trail in winter: Suitable for snowshoeing or backcountry skiing. The campground is not open in winter, so the Bisby Rd. trailhead would have to be used.

🚶 Distances: Trailhead near beach to Nicks Creek, 0.7 mi; to jct. with Remsen Falls Trail, 0.8 mi; to jct. with Nelson Lake Trail, 1.7 mi; to map board, 3.2 mi; complete circuit, 4.7 mi (7.5 km). 🪶

Moose River Plains Section

 The Moose River Plains Complex includes Moose River Plains Wild Forest (MRPWF, where the trails are, and thus referenced most frequently in this guide), Moose River Plains Camping Corridor, and Little Moose Wilderness. The Complex is a remote tract of land that includes a 50,000-acre piece purchased by the state from Gould Paper Company in 1963. It lies SE and E of Limekiln Lake, its S portion bounded by West Canada Lake Wilderness Area and its NE portion bounded by Blue Ridge Wilderness Area. Formerly called the Moose River Recreation Area, the complex is mostly drained by the South Branch of the Moose River. At its heart are the Moose River Plains, the principal floodplain of the South Branch, including that of lower Sumner Stream flowing W and S into the South Branch. The Plains are flat and largely open, with grass, bushes, and expanses of wetland.

A six-year field study begun in 1995 and conducted by Brian and Eileen Keelan of Rochester, N.Y., found that a 200-square-kilometer area centered on the MRPWF contained 522 species of vascular plants of 254 genera and 86 families. Under a special DEC permit, the Keelans collected hundreds of specimens, later donated to the State Museum in Albany, that were found for the first time in Hamilton and Herkimer Counties. Threatened species found included Farwell's water milfoil (two locations), alga pondweed (seven locations), and mountain goldenrod and balsam willow (three locations). Other finds, "uncommon but not really rare," included nineteen species of orchids. (See New York Natural Heritage Program website, acris.nynhp.org.)

A state brochure calls this "the largest block of remote land in the Adirondacks readily accessible by motor vehicle," but that depends on the season. The Limekiln Lake-Cedar River Rd. (Moose River Plains Rd.) is open from the Wednesday before Memorial Day to the last day of big-game hunting season in November. (Note drivers must have tire chains after October 1.) There are gates at Limekiln (W) and Wakely Dam (E, Indian Lake end). The road may be closed at other times if conditions—washouts, blowdown—warrant. In October 2006, more than fifty hunters were trapped by nearly 2 feet of snow and blowdowns. The area includes a deer yard where large numbers of deer spend the winter.

Although one of the last great wild areas to be cut, Moose River Plains Wild Forest is primarily second or third growth forest, most of it extensively logged before state acquisition. Some impressive conifer stands, especially white pine and balsam fir, remain in tracts purchased by New York State before the rest of the region was logged.

MRPWF has sizeable hills and a mountain range, with Little Moose Mt. reaching 3620 ft. The hiking trails covered in this guide do not climb these hills. Some of the ponds and lakes are unusually high, topped by Sly Pond at 2872 ft, one of the highest bodies of water in the Adirondacks (compare to Lake Colden at 2764 ft, or even Avalanche Lake at 2863 ft, both in the High Peaks). Sly Pond Trail, as well as several other trails in the eastern portion of MRPWF, are included in ADK's *Central Trails* and on *Trails Illustrated Map 744: Northville/Raquette Lake*.

The trails in this guidebook are all in or accessed from the western MRPWF. Two nearby trails accessible from the Plains but located in West Canada Lake Wilderness Area—trails leading to the Indian River and Balsam, Stink, and Horn Lakes (on *Trail Illustrated Map 745,* 2017 revision, as trails 72 and *Central Trails* trail 95—are described in the Western-Central Overlap Section of this guide.

The trails of MRPWF, maintained by DEC, are largely on old logging roads leading to ponds and lakes. and lakes. The Complex offers camping, with 116 primitive roadside campsites, including eight that are accessible; four accessible launches for paddlers; and biking on all roads and trails except those in the Little Moose Wilderness, where biking is prohibited. Construction of single-track biking trails is being considered (2016). In addition, the Complex features six designated horse trails totaling nearly 35 miles, cross-country skiing and snowshoeing are permitted on all hiking trails, and nearly 16 miles of trails have been designated for skiing only. Nature study, fishing, and hunting are among other uses.

No motorcycles, motorized bicycles, or all-terrain vehicles are allowed. Entry by foot or bicycle is permitted at any time. After the gates close in the fall, access for hikers is nearly shut off. Limekiln Rd. is plowed only to the area of the W gate, and Cedar River Rd. on the E is not plowed past the last home.

The W entrance to the MRPWF is reached by driving toward Raquette Lake from Inlet on NY 28. At 0.8 mi from the center of Inlet, turn R (S) down Limekiln Rd., then keep L when you see Limekiln Lake downhill, turning onto the unpaved road. From the control station at this entrance, MRPWF's through road, Moose River Rd., extends for 21.2 mi to the Cedar River (E) entrance. The latter is at the end of Cedar River Rd., which comes in 11.8 mi from NY 28/30, about 2 mi W of the village of Indian Lake.

As one drives along Moose River Rd. from the Limekiln entrance, Rock Dam Rd. heads SW at 4.6 mi (16.6 mi from the Cedar River entrance), and at 8.2 mi (12.9 mi from the Cedar River entrance). Otter Brook Rd. goes S, while Moose River Rd. goes L at each jct. Otter Brook Rd. proceeds 3.3 mi to a fork just across the bridge over Otter Brook, where it bears L (E) a short distance to its end. At the fork, Indian River Rd. goes R (W and SW).

A leaflet showing the roads, trails, and camping areas of MRPWF is available at the entrances. The trails usually bear DEC yellow markers and trailheads have signs. Parking is on the road or, in some cases, one can drive off the road a short distance to park.

A short suggested hike in this section is listed below.

SHORT HIKE
Rock Dam—2.8 mi (4.5 km) round-trip. Gentle traveling to the "rock dam" on the Moose River. See trail 71.

68 Limekiln Creek–Third Lake Trail

Trails Illustrated Map 745: O9

This trail connects Limekiln Rd. and South Shore Rd. It is designated as both a ski touring and hiking trail. It is a generally level route extending from the SW end of Limekiln Lake Public Campground along Limekiln Creek, then NW to Third Lake Creek and the trailhead at South Shore Rd. near Third Lake, a through hike of 5.6 mi. At the start the route follows the W segment of a DEC self-guided nature trail, which makes an interesting 1.5 mi trip in its own right. The longest section of the trail route, going NW toward Third Lake, passes through extensive wet areas heavy with mosquitoes through June.

▶Trailheads: To reach the E trailhead at Limekiln Rd. from the parking area in the center of Inlet, drive 0.8 mi on NY 28 toward Blue Mt. Lake, turn R on Limekiln Rd., and go 1.7 mi S. Turn R on the entrance road to the public campground and pay a day-use fee at the booth. With attractive Limekiln Lake on the L, drive the whole length of the campground to its SW end and park by Campsite 87. Because the campground is closed after Labor Day and reopened in early May, it is necessary to park near the gate during that period and go an additional 1.5 mi on foot.

To reach the South Shore Rd. trailhead from the parking area in Inlet, go one short block toward Raquette Lake and turn R at the first corner. Drive 5.5 mi (passing the Inlet Ski Touring Center and the Fourth Lake Picnic Area) on South Shore Rd. Turn L at the large clearing 0.3 mi past the picnic area.

To reach the South Shore Rd. trailhead from the Tourist Information Center in Old Forge, go S on NY 28 and turn L at the first corner. Keep L until you leave the lake headed SE. Go about 5 mi and turn R into the large parking area. ◀

From Campsite 87 at the E trailhead (0.0 mi), the yellow-marked trail goes S on a barricaded driveway for 100 yd, turns L past a pump house at the end of the field, and reaches the beginning of Old Dam Self-Guided Nature Trail at 0.2 mi. At the register, there are descriptive leaflets for the nature trail. On the L is a fish barrier dam in Limekiln Creek, just out of Limekiln Lake. The nature trail returns over the dam to this spot.

To the R (SW), the trail goes through tall conifers with a boggy pond on the L, following yellow ski trail markers. At 0.6 mi, the trail crosses Limekiln Creek at the site of the "old dam," used in the first half of the nineteenth century in connection with log drives down the creek to the South Branch of the Moose River. Forty yd beyond, the nature trail goes L (E) at a jct. The ski/hiking trail goes R and heads SW through tall conifers, paralleling Limekiln Creek and its wetland. At 1.3 mi, there is a good view R of a beaver meadow.

Beyond the wetland the trail follows above the creek in an attractive section at 1.5 mi, passing a small but pretty waterfall and pool, worth the bushwhack of a few yards down to them. At 1.6 mi the trail crosses a bridge over the creek. Approximately 100 yd downstream on the R bank, a larger waterfall can be seen. This is a good turnaround point for a round-trip hike.

The rest of the trail toward Third Lake goes generally NW. Beyond the bridge it passes through stately hardwoods and fields of ferns, which are much in evidence from here on. At 2 mi, the trail goes R onto a weedy snowmobile trail, follows it for 40 yd, and turns L off of it. (Be alert to this turn.) Herbaceous growth continues underfoot.

The trail enters a conifer forest at 2.3 mi and crosses a bridge over the outlet of Limekiln Swamp, which lies on the R. Shortly after the trail reenters the woods, one of the Limekiln Ski Routes (trail 69) comes in on the R at 2.8 mi. This trail can be used for a good loop ski trip.

For the next couple of miles, the route crosses mostly flat, swampy, or semi-swampy terrain in a mixed conifer-hardwood forest. In this section the trail follows a vehicle track, turns R off it at 3.7 mi where the footpath temporarily disappears in the ferns, and follows the edge of Third Lake Creek Swamp with nearly 0.5 mi of continuous wet footing. The trail then regains the vehicle track, following it for a little over 0.2 mi only to turn R off it again (be alert here), and then follow Third Lake Creek.

At 4.7 mi, the trail again regains the vehicle track on private land and follows it through dense conifers and along muddy places for 360 yd to a chain barrier. Just beyond, at 4.9 mi, the route turns R on a widened jeep road with ruts and mud puddles. The trail follows the road through deciduous woods to the trail's end at 5.6 mi at South Shore Rd., E of Third Lake. There is an open area for parking (formerly the site of Third Lake Campground) but there may be no trail sign.

✳ Trail in winter: DEC ski trail. The entire trail cannot be used easily for a loop trip, but the first 2.3 mi can be used in connection with the Limekiln Ski Routes (trail 81) for a good day's outing.

⚹ Distances: Limekiln Lake parking area to creek with waterfall, 1.6 mi; to Limekiln Ski Trail (trail 69), 2.8 mi; to W trailhead, 5.6 mi (9 km). Limekiln Rd., looping back via the longest Limekiln Ski Route, 8.6 mi. Nature Trail loop, 1.5 mi.

69 Limekiln Ski Routes

Trails Illustrated Map 745: P9

▶Trailhead: To reach the trailhead from the parking area in the center of Inlet, drive 0.8 mi on NY 28 toward Blue Mt. Lake (SE). Turn R on Limekiln Rd. and go 1.7 mi S. Park at the entrance road to Limekiln Lake Campground if space has been plowed. The route is marked with DEC yellow markers. ◄

Joanne Kennedy

In ski touring season, one may ski from Limekiln Rd. to Limekiln Creek–Third Lake Trail (trail 68) on two different routes. To reach the start of that hiking-skiing trail, just W of Limekiln Lake, ski W from Limekiln Rd. along the public campground's entrance road. Then follow the route of the yellow ski markers, which leaves the main campground road to make shortcuts nearer the lake through the remainder of the campground. An alternative to part of this route is to ski on Limekiln Lake from the boat launching site, which the main campground road passes, to the shore of the bay at the NW corner of the lake.

The other route, also marked with DEC yellow cross-country ski markers, leaves the W side of Limekiln Rd. at a point 1 mi S of the road's jct. with NY 28 and 0.7 mi N of the public campground's entrance road. The trail goes mostly SW for over 3 mi to end at Limekiln Creek–Third Lake Trail (trail 68) N of where the latter crosses the outlet of Limekiln Swamp. Near the start of the route, several trails go R as part of the town of Inlet's network, and thereafter a snowmobile trail is crossed at an angle (actually followed a short way).

At about 1.4 mi there is a jct. with signs, where a connecting ski trail goes L to Limekiln Lake Public Campground. This connecting trail, also with yellow ski markers, goes mostly SE, making turns at three jcts. with snowmobile trails, and reaches the NW area of the campground by Campsite 184. From there one should follow the ski and snowmobile markers L to a broad jct. at Campsite 47, and then descend toward the campground's beach to pick up the ski route through the campground, as described above.

Omitting the final approximately 3 mi of Limekiln Creek–Third Lake Trail, one has the choice of several circuit ski routes using these trails. Another option is to start at Fern Park on South Shore Rd. and follow the town's Trail No. 6 (shown on *Trails Illustrated Map 745* as the end of trail 69 nearest Inlet) along the E side of the town's network to the DEC ski trail W of Limekiln Rd., and then continue as desired, perhaps all the way to South Shore Rd. near Third Lake.

❉ Trail in winter: DEC ski touring trails.

❊ Distances: Vary by loops chosen.

70 Whites Pond Trail

Trails Illustrated Map 745: O10

A trail to a small pond and then over a ridge before a drop to Limekiln Lake.

Note that *Central Trails* trail 85, which goes to the shore of Limekiln Lake, is not easily accessed from the lake and is best hiked from its Moose River Rd. trailhead to the W. (See trail description in Western-Central Overlap Section of this guidebook, or in *Central Trails*.)

▶Trailhead: From the jct. of Moose River Rd. and Rock Dam Rd. (4.6 mi from the W entrance and 16.6 mi from the E entrance of the MRPWF), drive S on Rock Dam Rd. for 2.6 mi. The trailhead is on the R. There is a trailhead sign and parking for three cars. The trail is marked with DEC yellow markers. The route is well marked and generally not difficult to find.

One also may start from the Limekiln Lake end by renting a boat at Limekiln Lake Public Campground or bringing one to launch there. The landing is not very prominent at the trailhead; it is a little bit W of the creek.◀

After a short lead-in section from Rock Dam Rd. (0.0 mi), the route follows an old road. It contours along pleasant but dense forest, crossing several creeks.

At 0.5 mi, the route turns L and climbs, going S at first, then generally W. It turns R at 0.9 mi and climbs, sometimes steeply, until 1.1 mi. Shortly beyond, the old road crosses a marshy meadow. The route then leaves the old road and becomes more rugged. After more ups and downs, the trail skirts a nice marsh-ringed pond on the L.

Whites Pond appears on the R at 1.7 mi. There was once a cabin on the spruce-covered island in the middle of the lake.

Continuing beyond the beaver dam at the outlet, the trail becomes more obscure as it goes up the hillside N of Whites Pond. The route turns N, still climbing, then follows a ridge NE to the high point at 2.2 mi. A long downhill section leads to a creek crossing at 2.8 mi and the shore of Limekiln Lake at 3.2 mi. There are some possibilities for camping on the hill above the trail L.

❄ Trail in winter: Not very accessible, except by snowmobile. The Limekiln Lake end is somewhat steep.

🐾 Distances: Rock Dam Rd. to Whites Pond, 1.7 mi; to Limekiln Lake, 3.2 mi (5.1 km).

71 Rock Dam

Trails Illustrated Map 745: N10

An easy trail to the confluence of the Red and Moose Rivers, where a natural stone wall holds back much of the Moose.

Note that the relatively nearby East Shore Path and Snowmobile Trail (*Central Trails* trail 85) is described in Western-Central Overlap Section of this guidebook, as well as in *Central Trails*.

▶Trailhead: Start at the jct. of Moose River Rd. and Rock Dam Rd. (4.6 mi from the W entrance and 16.6 mi from the E entrance to MRPWF). Drive S on Rock Dam Rd. for 3.8 mi. The trailhead is on the L. Rock Dam Rd. is barricaded at private land about 0.4 mi S of the trailhead.◀

Moose River. Chris Murray

Leaving the trailhead (0.0 mi), the route cuts over a minor hump, joins an old woods road, and loops gently NE on the old road through well-established forest. At about 1 mi, the route leaves the old road, turns around, and heads S. An unofficial cutover of perhaps 50 yd on this unnecessarily long loop cuts more than 0.1 mi off each way. This end of the trail is generally wetter and rougher, but easy to follow.

The trail ends at 1.4 mi at a slight opening on the South Branch of the Moose River. An unmarked path L upstream along the river bank will bring the traveler even with the "dam" or out on the rocks below it. In times of low flow, sturdy hikers wade out to the dam, which is a broad, smooth rock formation blocking the river from a small island to the far bank with deeper water behind it upstream. Others may prefer to gaze at the formation from the rocks downstream. The Red River joins just above the dam L.

❋ Trail in winter: Not readily accessible except by snowmobile.

🏃 Distance: To Rock Dam, 1.4 mi (2.2 km).

72 Indian River Trail

Trails Illustrated Map 745: M9

See trails 95 and 95A in Western-Central Overlap Section for full description of the two trails leading from Indian Lake (on *Trails Illustrated Map 744: Northville–Raquette Lake*) to the Indian River and Balsam, Stink, and Horn Lakes. 🦫

Long Lake. Chris Murray

McKeever-Woodgate Section

 This section offers many trails to and along beautiful lakes and ponds, as well as scenic views from the summit of Woodhull Mt. and a ledge overlooking Bear Lake. This region is frequented by hunters in the fall.

The waters of the region mostly feed the Black River. Several of the lakes are or were dammed to store water for the Black River Canal, which supplied water to the Erie Canal. Smaller dams were also used by lumbermen to supply water for log drives down the river.

A dam and lumber mill existed on the Moose River just upstream of the NY 28 bridge until, rather late in life, the dam gave out in a gala performance, leaving the downstream bridge lodged solid with cut timber. The dam and mill were owned by John Dix, former governor of New York State.

A few suggested hikes for this section are listed below.

SHORT HIKES

Gull Lake: 6.8 mi (10.9 km) round-trip. This peaceful lake makes a beautiful setting for lunch. Return by the same route, or continue on the Gull Lake Loop, for a round-trip of 7.8 mi. See trail 80.

Bear Lake: 4 (6.4 km) mi round-trip. Offers a modest amount of climbing, and the lake is a very rewarding wilderness experience. Return by the same route. See trail 82.

MODERATE HIKE

Woodhull Lake: 9 mi (14.4 km) round-trip. The lake is large, and the lean-to is one of the largest in the Adirondacks. See trail 78.

HARDER HIKES

Sand Lake Falls: 15.2 mi (24.3 km) round-trip. Pleasant trip on gentle terrain to the lean-to at Sand Lake Falls. The falls are modest, but the scene is pleasant. See trail 79.

Woodhull Mt.: 15.2 mi (24.3 km) round-trip. The view from the fire tower is very nice, with panoramic views and, surprisingly, no trace of the facilities of the Adirondack League Club to the SE. As of 2014, the tower could be ascended to just below the cab; however, there is no assurance that it will remain climbable. (Although many towers in the Adirondacks and Catskills have been "adopted" by Friends groups, this one is challenged by the long trek necessary to get there.) See trail 76.

73 Round Pond–Long Lake Trail

Trails Illustrated Map 745: M4

▶Trailhead: From the NY 28 bridge over the Moose River near McKeever, take Moose River Rd. on the S side of the river, heading W, for 2.1 mi. The trailhead is an old woods road on the L (S), shortly before the high point on the road. Although marked, it is easy to miss. Park on the shoulder (almost room for one car) or on the S side at a wider spot at the top of the hill.◀

From Moose River Rd. (0.0 mi), the route follows the old road straight for 40 yd, then turns R and curves gently up a hill and over the top. It curves R again and meets an unmarked trail jct. Ahead from the jct., and then to the R, an old road leads quickly to the beautiful shore of Round Pond at 0.3 mi. The marked trail leads L (E) away from the old road at the jct., climbing gently. It continues generally S along a ridgetop woods road. The forest here is nearly all hardwood. Ignore a road fork on the R at 0.9 mi.

The route finally comes down off the ridge in a couple of moderate descents. For the final quarter mile, the route follows S near the Lost Pond–Long Lake stream.

The trail ends at a jct. at 1.7 mi with Brandy Lake trail (trail 74). From here, to the L it is 1 mi to NY 28 via trail 74 and 1.3 mi to Lakeview Rd. along Otter Lake via trails 74 and 75. To the R, Brandy Lake trail (trail 74) leads to Brandy Lake, 1 mi from the jct., and Round Lake Rd., 3.4 mi. Round Lake, S on Round Lake Rd., should not be confused with Round Pond near the start of this trail.

❋ Trail in winter: State snowmobile trail, otherwise suitable for snowshoeing or skiing.

🐾 Distances: Moose River Rd. to Round Pond, 0.3 mi; to Brandy Lake trail (trail 74), 1.7 mi (2.7 km).

74 Brandy Lake

▶Trailhead: From the bridge over the Moose River near McKeever, drive S on NY 28 for 3.6 mi. The snowmobile trailhead and woodsy parking for several cars are located in the trees to the R (W). Headed N, after passing through Woodgate, it is 3.6 mi from the Adirondack Park sign to the trailhead on the L.

It is also possible to canoe across Long Lake to reach a yellow-marked spur trail that connects to the main trail. From NY 28 at a 90-degree turn W of White Lake and Boy Scout Camp Russell, drive N. Take the next L onto Round Lake Rd., then turn R onto Long Lake Rd. at 0.5 mi from NY 28. Go 1.1 mi NNE, passing Camp Nazareth, to a gravel parking lot on the R with DEC markers at the intersection of Capron Rd., a few yards from the lake L. Paddle N (R from the put-in) less than 0.4 mi past a couple of islands (one behind the other) and turn L (NW) before the lake narrows, where the trail comes down to the shore on the L.◀

The route from NY 28 (0.0 mi) is an old woods road going gently down to Otter Lake outlet stream at 0.4 mi. On the other side, the trail climbs gently and meets a jct. on level ground at 0.5 mi. To the R is Otter Lake Outlet Trail (trail 75), leading to trailheads at Otter Lake.

Turning L, the trail goes SW, swings around a hill, and heads N to cross an inlet creek of Long Lake shortly before the jct. with Round Pond–Long Lake Trail (trail 73) at 1 mi. The route then heads L (SW) and starts a gentle climb, passing a rock pile perhaps 40 yd long. It soon levels out, continuing on easy terrain to a jct. at 1.4 mi. The route ahead looks better, but the marked trail turns abruptly L and begins a climb.

The trail crosses two snowmobile bridges, and at 1.7 mi where the wide snow-mobile trail is rising and bending R, there is a footpath L with a handmade sign and an old faded arrow. This blue-marked trail heads uphill, turns R, and continues rising slightly, eventually dropping to an informal campsite at the E shore of Brandy Lake at 2.1 mi. It continues along the side of a hill and across a wet area, and climbs into the woods until, at 2.3 mi, it reaches a large log across the trail. Although another log L is cut out, that is a trail to private land. The trail goes R, downhill, to the shore of Brandy Lake at 2.3 mi, passing a yellow-marked spur trail at L.

(This spur trail continues to Long Lake and can be used to reach the main trail by boat or canoe across Long Lake [see Trailhead, above]. It can function also as a carry from Long Lake to Brandy Lake. It heads generally S, then bends R uphill, passing some side trails with flagging, apparently leading to private property. It then goes along a ridge with some glimpses of Long Lake and between rock walls 6 to 8 ft high and about 20 ft apart at 0.5 mi from the jct. At 0.6 mi the trail drops L to near Long Lake and then turns R along the lake to end at an overhanging tree with a yellow trail marker at 0.7 mi.)

The main trail continues as a snowmobile trail SW and then S to a trailhead on Round Lake Rd. near Masonic Home Camp, approximately 2 mi farther.

❀ Trail in winter: Part is a snowmobile trail. Otherwise suitable for snowshoeing and skiing.

🐾 Distances: Trailhead to Otter Lake Outlet Trail (trail 97), 0.4 mi; to Round Pond–Long Lake Trail jct. (trail 73), 1 mi; to Brandy Lake campsite, 2.1 mi; to Brandy Lake shore, 2.3 mi (3.7 km). To Long Lake via spur, 3.1 mi (5 km).

75 Otter Lake Outlet Trail

Trails Illustrated Map 745: M4

▶Trailhead: At the Otter Lake settlement on NY 28 S of the Moose River, take Lakeview Rd. 1.4 mi to its end. A dirt road continues on to a tiny dam on Otter Lake outlet. The snowmobile trail starts on the S side, near the dam. Alternately, from the highway take Woods Rd. on the S side of Otter Lake for 0.4 mi. The snowmobile trail starts on the S side at a bend in the road. At the other end, the trail may be reached via Brandy Lake trail (trail 74).◀

From Woods Rd. (0.0 mi), go S a short way to a snowmobile trail jct. Turn R up the hill and continue in a gentle loop, to meet the trail from Lakeview Rd. at about 0.3 mi (0.1 mi from Lakeview Rd. to the R). That route goes S from the side of Lakeview Rd. about 50 ft before the dam.

The trail turns L and follows the Otter Lake outlet stream through hardwood forests and past huge boulders strewn about. At 0.8 mi, the route leaves creek bottomland and ascends to a broad shelf along a hillside. The trail remains almost level for the rest of the way to the jct. with the Brandy Lake trail (trail 74) at 1.1 mi. From here, trail 74 goes L to NY 28 in 0.5 mi; the route R goes around Brandy Lake and beyond to Round Lake Rd.

❀ Trail in winter: Snowmobile trail. Otherwise suitable for skiing and snowshoeing.

🐾 Distances: Woods Rd. to jct. near Lakeview Rd., 0.3 mi; to Brandy Lake trail (trail 74), 1.1 mi (1.8 km). (Lakeview Rd. trailhead to Brandy Lake trail, 0.9 mi.)

76 Woodhull Mt.

Trails Illustrated Map 745: M5

This trail to a fire tower is long for a day trip (15.2 mi round-trip) but it offers easy walking, much of it on an old railroad bed with gentle grades. Some people make the trip as a combined bike/hike, mountain biking for approximately the first 5 mi, securing their bikes, and hiking to the top of Woodhull.

The recommended day hike for the area is a loop trip: take Wolf Lake Landing Rd. (trail 77) from its McKeever trailhead to Bear Lake Trail (trail 82); follow this to Bear Lake; then take Bear Lake–Woodhull Lake Trail (trail 78) to Woodhull Lake and its lean-to. Then use Wolf Lake Landing Rd. (trail 77) N to the

Woodhull Mt. trail (trail 76), proceeding W to the starting point. Both lakes have fine scenery. Bear Lake has a nice sand and pebble beach, and Woodhull Lake has a grand lean-to. The full loop is 10.4 mi.

▶Trailhead: Go to McKeever Rd., on NY 28 S of Old Forge. Turn E toward McKeever, just S of the Moose River bridge. Go 0.3 mi to a jct. The pavement turns L. Leave it and continue straight ahead on a dirt road past the old railroad station. Cross the tracks and continue to the second parking lot, 0.8 mi from the highway. The first parking lot, at 0.6 mi, is for Wolf Lake Landing Rd. (trail 77).◀

From the parking lot and trail register (0.0 mi), the route continues beyond the barricade on a surprisingly smooth surface. This rebuilt roadway follows the roadbed of the former Moose River Lumber Company Railroad, which went to Number Four Camp near Woodhull Mt. To accommodate the railroad, the route was sloped gently and there are no sudden climbs.

At 0.7 mi, a trail R leads to Bear Lake and beyond (trail 82). At 2.6 mi, the yellow route crossing the trail leads L (N) to Remsen Falls and R (S) 0.3 mi to connect with Wolf Lake Landing Rd. (trail 77) about 100 ft before it turns R (S) on the way to Woodhull Lake.

(Remsen Falls, a 6.2 mi round-trip via this route, is a popular day hike. From the jct., the Remsen Falls spur trail L goes generally N, descending almost continuously with a gentle slope. It passes several camping spots and reaches the South Branch of the Moose River near Remsen Falls at 0.5 mi. Crossing the river at times of high water is out of the question, but the usual crossing otherwise is above the falls, where the trail reaches the river at an old road ford. Some hikers wade the stream at the Remsen Falls Lean-to [see trail 66], about 0.2 mi to the L, or just below it. In any case, the water may be more than knee deep. It becomes chest deep about 24 hours after a rain. The falls are not very high, but are worth the trip.)

Continuing E from the four-way jct., Woodhull Mt. Trail passes a small pond on the L at 2.9 mi. After some gentle climbing, the route levels off. It was in this area that the logging railroad crew headed for Number Four Camp would uncouple the moving cars from the engine and race ahead to pull off to the L on a Y. After the cars rolled by on the main line, they would back the engine on the second leg of the Y, rejoin the main line going in reverse, catch up with the cars, and hook on before applying the brakes at Number Four Camp. The train was thus reorganized for the return trip.

As it starts down the gentle slope, the road finally leaves the railroad bed and turns slightly L. The remains of the old railroad bed continue on ahead. A short distance farther on, the route becomes slightly rougher and the road finally ends in a sharp R turn on a creek bank at 5.1 mi. The trail turns L at the end of the road on the creek bottom, and crosses over the creek. The route continues from the creek bank as a narrow foot trail, fairly well marked with a combination of red DEC markers, red painted can lids, red tape, and finally orange and red rectangular markers.

From here on, the trail climbs steadily with very few level parts. At 5.6 mi, a red-marked hunting trail goes R, and the trail takes a sharp L. The route climbs more steeply and zigzags somewhat randomly. It drops into a swampy creek bed at 6.1 mi, goes up steeply for a short distance, and reaches a trail jct. at 6.4 mi. (The route straight ahead shows the heaviest use. This is a hunting trail, marked with red paint blazes, that leads 0.3 mi to the Wolf Lake Landing Rd. Extension.)

The red DEC trail turns L and continues climbing. A creek at 6.6 mi provides a brief level section, followed by more climbing through thickets and blowdown. As the trail levels out, it becomes bumpier and somewhat overgrown, finally leading to the fire tower near a huge boulder at 7.6 mi.

The only view from the ground may be obtained by going E on the summit for 200 ft to the site of a burned cabin, where a limited opening to the E gives a glimpse of unending forest and hills. A better view by far can be gained by climbing the tower, which is open to just below the cab. To the S, one can see part of Woodhull Lake, with Big Island visible at the near end. To the N, Nicks Lake is visible. Looking W, the South Branch of the Moose River appears nearby, passing through an interesting gorge on its journey W.

❋ Trail in winter: Snowmobile trail most of the way. Suitable for snowshoeing or backcountry skiing. Mountain section recommended only for experienced backcountry skiers.

🐾 Distances: To Bear Lake Trail jct. (trail 82), 0.7 mi; to Remsen Falls Spur and Wolf Lake Landing Rd. link, 2.6 mi; to road end, 5.1 mi; to summit and lookout tower, 7.6 mi (12.2 km). Ascent, 812 ft (247 m). Summit elevation, 2362 ft (720 m).

77 Wolf Lake Landing Rd.

Trails Illustrated Map 745: M5

There were once plans to abandon this trail, which had become terribly rutted. Vast improvements since have rehabilitated it for use by the disabled. It's quite smooth and suitable for bicycles as well—this being in a Wild Forest rather than a Wilderness Area, where bicycles are banned.

Funding from several sources, including a federal grant under the National Recreation Trails Fund Act, allowed improvements. One goal was to provide access to scenic destinations for the disabled on a multi-use trail. Improvements have made the trail into a road, open to the public with motor vehicles; however, ATVs are not allowed. The disabled can obtain permits to use gates for access to Remsen Falls (and a handicapped accessible privy, picnic table, and campsite) and the last several hundred yards to Woodhull Lake. For others, parking at the connecting trail to Remsen Falls would cut about 5 mi off a round-trip hike to Woodhull Mt. via trail 76. Contact the DEC office in Herkimer (315-866-6330) well in advance to arrange for a permit.

Once used by the Adirondack League Club to reach the steamboat at Wolf Lake Landing, it has effectively been replaced for that purpose by the private

Woodhull Lake lean-to. Norm Landis

Bisby Rd.

▶Trailhead: Go to McKeever Rd., on NY 28 S of Old Forge. Turn E toward McKeever just S of the Moose River crossing. Go 0.3 mi to a jct. The pavement turns L. Leave the pavement and continue straight ahead on a dirt road past the old railroad station. Cross the tracks and continue to the first parking lot, on the R 0.6 mi from the highway. The automobile road continues ahead a short distance to another parking lot used for the Woodhull Mt. trail (trail 76).◀

From the parking lot (0.0 mi), the route turns R (S) and soon curves E. At 1.1 mi, a jct. is created by the crossing of the blue-marked Bear Lake Trail (trail 104), on its way uphill from trail 76 as it continues R to Bear Lake and beyond.

At a jct. at 3.1 mi, a road L leads N to the Woodhull Mt. trail and the Remsen Falls spur (see trail 76). Just beyond the jct. Wolf Lake Landing Rd. turns R, passing some hunters' campsites. The road heads S in reasonably dry condition. An unmarked road L (E) at 4.8 mi is not a DEC trail but an abandoned old road that led to the region of the old Number Four lumber camp.

Beyond the jct., Wolf Lake Landing Rd. climbs over a minor hill and descends. At 5 mi, the L fork leads down to Wolf Lake Landing, a shoreline with a nice view, with the Woodhull Lake lean-to in sight on a point R. The landing was once a major transfer point for Adirondack League Club members going to camp. The R fork of the road continues S parallel to the lake.

A yellow-marked trail R at 5.5 mi is Bear Lake–Woodhull Lake Trail (trail 78). Just beyond, the trail crosses a creek, and 50 ft beyond that there is a terribly muddy, red-marked spur trail L (E) to Woodhull Lake Lean-to, a doublewide: where the end would normally be, there are a couple of posts and the shelter continues to about twice the length of a normal lean-to. Beyond this jct., the old road becomes Woodhull Rd. (trail 83).

✳ Trail in winter: Snowmobile trail. Suitable for skis and snowshoes, but the first segment should be bypassed by using trail 76 and the Landing Rd. link.

🚶 Distances: McKeever trailhead to Bear Lake Trail (trail 82), 1.1 mi; to crossover trail to Woodhull Mt. trail (trail 76), 3.1 mi; to extension, 4.8 mi; to Wolf Lake Landing, 5 mi; to Woodhull Lake Lean-to and Bear Lake–Woodhull Lake Trail (trail 78), 5.5 mi (8.8 km).

78 Bear Lake–Woodhull Lake Trail

Trails Illustrated Map 745: M6

This interior trail connects Bear Lake (see trail 82) and Woodhull Lake (see trails 83 and 87). It passes small Bloodsucker Pond near Woodhull Lake.

▶Locator: The W end of the trail intersects Bear Lake Trail (trail 82), 2.2 mi from its beginning at Woodhull Mt. Trail (trail 76). The E end is on Woodhull Rd. Trail (trail 83), 7.6 mi from the Bear Creek Rd. trailhead.◀

From Bear Lake Trail (trail 82) at the inlet to Bear Lake (0.0 mi), the yellow-marked trail goes E along the creek, then turns slightly S away from it to climb over the divide between Bear Lake and the much larger Woodhull Lake. At the top of the divide, there is a confusing turn to the R (S) along a wet area.

After the high point, the route is easier to recognize on an old road. It passes Bloodsucker Pond at 1.6 mi and reaches Woodhull Rd. trail (trail 83) at 1.7 mi, just 50 ft N of Bloodsucker Creek, which is itself 50 ft N of the side trail E to Woodhull Lake Lean-to, 0.2 mi away. The jct. with Woodhull Rd. is not marked. It is best located by its position just N of the creek and lean-to trail.

✳ Trail in winter: Suitable for snowshoers or good backcountry skiers.

🚶 Distances: Bear Lake to Woodhull Lake, 1.7 mi (2.7 km).

79 Sand Lake Falls Trail

Trails Illustrated Map 745: L7

This trail provides a through route from the Woodgate area, partly via trail 83, to North Lake. Sand Lake Falls is closer to the North Lake end, but the Woodgate trailhead leads to many other trails.

▶Trailheads: From Woodgate on NY 28, go E on Bear Creek Rd. Cross the railroad tracks and continue to the parking lot just over the line into Herkimer County, 3.1 mi from Woodgate, on the L. A badly rutted and rocky jeep road continues 3.7 mi to a small section of private land; this is trail 83, with which trail 79 shares the route at its start and also briefly midway.

The North Lake end of the trail is reached from Forestport on NY 28. Go E on

North Lake Rd., cross the railroad tracks at Forestport Station, and continue to the dam at Atwell at 15.4 mi. Turn L at the dam and go 0.3 mi to a snowmobile trailhead with a register where the trail heads immediately uphill L. ◀

From the parking lot and trail register on Bear Creek Rd. (0.0 mi), the trail shares its route with the Woodhull Rd. trail (trail 83). The blue-marked Chub Pond Trail (trail 81) departs R at 0.3 mi. The yellow trail 101 turns L off of the deeply rutted and muddy Woodhull Rd. at 0.4 mi. (Woodhull Rd. continues straight ahead, rejoining trail 79 at 2.6 mi, compared to 3.1 mi by the trail; one can choose to follow the road, but it is rough going. See below.)

Turning L off the road and going past a barricade, the trail follows an old woods road N. After a gradual descent, the trail becomes nearly level. At 1.2 and 1.4 mi, old roads L lead in 50 yd to the banks of Bear Creek.

Continuing NE on the R fork, the old road is nearly level, but ATVs have made the next 0.5 mi into a chain of hogwallows. At 2 mi, after two tiny brooks, the red trail to Gull Lake (trail 80) goes uphill R, while the yellow trail continues on ahead. There is little change in elevation along this part of the trail, because it follows the contours.

The yellow (and snowmobile) route turns R, and heads SSE to a jct. with Woodhull Rd. at 3.1 mi. The route then turns L and follows the muddy jeep road, which soon heads E and tilts upward, leaving the mud behind. This climb is not very steep or long. After topping the hill, the route levels and comes to an inholding of private land at 3.9 mi. There are several private camps here, once labeled "Village of Millbrook, population 0 (Dry town)." The road continues on past the cabin to the L as the red hiking (and snowmobile) Woodhull Rd. trail (trail 83). At the corner in the road just before the Millbrook site the route heading R (E) is the blue hiking (and snowmobile) trail 79 to Sand Lake Falls.

After the wet Millbrook area, conditions improve as the trail climbs a slight hill, then drops. At 6.9 mi, the trail finally reaches a high point, turns almost S, and heads down. The downhill continues on a mostly gentle slope to a lean-to at 7 mi. Sand Lake Falls is just beyond the lean-to.

The falls are in a very pleasant setting, with the water gliding over a smooth rock slab for a 10 ft descent. Smaller falls on the stream above and below this site make for pleasant exploring. In summer, the stream is small, but still high enough to top your boots (but no crossing is necessary). The blue-marked trail continues through woods past the lean-to, then emerges on the banks of the creek at a long beaver meadow at 7.3 mi.

Depending on the time of year, the next 0.7 mi can be soggy going. The trail follows the L edge of a vlei, crosses a point of land, continues along the edge, crosses another point of land, then proceeds on a snowmobile bridge over a tributary. Following the edge of a vlei again, the trail bends R and proceeds over a bridge (sometimes under water) of nearly 40 yd, crossing two streams. To the L, signs indicate the private property boundary of the Adirondack League Club as the trail heads uphill. It ascends, bends R and L, and drops to Grindstone Creek at 8.9 mi. Grindstone Creek can be crossed on a bridge.

The next segment is pleasant walking on an old road in good condition, which is marked for snowmobiles. At 9.9 mi on the R (SW), Little Woodhull Lake Trail (trail 85) leads to Little Woodhull Lake, while trail 101 continues SE, crossing several brooks, before finally descending to North Lake Rd. at 11.9 mi.

❄ Trail in winter: Snowmobile trail, probably lightly used. Suitable for strong backcountry skiers and snowshoers.

🐾 Distances: Bear Creek Rd. trailhead to Chub Pond Trail (trail 81), 0.3 mi; to split from trail 83, 0.4 mi; to return to trail 83, 3.1 mi; to jct. at Millbrook site, 3.9 mi; to lean-to and falls, 7 mi; to Grindstone Creek, 8.9 mi; to Little Woodhull Lake Trail (trail 85), 9.9 mi; to North Lake Rd., 11.9 mi (19 km).

80 Gull Lake Loop

Trails Illustrated Map 745: L5

▶Locator: This interior trail begins at 2 mi on Sand Lake Falls Trail (trail 79). Take Bear Creek Rd. E from Woodgate on NY 28. Cross the railroad tracks and continue to the parking lot on the L, at 3.1 mi from Woodgate.

A badly rutted and rocky jeep road (Woodhull Rd., trail 83) continues on for another 3.4 mi to a small section of private land. ◀

From the parking lot (0.0 mi), follow Sand Lake Falls Trail (trail 79) past its jct. with the blue-marked Chub Pond Trail (trail 81) on the R at 0.3 mi (a loop trip returns to this jct.), being sure to follow it L off Woodhull Rd., trail 83) at 0.4 mi. The red-marked Gull Lake Loop leaves this trail at a jct. R at 2 mi.

Heading SE, the red-marked trail goes gently uphill for 0.3 mi to a crossing of Woodhull Rd. (trail 83). Past Woodhull Rd., 4WD vehicles occasionally mangle the route, an old woods road, on their way SE to Gull Lake. It is marked in red as both a snowmobile trail and a foot trail.

The route is easy going to a jct. at 1 mi. To the L, a yellow foot trail follows an old woods road for a short way, then continues across rougher terrain to the lean-to at 1.4 mi. It is well located on a point of land, with fine views of a peaceful wilderness lakeshore and clean water. A return to the trail takes only a few minutes. (Total trip distance from the trailhead to this point is 3.8 mi.)

The trail briefly skirts the lake near an unofficial boat landing, plunges into the woods with little ups and downs, and then crosses the lake outlet stream on a snowmobile bridge. The route continues generally W. A short herd path leads through the woods to the swampy S shore of Gull Lake.

The main trail bends R (S), and finally SW, continuing through open woods to a jct. with the blue-marked Chub Pond Trail (trail 81) at 4.2 mi. From here, the loop trip follows the blue trail R (W) on a smooth, pleasant woods road, reaching the trailhead at 7.8 mi.

❄ Trail in winter: Snowmobile trail. Suitable for backcountry skiing and snowshoeing.

Beaver and lodge. Joanne Kennedy

🦫 Distances: Parking lot/trailhead to trail via Sand Lake Falls Trail (trail 79), 2 mi. Sand Lake Falls Trail to Gull Lake lean-to spur, 1 mi; to lean-to, 1.4 mi; to Chub Pond Trail, 4.2 mi (6.7 km). Full loop to parking lot, 7.8 mi (12.5 km).

81 Chub Pond Trail

Trails Illustrated Map 745: K5

▶Trailhead: See trail 79.◀

From the parking lot and trail register (0.0 mi), the route follows Woodhull Rd. for 0.3 mi, then turns R on another old road marked as a blue foot trail (and snowmobile trail). At 1.2 mi, a trail on the R with two old paint blazes leads past a beaver pond on Gull Lake Outlet stream and into unknown territory. Shortly afterward, the trail turns R and crosses Gull Lake Outlet stream on a snowmobile bridge. The stream meanders quietly beside grass hummocks.

At 2 mi, Gull Lake Loop (trail 80) joins on the L. Continuing past this jct., at 2.2 mi the route crosses a stream and turns L, the snowmobile route following the old road through a miserably wet section, and the foot trail paralleling it on the hillside. At 2.6 mi, the routes rejoin. At 3 mi, a short path leads R to the open marsh at the upper end of Buck Pond.

The trail splits at 3.7 mi. The L fork is marked for snowmobiles and as a red foot trail; the R fork continues as a blue foot trail only (see below). The L fork (red) leads down a mostly gentle hill to the shore of Chub Pond at 4.2 mi. A spur trail leads L to a lean-to, Chub Pond 2, on the shore of the lake at 4.4 mi. The setting is idyllic. The pond is gravel-bottomed, and lined with evergreens.

The snowmobile trail continues around the shore of the lake, passing lean-to #1 (see description below) in the midst of old blowdown on the S side, and ending on the S shore of the lake.

The blue trail continues from the jct. at 3.7 mi as a foot trail. At 4 mi, the route starts down gently, then steeper, to a jct. with the snowmobile trail around the lake at 4.3 mi. Continuing R (SW) around the lake, the trail reaches a bridge across an old dam at the outlet at 4.8 mi. A tornado in 1984 took down nearly every tree in this area. The debris is now hidden by fields of ferns, bushes, and young trees.

At 5.2 mi, the yellow trail to Stone Dam Lake (trail 84) joins on the R (S). It may be difficult to find in the heavy bushes. The snowmobile trail continues ahead and ends in woods at the S shore of the lake. A side trail R at 5.3 mi leads a short distance to Chub Pond Lean-to 1. The lean-to has to be seen to be believed. Built in 1961 (DEC lean-to permit #193, according to a sign) by a private group as a sort of wilderness palace, it has bunks, tables, shelves, and skylights (normally covered to prevent damage). It was refurbished in 1986 with a porch added for stability after the structure was damaged by trees falling on it during the 1984 tornado. Nonetheless, its setting is deep in the woods, while Chub Pond Lean-to 2 overlooks the lake.

Gull Lake Outlet was reportedly dammed by canal authorities in the early part of the twentieth century to store water for the Black River Canal. Most of the earthen parts of the very small dam remain.

(For travelers continuing on to Stone Dam, the yellow trail, trail 84 at 5.2 mi, near Chub Pond Lean-to 1, leads S over a small hill and across rolling terrain to Stone Dam Lake at 7.8 mi. The route is marked with yellow foot trail markers. It provides a real sense of wilderness, and offers a through hike from Black Creek Rd. to North Lake Rd. The trail does not stop at Stone Dam Lake, or at Stone Dam, which is washed out. Be alert for the water seen through the trees L at 7.8 mi [2.6 mi from Chub Lake]. The former Stone Dam Lake Camp is now no more than detectable foundations [10 x 12 ft] hidden in the woods. After crossing Woodhull Creek at 10.3 mi, the route follows a smooth and broad woods road, with obviously greater usage. The end of the trail, at 11.4 mi, is on North Lake Rd. [see trail 84].)

❄ Trail in winter: Snowmobile trail. Suitable for snowshoeing or backcountry skiing. The descent to Chub Pond on the N side has some steep parts, but the trail via Chub Pond Lean-to 2 is gentle.

🐾 Distances: Trailhead to split from Woodhull Rd., 0.3 mi; to Gull Lake Loop (trail 80), 2 mi; to Buck Pond spur, 3 mi; to Chub Pond Lean-to 2, 4.4 mi; to Lean-to 1 near Chub Pond, 5.3 mi (8.5 km). Continuation to Stone Dam Lake, 7.8 mi; to North Lake Rd., 11.4 mi (18.2 km).

82 Bear Lake Trail

Trails Illustrated Map 745: M6

Bear Lake Trail connects the Woodhull Mt. trail (trail 76) on the N with Woodhull Rd. Trail (trail 83) on the S. It passes Bear Lake, which is remote and beautiful, and has a connecting trail in its middle for access to the lean-to on Woodhull Lake. A very nice loop trip can be had by taking Woodhull Mt. and Bear Lake Trails from McKeever to Bear Lake, Bear Lake–Woodhull Lake Trail to the lean-to on Woodhull Lake, Wolf Lake Landing Rd. to connect on the N, and Woodhull Mt. Trail to return (trails 76, 82, 78, 77, and 76). Longer loop trips can be made using all of Woodhull Rd. (trail 83).

▶Locator: This interior trail's N end is on Woodhull Mt. trail (trail 76), 0.7 mi from the McKeever trailhead, and its S end is on Woodhull Rd. (trail 83), 7.5 mi from the Bear Creek Rd. trailhead.◀

The yellow-marked Bear Lake Trail begins (0.0 mi) on the R (S) at 0.7 mi on the Woodhull Mt. trail (trail 76). It heads S, crossing Wolf Lake Landing Rd. (trail 77) at 0.2 mi. After the road, the route crosses some marshy ground and begins a mild climb while weaving a bit. At 0.8 mi, after descending a little, the route turns L and starts more steeply downhill. There is a lookout next to the corner giving a view through the trees of Bear Lake and the hills beyond.

At the bottom of the descent, at 1.2 mi, the trail comes close to the lake at an enjoyable sand and pebble beach. A little farther E around the lake, an unofficial campsite makes a good place to stay. Continuing beyond that, the route turns gradually S and meets the main inlet stream at 1.7 mi. A spur trail R leads to an unofficial campsite at the lake near the inlet stream.

On the S side of the bridge over the stream, the yellow-marked Bear Lake–Woodhull Lake Trail (trail 78) goes L (E). To the S beyond this jct. Bear Lake Trail passes through an old lumber clearing, strikingly bordered by fir trees, at 2.1 mi. The trail turns L, climbs a hillside, goes sharply L, and continues uphill to a saddle below Neejer Hill, where the trail joins Woodhull Rd. Trail (trail 83) at 3.4 mi. To the R, it is 4.7 mi to the Bear Creek Rd. trailhead.

❄ Trail in winter: Suitable for snowshoeing or intermediate-level backcountry skiing. There are some ups and downs, including a rather steep descent to Bear Lake.

🦌 Distances: McKeever trailhead via trail 76 to Bear Lake Trail, 0.7 mi. Trail 76 to Bear Lake, 1.2 mi; to Bear Lake–Woodhull Lake Trail (trail 78), 1.7 mi; to Woodhull Rd. Trail (trail 83), 3.4 mi (5.4 km).

83 Woodhull Rd.

Trails Illustrated Map 745: L5

This old road, now mainly a trail, once gave access to the landing on Woodhull Lake for travel to Adirondack League Club land as well as later access to the dam on the lake. The dam is on private, posted land, but the route still allows access to state land on Woodhull Lake (not the shortest route) and to many other backwoods lakes and streams. The road is still used by 4WD vehicles to reach a private plot of land on Mill Brook, about halfway to Woodhull Lake.

▶Trailhead: From Woodgate on NY 28, go E on Bear Creek Rd. Cross the railroad tracks at 0.8 mi, and continue to the end of the good road and a DEC parking lot at 3.1 mi.◀

Beginning at the register by the parking lot (0.0 mi), the route starts on a jeep road. In a short distance, the blue-marked Chub Pond Trail (trail 81, used also for the Gull Lake Loop) joins on the R. Woodhull Rd. continues straight.

At 0.4 mi, Sand Lake Falls Trail (trail 79) goes L as the road continues ahead. They rejoin later; the hiker can avoid the muddy road by taking trail 79, although the trail is 0.5 mi longer.

At 1.9 mi, a trail on the R leads to Gull Lake (trail 80). At 2.6 mi, trail 101 rejoins the road. After climbing E up a hill, the road turns L and a not-too-prominent blue-marked trail connects on the R at 3.7 mi. This is the continuation of Sand Lake Falls Trail (trail 79) to the E.

Woodhull Rd. Trail continues N on the L branch, through "Village of Millbrook, Population 0 (Dry town)." This is a collection of private camps on a private plot surrounded by state land. Beyond the camps, the trail crosses Mill Brook and begins a long gentle climb along the flank of Neejer Hill. After ascending, the trail turns E across a broad hilltop. At 4.7 mi, Bear Lake Trail (trail 82) joins on the L.

At 6.2 mi, the trail meets an old road jct. (Straight ahead, the old road heads E, then curves to the SE, headed for Woodhull Dam. It reaches private posted land 1.1 mi from the jct.) The trail continues L (NW) from this jct. with some muddy areas.

At 7.4 mi, a spur R leads to the gigantic Woodhull Lake Lean-to in 0.2 mi. The view from this lean-to and from rocks on the shoreline is very good. The old road continues on past the jct. toward Wolf Lake Landing (reaching trail 78 in 0.1 mi) and returns to NY 28 as Wolf Lake Landing Rd. (trail 77).

❋ Trail in winter: Snowmobile trail. It is an easy ski route, with the hill before Millbrook and a few modest slopes in the Mill Brook area.

🚶 Distances: Bear Creek Rd. trailhead to jct. with Gull Lake Loop (trail 80), 1.9 mi; to Sand Lake Falls Trail (trail 79), 3.4 mi; to Bear Lake Trail (trail 82), 4.7 mi; to Woodhull Lake lean-to, 7.6 mi (12.2 km).

NY 8 and North Lake Road Section

The West Canada Lake Wilderness Area covers a vast area N of NY 8 from Nobleboro to Piseco Lake. There are only four official trails into the wilderness from the S, but several additional access points allow extensive possibilities for the experienced wilderness traveler.

The remainder of the area between NY 8 and North Lake Rd. is mostly state land in the Black River Wild Forest. Hikers here need to be a bit more self-reliant, with a sense of direction and expectations for close forest scenery rather than sweeping views. This is the country of Adirondack French Louie, Nat Foster, Jock Wright, Atwell Martin, and a host of ragged, rugged lumberjacks, trappers, and hermits who tangled with the upper reaches of the Black River. It is the home of several of the earliest sportsmen's clubs in New York State.

The importance of the waters in this section may have been a principal factor in the creation of the Adirondack Park. The water fed the Erie Canal, which was chronically short of water in the summer. The larger lakes in this section still store and supply water for the canal. The water is tapped off from Kayuta Lake at Forestport and sent down the old Black River Canal, past Boonville to Delta Lake, and on into the high point of the Erie Canal at Rome. West Canada Creek sends water into storage in the Hinckley Reservoir and then on to the canal at Herkimer.

Access to some trailheads is difficult along NY 8. Anyone expecting to drive Haskell Rd. N of Nobleboro should be aware of its sometimes rough condition, best suited to jeeps and pickups. The road to North Lake, however, is in reasonably good condition most of the year, with trailheads to Stone Dam, Twin Lakes, Little Woodhull Lake, North Lake, South Lake, and Sand Lake Falls readily accessible to passenger cars.

North Lake Tract

In 1990, the Nature Conservancy helped arrange a New York State–owned conservation easement on this 11,490-acre tract of land, formerly known as the J. P. Lewis Tract. Once posted by the Adirondack League Club (ALC), this area surrounds the N end of North Lake and contains the former ALC exclusive, Ice Cave Mt. The owner has the right to continue to man-

North Lake. Courtesy of DEC

age the forest for timber harvest. The easement allows the owner to close any zone within the tract while timber harvesting is in progress.

Otherwise, the tract is open to public recreational use with the exception of motorized vehicles such as motorcycles, ATVs, and snowmobiles. Cars are allowed only on the loop road extending into the heart of the tract, but must give way to lumber trucks as necessary. Camping is "first come, first served," including the designated camping sites along North Lake. Trails 87A through 87J—all logging roads—are located within this tract. These are not DEC trails. The agreement allows the DEC to mark and maintain seven trails, but they may or may not follow any of these routes. Updated information may be obtained from DEC foresters in the Herkimer office (315-866-6330).

Pratt-Northam Memorial Tract and Park

Pratt-Northam Memorial Tract was given to New York State as silviculture (tree-cutting) land. Located S of South Lake Rd. near South Lake, it is currently managed in the same manner as the surrounding Wild Forest lands. South Lake Trail (trail 88) passes through this tract.

Within Pratt-Northam Memorial Tract is Pratt-Northam Memorial Park. Given to the state as a park, this land provides recreational access to South Lake. There is a small, informal picnic site just S of South Lake Rd. where it first meets South Lake. This site can also be reached by a side trail from trail 88 (South Lake Trail) shortly after the trailhead.

A few suggested hikes for this section are listed below.

SHORT HIKE

Vista (Keegans) Trail to Ledge Mt. Overlook: 1.6 mi (2.6 km) round-trip. Short, well-marked trail with moderate grades to small lookout over West Canada Creek and forest. See trail 91.

MODERATE HIKE

Twin Lakes: 6.2 mi (9.9 km) round-trip. Easy walking, but sometimes wet. Crosses through a small swamp, and ends near the remains of a small dam once used to impound water for the Erie Canal. See trail 86.

HARDER HIKE

Little Salmon Lake: 12.6 mi (20.2 km) round-trip. An old road and old logging road lead to a pleasant, remote lake. See trail 93.

84 Stone Dam Trail

Trails Illustrated Map 745: J6

Initially gentle, this route becomes somewhat rough and is apparently less used after it crosses Woodhull Creek. Pay careful attention to the yellow markers. Fairly open older hardwoods give way in places to evergreens, with only an occasional muddy spot. The trail does not reach any reliable landmarks until it passes Stone Dam Lake (seen through the trees on the R). If your goal is to reach the lake, keep a careful watch or you may go much farther than intended. The lake and dam site must be reached by bushwhack. The route ahead goes to Chub Pond and can be used as a through trip to Bear Creek Rd. at Woodgate or the McKeever trailhead.

▶Trailhead: From the highway jct. at Forestport, on NY 28, take North Lake Rd. E to the railroad tracks at Forestport Station. Continue straight ahead (E) on North Lake Rd. The trailhead is on the L (N) just after a bend in the road, 6.5 mi from Forestport Station. Park in a three-car parking lot just off the road (somewhat lower than the road), or on the shoulder beside the trailhead.◀

From the trailhead on North Lake Rd. (0.0 mi), the yellow-marked route heads N on an old road with a soft, broad pathway. At 1 mi, the trail crosses Woodhull Creek on a nice log bridge with a cable for a handrail. Beyond this, the trail becomes rough, and is less used.

At 1.8 mi, a thick group of large spruce trees dominates the trail, but doesn't last long. Open hardwoods again prevail. A particularly magnificent birch sits right by the trail at 3.2 mi, at the top of a climb. A modest downhill slope after that should encourage attention to Stone Dam Lake through the trees R at 3.5 mi. A short bushwhack through the forest will reveal the shore. On a slight peninsula of the N shore is the site of the former Stone Dam Lake Camp, one of the smallest imaginable sportsmen's camps.

The yellow trail continues past Stone Dam Lake, climbing a little before crossing an inlet brook. The route winds over small bumps and crosses several little creeks, often passing through open, well-established forest. It finally takes a distinctly downhill trend and joins the blue-marked Chub Pond Trail (trail 81) at 6.2 mi. Trail 81 goes R for 0.3 mi to Chub Pond Lean-to 1, and L 1.4 mi around the lake to Chub Pond Lean-to 2. Lean-to 2 has by far the better scenery.

For continuation to Bear Creek Rd., see Chub Pond Trail (trail 81).

❄ Trail in winter: Suitable for backcountry skiing and snowshoeing. The trail is lightly marked and remote. Trailhead parking may be a problem.

🚶 Distances: North Lake Rd. trailhead to Woodhull Creek, 1 mi; to Stone Dam Lake, 3.5 mi; to Chub Pond Trail, 6.2 mi (9.9 km). To Bear Creek Rd. trailhead, 11.4 mi (18.2 km).

85 Little Woodhull Lake Trail

Trails Illustrated Map 745: K7

▶Trailhead: From the highway jct. at Forestport, on NY 28, take North Lake Rd. E to the railroad tracks at Forestport Station. Continue straight ahead (E) on North Lake Rd. Check the distance carefully. The trailhead is an old road on the L (N), 14 mi from NY 28. Park at the snowmobile trailhead on the R just beyond.

The other end of the trail is on Sand Lake Falls Trail (trail 79), 2 mi from its trailhead on North Lake Rd. near North Lake. It is 1.8 mi between the trailheads for trails 79 and 85 along North Lake Rd., making a loop possible. ◀

From the trailhead on North Lake Rd. (0.0 mi), the route heads NW on an old road with an easy pathway under yellow DEC markers. It gradually turns N, gently climbing a ridge. At 1 mi, the trail tops out, turns L, and descends somewhat.

At 1.2 mi, the old road (with blue markers) goes straight ahead into the brush and blowdown, but the yellow-marked trail follows another old road turning sharply R. The path is mostly easy and pleasant, if not always well marked. There is an occasional old snowmobile marker and a footpath on the old road, which heads N, then swings W.

The trail finally curves W and reaches Little Woodhull Creek at 2.4 mi. At the creek, the vlei ahead seems to be the expected direction, but as it emerges, the trail instead turns L and follows along the margin of the woods in tall marsh grass. At the end of the soggy meadow, the trail turns inland L on a boulder-strewn, moss-covered old road (obscure; look carefully for markers). The route turns L off this old road at 2.5 mi. Look carefully for the markers, some of which are homemade.

The route soon becomes more obvious and follows Little Woodhull Creek, just S of it but not within sight of it. At 3 mi, the trail turns R and crosses the creek at the site of a former snowmobile bridge. The path straight ahead along the creek leads to an informal campsite in approximately 175 yd. There is a path W to the lake, which is pretty and has a strong sense of remoteness.

Continuing N from the creek, the now red-marked trail continues on gentle ground. In about 100 yd, the lake comes into view through the open woods to the L. At the first tiny creek crossing, there is an obscure trail L to the lake.

The trail continues on easy ground and then climbs gently up a hill. The route is faint here but has red DEC and red paint markers, as well as homemade markers. The hill is fairly open. The trail skirts to the R of the broad hilltop and meets Sand Lake Falls Trail (trail 79), an obvious old road, at 4.9 mi. To the L, it is 0.7 mi to the crossing of Grindstone Creek on the way to Sand Lake Falls, and to the R it is 2 mi to North Lake. To complete a round-trip hike, go R to North Lake at 7 mi, turn R and walk to the dam at 7.4 mi, then turn R and walk down the road to your car at 8.8 mi.

❄ Trail in winter: Snowmobile trail, probably not used. Suitable for backcountry skiing and snowshoeing. This trail is far from civilization. Prepare well for your trip.

🐾 Distances: Trailhead to Little Woodhull Lake, 3 mi; to Sand Lake Falls Trail (trail 101), 4.9 mi (7.8 km). To Sand Lake Falls, 6.2 mi; to North Lake, 7 mi; complete loop trip via North Lake, 8.8 mi (14.1 km).

86 Twin Lakes Dam Trail

Trails Illustrated Map 745: J7

▶Trailhead: From NY 28 at Forestport, go E to Forestport Station. Continue straight ahead across the railroad tracks on North Lake Rd. The road narrows at 5.1 mi from the railroad tracks. At 10 mi from the tracks, turn R on the gravel road to North Wilmurt. The trailhead is 0.4 mi down this road on the L (E). There is parking for three cars.◀

The route begins at the DEC-marked trailhead in a hardwood forest (0.0 mi). An old woods road is used for this section, marked now and then by DEC snowmobile trail markers. An occasional mudhole and adjacent bog make the route more interesting.

At 2.1 mi, the route leaves the smooth old road and ascends slightly through evergreens before dropping again to a beaver meadow at 2.5 mi. This crossing may muddy your feet slightly. If the beavers return (flooding the area), you will probably have to make a bushwhack detour around the pond, going R.

The trail continues from an enormous stump at the E side of the meadow, through evergreens and over another small hill to the Twin Lakes outlet at 3.1 mi. The dam rotted out many years ago, but the remains can be inspected just a little way down from the trail's end. The rock and concrete frame for the gate is still in place, and the rotten stub ends of the wooden dam can be seen sticking out from the bank on the opposite side of the creek. This dam was used to store snowmelt, which could be let out later in the summer to maintain a sufficient water level in the Erie Canal (by way of the Black River Canal). Beavers have dammed the stream here in the past, and no doubt will return when enough small trees reappear in the meadow to provide food for them.

❄ Trail in winter: Snowmobile trail. Otherwise suitable for snowshoeing or backcountry skiing.

🚶 Distances: To departure from woods road, 2.1 mi; to Twin Lakes, 3.1 mi (5 km).

87 North Lake Tract Easement

Trails Illustrated Map 745: L7

"Trails" 87A–87J are old logging roads in the North Lake Tract and not DEC trails. Open for public use, they have no markers and are not maintained. Signs should be posted on the road along the N shore of North Lake if logging is under-way, restricting access.

Unless indicated otherwise, these trails are suitable for backcountry skiing and snowshoeing. The trails are not marked, but the roadways are prominent. The road along the length of North Lake is not plowed, thus adding between 3.3 and 4.5 mi to the trips in the winter. Trailhead parking may be a problem in the winter.

87A Grindstone Creek Trail (unmaintained)

Trails Illustrated Map 745: L7

▶Trailhead: Starting from Forestport on NY 28, go E on North Lake Rd., cross the railroad tracks at Forestport Station, and continue to the dam at Atwell at 15.4 mi. Turn L at the dam and travel 3.3 mi to the first parking lot on the L. The trailhead is 0.2 mi S of the parking lot.◀

This logging road is now grass-covered, and very easy walking. From the trail-head (0.0 mi), it follows the course of Mud Pond Outlet for the first 0.5 mi, until the creek turns S and the road continues W up the mild slope of the hill. There is a 40 ft wide dugout pit on the L at 0.9 mi. This is a useful landmark for locating the start of Mud Pond Trail (trail 108B), which is another 0.1 mi ahead on the L at 1 mi.

The main road continues over a gentle high point and descends very slowly.

Numerous narrower old logging roads go L and R along the route.

At 2.2 mi, the road turns R while a lesser road continues straight ahead. After the turn, the route is downhill to a turnaround at 2.4 mi. A less prominent old road continues ahead to cross Grindstone Creek in another 100 ft. That road turns L and continues downstream along the creek. Another older road turns R at the turnaround and goes 300 ft upstream along the upper edge of a grassy marsh. After emerging from the wet grassy area, the road crosses a small creek and continues up the end of Golden Stair Mt. The creek just crossed is fed by a two-ended marsh to the E; it sends water E to Golden Stair Creek and W to Grindstone Creek. Back at the turnaround, still another easy old logging road goes L from the end of the road to follow downstream along Grindstone Creek.

🏃 Distances: Trailhead to jct. of Mud Pond Trail (trail 87B), 1 mi; to turnaround, 2.4 mi (3.8 km).

87B Mud Pond Trail (unmaintained)

Trails Illustrated Map 745: L8

Mud Pond is a scenic but shallow lake surrounded by a boggy shoreline. Thick and treacherous bogs at the N and S ends make access difficult; a stroll around the lake is out of the question. Adventurous bushwhackers can approach the lake from the W side by taking the R uphill branch on the road at 0.4 mi.

▶Locator: On Grindstone Creek Trail (trail 87A).◀

Starting from the jct. on Grindstone Creek Trail (0.0 mi), the route is nearly level, heading SW. At 0.4 mi, at a Y jct., the route bears L, going downhill. At 0.6 mi, the old road reaches a small clearing and turns sharp R. Beyond that, it continues S over a slight hill at 0.8 mi.

The best route to Mud Pond is from this slight hilltop. Turn sharp R and bushwhack 0.1 mi through the evergreens to the rim above Mud Pond.

The old road continues beyond the hilltop, down across Mud Pond Outlet creek, turns R at 1 mi, and continues onto the tabletop behind Sugarloaf Mt., which overlooks North Lake.

🏃 Distances: Grindstone Creek Trail (trail 87A) to Mud Pond bushwhack turnoff, 0.8 mi (1.3 km). To Mud Pond, 0.9 mi (1.4 km).

87C Canachagala Trail (unmaintained)

Trails Illustrated Map 745: L8

▶Trailhead: See Grindstone Creek Trail (trail 87A). From the dam, go 3.6 mi to the second parking lot on the L, where the road makes a sharp R bend. The trailhead is on the E edge of the parking lot.◀

From the road corner in front of the parking lot (0.0 mi), the old road goes NW past a gate on nearly level ground, then begins a gentle climb to the terrace above a creek. Once on the terrace, the route wraps around Canachagala Mt. A small pond on the L at 0.6 mi is the E end of the extensive swamps surrounding Golden Stair Creek.

After a mild climb, the trail reaches Golden Stair Mt. Trail (trail 87D) on the L at 1.2 mi. Continuing N, the trail parallels the unnamed creek, turns uphill at 1.4 mi, and reaches the boundary of Adirondack League Club land at 2 mi. There is a high point in the valley just ahead. Canachagala Lake is on the other side, and does not contribute to the creek followed by this trail.

🔀 Distances: Parking lot to Golden Stair Creek swamp, 0.6 mi; to Golden Stair Mt. Trail (trail 87D), 1.2 mi; to boundary of Adirondack League Club, 2 mi (3.2 km).

87D Golden Stair Mt. Trail (unmaintained)

Trails Illustrated Map 745: L8

This area is of special interest for its extensive flower fields.
▶Locator: On Canachagala Trail (trail 108C).◀

From Canachagala Trail (0.0 mi), the trail heads W across the lay of the land, drops down once to cross the nearby creek, crosses over a slight hill at 0.4 mi, drops down again to cross Golden Stair Creek, and finally proceeds up Golden Stair Mt. The primary road ends at 0.9 mi on the lower slopes of the mountain, where the steep hillside begins.

🔀 Distances: Canachagala Trail (trail 108C) to end of road at Golden Stair Mt., 0.9 mi (1.4 km).

87E North Branch Trail (unmaintained)

Trails Illustrated Map 745: L8

This trail leads to an interesting backcountry section of the upper Black River, and provides the shortest access to Ice Cave Mt. The Ice Cave is actually a 96 ft deep trench on the SW end of the mountain that collects winter snows and remains icy into the summer months. Ice Cave Mt. seems to have a severe case of fracture throughout its length. The summit is mostly a jumble of boulders covered by a thin quilt of soil that doesn't quite fill the gaps. There are many boulders standing along the ridge where they have broken away and begun to slide off. One gigantic boulder stands precariously on the very steep W slope about 0.4 mi NE of the cave. For another approach to the cave, see Ice Cave Creek Trail (trail 87F).

▶Trailhead: See Grindstone Creek Trail (trail 87A). From the dam, go 4.5 mi to the third parking lot on the R at the end of the road. The trailhead is the straight continuation of the road at the end of the parking lot. (Eastside Trail, trail 87G, turns R at the same location.)◀

Leaving the parking lot (0.0 mi), the old road heads due N, then climbs gently as it curves to head NE. There is a jct. with trail 87F on the L at 0.5 mi. At 1.2 mi, the road crosses a small creek. This seems to be the most popular spot to begin bushwhacking up Ice Cave Mt.

(Ice Cave: Turning L off the road, this is the shortest Ice Cave route, but it is very steep. To reach the Ice Cave, go due N to the summit, then turn L in the middle of the ridge and make your way cautiously to the SW tip. The Ice Cave is on the W side of the tip. It is deep and dangerous. Be careful when you lean out to look.)

Past the creek and turnoff for the Ice Cave, at about 1.4 mi, an old road joins on the L, faintly marked by ancient red blazes. This is overgrown, but leads NW along the base of Ice Cave Mt. A L branch near the start may have been an ancient route to the Ice Cave. With a 0.5 mi bushwhack where the R branch gives out, one could reach the W end of the old Gould lumber road, which continues along the valley of the North Branch of the Black River to join a spur of the Horn Lake Trail (*Central Trails*, trail 95A; see Western-Central Overlap Section of this guidebook) near Horn Lake.

Beyond the old road, North Branch Trail continues along easy terrain until crossing a creek in a culvert at 1.6 mi. After the creek, the road becomes rough and overgrown, and finally ends beside the North Branch of the Black River at 1.8 mi, where the river splashes as it tumbles over boulders and slight cascades.

🐾 Distances: Parking lot to trail 87F, 0.5 mi; to take-off point for Ice Cave bushwhack, 1.2 mi; to North Branch of the Black River, 1.8 mi (2.9 km).

87F Ice Cave Creek Trail (unmaintained)

Trails Illustrated Map 745: L8

There is a large clearing at the end of this road where one could camp and explore the area. It also provides a second and not-so-steep access route to the Ice Cave on Ice Cave Mt. (see introduction to North Branch Trail, trail 87E). The Ice Cave Mt. area is mentioned by David Beetle in *Up Old Forge Way*, when he describes tractors being used for the first time to replace horses in large-scale logging operations.

▶Locator: On North Branch Trail (trail 87E), 0.5 mi NE of the parking lot.◀

From the jct. with North Branch Trail (0.0 mi), the old road goes W uphill for 0.2 mi, then levels off and passes the S tip of Ice Cave Mt. At 0.4 mi, the route crosses Ice Cave Creek near a beaver dam and turns N. The grassy old road passes a tiny waterfall dripping over bare rock L along the lower edge of Canachagala Mt. A little farther on, the road enters a large lumber clearing along its upper edge at 1.3 mi.

(To reach the "cave" on Ice Cave Mt., go downhill across the clearing and locate the lumber road crossing Ice Cave Creek [no bridge]. Follow it SE up the hill. At 0.2 mi from the creek, another old tote road goes uphill L, possibly marked with red tape on a tree overhead. Follow it uphill, approximately 60 degrees by compass. This takes you up the gentlest slope on the end of Ice Cave Mt. As it nears the top, the tote road goes into a slight notch to the L of the cliffs on the end of the mountain. Follow along the nearly level ground below the cliffs for another 0.1 mi until the cliffs disappear and you can climb onto the summit ridge with ease. Turn R and go along the middle of the ridge until you reach the Ice Cave at the end, approximately 2.7 mi from the trailhead. The route along the edge of the cliffs is annoyingly uneven and difficult going, not to mention dangerous. Take care with your footing on the summit. It is a jumble of broken rock, half covered by soil. You can drop a leg into many a crevice. The Ice Cave is a vertical cleavage in the rock of the mountain, no doubt being slowly forced apart by expansion of the ice at its bottom in winter. It is about 96 ft deep. A careless visitor could be killed by a fall into what seems at first glance to be only a slight gap in the rock. The safest view is from the far [SW] end.)

Trail in winter: Suitable for backcountry skiing and snowshoeing, though the Ice Cave Mt. part is hard to follow and sometimes a bit steep for skiing.

🏃 Distances: North Branch Trail (trail 87E) to Ice Cave Creek, 0.4 mi; to clearing on Ice Cave Creek, 1.3 mi (2.1 km). To Ice Cave, 2.7 mi.

87G Eastside Trail (unmaintained)

Trails Illustrated Map 745: L8

Overnight campers may find this route very much to their liking for its eight primitive campsites and two lean-tos along the E shore of North Lake.

▶Trailhead: See Grindstone Creek Trail (trail 87A). From the dam, go 4.5 mi to the third parking lot on the R at the end of the road. The trailhead is the gate on the R at the N end of the parking lot.◀

From the gate (0.0 mi), continue along the loop road extension. At 0.3 mi, this crosses the North Branch of the Black River and turns SW to follow the river along its upper bank. At 1.1 mi, Black River Middle Branch Trail (trail 87H) curves L and starts gently uphill, while the Eastside Trail road turns R off the main road and continues SW along level ground above the N end of North Lake.

The Middle Branch of the Black River crosses under the road at 1.4 mi. At 1.5 mi, the trail passes within 200 ft of the lake R. A slight two-track road R leads to a campsite with a steel fire ring.

At 1.9 mi, the trail crosses Jocks Brook, named after Jonathan "Jock" Wright. The road going uphill on the L is trail 87I, the Jocks Brook trail. Continuing S past the jct., the old road becomes overgrown for a short distance. At 2.2 mi, the road crosses a culvert. There is another campsite with a fire ring 200 ft R at the edge of the lake.

The haul road ends at 2.3 mi, but a rutted skid road continues on. At 2.6 mi, the skid road passes a private cabin downhill by the lake. There is another camping site slightly farther S, at 2.7 mi. This is the end of the trail. (If one is willing to bushwhack another 0.5 mi along the steep slope above the lake, two lean-tos are set on state land. The state land boundary is at 3 mi, but the old road goes only as far as the last campsite at 2.7 mi.)

   🐾 Distances: Parking lot to Black River Middle Branch Trail (trail 87H) jct., 1.1 mi; to Jocks Brook Trail (trail 87I), 1.9 mi; to campsite at end of trail, 2.7 mi (4.3 km).

87H Black River Middle Branch Trail (unmaintained)

Trails Illustrated Map 745: L8

►Locator: On Eastside Trail (trail 87G), 1.1 mi from parking lot.◄

At the jct. (0.0 mi) on Eastside Trail, where Eastside Trail turns R and goes downhill to cross the Middle Branch, Black River Middle Branch Trail curves L (E) and starts gently uphill. At 0.6 mi, the Loop Rd. Extension (trail 87J) starts R. At 0.8 mi, Middle Branch Trail starts up more steeply, then alternates down and up as it crosses streams and climbs hillsides. It meets a corner of Adirondack League Club land on a hilltop at 1.9 mi and ends on another hillside at 2.5 mi. There is a small pond on the Black River just a little S of the end of the trail. Private land is only a little farther on the S, E, and N.

   🐾 Distances: Eastside Trail (trail 87G) to jct. with Loop Rd. Extension (trail 87J), 0.6 mi; to end of trail, 2.5 mi (4 km).

87I Jocks Brook (unmaintained)

Trails Illustrated Map 745: L8

►Locator: On Eastside Trail (trail 87G). ◄

This old road leaves Eastside Trail near the Jocks Brook inlet into North Lake (0.0 mi) and heads uphill parallel to the brook. There is a Y jct. at 0.4 mi. The R fork, which once went all the way to Honnedaga Lake Rd., disappears in the brush. The L fork goes downhill to Jocks Brook at 0.5 mi and continues across the brook and up the slopes of Hardscrabble Mt., into many branches that end at various points on the slope.

   ❄ Trail in winter: Steep, but otherwise suitable for experienced backcountry skiers and snowshoers. Very remote.

   🐾 Distance: Eastside Trail (trail 87G) to Jocks Brook, 0.5 mi (0.8 km).

87J Loop Rd. Extension (unmaintained)

Trails Illustrated Map 745: L8

►Locator: W trailhead on Black River Middle Branch Trail (trail 87H), 0.6 mi from Eastside Trail (trail 87G) (1.7 mi from parking lot).

   To reach the E trailhead, start from Forestport on NY 28, go E on North Lake

Rd., cross the railroad tracks at Forestport Station, and continue to the dam at Atwell at 15.4 mi. Continue on across the dam and along the gravel road, now called South Lake Rd. Pass South Lake and continue on Honnedaga Lake Rd. to the locked gates at a Y in the road at 19.4 mi. The loop road extension is on the L (NW) side of the road about 200 ft back from the Y jct. ◀

Starting at the W trailhead, the trail leaves Black River Middle Branch Trail (87H) on the R, goes downhill, and crosses the Middle Branch of the Black River. A long, gentle, but steady climb leads past a slight view of Hardscrabble Lake end-on (L) to a saddle at 0.5 mi in the hills above Hardscrabble Lake (downhill L). At 0.7 mi, the road makes a sharp R turn where a side route goes L to private land at Honnedaga Lake. From here, the route is downhill to Jocks Brook, where the culvert is washed out. Once across the brook, it is an easy trip around the headwater swamp and up to Honnedaga Lake Rd. (1.7 mi), just W of the gates that halt public access to the private lands around Honnedaga Lake.

🐾 Distances: Black River Middle Branch Trail (trail 87H) to saddle overlooking Hardscrabble Lake, 0.5 mi; to Jocks Brook, 1.1 mi; to Honnedaga Lake Rd., 1.7 mi (2.7 km).

88 South Lake Trail

Trails Illustrated Map 745: J9

The major portion of this trail lies within the Pratt-Northam Memorial Tract, which was donated to the state with the condition that it not be part of the Forest Preserve. The land surrounding South Lake is a park (Pratt-Northam Memorial Park), while the remainder is silviculture land, currently treated in the same manner as Wild Forest land.

▶Trailhead: From Forestport on NY 28, go E on North Lake Rd., cross the railroad tracks at Forestport Station, and continue to the North Lake Dam at Atwell in 15.4 mi. Continue across the dam past private homes and into the woods again. At 17.6 mi, just before reaching South Lake, park in the weedy open space beside an old road R. This road is the trail. The main road continues on to South Lake in 0.1 mi, becomes Honnedaga Lake Rd., and enters barricaded private land in about 2 mi. There is a nice picnic spot in the Pratt-Northam Memorial Park on the R, just as the main road reaches South Lake. ◀

From North Lake Rd. (0.0 mi), the route, marked with DEC snowmobile markers, heads S near the W end of South Lake. A branch to the L goes to the picnic spot on the lake nearby. About 350 yd past this branch, an unmarked trail joins on the R. That trail is on private land.

Continuing straight ahead on the main trail, at 0.6 mi there are some wet dips as the old road curves L around the corner of the lake (out of sight). Modest ups and downs continue, still following the S shore out of sight of the lake. A small bridge across an outlet creek crosses near a low spillway holding back the water of South Lake at 2.5 mi. Because of the artificial damming, South Lake has two outlet streams which join a little farther downstream.

At the top of the climb from the creek, an unofficial trail goes L 375 ft to the shore of the lake beside the outlet arm. There is a good view of the lake. Back on the main trail, another side trail L at 2.6 mi leads L 450 ft to the main dam (of modest size).

The main trail soon crosses the outlet stream on a snowmobile bridge. Shortly beyond, at 2.8 mi, an old road goes L, while the trail goes R (S). Following along the flatlands of the South Lake Outlet, the road passes through an old lumber clearing. Beyond the clearing, one road in fairly good condition goes S, but the snowmobile trail takes a L fork at 3.2 mi and starts uphill, curving E. By 3.5 mi, the route has turned to the NE and reached a jct. The route straight ahead soon disappears, while the trail takes a sharp R turn and continues uphill a little farther.

The trail reaches another old road at 3.9 mi and turns R on that road, heading S. Jones Brook (one of many by that name) is crossed near the bottom of the hill, followed soon by Little Salmon Outlet at 4.6 mi. Just beyond, the remains of an old cabin in a clearing signal a R turn and a short diversion to the W. After this short excursion on level ground to another jct. at 4.8 mi, the old road ahead leads along Little Salmon Outlet, while the trail goes uphill on the L branch.

At 5.2 mi, the snowmobile trail turns uphill L. (The old road straight ahead leads over the top of a small hill and to a jct. L at 5.5 mi. Both branches soon disappear into thick undergrowth.) Continuing on the snowmobile trail, the route heads SE, going steadily upward on an old road. As it curves L and heads NE, the trail levels off. After another 0.3 mi, the route curves R and heads steadily but gently uphill across a wet hillside, finally leveling out to meet Little Salmon Lake Trail (trail 93) at 7.1 mi. Summit Camp (private) is straight ahead through the woods, but not visible from the jct.

Baby Lake Falls Trail (trail 96), extending another 2.8 mi to Baby Lake Falls, can be reached by going about 300 ft R (S) on Little Salmon Lake Trail (trail 93) and then taking an unmarked primitive road L past Summit Camp. Continuing S on Little Salmon Lake Trail leads to Cement Bridge at 2.5 mi and Haskell Rd. at 5.2 mi. From the jct. of South Lake (trail 88) and Little Salmon Lake Trails, a turn to the L (N) leads to Little Salmon Lake in 1.1 mi.

❅ Trail in winter: Easy skiing most of the way, suitable for intermediate skiers familiar with wilderness travel. Expect some snowmobile usage, and keep out of the way.

🐾 Distances: North Lake Rd. to South Lake dam, 2.6 mi; to Little Salmon Outlet, 4.6 mi; to Little Salmon Lake Trail (trail 93), 7.1 mi (11.4 km). To Haskell Rd. via trail 93, 12.3 mi (19.7 km).

89 Middle Branch Marsh (unmaintained)

Trails Illustrated Map 745: H7

The Middle Branch Marsh trail does not have markers and is not a DEC trail. It is used by owners of a private camp S of Middle Branch Marsh.

▶Trailhead: From the jct. of NY 8 and NY 365, 28 mi NE of Utica, go W on NY 365 for about 300 ft to Hooper Dooper Rd. Turn N on that road and go 1.1 mi to a snowmobile trailhead R.◀

Take the road W at the jct. near the trailhead. Continue on the most heavily used route for approximately 0.4 mi W from the jct. The principal route turns N and continues through private land, finally reaching state land at about 1.4 mi. The old road reaches a private camp at about 4.5 mi, and Middle Branch Marsh at about 5.2 mi. The scene is quite remote and the region beyond the marsh is said to be very wild and beautiful. There are no special lakes or viewpoints; this trip would appeal mostly to wilderness explorers.

❋ Trail in winter: Not a DEC trail, but may have snowmobile traffic. Suitable for snowshoeing and backcountry skiing, if a parking place can be found farther down Hooper Dooper Rd.

🚶 Distance: To state land, 1.4 mi; to Middle Branch Marsh, approximately 5.2 mi (8.3 km).

90 Mad Tom Trail (unmaintained)

Trails Illustrated Map 745: I8

This trail leads along the ridge above Mad Tom Brook to provide access to Mad Tom Lake (tiny, but nice), Mill Creek Lake, Black Creek Lake, Crosby Vlei, and Burp Lake. Black Creek Lake, 0.5 mi long, is the largest of the lakes reached directly from NY 8.

▶Trailhead: From the jct. of NY 8 and NY 365, 28 mi NE of Utica, go E on NY 8 for 1.1 mi to Remonda Rd. (This is 4.2 mi W from Haskell Rd. at Nobleboro near the West Canada Creek scenic overlook.) Turn L (N) and go 0.2 mi to the end of the road, where there is a snowplow turnaround and parking (except in snowplow season). Mad Tom Trail is the old and narrower continuation of this road.◀

From the end of the paved road (0.0 mi), the route goes N on the old road and passes an old cabin at 0.4 mi. Owners of the cabin have retained the right to drive past the open gate, but all others must park on state land on Remonda Rd.

The trail continues N on the old road, climbing gently until reaching the hill W of Mad Tom Lake at 1.6 mi. Descending gently from the hill, the trail passes through a small clearing, crosses a stream, and reaches a jct. at 2.1 mi. The route to the R is a side trail leading to Mad Tom Lake at 2.3 mi.

The main trail forks L and continues on easy terrain. At 3.1 mi, there is a T jct. with the old Black Creek Lake Rd. To the R, Mill Creek Lake Trail (trail 92) leads to Mill Creek Lake (about 1 mi), which has two private plots on its E end. (Mill Creek Lake Trail continues on past Mill Creek Lake to a trailhead off NY 8, making a loop hike possible with a car spotted at the S trailhead for Mill Creek Lake Trail.)

To the L, the Mad Tom Trail follows Black Creek Lake Rd. uphill past a jct. with Milk Can Trail at 3.2 mi. (Milk Can Trail leads to the private Shanty Mt. Camp in another 1.3 mi.) From the jct., the Mad Tom Trail climbs NE, gaining about 400 ft in the next half mile. After a level section, it goes up again to follow the hillside above Little Black Creek, crossing it at 4.7 mi. A slight additional climb leads to a broad hilltop and later a relatively gentle downhill run to Black Creek Lake.

The trail reaches a private land boundary at 5.4 mi. The old road goes downhill inside that boundary, which is prominently posted. To avoid the posted private land, turn L and bushwhack through open forest WNW to the lake at 5.7 mi. Partway along this bushwhack route, you will encounter a well-worn path leading WSW across the S end of the pond at Crosby Vlei. Privately maintained trails also lead around Black Creek Lake to give access to Burp Lake. The private land-holding on Black Creek Lake is approximately the middle third of the lakeshore on the S side.

✴ Trail in winter: Snowmobile trail.

🏃 Distances: Trailhead to Mad Tom Lake, 2.3 mi; to Black Creek Lake Rd., 3.1 mi; to Black Creek Lake, 5.7 mi; to Burp Lake, 6.9 mi (11 km).

91 Vista (Keegans) Trail to Ledge Mt. Overlook

Trails Illustrated Map 745: H8

Formerly a bushwack, this spot is sure to become popular now that a trail has been built. Keegan Roberts, now a guide, built this route as an Eagle Scout project. It provides a pleasant climb with gentle to moderate grades to a small ledge overlooking mixed forest and part of West Canada Creek. (The ledge has a big drop, so don't get too close.) The state calls this the Vista Trail, since it can't name a trail after a living person.

▶Trailhead: From the jct. of NY 8 and Haskell Rd. in Nobleboro, go 3.3 mi W on NY 8. Turn R just before the entrance to a gravel pit where there is extra pavement along the N side of the road. Or eastbound from the jct. of NY 365 on NY 8, go 2.4 mi E to a dirt road just beyond (E of) a gravel pit. The state's massive sign, stolen within a couple weeks of installation, is not likely to be replaced soon. On that dirt road go in 0.3 mi, staying L at a Y, through brush and small trees to a parking area on the L, suitable for about four vehicles, where yellow markers begin on the N side. Note that the road may be "tight"; brush may scrape the side of your vehicle and ruts may be bad. You may want to check first, or just park in the wide area along the road and hike that extra 0.3 mi (each way). If you enter forest on the roadway, you've gone too far.◀

From the parking lot (0.0 mi), until signs are installed, look for flagging on the N end (avoiding a more obvious trail on W side). In about 20 yd, yellow foot trail markers start, and the trail drops through a gully to near a property boundary (keep L), then climbs to a small ridge and bends L. There are many slight bends along the trail to keep grades gentle and prevent the erosion that occurs on steeper trails, so users should look ahead for markers and not take shortcuts.

At 0.2 mi, a moderate climb starts. The trail crosses a one-step stream, bends around a rock pile at 0.4 mi, and in another 100 yd passes a 7 ft high boulder, the only one seen this low on the mountain. The trail crosses a three-step stream on rocks. A steeper section at 0.5 mi leads to the back side of the end of a ridge where slippery moss-covered rocks may be hidden by ferns at 0.6 mi. Generally easy grades begin W, with the trail crossing WSW to the "front" (S) of the ridge, and another 35 yd later dropping to the small lookout at 0.8 mi.

Caution should be used along the edge: The drop-off is large—higher than the trees below—and the trees along the edge don't have much soil to hold onto, and so may not hold hikers.

❇ Trail in winter: Possible snowshoe. Park on NY 8 as best one can manage, adding another 0.3 mi distance and 40 ft elevation.

🐾 Distance: Road to ledge, approximately 0.8 mi (1.2 km). Ascent from parking lot, 130 ft (40 m). Elevation (high point of trail), 1776 ft (541 m).

92 Mill Creek Lake Trail

Trails Illustrated Map 745: H9

▶Trailheads: To reach the N trailhead, from NY 8 at Nobleboro go N on Haskell Rd., which becomes a gravel road, for 1.4 mi. The trail starts on the L with grassy parking for at most a couple of vehicles. The former snowmobile trail is an old road heading NW, with no trailhead sign, but there is a sign prohibiting vehicle travel. After a while, there are a few snowmobile markers, then flagging.

To reach the S trailhead, go 4.5 mi E from the jct. of NY 365 and NY 8 on NY 8 (or 0.8 mi W from Haskell Rd. at Nobleboro by the scenic overlook at West Canada Creek) and look for a dirt lane known as Flansburg Rd. There is no sign. There's a clearing with a garage just W of it and after about 50 ft of woods a clearing E of it. To make sure, check that the utility pole is NG 241. The dirt road leads 0.7 mi to parking in a clearing next to a small pond. Alternatively, there is a wide spot near the start of the road for possible parking; be careful not to block the road. ◀

From the N trailhead (0.0), go N on the old road. The route climbs around a hill, heads NW along a creek, then goes briefly W away from the creek to reach level ground. From there, it heads generally W on gentle ground. Starting at 0.7 mi, there is a series of four old snowmobile bridges (or the remnants thereof). To 1 mi, the way is somewhat thick and boggy. After that, it is decently dry but more obscure, even though the forest is fairly open. There is flagging, however, the rest of the way to Mill Creek.

At 1.8 mi, the trail turns R on a very old road and soon comes to the red blazes of a privately marked trail. To the L on that trail it is about 200 yd to a small, home-built footbridge (with two sections each side of an island) over Mill Creek. Continuing on the marked snowmobile route, the path is open and fairly easy to follow. It curves around and over the slight hill L, and reaches Mill Creek at 2 mi. There, two creeks, one the outlet from the lake and another coming in from the NE, join and flow SE. The beaver meadow is flooding well away from the creeks. Crossing the section flowing SE may be possible on a beaver dam, or hikers can work their way back downstream to the narrow footbridge.

Across the creek, there are two routes S. The old snowmobile route goes SW to a jct. with a red trail (see below for red trail), where it turns L along the creek for about 100 yd before curving R and climbing the hillside. There are few markers and this route may be difficult to follow. Also, it goes through the woods and does not offer any view of the lake. The route winds S uphill to a road at 2.4 mi. Following this private road to the L, it is only a short distance to the main dirt road. Turn L to reach the S trailhead. To the R, this road leads W past side trails to private camps on Mill Creek Lake and goes on to meet the Mad Tom Trail (trail 90) in another 1.3 mi.

From the footbridge (or farther W if the beaver dam crossing is used closer to where the creeks merge), blazes indicate a privately marked trail on public land heading SW along Mill Creek to the outlet of Mill Creek Lake. Views of the lake are easiest here, but there is no convenient access. A trail going R across an impressive bridge over the outlet leads to a private camp on the NE corner of the lake.

The red trail continues along the E side of the lake, eventually reaching a private camp on the SE side. Turn L near that camp to reach the main dirt road at 2.5 mi. (Northbound travelers may have difficulty finding a turnoff R [N] from the private road to the camps. If you miss it, continue down the road until you approach the house. Turn R, staying away from the private land, and then go L again to Mill Creek Lake until you reach the red-blazed trail.)

On the road to the R, it is about 1.2 mi to the Mad Tom Trail (trail 90). To the L, the trail follows a rocky snowmobile road (which may have vehicle traffic to the camps) SE and then S downhill, dropping about 300 ft in 1.4 mi to reach the S trailhead. Note that the hiking trail ends here at the pond. The roadway E is a snowmobile route that crosses private land and hikers should not use it.

❇ Trail in winter: N section is no longer used or maintained as a snowmobile trail, but S portion along the old road is used. Easy backcountry skiing and snowshoeing. Haskell Rd. may not be plowed to N trailhead and the 0.7 mi dirt road to S trailhead probably will not be plowed.

🐾 Distances: N trailhead to Mill Creek, 2 mi; to Mill Creek Lake via red trail, about 2.3 mi; to main dirt road via red trail, 2.5 mi; to S trailhead, 3.9 mi (6.2 km).

93 Little Salmon Lake Trail

This old road dates from the 1800s, when it was used to bring the public to the privately run Forest Lodge on Honnedaga Lake. That was a grueling carriage trip with an overnight stop at Nobleboro. The hotel was taken over as a private facility by the Adirondack League Club after the club's formation in 1890. Access from the S was eventually abandoned, and the club uses a short private road at the end of North Lake Rd. The remains of the sturdy concrete bridge (known as Cement Bridge) across Big Brook attest to continuing use of Herkimer Landing Rd. through WWII, when a USGS survey marker was placed on the bridge.

The more recent extension of Haskell Rd. along West Canada Creek beyond Herkimer Landing Rd. was used for lumbering, but is now falling into disrepair. Two private camps still stand along Little Salmon Lake Trail route, and several more along the Haskell Rd. extension N.

▶Trailhead: From NY 8 at Nobleboro, go N on Haskell Rd. This becomes a gravel road. Continue for 2.6 mi to the end of the gravel road at an open field known as Haskell Place. You may wish to park your car here; the remainder of the road is rough. Continue on the dirt road for another 0.9 mi to the trailhead on the L. Haskell Rd. continues along West Canada Creek for another 6 mi to private land in Miller Park, but is exceedingly rough and suitable only for high-clearance 4WD. Honnedaga Brook Trail (trail 95) is near the end of this road.◀

As Haskell Rd. turns R and descends past the trailhead, the trail turns L (0.0 mi) and climbs a slight hill on a rocky old road, gradually turning W. At 0.6 mi, the old road levels off and turns N to follow the contour of the hill. A side trail R (N) at 1.2 mi leads down steeply to a private camp on Big Brook.

After a moderately steep descent, a small creek at 2.4 mi must be crossed by wading (or push upstream 30 ft and step across). Beyond that, some gentle ups and downs lead to the site of the Cement Bridge, a landmark at Big Brook at 2.7 mi. This formerly sturdy concrete bridge makes it clear that this was once a well-used road.

Just before the bridge there is a jct. The trail L is Round Top Trail (trail 94), which connects to the Mad Tom Trail (trail 90). Just 370 ft N of the bridge on the R, a road leads a short distance to a clearing L and a camping location R.

The trail soon starts uphill, with mild climbing to a high point on the hill above Whiskey Spring Vlei at 4.3 mi. On the next hilltop, above Threemile Vlei, the trail proceeds on a less used track at 5.2 mi, while the road R shows more use. It goes to Summit Camp, a private camp on the edge of the hill. Baby Lake Falls Trail (trail 96) starts at the rear (NE) corner of the clearing at Summit Camp. When using that trail, please do not disturb the private camp or use its facilities.

Trail 93 continues N through grass. South Lake Trail (trail 88) comes in on another old road L; it leads NW around the S shore of South Lake to South Lake Rd. and Atwell (7.1 mi to the road). Just beyond this jct., on the R at 5.4 mi, is

Chipmunk. Joanne Kennedy

a second road R leading to Summit Camp.

The trail continues NE downhill, crosses a creek, and ascends slightly. Just after it levels off, a faint trail L is the route to Little Salmon Lake at 5.9 mi. It is an unmarked, unofficial cutoff. The official trail connection is 300 ft farther down the hill, just at the flats before a creek. There is a snowmobile trail sign pointing L, but there is absolutely no trace of a trail and the trail markers are difficult to spot. If you reach this point and want to visit the lake, go back 300 ft to avoid a thick bushwhack.

The well-worn road continuing N from this jct. leads to a crossing of a wetland. Beyond that, the road goes onto posted private land of the Adirondack League Club, headed for Herkimer Landing on Honnedaga Lake.

The cutoff trail L (NW) leads down the hill 200 ft to level ground. The official trail route connects on the R at this spot, but that 200 ft section is not usable. From here, the trail heads W, winding through the woods with a slight footpath and sufficient markers. Just before the lake, a hill on the L with semi-level ground provides some possibilities for camping.

The trail ends on the E end of Little Salmon Lake at 6.3 mi. This lake is pleasant and remote, with a fairly abrupt shoreline but thick surrounding growth.

The S side has many magnificent trees in a long-established and fairly open forest. Possible campsites are more numerous on the S side, especially toward the W end of the lake. Hikers wishing to bushwhack W to South Lake Trail (trail 88) should keep well above the creek on the S side. The other side is reported to have an ATV trail to the lake; if you don't find it, the way is thick and wet.

✴ Trail in winter: Snowmobile trail. Haskell Rd. is not plowed. Easy backcountry skiing and snowshoeing, with one somewhat steep slope, but the remoteness of the region and the long distance to the lake make this trail best suited for groups with strong backwoods winter experience. On the return ski, there are two long glide slopes.

🐾 Distances: Haskell Place (winter trailhead) to trailhead, 0.9 mi; trailhead to Round Top Trail (trail 94) and Cement Bridge, 2.7 mi; to South Lake Trail (trail 88), Summit Camp, and Baby Lake Falls trail (trail 96), 5.2 mi; to Little Salmon Lake, 6.3 mi (10.1 km). To Baby Lake Falls via trail 96, 8 mi. To South Lake Rd. via trail 88, 12.3 mi.

94 Round Top Trail

Trails Illustrated Map 745: I8

This is a woodsy cutover trail that connects Little Salmon Lake Trail (trail 93) and Mad Tom Trail (trail 90), both snowmobile and ATV trails. However, ATVs are not allowed on this one because it crosses private land. It is shaded nearly the entire route. A snowmobile trail, it is fairly easily followed.

▶Locator: The E end is on Little Salmon Lake Trail (trail 93) and the W end is on Mad Tom Trail (trail 90).◀

At the 2.7 mi point on Little Salmon Lake Trail, just before the Cement Bridge, Round Top Trail bears L (0.0 mi), passes a "motorized vehicles prohibited" sign, and climbs uphill, generally SW. It crosses a few rocky areas that make it interesting for hikers, although they wouldn't concern snowmobilers. There are a couple of switchbacks, but stumps several inches high reveal where the route was cut.

In less than 0.5 mi the trail becomes much more moderate and flattens out after climbing about 660 ft to skirt N of the top of Round Top. The trail crosses private land and then a couple of wet spots as it gradually descends to the Mad Tom Trail (trail 90) about 0.8 mi S of where that trail hits the private land boundary, which hikers must bypass for access to Black Creek Lake and Burp Lake.

✴ Trail in winter: Remote trail far from trailheads. Marked as a snowmobile trail. Suitable for snowshoeing or use by advanced skiers.

🐾 Distance: Little Salmon Lake Trail (trail 93) to Mad Tom Trail (trail 90), 2.8 mi (4.5 km).

95 Honnedaga Brook Trail (unmaintained)

Trails Illustrated Map 745: J10

This trail goes up Honnedaga Brook, passes Beaverdam Pond, and continues to a jct. The R branch goes along Jones Brook to private land in Miller Park. It seems most suitable for fishermen from the private land nearby. The L branch goes along Honnedaga Brook to Falls Camp and Baby Lake Falls. Access by road is too difficult for casual day hiking, but the region is clearly remote and this may be a good starting place for hardy adventurers. The Baby Lake Falls trail (trail 96) is a longer but better maintained and more accessible route to Baby Lake Falls.

▶Trailhead: From NY 8 at Nobleboro, go N on Haskell Rd., which becomes gravel. Continue for 2.6 mi to the end of the gravel road at an open field. Parking is allowed here. This is the end of the town-maintained road. From here on, the road gets progressively rougher, passable by 4WD vehicles, preferably with high clearance. Continue through rock and mud until the road crosses a stream bridge at 7.8 mi, with a house uphill L just before the stream. On the N side of the stream, an old road goes L (the trail). Park near the entrance to that side road. This is an unofficial trail with no markers.◀

Starting uphill on the old road NW from Haskell Rd. (0.0 mi), the route soon levels off, crosses an outlet stream, and loops around Beaverdam Pond on the hillside above. The view is pleasant through the trees.

The old road turns R at 1 mi to continue N along Jones Brook to private land at 1.7 mi. At the turn, Honnedaga Brook Trail goes straight (NW). It is much fainter than the trail to the R. Now a somewhat obscure old road, the trail continues parallel to Honnedaga Brook (100 yd L) to the confluence of Honnedaga and Jones brooks at 1.2 mi. The route crosses Jones Brook (no bridge and rather deep water) and continues on the N side of Honnedaga Brook, finally crossing that brook at 2.1 mi to join the Baby Lake Falls trail (trail 96) at Falls Camp (a clearing). Baby Lake Falls is 0.6 mi to the R on that trail.

The old road beyond Jones Brook is now very obscure; travel is for experienced bushwhackers. Jones Brook is wide and has fairly deep water.

✽ Trail in winter: The winter trailhead is at Nobleboro, 7.8 mi S of the summer trailhead. Easy traveling as far as Jones Brook. Shortest route to Baby Lake Falls (10.5 mi). The 1 mi section from Jones Brook to Falls Camp is a bushwhack. The entire route is otherwise easily skied.

⚹ Distances: End of town road to trailhead by jeep road, 5.2 mi; trailhead to Beaverdam Pond, 0.3 mi; to trail jct., 1 mi; to crossing of Jones Brook, 1.2 mi; to Falls Camp, 2.1 mi; to Baby Lake Falls, 2.7 mi (4.3 km).

96 Baby Lake Falls

Trails Illustrated Map 745: J9

These beautiful falls are located on Honnedaga Brook, which is the outlet of Baby Lake and Honnedaga Lake. Although the falls are not straight down, and the highest cascade is only about 30 ft, the entire 200 ft of descending water, flanked by moss-covered giant boulders, forms an exceptional scene. The shorter Honnedaga Brook Trail (trail 95) also goes to the falls, but its trailhead is reachable only by 4WD vehicles, 1 mi of the trail is very obscure, and a wide, deep stream must be crossed without a bridge.

▶Locator: See Little Salmon Lake Trail (trail 93). Baby Lake Falls Trail starts at Summit Camp on Little Salmon Lake Trail near Little Salmon Lake. There are no trail markers to Baby Lake Falls.◀

From Little Salmon Lake Trail (0.0 mi), the trail continues from the L rear corner (NE) behind Summit Camp, a private cabin. (Please do not disturb the cabin or use the facilities.) The way is slightly obscure, but recognizable in the beginning as an old road going downhill. Do not confuse it with another trail heading NW from the same spot, which goes on level ground to rejoin Little Salmon Lake Trail.

After a short descent, the trail climbs slightly to pass along the hill above Threemile Vlei. There are no markers, but the route is easy to follow. At the SE end of the hill, at 0.9 mi, a long descent begins, with a steady, moderate grade. At 1.8 mi, the trail levels briefly and passes a small bog on the R.

The route goes briefly L and then NE down the hill, before the trail bottoms out at a clearing on Honnedaga Brook at 2.2 mi. This is the site of the former Falls Camp, now just a slight clearing. Honnedaga Brook Trail (trail 95), coming from the E, crosses the brook here.

On the N side of the clearing there is a trail continuing to the falls. It is overgrown at the start. Search carefully for a slight footpath in open woods. It goes N along the base of the hillside L until it crosses a side stream. After crossing, it turns R and descends to a wet grassland. Stay L around the edge of the grassland to avoid water in the middle. At this point, the falls can be heard ahead.

The trail heads NE into the woods for another 200 ft to the bottom of Baby Lake Falls, 2.8 mi from Summit Camp and 0.6 mi from Falls Camp. If you wish to see the flume and the peaceful meadow at the top of the falls, climb the hill 30 ft on the L, away from the stream, to avoid destroying the beautiful moss covering the rocks at the side of the falls. Take care at the top. If you slip into the fast-running flume, your body will be recovered at the very bottom.

❊ Trail in winter: The winter trailhead is at Nobleboro, 3.5 mi before the summer trailhead. Most of the route is a lightly used snowmobile trail. The distance is definitely pushing the limits for winter day trips, even for strong groups, but the trail is otherwise suitable for snowshoeing. Little Salmon Lake Trail (trail 93) is suitable for backcountry skiing, but the steepness of some hill sections makes it most suitable for intermediate skiers. The return trip has two long glide sections. The Baby Lake Falls trail has a long downhill section with thick undergrowth, suitable only for snowshoers or very good skiers.

🏃 Distances: Little Salmon Lake Trail (trail 93) to descent, 0.9 mi; to Honnedaga Brook, 2.2 mi; to Baby Lake Falls, 2.8 mi (4.5 km).

West Canada Lake. ADK archives

Morehouseville Wilderness Access

Trails Illustrated Map 745:110

There are no trails in this region, but the road crossing the South Branch of West Canada Creek at Morehouseville provides access to the trailless interior of the West Canada Lake Wilderness Area.

▶Locator: From the center of Morehouseville on NY 8, turn N on Fayle Rd. Follow this gravel road downhill across a bridge and uphill again for about 0.5 mi. Fayle Rd. turns W upon reaching level ground and soon enters private land. Park along the road just after it reaches the high ground. Note that past the bridge, Fayle Rd. is seasonal and unplowed in winter, and may not be passable until after spring thaw.◀ 🦶

Stillwater fire tower trail. Nancie Battaglia

Beaver River–Stillwater Section

The lands around Stillwater Reservoir are mostly state-owned, and tend to be used by the public for canoe and motorboat camping. Weekend use has increased greatly in recent years, with campsites filled to capacity. Even so, the reservoir is reputed to be the largest loon breeding area in the state.

Remote and wild, the 6700-acre reservoir has not been as seriously affected by acid rain as some of the interior ponds and still supports a sizeable fish population. This is attested to not only by the presence of anglers but also by the presence of the loons, plus the frequent occurrence of that even more dedicated fish eater, the cormorant. There are numerous attractive designated primitive campsites along the shores of the reservoir.

The reservoir was once a collection of small ponds along the Beaver River. New York State erected a small dam in the Stillwater area in 1864 for logging purposes. In 1882–86, the Department of Transportation built a larger dam to serve the Black River Canal and the mills along the lower reaches of the Black River. A still higher dam was built in 1922–24 to serve water-powered mills downstream. Today the reservoir is part of a series along the Beaver River used to generate electric power. Besides the DEC forest ranger station, the community near the dam at Stillwater offers boat rentals, a store, a restaurant-hotel, and a bed and breakfast.

Several hiking trails are accessible from the lake. The Red Horse Trail and the trails at Beaver River Station must normally be reached by boat. Farther W, the Pepperbox Wilderness Area is reached by a bridge across the Beaver River at Moshier Falls or the bridge below Stillwater Dam.

Beaver River Station can be reached overland via Beaver River Trail from Twitchell Lake (6.6 mi) or the old railroad bed from Big Moose Station (8.2 mi). The latter is listed as a snowmobile trail but walking on the tracks may not be legal. Beaver River Station can also be reached by boat from Stillwater (approximately 6 mi by water, or 1.2 mi by water and 5.6 mi on Flow Rd.). The Norridgewock, a lodge at Beaver River Station, operates water taxis and scheduled summertime cruise boats between Stillwater and Beaver River Station. Boats can also be rented at Stillwater.

The old Carthage Military Rd. along the Beaver River passed close to the contemporary community of Beaver River Station, but the earliest occasional homes and camps were mostly nearer the river. The community owes its formal existence to W. S. Webb, builder of the Mohawk & Malone Railroad, which became the Adirondack & St. Lawrence Railroad (Adirondack Division of the New York Central). A lumber mill was established at Beaver River Station in 1893 by Firman Ouderkirk to process timber from Webb's land in the area. Webb had sued the state, contending that the 1886 dam on the river had blocked lumbering in the area and that the railroad was not a feasible means of shipping the timber.

After he won, the lumber was, of course, shipped on Webb's railroad. Cutting was completed by 1904, Webb sold the surrounding land to the state, and the community shrank to just a few remaining families.

The Carthage Rd.—the remains of which is now called Six Mile Rd.—once gave access by car from the W, but the rising waters of then-newly enlarged Stillwater Reservoir cut off that route by 1924. At the same time, the new and higher dam required the clearing of all the land to be flooded. Beaver River Station again became a booming lumber town from 1922 to 1924, then again declined. The railway station was closed in 1943, and the railroad itself ceased all Adirondack operations in 1971. This compact 0.6 square mi piece of private land is again reduced to a full-time population of only a few people, but it is chock full of summer cottages. Dilapidated old trucks without license plates ply the short road from the center of town to the boat landing at Grassy Point; the community has no road access to the outside world.

State lands N of the Beaver River are likely to remain nearly trailless. Private landholders at Raven Lake still use the old timber company road from Stillwater. This road—the Raven Lake Primitive Corridor—is not open to other vehicle traffic, and serves as an access route for foot travel to reach the E part of the Pepperbox Wilderness Area and W part of the Five Ponds Wilderness Area. It separates the two Wilderness Areas. The road is barricaded at the S tip of Raven Lake where maintenance ends. There are old roads beyond that. Canoe carries between Stillwater Reservoir, Raven Lake, Lyon Lake, and Bear Pond are marked and signed.

A few suggested hikes for this section are listed below.

SHORT HIKE
Colvin Rock: 0.1 mi (0.2 km). A short walk 600 ft from Grassy Point landing with 300 ft of trail to a rock with some faint markings from the Colvin Survey Party. (Not to be confused with Colvin Memorial, a rock with a plaque at the N end of Norridgewock Lake.) See trail 103.

MODERATE HIKE
Norridgewock Lake Trail: 1.8 mi (2.9 km). An easy walk around the lake and across the causeway passing Colvin Memorial. Crossing the causeway may not be possible in times of high water, however, as it involves a stream crossing at S end. See trail 102.

HARDER HIKE
Red Horse Trail: 5.3 mi (8.5 km). A remote trail accessible by boat on the N side of Stillwater Reservoir, with a lean-to at its start. The trail passes Salmon and Witchhopple Lakes, and ends at Clear Lake. See trail 100.

97 Pepperbox Wilderness Access and Moshier Falls

Trails Illustrated Map 745: S4

▶Trailhead: Go to Moshier Rd., which is 2.1 mi E of Number Four on the Stillwater Rd. and 5.9 mi W of the jct. of Stillwater Rd. and Big Moose Rd. Turn N on Moshier Rd. for 0.6 mi. As you approach the power station water-surge tower, there is a DEC parking lot on the R. The trail starts just across the road.◀

From the road (0.0 mi), the blue-marked trail goes down a bank between the road and Sunday Creek, then turns R and follows the creek a short way to a bridge over the creek. At the far end of the bridge, at a T, the L fork is a canoe carry to Beaver River. (This spur turns L in a short distance, goes to a private road, turns R on the road, crosses a bridge without handrails, and turns L to the put-in at 0.3 mi from the main trail. This is a nice grassy area, perfect for a picnic.)

Pepperbox Trail turns R at the spur jct., follows the stream, then curves to meet a second bridge across the Beaver River. On the second bridge, one can view the power station outlet and the final cascades of Moshier Falls.

The trail then plunges into the woods to reach a power-line route, now quite overgrown. The trail keeps to the edge of the "clearing" parallel to the power line. When the power line makes a L turn, the trail crosses the power-line path and ends at a trail sign on the other side at 0.5 mi. This puts the hiker onto state land at the border of the Pepperbox Wilderness Area. There are no official trails beyond this point. You are on your own, and should certainly know how to use your map and compass.

To view Moshier Falls, follow the herd path N past the power line for about 100 ft, then bushwhack R (E) to the water's edge. This water is fast-flowing, powerful, and dangerous, and the banks are treacherous. Do not attempt to reach the very edge. Stay safely back and enjoy the view.

❋ Trail in winter: Suitable for wilderness experts on skis or snowshoes. There are no trails in the Pepperbox Wilderness Area. The parking lot may not be plowed in winter.

⚹ Distances: To Wilderness Area boundary, 0.5 mi (0.8 km). To Moshier Falls, 0.6 mi (1 km).

98 Sunday Creek Trail

Trails Illustrated Map 745: S4

▶Trailhead: See Pepperbox Wilderness Access and Moshier Falls (trail 97).◀

The route starts in the NE corner of the parking lot (0.0 mi) and goes over a small rise. It continues E along the N bank of Sunday Creek until reaching the state land boundary at 0.3 mi. A sign indicates this is the Pepperbox Wilderness, however, it is the Independence River Wild Forest. The trail ends abruptly, leaving one to wonder why; it allows anglers to reach state land along the creek without trespassing.

❋ Trail in winter: Suitable for wilderness skiers or snowshoers, but the trail is very short. Only expert skiers or snowshoers should enter the wilds beyond the trail.

🏃 Distance: To state land boundary, 0.3 mi (0.5 km).

99 Raven Lake Jeep Trail

Trails Illustrated Map 745: T6

This gated jeep trail primarily provides access for the owners of a small private inholding at Raven Lake. It also allows hiker penetration of an otherwise trailless, remote area of the Forest Preserve.

▶Trailhead: Access is from Stillwater Reservoir, on Stillwater–Number Four Rd., 27 mi E of Lowville. Just before the reservoir, turn L at Stillwater Restaurant. Take this gravel road 1.2 mi to a DEC parking area on the R, just before a gated wooden bridge spanning the Beaver River and just after the dam itself is visible to the R. A trail register is located here and the unmarked trail begins over the bridge.◀

From the bridge (0.0 mi), the jeep trail begins a series of rolling ascents over hardwood-covered ridges. After a large gravel pit opening at the outset, the forest is mostly an intermediate one in the process of maturing. For part of the way, the jeep trail forms the boundary between the Five Ponds Wilderness Area and the Pepperbox Wilderness Area.

As the trail continues over several hills, the forest displays signs of logging from the 1990s. One bonus from this heavy cutting is the profusion of blackberry and red raspberry bushes along the road.

At 2.1 mi Shallow Pond comes into view on the L. It is connected by a short channel to Raven Lake, a handsome 70 acre body of water with hills on one side. Evergreens are common along the two shorelines, in contrast to the ridges, which are generally clothed in hardwoods.

This is the highlight of the jeep trail, but the route does go approximately 1 mi farther, ending at a large log landing. Before that, another jeep road goes R at approximately 2.5 mi to arrive at Slim Pond at 3.4 mi. Slim Pond is another long, shallow body of water nestled between wooded ridges. The path of the jeep trail

Signs of beaver activity along the trail. Joanne Kennedy

is blocked by boulders just after Shallow Pond, as the right-of-way of the private inholding terminates here; the condition of the trail from Shallow Pond to Slim Pond can be expected to deteriorate barring any unforeseen circumstance.

❄ Trail in winter: The entire jeep trail to Slim Pond makes for an excellent round-trip ski jaunt in winter. Exercise caution going over the bridge at the outset.

🚶 Distances: Trailhead to Shallow Pond, 2.1 mi; to Slim Pond, 3.4 mi (5.4 km).

100 Red Horse Trail

Trails Illustrated Map 745: U8

This blue-marked DEC trail, accessible only by boat, leaves the N shore of Stillwater Reservoir and passes several impressive medium-sized glacial lakes on its way to Clear Lake. It is the only trail that gives access to the remote and wild S portion of the Five Ponds Wilderness Area.

▶Trailhead: The trailhead is reached only by a 5.5 mi boat trip up Stillwater Reservoir from the DEC launch site at the hamlet of Stillwater, 27 mi E of the Lewis County village of Lowville on Stillwater–Number Four Rd.◀

The trail begins at Trout Pond on the N shore of Stillwater Reservoir (0.0 mi). If the water level of the reservoir is low, the starting point is at Big Burnt Lake, approximately 0.3 mi before and R of Trout Pond. Trout Pond and Burnt Lake, both formerly interior lakes, became bays of Stillwater Reservoir with construction of the dam at Stillwater.

From Trout Pond (0.0 mi), the trail proceeds along the bank of Red Horse Creek; a lean-to is just N of the head of Trout Pond. The trail reaches Salmon Lake at 1.1 mi. The magnificent stand of climax spruce, hemlock, and yellow birch is dwarfed by the occasional gigantic white pine on the shores of the creek.

The trail now skirts the shore of Salmon Lake, passing two former lean-to sites that are now campsites at its head. The trail leaves the lake and passes through a continuous stand of impressive climax forest, crossing an extensive beaver-created wetland on a plank at 1.9 mi. The trail gradually begins to ascend a modified esker with large spruce and hemlocks. It descends from the low ridge to cross several parallel wetlands before reaching Witchhopple Lake at 3.3 mi. The wooden planks used to cross these wetlands can be quite slippery after a rain, so caution should be used.

The trail leaves Witchhopple Lake and proceeds through the same impressive climax forest as before until reaching the shore of Clear Lake at 5.3 mi. Wet spots are encountered in several areas just before the pond. Summit Mt. looms protectively over the pond.

❀ Trail in winter: Hazardous skiing along Stillwater Reservoir to the trailhead. Remoteness and occasional rough topography limit skiing from the trailhead.

❀❀ Distance: Stillwater Reservoir, Trout Pond trailhead to Salmon Lake, 1.1 mi; to Witchhopple Lake, 3.3 mi; to Clear Lake, 5.3 mi (8.5 km).

101 Beaver River–Twitchell Trail

Trails Illustrated Map 745: S8, T8

The trail goes from Beaver River Station on Stillwater Reservoir to Twitchell Lake near Big Moose. The S trailhead at Twitchell Lake is accessible by car, but the N trailhead at Beaver River Station is accessible only by boat from Stillwater. A water taxi is available from Stillwater to Grassy Point. And a barge goes from Stillwater to the W end of Flow Rd., the old Carthage Rd., so you can take your vehicle to Beaver River with barge reservations (there's no set schedule) through Norridgewock III by calling 315-376-6200.

Beaver River, as noted in the introduction to this section, is interesting to visit in its own right. Hardy travelers who start early could walk the 6.6 mi Beaver River–Twitchell Trail from Twitchell Lake, visit Beaver River Station, perhaps have lunch at the Norridgewock or hotel, and return to Twitchell Lake by nightfall. This is a fairly long hike. For the less hardy, a two-car trip can be arranged by taking the cruise boat from Stillwater to Beaver River, then continuing on to Twitchell Lake via Beaver River–Twitchell Trail, or the other way around.

▶Trailheads: To reach the trail at its S end, drive NW from Eagle Bay on Big Moose Rd. to Big Moose (Station). At 7.3 mi from NY 28, just before the road crosses the railroad tracks, turn R onto Twitchell Rd. and drive 2 mi to a parking lot on the lake at the end of the road. The trail starts on the L (W) end of the parking lot and is marked with blue markers.

The N end of the trail is in Beaver River Station, accessed by boat from Stillwater. To get to Beaver River Station from Stillwater, see trailhead information for trail 103. (After debarking at Grassy Point, go up the landing road for 0.8 mi to Beaver River Station.)

From the Norridgewock III in the center of town, proceed N along the tracks for 0.1 mi, turn R on a road, cross the causeway, and continue along the road. At 0.3 mi, there is a rock with a plaque honoring Verplanck Colvin. Turn R at the jct. at 0.5 mi. At 0.7 mi, the road makes a R turn, while the trail goes straight ahead along the edge of lawn for a cottage R. There is a sign on the tree pointing to Twitchell Lake. ◄

Beaver River. Betsy Tisdale

Starting at the S trailhead parking lot (0.0), the trail follows a woods road W on level ground. (This is also Razorback Pond Trail, trail 26.) At 0.4 mi, the trail turns R onto a footpath and starts steeply up a hill. The hilltop at 0.8 mi is sharply pointed, and the trail starts steeply down again. This steep maneuver is necessary because the trail manages to squeeze between the corners of two private tracts of land; without it there would be no public access. The trail continues on a much easier grade and crosses the outlet stream for Oswego Pond at 1.3 mi.

The route continues on fairly easy terrain to the pointed N end of Twitchell Mt. at 2.7 mi. The trail follows the base of the mountain, heads W for 0.3 mi to bypass a swampy creek bottom, then crosses the creek near its upper end. Signs at 3.2 mi mark a sharp L turn.

The route is low for a while but then climbs steadily on mostly gentle grades to the high point at 4 mi. The way from here is down, gently at first, until 5 mi, where a somewhat steep descent begins.

The trail reaches the register at 5.9 mi and then civilization on level ground at 6 mi. Turn R on Norridgewock Lake Trail (trail 102) and follow the road to a T intersection. Then turn L to cross over the causeway to reach the railroad tracks at 6.5 mi. Turn L into the center of town, reached at 6.6 mi.

❅ Trail in winter: Snowshoe and ski experts only. The remoteness of the trail and the strenuous, steep climbs make this a real challenge.

🏃 Distances: S trailhead to turnoff onto footpath, 0.5 mi; to Oswego Pond outlet, 1.3 mi; to Twitchell Mt., 2.7 mi; to jct. with Norridgewock Lake Trail (trail 102), 6 mi; to center of Beaver River Station, 6.6 mi (10.6 km).

102 Norridgewock Lake Trail

Trails Illustrated Map 745: T8

This is a loop trail, circling Norridgewock Lake. It is an easy stroll, best suited for those staying in Beaver River Station.

▶Trailhead: Located at the center of town at Beaver River Station. To reach Beaver River Station, see trailhead information for Colvin Rock trail (trail 103).◀

Starting at the tracks in front of the hotel known as Norridgewock III (0.0 mi), go N along the tracks for 0.1 mi and turn R (E) on the road. Cross the causeway, passing a plaque commemorating Verplanck Colvin. Turn R at a jct. at 0.5 mi and go along the E shore of the lake. At 0.6 mi the road meets a T jct. Beaver River–Twitchell Trail (trail 128) goes straight ahead at this jct., headed for Twitchell Lake 6 mi away.

Turn R and continue on the dirt road, which ends at 0.9 mi. Turn sharp L around a red building and follow the footpath. A private footpath turns R just after the building and crosses the creek to a private camp. Continue ahead (SE) on the less used footpath for another 300 ft, where it finally turns W to cross the creek on a small bridge. The footpath is marked occasionally with DEC markers and is easy to follow. It winds among old forest, crosses the W branch of the Beaver River (a creek), and swings N to meet an old road at 1.5 mi. Continue along this road to the jct. at 1.6 mi. Turn L, go to the next jct., and turn R. This returns you to the center of town at 1.8 mi.

❋ Trail in winter: Suitable for a ski or snowshoe.

🏃 Distances: Norridgewock III to center of causeway, 0.3 mi; to Beaver River–Twitchell Trail (trail 128), 0.6 mi; to end of village roads, 0.9 mi; complete circuit, 1.8 mi (2.9 km).

103 Colvin Rock

Trails Illustrated Map 745: T8

This is a very short trail at Beaver River Station, going to a witness rock carved by the Verplanck Colvin survey party. Colvin led a state survey of the Adirondack region in the late 1800s and is credited with advocating for the creation of the Adirondack Forest Preserve and Park. On its side facing the trail, various initials and data are carved. The survey mark is on the survey line that separates the Totten and Crossfield Purchase from John Browns Tract.

▶Locator: The most common way to reach this trailhead is by boat from Stillwater. To reach the boat landing at Stillwater from Lowville, go E on Number

Four Rd. to Number Four, turn R onto Stillwater Rd., and continue to the jct. with Big Moose Rd. Bear L to Stillwater. From Eagle Bay on NY 28, go NW on Big Moose Rd. Continue past Big Moose Station to the jct. with Stillwater Rd. Turn R into Stillwater. Park at the boat launch site by the ranger station and obtain a map of Stillwater Reservoir at the registration booth in front of the ranger station.

Go by boat to Grassy Point near Beaver River Station. Beach your boat; the docks are private. Go 600 ft up the road toward Beaver River Station. The trail starts on the L (E) and is 0.7 mi from Beaver River Station. ◀

Leaving the road (0.0 mi), the trail goes gently up a slight hill heading NE. At a bit under 0.1 mi, there is an exposed rock on the L with some faint carving on it. This is the Colvin Rock. The trail continues on past the rock, gradually dimming from an ATV trail to a faint herd path. It arrives at the reservoir on the point of a small peninsula. If the water is high, you may not see the meadow ahead strewn with large boulders.

✴ Trail in winter: Gentle terrain, but hardly worthy of a winter trip.

🐾 Distances: Grassy Point to trailhead, 600 ft; from Beaver River Station to trailhead, 0.7 mi; from trailhead to Colvin Rock, 0.1 mi (0.2 km). 🍃

Lake Lila from Mount Frederica. David Hough

William C. Whitney Wilderness Area and NY 30 Section

 With the purchase by the state of nearly 15,000 acres from Whitney Park in 1997, many new trails and canoeing opportunities became available to the public. This purchase and the former Lake Lila Primitive Area were combined in 2000 to create the William C. Whitney Wilderness Area. Lying W of NY 30 between Long Lake and Tupper Lake, the area includes mostly rolling hills, low mountains, and many lakes and ponds.

Historically, this area has been one of the most intensively logged in the Adirondacks. This plus clean-up from the devastating microburst storm of 1995 means that most of the trails are old (and in a few cases, recent) logging roads. While many of the destinations—often a lake or pond—are beautiful, sometimes the routes can be less than spectacular. The logging roads are often lined with young hardwoods such as yellow birch, black cherry, and red maple. Over time, as the woods age, these roads will narrow into trails and develop character. In the short run, advantages include the wonderful berries available during the late summer months along the routes and in the log staging areas.

Constructed to accommodate log trucks, the trails generally are wide and double-tracked with gentle grades. They are often suitable for large-tired strollers, allowing the entire family to enjoy the wilderness. Sometimes the trails follow old skid tracks, which were used to drag trees to the landing areas. These trails are rougher and have healed faster than the gravel logging roads. In a few instances trails follow old railroad grades. More typical hiking trails, such as those that go up Coney Mt. and Frederica Mt. provide beautiful overviews. The many ancillary logging roads and skid trails open myriad possibilities for exploration off-trail, but can lead to confusion as to the right way to proceed. Overall, the area presents a great number of exciting destinations for forest exploration.

Trails in areas adjacent to the William C. Whitney Wilderness Area have also been included in this section. Two interesting trails, Owls Head Mt. (trail 104) and Lake Eaton (trail 105), are in the area of Lake Eaton near the hamlet of Long Lake. These trails and loops travel generally through a handsome, mature forest of mixed hardwoods and conifers. The Owls Head Mt. trail offers a fairly sharp ascent up a modest-sized mountain to overlook the shores of Long Lake. Owls Head is one of the area's highest eminences. There is a state campground at Lake Eaton.

The trail to Coney Mt. (trail 106), which is located S of Tupper Lake just off NY 30 before the turnoff to William C. Whitney Wilderness Area, is a short climb for a great view and a good trip for children.

A few suggested hikes for this section are listed below.

SHORT HIKE
Coney Mt.: 1.1 mi (1.8 km) round-trip. A short climb for a great view; a good trip for children. See trail 106.

MODERATE HIKES
Owls Head Mt.: 6.2 mi (9.9 km) round-trip. Except for a difficult pitch just before the summit, this is a not-too-difficult climb that provides outstanding views. See trail 104.

South Shore Trail: 8.6 mi (13.8 km) round-trip. Gentle grades on a rolling trail with a nice picnic spot on Little Tupper Lake; berries are great in the late summer. It is accessible for strollers with large tires. See trail 108.

HARDER HIKE
Lilypad Pond: 16.8 mi (26.9 km) round-trip. This is a harder hike not because of the terrain, but because of length. It negotiates gentle grades on rolling woodland with both Lilypad Pond and Little Salmon Pond at the end. See trail 109.

Trail Described		Total Miles (one way)	Page
104	Owls Head Mt.	3.1 (5.0 km)	160
105	Lake Eaton	0.4 (0.6 km)	162
106	Coney Mt.	1.1 (1.8 km)	162
107	Goodman Mt.	1.6 (2.6 km)	163
108	South Shore Trail	4.3 (6.9 km)	164
109	Lilypad Pond	8.4 (13.4 km)	165
110	Camp Bliss	1.0 (1.6 km)	166
111	Rock Pond	3.3 (5.3 km)	167
112	Hardigan Pond	1.6 (2.6 km)	167
113	Shingle Shanty Brook–Lilypad Pond Carry	0.8 (1.3 km)	168
114	Lilypad Pond–Little Salmon Lake Carry	0.4 (0.6 km)	168
115	Salmon Lake Outlet–Hardigan Pond Carry	0.3 (0.5 km)	169
116	Hardigan Pond–Rock Pond Carry	1.8 (2.9 km)	169
117	Rock Pond–Little Tupper Lake Carry	0.1 (0.2 km)	170
118	Lake Lila to Frederica Mt.	4.4 (7.0 km)	170

104 Owls Head Mt.

Trails Illustrated Map 745: U15

The red-marked trail to the top of Owls Head Mt. starts at the outskirts of Long Lake village. This is one of the isolated peaks of this region and a panoramic view of the surrounding area can be had from the summit.

▶Trailhead: Take NY 30 N from the center of Long Lake to Endion Rd. on the L at the edge of the village. It is 1.6 mi on Endion Rd. to the trailhead on the R. ◀

There are two more or less parallel trails at the outset (0.0 mi). The trail to the R is marked as a snowmobile trail. The L trail immediately begins a steep climb under large hemlock and yellow birch. It levels off as sugar maple becomes prominent. A snowmobile trail comes in on the R just before height of land at 0.5 mi; the two trails now run concurrently, descending into the Lake Eaton drainage.

At 0.9 mi, the trail reaches a jct. with DEC signs. The trail R is an abandoned trail used as access by snowmobile to Lake Eaton. This trail joins the unmarked Lake Eaton trail (trail 105) in 0.1 mi and reaches Lake Eaton in 0.4 mi.

The Owls Head Mt. trail proceeds L. It is now marked with both red hiking trail markers and the larger red snowmobile trail markers because the hiking trail and snowmobile trails are simultaneous for the next quarter-mile. To add somewhat to the confusion, an occasional yellow snowmobile trail marker appears. These were used by DEC until being supplanted by the red markers. The signs for the Owls Head Mt. trail at subsequent junctions are clear, however, so the variations in trail marker colors should not prove troublesome.

At 1 mi, an unmarked jct. R indicates the Lake Eaton trail (trail 105), a short, sporadically marked trail that leads to the shore of Lake Eaton. The Owls Head Mt. trail continues under a canopy of hemlocks. Occasional telephone poles still stand as testimony to the staffed fire tower that once stood on top of Owls Head Mt.

At 1.1 mi, the trail reaches another marked DEC jct. The abandoned snowmobile trail goes L to Forked Lake in 8.2 mi while the Owls Head Mt. trail continues straight. Small red trail markers point the way; the red and yellow snowmobile disks indicate the trail to Forked Lake.

At 1.8 mi, a steep ravine can be seen L. Spruce now begins to come into the canopy. At 2 mi, the trail begins to climb, getting rockier and steeper at 2.5 mi. After another ravine on the L, the trail encounters large beech trees. At 2.7 mi, the way is encumbered slightly by blowdown until at 2.8 mi the trail reaches the remnants of the fire observer's cabin in an open glade underneath the pinnacle of Owls Head.

The trail now begins a very steep scramble to the top, starting to rise just past the open glade. This last ascent is somewhat strenuous and may entail the use of one's hands. The summit with its small open area surrounded by conifers is at 3.1 mi. From the 2780 ft peak, Owls Head Pond is immediately below with good views of Raquette Lake and Forked Lake to the SW. The hazy summit of Blue Mt. is just E of S, while Kempshall Mt. looms ahead in the distance. The 14 mi of Long Lake itself, so close by, are mostly hidden from view.

❋ Trail in winter: Not suitable in winter, especially past 2 mi, because of its steepness.

🐾 Distances: Endion Rd. to jct. with unmarked Lake Eaton trail (trail 105), 1 mi; to summit of Owls Head Mt., 3.1 mi (5 km). Ascent, 1168 ft (356 m). Elevation, 2812 ft (857 m).

105 Lake Eaton

Trails Illustrated Map 745: U15

▶Locator: This short, mostly unmarked trail to Lake Eaton begins at a currently unmarked jct. at 1 mi on the Owls Head Mt. trail (trail 104).◀

From the jct. (0.0 mi), the trail proceeds through a mixed, mostly mature forest on its drop toward the lake. At 0.1 mi, just before the trail joins with a snowmobile trail from the R, a homemade sign with an arrow indicating the direction to Owls Head can be seen high on a tree by hikers coming from Lake Eaton.

The trail now passes through a low wet area and after a small rise continues downward toward the lake. Just before it reaches the shore at 0.4 mi, a trail following the shore joins from the R. Turn L and look for a short trail to a canoe landing spot on the shoreline. A small sandy beach is here, along with a canopy of large conifers—mainly white pine. These conifers circle the rim of the lake for a good part of its circumference. Across the lake is the developed DEC Lake Eaton Campground. At the landing there is another homemade sign high in a tree with an arrow indicating the way to Owls Head.

❋ Trail in winter: Generally not practical for winter use owing to brevity and to steep terrain on the trail that leads to trailhead.

🚶 Distance: Owls Head Mt. trail to Lake Eaton, 0.4 mi (0.6 km).

106 Coney Mt.

Trails Illustrated Map 745: X14

This trail on state land provides a beautiful view after a circular climb around Coney Mt. of only 1.1 mi.

▶Trailhead: Access is from a small parking lot on the E side of NY 30 just N of the Franklin-Hamilton county line, before the snowplow turnaround area on the W side of NY 30. From the N, this is approximately 1.5 mi S of the jct. with NY 421; from the S it is 1.1 mi past the jct. with Sabattis Circle Rd. (CR 10A). ◀

From the parking area (0.0 mi), the blue-marked trail climbs SE through mostly mixed hardwoods. It circles around a small drainage to the L, slowly turning NW then N along the rock talus base of the mountain. The trail picks through rocky terrain until at 0.5 mi it turns E and climbs to a pass between Coney Mt. and a small hill to the N. The trail continues to circle the mountain and climb as it now turns to the SE, then S, reaching a pass at 1 mi. Here the trail meets the Franklin-Hamilton county line, marked with paint blazes, then turns and continues NW up a steep climb to the open peak at 1.1 mi.

The view from the top is clear in all directions. Round and Little Tupper Lakes can be seen to the W and SW, and the High Peaks to the E. Tupper Lake is visible to the N, along with Goodman Mt. This summit, formerly known as Litchfield Mt., was renamed for Charles Goodman and his grandson Andrew Goodman, a civil rights worker murdered while working in a voter registration campaign in

View from Coney Mountain. Chris Murray

Mississippi in the early 1960s. The Goodman family owned a summer home at the base of the summit from 1933 to 1989.

❄ Trail in winter: Not suitable owing to steep terrain.

🏃 Distances: NY 30 to summit of Coney Mt., 1.1 mi (1.8 km). Ascent, 548 ft (171 m). Elevation, 2280 ft (695 m).

107 Goodman Mt.

Trails Illustrated Map 745: Y14

This trail on state land provides a view to the S after a hike up an abandoned highway that circles the mountain. Formerly known as Litchfield Mt., Goodman Mt. was renamed for Charles Goodman and his grandson Andrew, a civil rights worker murdered while working to educate and register disenfranchised voters in Mississippi in the early 1960s. The trail was dedicated to Andrew Goodman in August 2014, and President Obama awarded Goodman the Presidential Medal of Freedom posthumously in November 2014. A kiosk in the parking area tells the history of Andrew Goodman. To the SE of the parking lot is Lumberjack Spring, a watering stop for stagecoaches and wagons during the 1800s.

▶Trailhead: Access is from a spacious parking lot at Lumberjack Spring, on the E side of NY 30 approximately 0.4 mi S of the jct. of NY 30 and CR 421 and 2.2 mi N of the jct. of NY 30 and Sabattis Circle Rd. (CR 10A). ◀

The trail starts toward the NE from the parking lot (0.0 mi) on an abandoned section of old NY 30. It immediately crosses a wide bridge on Cold Brook. The first 1400 ft of the trail is suitable for use by persons with limited mobility. The trial continues through a mostly pine forest along the old pavement on a gentle incline. At 0.2 the trail steepens and narrows, and access for those with limited mobility ends.

The trail continues climbing until 0.7 mi, where it turns sharply L up a steep bank to the NW. The forest is now mixed hardwoods with beech trees predominating. The trail climbs along a slight ridge turning L then sharply R at 1 mi, continuing its circular path around the mountain. In the fall, after the leaves have fallen, Tupper Lake can be seen through the trees at 1.3 mi. The trail now steepens, turning S and climbing to a false peak on the NW side of the mountain at 1.5 mi. The trail continues to a short scramble up patches of bare rock to reach the summit at 1.6 mi. The view is mostly in the southern direction, with Coney Mt. the closest peak.

❄ Trail in winter: Lower section of the trail on the road is suitable for winter use but higher sections are not, owing to steep terrain.

𝄪 Distances: Parking lot on NY 30 to end of limited mobility access 0.2 mi; to turn from abandoned road, 0.7 mi; to summit of Goodman Mt., 1.6 mi (2.6 km). Ascent, 581 ft (177 m). Elevation, 2178 ft (664 m).

108 South Shore Trail

Trails Illustrated Map 745: W13

This trail parallels the S shore of Little Tupper Lake, though not always within view of it. The route follows an old logging road and is marked sporadically with yellow horse trail markers and signs mounted on posts at some trail jcts. The DEC has noted that bears often knock down these signs. The terrain is rolling with many branching intersections and old skid trails. In most cases the hiker should take the most traveled branch. The trail ends at a clearing near two campsites on Little Tupper Lake.

▶Trailhead: Access is from NY 30. From the S, turn L onto CR 10 (Circle Rd., also the access to the DEC Little Tupper Lake Headquarters), 7.1 mi N of the NY 30/28N intersection in Long Lake, and travel 2.9 mi to the trailhead on the L. There is a small parking area with a DEC sign and room for two to three cars.

From the N, bear R onto CR 10A (Sabattis Circle Rd.) 11.2 mi S of the NY 30/3 intersection in Tupper Lake; at a fork 3 mi from NY 30, do not continue R toward the DEC Little Tupper Lake Headquarters, but turn L. Cross Bog Stream and pass a private drive on the R side of the road to reach the trailhead, also on the R side. Distance from NY 30 via this route is 3.4 mi.◀

The trail starts (0.0 mi) on the level and passes through young yellow birches and black cherry trees. Continuing on rolling terrain, at approximately 0.5 mi it reaches a small clearing and jct. The route continues straight ahead. At 0.6 mi, a private property sign appears on the N side of the trail. This indicates Camp on the Point, one of two private holdings on Little Tupper Lake.

After a small creek at 1 mi, the trail reaches a large clearing with a major intersection at 1.5 mi. The setting makes for good growth of blackberry and raspberry, notable for those hiking in the late summer. A sign indicates a turn to the R (W). At 2.4 mi, at a large clearing, the trail again bears R. At 2.6 mi, at another large clearing, Little Tupper Lake is in view to the N (R). A short trail leads to a landing in a bay located SW of the DEC Little Tupper Lake Headquarters across the lake on the N shore.

At this point there is a major split in the trail. The route continues to the L, ascending on a gentle grade. At 3.2 mi, at a jct., the trail bears R. At 4.2 mi a DEC sign marks a final jct. The trail goes R down toward Little Tupper Lake, reaching a clearing at 4.3 mi. The lake can be reached by bushwhacking downhill to the shore. There are two primitive campsites near this point. Number 21 is SE along the shoreline; blowdown and regrowth of small trees make this short bushwhack difficult. Campsite 22 is on an island off the shore.

❄ Trail in winter: Well suited for cross-country skiing and snowshoeing owing to the gentle terrain.

❅ Distances: Parking area to first large clearing, 1.5 mi; to clearing in view of Little Tupper Lake, 2.6 mi; to end of trail, 4.3 mi (6.9 km).

109 Lilypad Pond

Trails Illustrated Map 745: W12

This red-marked trail follows the N shore of Little Tupper Lake past Bum Pond and then traverses rolling forest to Lilypad Pond.

▶Trailhead: Access is from NY 30 via Sabattis Circle Rd. or Circle Rd. (see South Shore Trail, trail 108). At a fork with a large DEC sign indicating Little Tupper Lake Headquarters and Lake Lila, head W 5.8 mi. The Burn Rd. trailhead is located on the L (S) side of the road. This is a large parking area.◀

The red-marked trail starts at a locked gate (0.0 mi) on a logging road. It drops gradually through young mixed hardwoods and pines to the outlet of Otter Pond at 0.4 mi. The trail now turns to the S and Little Tupper Lake comes into view at 0.9 mi. At 1 mi, by a large sign with a "1," is a large boulder on the R. Campsite 5 is S on Little Tupper Lake.

The trail continues SW, following a marshy inlet and leaving Little Tupper Lake, then turning SE and dropping to cross a marshy inlet at 1.4 mi. The lake comes back into view at 1.7 mi, and the turnoff for Campsite 8 is at 2 mi.

The trail continues parallel to the shore of Little Tupper Lake to an unnumbered campsite with a green outhouse at 2.4 mi. A nice beach at Campsite 9 on little Tupper Lake can be reached from this site by bushwhacking S to the lakeshore.

The trail leaves the lake, bearing W, then turns L at 2.9 mi in a SW direction, leaving the road indicated on the Little Tupper Lake USGS Quadrangle. A bridge crosses Charley Pond Stream at 4 mi and the route passes a sandpit at 4.5 mi before crossing a creek with a small pond on the W (R) side of the trail. A small pond—created by the logging road—is encountered at 4.6 mi. The jct. with the Camp Bliss trail (trail 110) diverging to the L (S) is marked with a sign at 4.7 mi.

The trail now turns W and at 5 mi makes a sharp turn to the S at a large boulder called Fivemile Rock. Continuing to the S on a relatively flat stretch, the trail reaches the jct. with Rock Pond Trail (trail 111) going L at 5.3 mi. At 5.9 mi the trail arrives at another jct., and a short track leads L back to Rock Pond Trail. This trail creates a small triangle SW of Bum Pond and is 0.5 mi in length.

Lilypad Pond Trail continues to the R and turns W. At 6.2 mi it leaves the road, bearing SW (L) and enters a landscape of open meadows and forested clumps, the result of past forest fires. Shortly after a large clearing, the trail crosses a creek at 6.8 mi. The trail crosses a feeder stream to Lilypad Pond and enters a nice stand of white pines at 8.1 mi. It intersects the carry trail from Lilypad Pond to Little Salmon Lake (trail 114) at 8.3 mi. Continuing straight briefly, it turns W (R) just before the logging road crosses the outlet to Little Salmon Lake and descends to a marshy canoe put-in on Lilypad Pond at 8.4 mi.

✳ Trail in winter: Well suited for cross-country skiing and snowshoeing owing to its width and gentle, rolling terrain.

👣 Distances: Parking area to lake view, 0.9 mi; to Campsite 8 turnoff, 2 mi; to L turn from road, 2.9 mi; to Camp Bliss trail, 4.7 mi; to Rock Pond trail, 5.3 mi; to "triangle trail" to Rock Pond trail, 5.9 mi; to Lilypad Pond, 8.4 mi (13.4 km).

110 Camp Bliss

Trails Illustrated Map 745: V12

This 1 mi trail connects Lilypad Pond Trail with the former Camp Bliss on the S end of Little Tupper Lake.

▶Locator: This trail begins at the 4.7 mi point on Lilypad Pond Trail (trail 109), which starts at the Burn Rd. trailhead on Sabattis Rd.◀

From the jct. (0.0 mi), the trail heads E up a small hill, continuing through gently rolling terrain until Bum Pond can be seen S (R) through the trees at 0.3 mi. A sign marks a path to the pond. The trail continues E, then turns NE to reach Camp Bliss on Little Tupper Lake. This was formerly the location of a camp owned by the Whitney family; the camp was removed after the purchase of the property by the state. A campsite at this location provides a beautiful view of the lake through the pines surrounding it and has a nice beach.

✳ Trail in winter: Well suited as an intermediate destination with a good vista or as a side trip as part of a winter outing on Lilypad Pond Trail.

👣 Distances: Lilypad Pond Trail to Bum Pond, 0.3 mi; to Camp Bliss site, 1 mi (1.6 km).

111 Rock Pond

Trails Illustrated Map 745: V12

This spur trail off the Lilypad Pond trail crosses the outlet to Bum Pond, passes Frenchmans Mine, then crosses the outlet of Rock Pond before ending at a campsite on the NE shore of Rock Pond.

▶Locator: This trail begins at the 5.3 mi mark on the Lilypad Pond trail (trail 109), which starts at the Burn Rd. trailhead on Sabattis Rd.◀

The blue-marked trail descends from the Lilypad Pond trail (0.0 mi) toward the S, reaching small streams at 0.2 mi and 0.5 mi. At the second stream, a short side trail E (L) leads to the dam on Bum Pond.

Continuing S, the trail enters a clearing at 0.8 mi and meets a short trail entering from the NW. This is a 0.5 mi path that joins the Lilypad Pond trail, forming a triangle.

The trail continues S, passing a large gravel pit called Frenchmans Mine that produced the gravel used to construct the logging roads in the area. At 1.4 mi it crosses a creek on a bridge and comes to the jct. with the Hardigan Pond trail (trail 112). The Rock Pond trail continues L and reaches Rock Pond outlet at 2.4 mi. The carry trail from Rock Pond to Little Tupper (trail 117) crosses shortly after a bridge over the Rock Pond outlet.

The trail now follows a steep logging road to the R along the hillside on the NE shore of Rock Pond. At 3.2 mi the trail branches R on a logging road spur downhill, reaching Campsite 30 on Rock Pond at 3.3 mi. The campsite is located just SE of a peninsula that juts into Rock Pond on the NE shore.

❋ Trail in winter: Well suited for cross-country skiing and snowshoeing, but begins a good distance from the Burn Rd. trailhead.

🚶 Distances: Lilypad Pond trail to side trail to Bum Pond, 0.5 mi; to Hardigan Pond trail, 1.4 mi; to Rock Pond outlet, 2.4 mi; to campsite on Rock Pond, 3.3 mi (5.3 km).

112 Hardigan Pond

Trails Illustrated Map 745: V12

This yellow-marked spur trail off the Rock Pond trail, which itself branches off the Lilypad Pond trail, ends on the shore of Hardigan Pond 1.6 mi after leaving the Rock Pond trail.

▶Locator: This trail begins at the 1.4 mi mark on Rock Pond Trail (trail 111); this is 6.7 mi from the Burn Rd. trailhead on Sabattis Rd., via Lilypad Pond Trail (trail 109).◀

Leaving the Rock Pond trail (0.0 mi), the route heads S up a small hill. The trail then drops, only to climb to a low divide and then descend into the watershed of Louie Pond. At 0.9 mi, just over a small rise, an unmarked fork L leads to Louie Pond. The Hardigan Pond trail bears R. At 1.3 mi, it meets the carry from

Hardigan Pond to Rock Pond (trail 116), with which it shares ground the rest of the way to Hardigan Pond. The way to Rock Pond continues straight through the intersection to the E, while the route to Hardigan Pond turns S (R) and at 1.4 mi leaves the logging road it has been tracing and becomes a footpath on an old logging railroad grade. Many railroad ties are still in place, some with a steel "S" pounded onto their ends. The ties make the hiking awkward through mixed pines and hardwoods. Hardigan Pond comes into view on the R at 1.6 mi.

❀ Trail in winter: Well suited to winter muscle-powered transit owing to its width and the gentle rolling terrain, but the trail begins a good distance from the Burn Rd. trailhead.

🐾 Distances: Rock Pond trail to fork to Louie Pond, 0.9 mi; to canoe carry to Rock Pond, 1.3 mi; to Hardigan Pond, 1.6 mi (2.6 km).

113 Shingle Shanty Brook–Lilypad Pond Carry

Trails Illustrated Map 745: V11

This trail connects Shingle Shanty Brook with Lilypad Pond; its primary use is as a canoe carry.

▶Locator: Access is through Lake Lila (trail 118) and up Shingle Shanty Brook, or from the NW bay of Lilypad Pond. The route is described from W (Shingle Shanty Brook) to E (Lilypad Pond). ◀

The trail begins at a point where Shingle Shanty Brook is blocked by a downed tree and posted signs on a cable stretch across the brook (0.0 mi). There is a steep sandy beach on the R bank (L bank as one heads upstream).

The trail turns NE in a downstream direction among large pines. It then bears E, alternately turning S and climbing steeply, then turning E again along the contours of a hill. The trail passes through open meadows alternating with wooded areas, the result of past forest fires. At 0.2 mi, the trail passes over bedrock outcrops and joins a logging trail.

After height of land at 0.3 mi, the trail begins a gradual drop, passing through mostly open meadow until 0.5 mi, where it leaves the logging trail by turning S (R). The trail now drops more rapidly and the number of white pines increases until it terminates at the NW bay of Lilypad Pond at 0.8 mi.

❀ Trail in winter: Not worthwhile, owing to a few steep stretches as well as its remoteness and short length.

🐾 Distances: Shingle Shanty Brook to Lilypad Pond, 0.8 mi (1.3 km).

114 Lilypad Pond–Little Salmon Lake Carry

Trails Illustrated Map 745: U11

Marked with red disks where it corresponds with Lilypad Pond Trail (trail 109), this short trail connects Lilypad Pond with Little Salmon Lake and is used primarily as a canoe carry.

▶Locator: Western access is from Lilypad Pond in a bay on the SE shore of the pond just N of the inlet from Little Salmon Lake; E access is at the outlet of Little Salmon Lake. The route is described from W to E.◀

The trail begins in a boggy area on Lilypad Pond (0.0 mi) and may be marked with survey tape. It soon reaches drier ground, passing large white pine stumps and joining a skid trail. This is the red-marked Lilypad Pond Trail (trail 109). At 0.1 mi, the route attains a gravel logging road; the road continues S, crossing the outlet to Little Salmon Lake and leaving public property, but the route to Little Salmon Lake follows the road N and in a few yards leaves Lilypad Pond Trail, following another gravel logging road E (R). At 0.4 mi, the carry trail leaves the logging road to the S (R) and reaches the outlet of Little Salmon Lake at a designated campsite. Hikers or canoeists with extra time may want to follow the outlet downstream to view a washed-out hand-laid mortarless dam.

❋ Trail in winter: Not recommended owing to its remoteness and short length.

🐾 Distances: Lilypad Pond to logging road, 0.1 mi; to Little Salmon Lake, 0.4 mi (0.6 km).

115 Salmon Lake Outlet–Hardigan Pond Carry
Trails Illustrated Map 745: U12

This trail connects Salmon Lake Outlet to Hardigan Pond along a railroad grade and is used primarily as a canoe carry.

▶Locator: SW access is from Salmon Lake outlet just below Touey Falls; NE access is at the beaver dam at the outlet of Hardigan Pond. The route is described from SW to NE.◀

The carry, which may be marked with orange survey tape, begins on the Salmon Lake Outlet just below Touey Falls at a collapsed boathouse (0.0 mi). It proceeds N to NE along an old railroad grade, turning off to the W (L) at 0.2 mi. This turn could be missed; watch for it carefully.

The trail continues up a small rise through a logged-out area then drops, turning N into a marshy area and arriving at a beaver dam on the outlet of Hardigan Pond at 0.3 mi.

❋ Trail in winter: Not recommended owing to its remoteness and short length.

🐾 Distances: Salmon Lake Outlet to Hardigan Pond, 0.3 mi (0.5 km).

116 Hardigan Pond–Rock Pond Carry
Trails Illustrated Map 745: U12

Marked with yellow disks and possibly orange survey tape, this trail connects Hardigan Pond and Rock Pond and is used primarily as a canoe carry.

▶Locator: W access is from the shore of Hardigan Pond near its NE tip; E access is from the NW corner of Rock Pond's SW bay. The route is described from W to E. ◀

The yellow-marked trail begins on the railroad grade on the NE shore of Hardigan Pond (0.0 mi). This part of the route corresponds with the Hardigan Pond trail (trail 112). Many railroad ties are still in place, some with a steel "S" pounded onto their ends. The ties make for awkward hiking through mixed pines and hardwoods.

At 0.3 mi, the trail joins a logging road at a yellow marker and a sign pointing to Hardigan Pond. The trail continues on the logging road until a cairn indicates Hardigan Pond Trail turning W (L). The carry trail turns E (R).

At 0.5 mi the logging road branches; the carry trail continues L (N). At 0.8 mi, at a clearing, the trail bears L again. The DEC has placed rock cairns to mark the route. The trail crosses the outlet of Louie Pond at 1.2 mi and climbs to height of land and bedrock outcrops at 1.5 mi. The trail now drops steeply at times, crossing bedrock outcrops with Rock Pond coming into view at 1.7 mi. The trail proceeds straight through a boggy area before reaching the pond at 1.8 mi.

❋ Trail in winter: Not suitable mainly because of its remoteness, but also owing to a few steep stretches on the Rock Pond end.

✺ Distances: Hardigan Pond to split from Hardigan Pond trail, 0.4 mi; to Louie Pond outlet, 1.2 mi; to Rock Pond, 1.8 mi (2.9 km).

117 Rock Pond–Little Tupper Lake Carry
Trails Illustrated Map 745: V12

Marked with yellow canoe carry disks, this short trail connects Little Tupper Lake and Rock Pond and is used primarily as a canoe carry.

▶Locator: Canoeists coming from Little Tupper Lake will find the N trailhead along the Rock Pond outlet, near where it meets Rock Pond; canoeists on the pond will find it where the pond narrows to the outlet. The route is described from Rock Pond to Little Tupper Lake. ◀

The carry trail starts on the N (R) side of the Rock Pond outlet at a collapsed boathouse (0.0 mi). It continues on level ground through mixed hardwoods and pines, crossing a logging road (this is the Rock Pond trail, trail 111). The trail passes a large white pine and reaches an arm of Little Tupper Lake at 0.1 mi.

❋ Trail in winter: Not recommended owing to its remoteness and short length.

✺ Distances: Rock Pond outlet to Little Tupper Lake, 0.1 mi (0.2 km).

118 Lake Lila to Frederica Mt.
Trails Illustrated Map 745: V11

This blue-marked trail provides access to the largest lake wholly contained within the Forest Preserve, while traversing what was once one of the largest private parks in the Adirondacks: Nehasane Park.

▶Trailhead: Access is from NY 30 via Little Tupper Lake (see South Shore Trail, trail 108). The access road to Lake Lila is on the L at 7.7 mi on Sabattis Rd. Marked with a DEC sign, this is locally known as Charley Pond Rd. A DEC parking lot and metal barrier barring any farther travel by unauthorized vehicles are at 5.8 mi. ◀

The trail starts immediately past the barrier (0.0 mi). It is mainly level with occasional spruce and pine until it starts to rise at 0.7 mi amid medium-sized hardwoods. At 1.5 mi, it comes to the shore of Lake Lila (at the parking lot, a 0.3 mi yellow-marked canoe carry also provides access to the lake). Several of the forested islands of the lake can be observed here, as can the low hills encircling the lake on the W.

The trail now starts along the lakeshore with occasional large white pine present. At 1.9 mi, it crosses Harrington Brook as the brook empties into the lake. At 2.6 mi, a logging road goes off R to reach the site of a railroad station of the Remsen–Lake Placid line. At 2.8 mi a lean-to can be seen on the L at the lake shore.

At a jct. at 3 mi, the trail to Frederica Mt. goes R. (Straight ahead about a quarter of a mile is the site of the old Nehasane Lodge. This short trail has yellow markers. Nehasane Lodge, one of the "Great Camps" of the Adirondacks, was destroyed by the DEC in 1984 in compliance with the State Land Master Plan.)

The trail starts to rise through large hemlock and sugar maple at 3.2 mi. It then descends with yellow birch and red maple saplings lining its sides.

At 3.5 mi, the trail crosses the railroad grade. The railroad corridor is not part of the Whitney Wilderness Area and is used by snowmobilers in winter. At 3.6 mi, a wooden bridge crosses over a creek with an old beaver pond on the R. The trail continues to a sign for Frederica Mt. on the R at 3.8 mi. From here, the trail ascends through a mixed forest of softwoods and hardwoods to the overlook on Frederica Mt. at 4.4 mi.

From the top of Frederica Mt. an unequaled view of Lake Lila below and all the surrounding Wilderness Area may be had. Viewing all these verdant acres today, it is hard to believe that the entire Nehasane Park together with the adjoining hamlet of Sabattis (then called Long Lake West) was severely burned by a disastrous forest fire in 1908.

❄ Trail in winter: Suitable for cross-country skiing to the base of Frederica Mt. (3.8 mi from the parking lot) and can be snowshoed from there by accomplished snowshoers. Another 5.8 mi will have to be traversed from Sabattis Rd. if the access road is not plowed (it usually is not) and if parking is possible on Sabattis Rd.

🚶 Distances: Parking lot to Lake Lila, 1.5 mi; to spur to Nehasane Lodge site, 3 mi; to base of Frederica Mt., 3.8 mi; to summit, 4.4 mi (7 km). Ascent from trailhead, 414 ft (126 m). Elevation, 2195 ft (669 m). 🪶

View of ranger cabin from the firetower on Mt Arab summit. Mark Bowie

Tupper Lake Section

The village of Tupper Lake, one of the largest in the Adirondack Park, is at the center of a varied group of interesting trails. The village was once the core of the lumbering and wood-based industry in the Adirondacks; today, tourism and recreation are also important here. The trails in many cases join some of the area's numerous ponds and lakes, occasionally forming a chain linking these glacial relics to each other. Other trails ascend the region's isolated mountains, offering stunning views of the pond-strewn sprawling woodlands unfurled below.

Some of the forests through which the trails pass are themselves quite spectacular. Probably no other part of the Adirondack Park (with the exception of the remote Five Ponds Wilderness to the W) possesses such an abundance and variety of old-growth forest as do some of the woodlands here. Especially noteworthy in this regard are the forests along the Otter Hollow and Floodwood loops.

Two very large DEC campsites are located in this area: Fish Creek Pond and Rollins Pond.

A suggested hike in this section is listed below.

HARDER HIKE
Otter Hollow Loop: 10.6 mi (17 km). This hike is difficult not because of its terrain—mostly gently undulating through mixed forest with many ponds in view—but because of its distance (trail 122).

Trail Described	Total Miles (one way)	Page
119 Trout Pond	1.4 (2.2 km)	173
120 Mt. Arab	1.1 (1.8 km)	174
121 Floodwood Loop	9.0 (14.4 km)	175
122 Otter Hollow Loop	8.4 (13.4 km)	176

119 Trout Pond

Trails Illustrated Map 745: X12

This red-marked DEC snowmobile trail goes through the Horseshoe Lake Wild Forest, giving access to a deep two-tiered lake that provides habitat for both brook trout and lake trout.

▶Trailhead: Access is from Horseshoe Lake Rd. (NY 421). At 6.4 mi S of the Tupper Lake DEC boat launching site, NY 421 turns W off NY 30 and proceeds approximately 6 mi to the end of the pavement. The dirt road on the L, 1 mi past the end of the pavement, has been upgraded so that the 0.8 mi to the Lower Dam can be driven with care. (This road is not likely to be plowed in winter.) Cars may be parked here at the side of the road. ◄

Shortly after crossing the dam (0.0 mi), the trail begins to climb among mature hardwoods. At 1.1 mi it reaches the crest of a hill after a steady ascent. This hill is crowned with majestic mature beech, apparently in good health. A steep ridge to the L across a swale is adorned with magnificent white pine and hemlock.

At 1.4 mi the trail reaches Trout Pond, long and narrow with white pine fringing its shore. This isolated body of water received its name from the large lake trout lurking in its depths.

❄ Trail in winter: Suitable for skiing and snowshoeing its entire length with a noticeable ascent near its end, but be prepared for an extra 0.8 mi from NY 421.

👣 Distances: Dam to crest of hill, 1.1 mi; to Trout Pond, 1.4 mi (2.2 km). In winter, add 0.8 mi (1.3 km) at start.

120 Mt. Arab

Trails Illustrated Map 745: AA13

The Mt. Arab trail, marked in red, leads to a restored fire tower. Built in 1918, the last fire observer occupied it in the 1980s; it was condemned for public use in 1993. In 1997 a group of concerned citizens founded the Friends of Mt. Arab to restore the summit facilities and undertake other projects on the mountain. Through the efforts of this Friends group, hikers can now climb the restored tower, in which a volunteer interpreter is stationed on some days, and enjoy its beautiful view.

The summit is Forest Preserve land, but the trail passes through private property. A conservation easement has been obtained to allow access. The trail was rebuilt in 1990 and the Friends group has made improvements ever since (2016), including extensive trail work on the steeper sections in more recent years. Stones have been moved to form steps where there were muddy banks and washouts. At the top of the steepest section, a series of wooden steps has been built.

▶Trailhead: Access is off Conifer Rd., which intersects NY 3 approximately 7 mi W of the NY3–NY30 intersection in Tupper Lake and 10.4 mi E of Seveys Corners (the intersection of NY 3 and NY 56). Take Conifer Rd. 1.7 mi S to Mt. Arab Rd. on the L. Take this road 0.9 mi to the trailhead on the L, with parking R. The start is 0.3 mi after a railroad crossing. ◄

Leaving the road (0.0 mi), the trail passes through a stand of medium-sized hardwoods, beginning to ascend immediately. At 0.3 mi it enters the Forest Preserve, having traversed private lands on an easement.

The trail continues the steep climb until 0.8 mi, where it begins to level off amid large outcrops of mangerite. It then begins to circle, reaching the summit at 1.1 mi. The usual growth of stunted red spruce mantles the 2545 ft summit here, just as it does the other low mountains of this area of the Adirondacks. Mountain ash is also present on the summit, which was severely burned over in the early years of the twentieth century.

In the center of the small clearing at the top stands the restored fire tower, open to the public, and the observer's cabin. Mt. Arab Lake and Eagle Crag Lake are nearby to the SSE. Mt. Matumbla, the highest point in St. Lawrence County, is directly N. To the NNE, Raquette Pond and Tupper Lake Village can be clearly seen; Mt. Morris looms ahead to the SE. Moosehead Mt. can be seen NNW. The summits of these surrounding peaks are all on private land or made inaccessible by private land and are therefore unavailable to the hiking public. All are of approximately the same elevation as Mt. Arab.

❄ Trail in winter: Not suitable owing to steepness of terrain.

🚶 Distance: Road to summit, 1.1 mi (1.8 km). Ascent, 764 ft (233 m). Elevation, 2545 ft (776 m).

121 Floodwood Loop

Trails Illustrated Map 746: CC17

This is a rather lengthy loop, linking some of the myriad glacial ponds in an entrancing region of alternating ridges and water—both a legacy of the receding glacier that once mantled the area. To add to the allure, much of the forest crowning the ridges is imposing; some of it appears to be truly first growth.

▶Trailhead: The trail starts at Fish Creek Pond Campground, whose entrance is on the L of NY 30 5.5 mi N of Wawbeek Corners. A gate is on the R opposite Campsite 23, 0.2 mi inside the campground entrance. Begin here.◀

Follow the red disks around the gate (0.0 mi) and make a sharp R at 0.1 mi. The path straight ahead also turns R over a rise and is the return leg of the loop.

The way is marked by the splendid specimens of hemlock and yellow birch so prevalent in this region. Majestic red spruce is also present, but some of it appears to be succumbing to unknown ravages (some suspect acid deposition).

The trail makes a moderate ascent up a glacial knoll as it arrives at the first canoe carry at 0.9 mi. Fish Creek is to the L, Follensby Clear Pond to the R. The latter is one of the area's largest lakes and is adorned with a number of pine-clad islands.

The trail proceeds through a

James Bullard

spruce swamp for a short distance and then rolls on to make a sharp L and then another L to reflect the contour of one of the bays of the aptly named Horseshoe Pond. The next canoe carry is at 2.6 mi: atop a ridge after the outlet of Little Polliwog Pond, the carry to that tiny glacial pool goes L. At 2.9 mi a canoe carry connecting Little Polliwog and Polliwog Ponds crosses the route.

At 3.7 mi, the red-marked trail turns L on the canoe carry from Middle Pond to Polliwog Pond. To the R it is a short way to sprawling Polliwog Pond, whose sentinel white pines have hosted nesting osprey. At 4 mi the loop trail goes R as yellow canoe carry disks go straight ahead to Middle Pond. The trail arrives at Floodwood Rd. at 4.2 mi.

The trail goes L on Floodwood Rd. along Middle Pond until 5.2 mi, where it turns L and reenters the forest, heading S. The trail undulates as it crosses a wet spot spanned by a wooden bridge before coming to the intersection with yet another yellow-marked canoe carry. The loop trail bears R here; the way L leads to the S shore of Middle Pond.

At 6.3 mi, the loop trail turns L following the red disks; the yellow-marked canoe carry to the R arrives at Floodwood Pond in 400 ft. At 6.6 mi Otter Hollow Loop Crossover is a short link crossing Fish Creek to connect Floodwood Loop and Otter Hollow Loop (trail 122). The trail continues over rolling ridges with Little Square Pond on the R.

At 8.5 mi the trail crosses one final canoe carry. Fish Creek is on the R while the carry to the L goes to Follensby Clear Pond. The trail proceeds through a forest of pioneer white and grey birch, then makes a sharp L to reach its point of origin at 9 mi.

❊ Trail in winter: Snowmobile use is occasionally heavy, but this trail is well suited to cross-country skiing. Magnificent old-growth forest and hobblebush understory add to the allure of the trip. Glacial knolls in the 2 mi before Floodwood Rd. are more frequent and steeper than at the start, and the trail is narrow throughout. The campground road is plowed to the caretaker's cabin (0.1 mi from the entrance); no fee is charged after November.

🐾 Distances: Campground trailhead to Follensby Clear Pond, 0.9 mi; to Little Polliwog Pond, 2.6 mi; to Polliwog Pond, 2.9 mi; to Middle Pond, 3.7 mi; to Floodwood Rd., 4.2 mi; to Floodwood Rd. turnoff, 5.2 mi; to Floodwood Pond, 6.3 mi; to Otter Hollow Loop Crossover, 6.6 mi; to trailhead, 9 mi (14.4 km).

122 Otter Hollow Loop

Trails Illustrated Map 746: CC16

▶Trailhead: Otter Hollow Loop begins in Fish Creek Pond Campground on NY 30, 5.5 mi N of Wawbeek Corners, and links an assortment of glacial ponds under a towering arboreal canopy. The start is on the R opposite Campsite 104, 1.1 mi inside the campground entrance. The large body of water here is Square Pond.◀

he trail starts inside a gate (0.0 mi) and, traveling counterclockwise, follows d DEC disks under an impressive mixed growth forest of hemlock and yellow rch. At 0.3 mi a side trail L leads to dark, conifer-ringed Black Pond. At 0.5 mi e trail veers sharply L as a canoe carry goes straight ahead a short distance to opperas Pond.

At 0.9 mi the trail goes R at a fork. To the L is a short canoe carry leading to 'hey Pond. A linear-shaped pond, Whey is noted locally for the quality of its ook-trout fishing. The trail now begins to descend slightly and enters an ex-nsive conifer swamp for a distance, crossing on wooden corduroy in two aces, the last being the inlet to Little Square Pond, which lies off to the R at 2 mi.

The trail now rises as it ascends one of the glacial ridges and knolls so preva-nt in this area. A mature sugar maple, yellow birch, and hemlock forest arches acefully over the trail. As the trail descends again, a DEC sign at 2.9 mi points e way to a crossover to Floodwood Loop (trail 121) on the other side of Fish reek. Medium-sized white birch trees denote intensive fires early in the twen-th century. Floodwood Pond, one of the area's larger bodies of water, is visible in a number of spots for the next mile.

At 4.5 mi the trail reaches Rollins Pond Campground beside Campsite 256. his completes the link between the two large state campgrounds. The trail now ads S following the vehicle access road joining the two campgrounds. For a stance it follows the shore of Rollins Pond, another of the area's larger ponds. e extensive red pine plantation contrasts vividly with the native red pine nds on the E shores of some of the lakes and ponds in this vicinity. Large white ne and white birch line the roadway.

The trail descends with the far shores of Whey Pond visible L at 6.6 mi. A gate 7.1 mi is generally considered the end of Rollins Pond Campground and the ginning of Fish Creek Pond Campground. At 7.9 mi, the trail bears L at a Y tersection (R leads to NY 30). The route continues to 8.4 mi, where the begin-ng of the loop is reached on the L. Square Pond with all of its many designated mpsites is on the R. Straight ahead 1.1mi is the trail's winter terminus at the retaker's cabin.

✤ Trail in winter: Begins at the caretaker's cabin 0.1 mi inside the entrance. is is generally the limit of plowing and adds 1 mi to the loop in both directions ' a total distance of 10.4 mi. The grade and width of the loop are generally well ited to skiing and snowshoeing, with snowmobile activity only moderate.

⚹⚹ Distances: Trailhead to Copperas Pond, 0.5 mi; to Whey Pond, 0.9 mi; to tle Square Pond, 2.2 mi; to Floodwood Loop crossover, 2.9 mi; to Rollins Pond mpground, 4.5 mi; to gate, 7.1 mi; to trailhead, 8.4 mi (13.4 km). In winter d 1 mi in each direction for total distance of 10.4 mi (16.6 km). 🍃

Hoel Pond view. Joanne Kennedy

Floodwood Road Section

Floodwood Rd. joins NY 30 some 9.4 mi N of Wawbeek Corners, the intersection of NY 30 and NY 3, 6 mi E of the village of Tupper Lake. Paved at the outset, Floodwood Rd. is primarily a gravel town road that, after passing some camps in the first 0.5 mi, proceeds 5.6 mi through the Forest Preserve before dead-ending at the gates of a large private estate. It has a delightful network of trails clustered around it. Many of the trails link some of the glacial ponds that are so bounteous in this area. Others ascend moderate-sized peaks from which rich views of the entire area can be had.

This section of the Adirondacks has an abundance of marked canoe carries linking many of the myriad bodies of water. These carries are usually short and all are marked by DEC yellow markers. The carries described are both representative of the other carries as a whole and make appealing hikes on their own merits. This is due mostly to their moderate length (longer than most carries) and also to the beauty of the terrain they traverse. Some of the trails described are reached by the town road; others are accessible only by canoe.

Most of the Forest Preserve land N of Floodwood Rd. and the railroad tracks is designated as the St. Regis Canoe Area—unique so far in the Adirondack Park. For the most part, this Canoe Area is administered as a Wilderness Area, and motorboats are banned. The Forest Preserve land S of Floodwood Rd. and E of the railroad tracks is in the Saranac Lakes Wild Forest.

Drainage is almost entirely through the West and Middle Branches of the St. Regis River. St. Regis also lends its name to the area's most imposing pinnacle, which looms impressively over the conifer-clad, water-strewn lowland forests extending in all directions from its base (see St. Regis Mt., trail 135). The St. Regis Canoe Area holds many of the trails here, with the remainder in the Saranac Lakes Wild Forest.

A few suggested hikes for this section are listed below.

SHORT HIKE

Noel Pond: 1.6 mi (2.6 km) round-trip. This largely flat canoe carry leads to one of the many ponds in the St. Regis Canoe Area. See trail 123.

MODERATE HIKE

Floodwood Mt.: 3.8 mi (6.1 km) round-trip. A walk on a woods road followed by a gradual climb that reveals the wonders of numerous wild, little-known mountains. See trail 126.

123 Hoel Pond

Trails Illustrated Map 746: DD17

▶Trailhead: Access is from Floodwood Rd., 1 mi from its jct. with NY 30. The trail, marked with yellow disks by DEC as a canoe carry, starts at a small DEC sign on the R.◀

From the sign (0.0 mi), the trail, narrow and undulating, proceeds through a mostly mature forest of yellow birch, hemlock, and sugar maple for its first half. The presence of sugar maple indicates that the substrate over bedrock might be glacial till here, instead of the glacial outwash that is so common in this area.

At 0.7 mi the trail meets and runs alongside a golf course for a short distance. Whiteface and Moose Mountains can be clearly seen looming impressively to the E. At 0.8 mi the trail reaches Hoel Pond, with Long Pond Mt. towering above it on the far shore. Hoel Pond, actually an attractive, fairly large lake, is mostly in the Forest Preserve, with an area of private development on one shore.

❄ Trail in winter: Suitable for skiing and snowshoeing, but relatively short. Because it is narrow and curves sharply in places, caution should be exercised.

🐾 Distances: To golf course, 0.7 mi; to Hoel Pond, 0.8 mi (1.3 km).

124 Long Pond Canoe Carry

Trails Illustrated Map 746: DD16

▶Trailhead: Access to this trail is from Floodwood Rd. Take it W from NY 30 for 4.1 mi to a DEC sign on the R just past a railroad crossing. This is the start of the trail. (Note that there is also another canoe launch on Long Pond, at the W end, with a 0.3 mi carry. To reach it, continue W on Floodwood Rd. approximately 1.3 mi to the parking area on the R at the W end of the pond.)◀

From the sign (0.0 mi), the trail proceeds through a mature hemlock and yellow birch forest before crossing a beaver pond on corduroy at 0.4 mi. Some extra-large white pines are also in evidence. The trail continues in an undulating manner, passing a large creek at 0.6 mi. It traverses a mature forest to Long Pond at 1.1 mi. Long Pond is the start of a canoe excursion to Hoel Pond, near the start of Flood-

View from end of Long Pond Carry. Joanne Kennedy

wood Rd., via Slang and Turtle Ponds, utilizing only one short carry.

❊ Trail in winter: Provides a brief round-trip, or may be utilized as the first leg of an extended ski tour to Nellie Pond (trail 127).

❧ Distances: Floodwood Rd. to corduroy, 0.4 mi; to Long Pond, 1.1 mi (1.8 km).

125 Rollins Pond

Trails Illustrated Map 746: DD15

▶Trailhead: Access is from an extension of Floodwood Rd. 0.8 mi from a caretaker's cabin, R, that marks the former end of Forest Preserve lands and the end of the town road. State acquisition of the Floodwood Boy Scout Camp extended the state boundary on the S side of the road. Access is from a rough parking area on the L. In winter, if the road is unplowed, the trail begins at the caretaker's cabin and proceeds along the road, increasing the distance 0.8 mi each way. ◀

The trail, actually a private road, begins (0.0 mi) on the L by going through old fields in the process of being reforested after a severe fire. The boreal aspect of this region is reinforced by the balsam fir and black spruce reseeding directly here, in addition to the usual aspen, blueberries, and spirea.

At 0.4 mi the road crosses a creek on a bridge and proceeds uphill to a L turn at 1 mi that leads to the Floodwood Boy Scout Camp and the land they have retained in private ownership. The trail continues straight ahead through a forest of mainly second-growth hardwoods. At 1.1 mi the Floodwood Mt. trail (trail

126) branches R.

At 1.4 mi, the private Boy Scout lands end on the L. The road gradually becomes somewhat steeper as it undulates and crosses over several ridges. A number of creeks cross the trail, all draining into Floodwood and Rollins Ponds as part of the Saranac River drainage. At 2.1 mi, a pond with extensive marshes on the L is the headwaters of Rollins Pond.

At 3.2 mi the old Remsen-to-Lake Placid railroad bed marks the end of Forest Preserve land. The last 0.2 mi straight ahead has been retained by the Scouts. The Scouts are not in residence during the winter, however, so Rollins Pond can be reached easily then.

❊ Trail in winter: Primarily used as a cross-country ski route.

❧ Distances: Floodwood Rd. extension parking area to fork, 1.1 mi; to marshes, 2.1 mi; to railroad bed, 3.2 mi; to Rollins Pond, 3.4 mi (5.4 km). Floodwood Rd. to Rollins Pond, 5 mi (8 km).

126 Floodwood Mt.

Trails Illustrated Map 746: CC15

This is a relatively moderate climb to the top of one of the area's minor peaks where, on a clear day, a mega-view can be had for a modest effort.

▶Locator: Access is on the R at 1.1 mi on the Rollins Pond trail (trail 125), approximately 200 yd past a L turn to the privately held Boy Scout camp. At a low glacial boulder the trail, clearly marked by the red disks of the Floodwood Boy Scouts, departs.◀

The trail starts (0.0 mi) by gradually climbing through a second-growth forest of white ash and maple. The tread of the path is quite clear in most places, but in any event the red disks are clear all the way to the top. The trail runs along a babbling brook for a fair distance, crossing it in several places. The trail goes W upon reaching a shoulder of the mountain just under a point where a steep semi-cliff guides the last 0.2 mi. It turns sharply S for a distance and then goes W again before finally breaking out to the summit.

An interesting feature in this hardwood forest is the size of some of the sugar maples and beech that can be found almost up to the crest of the peak. Trees do not diminish in size until just before the top, in marked contrast to most of the area's mountains. Slope exposure providing a favorable micro-climate probably accounts for this.

The view from the summit is superb, especially when the leaves are off the trees. Equal views are available just below the peak when the trees are leafless. There is another viewpoint past the summit, after a steep descent and ascent. St. Regis Mt. and Bay Pond Mt. to the N, Mt. Matumbla to the S, and Iron Mt. in the SW foreground all give a glimpse of how the area's peaks are arranged. Countless water bodies—relics of the glacier ice strewn below—including Rollins and Floodwood Ponds, lie near the mountain's base. On an especially clear day the

Seward Range can be seen in the distance to the S.

❋ Trail in winter: Not suitable for skiing owing to steep terrain.

🏃 Distances: Rollins Pond trail to start of path marked with red disks, 1.1 mi; to summit, 1.9 mi (3 km). Ascent from Rollins Pond trail, 659 ft (201 m). Elevation, 2316 ft (706 m).

127 Nellie Pond Canoe Carry

Trails Illustrated Map 746: DD16

▶Locator: The designated parking area is just off Floodwood Rd., to the R approximately 1 mi past the railroad crossing. To reach this trail it is necessary to canoe the length of Long Pond, which is reachable via Long Pond Canoe Carry (trail 124) or from the canoe launch on the W end of Long Pond.◀

The start of the trail is indicated by a DEC white wooden canoe carry sign on the N shore of Long Pond (0.0 mi). The trail, somewhat boggy in spots, proceeds on the level through a conifer swamp, passing a beaver pond on the L. It starts to ascend the shoulder of a beech- and maple-crowned hill at 0.8 mi. It then descends and proceeds through another swamp, passing a side trail leading to Bessie Pond at 1.1 mi. At 1.4 mi it ends at the shore of Nellie Pond, which, in addition to the usual conifers, is framed by a cliff on the E.

❋ Trail in winter: Can be skied as the final segment of an extended cross-country ski round-trip using the frozen waters of Long Pond as a pivot. Ski 1.1 mi down the Long Pond trail (trail 124) to the S shore of Long Pond. Ski due E on Long Pond until the lake veers sharply to the N in 0.5 mi. Now ski directly N for approximately 2 mi into a large bay on the far shore. A white wooden canoe carry sign here indicates the start of the trail to Nellie Pond, which sports several steep pitches.

🏃 Distances: In summer, Long Pond to Nellie Pond, 1.4 mi (2.2 km). In winter, Floodwood Rd. to Long Pond, 1.1 mi; Long Pond to start of Nellie Pond trail, 3.6 mi; to Nellie Pond, 5 mi (8 km).

128 Long Pond Mt.

Trails Illustrated Map 746: DD16

▶Locator: This trail is reached only by canoe on Long Pond after a 0.3 mi carry from a parking lot 5.4 mi from NY 30 on the N side of Floodwood Rd. Paddle due E on Long Pond for 2 mi until the lake turns N. It is 1.5 mi of further paddling to a bay on the far N shore where there may be a sign for the canoe carry to Mountain Pond. Begin hiking here.◀

From the pond (0.0 mi), the trail ascends fairly steeply through a conifer plantation and then descends to a small clearing on the shore of Mountain Pond at 0.5 mi. Follow a path made by anglers to the R as it encircles the pond. At 0.6 mi

En route to Long Pond Mountain. David Hough

the trail leaves the pond and begins to climb gradually.

The climbing becomes quite steep in several sections, through a mixed northern hardwood–hemlock forest with occasional large specimens of hardwoods rising above the general canopy. Rock outcrops and cliffs have to be skirted in a number of places. The route generally parallels a hemlock ravine for a distance before leveling off briefly at a false summit. At 1.4 mi, the level, grassy summit is finally reached.

The view on top can be outstanding on a clear day. Mt. Matumbla is to the SW, and the forests to the N lead up to St. Regis Mt. Many of the lakes and ponds of the St. Regis Canoe Area are clearly visible, as are the towers of Tupper Lake to the SW. On a really good day, Whiteface Mt. can be seen in the distance clearly defined by its rock slides and the cirque near the summit. Adding to the charm of the trip is the pink corydalis in bloom among crevices in the cliffs just under the summit.

❀ Trail in winter: Generally not suitable for cross-country skiing, except for 3.5 mi on the surface of Long Pond when conditions permit. Steepness is the main impediment.

ᛤ Distances: To Mountain Pond, 0.5 mi; to summit, 1.4 mi (2.2 km). Ascent from Long Pond, 928 ft (283 m). Elevation, 2529 ft (771 m).

129 Clamshell Pond

Trails Illustrated Map 746: DD17

▶Locator: Take the first R turn on Floodwood Rd. at 0.3 mi and proceed along a golf course to arrive at the edge of the woods. Turn L and drive 0.1 mi down the gravel road to a parking area by the canoe put-in on Hoel Pond. (In winter, it is necessary to park carefully by the turn and ski or snowshoe the 0.1 mi to the put-in.) Paddle NW approximately 1.5 mi to a railroad embankment. Carry over it to Turtle Pond. A paddle NW to nearly the end of the pond leads to the start of the trail marked with a small DEC canoe carry sign on the shore R.◀

The trail leaves the pond (0.0 mi) among impressive white pines. At 0.1 mi, the trail passes a Norway spruce plantation, and at 0.3 mi it passes large native red spruce as it crosses a swamp on corduroy. A large beaver vlei is to the L. The trail then ascends a hill crowned with mature birch and sugar maple at 0.5 mi before starting a descent to reach the conifer-rimmed shores of Clamshell Pond at 1.3 mi. An abundance of freshwater mussels gave this pond its name.

❄ Trail in winter: May be used as the last segment of an extended cross-country ski round-trip across Hoel and Turtle Ponds. The terrain on the carry trail is rugged, and caution should be exercised.

🔆 Distances: In summer, Turtle Pond to corduroy, 0.3 mi; to Clamshell Pond, 1.3 mi (2.1 km). In winter, Hoel Pond put-in to railroad embankment, 1.5 mi; to Turtle Pond trailhead, 2.5 mi; to Clamshell Pond, 3.8 mi (6.1 km).

View from St. Regis Mountain. Stephanie Graudons

Paul Smiths Section

Paul Smith's College, noted for its forestry and hotel management programs, is the site of the Adirondack Park Visitor Interpretive Center (VIC) with its network of trails, and an attractive nature trail on the grounds of the college. In addition, there is a small series of trails in the St. Regis Canoe Area surrounding the college. The St. Regis Canoe Area embraces over 18,000 acres and is essentially managed as a Wilderness Area. These trails link the area's glacial ponds and one ascends a modest but dramatic mountain. The isolated Azure Mt. is also included in this section.

A few suggested hikes for this section are listed below.

SHORT HIKE
Azure Mt.: 2 mi (3.2 km) round-trip. A short but steep ascent leads to an open summit with marvelous long-distance views in all directions from the restored fire tower. See trail 136.

MODERATE HIKE
Fish Pond Truck Trail: 10.2 mi (16.3 km) round-trip. This nearly level route is intersected by several canoe carries leading to the shores of ponds in the St. Regis Canoe Area. See trail 130.

HARDER HIKE
St. Regis Mt.: 6.8 mi (10.9 km) round-trip. A strenuous climb is rewarded with superb panoramas of peaks and ponds. See trail 135.

130 Fish Pond Truck Trail

Trails Illustrated Map 746: DD17

This is a former state truck trail now barred to vehicular traffic in conformity with the State Land Master Plan. The unmarked but easily followed DEC trail, mainly undulating with one moderately steep section, goes through the heart of the St. Regis Canoe Area to a wild, remote lake fashioned by the last retreating glacier.

▶Trailhead: Access is from Fish Hatchery Rd., a short loop road that leaves NY 30 11.3 mi N of its intersection with NY 3 at Wawbeek Corners. A marked DEC trailhead is on the L here. Turn L off the loop road, then L again at the railroad crossing. Proceed about 0.5 mi past numbered campsites to a R turn; the truck trail gate is just ahead to the L of the parking lot.◀

The trail begins (0.0 mi) by passing through an area of mature yellow birch with young conifers coming in underneath. The route passes large white pines at 1 mi, and crosses a beaver pond just above the dam at 1.3 mi. Beaver activity is common along this trail, but since most of the crossings are over culverts on the former truck route, flooding is not usually a problem.

At 1.6 mi, the trail passes through a spruce-cedar swamp and shortly thereafter begins to ascend, reaching a height at 2 mi. At 2.2 mi a large grey bedrock outcrop is on the L. The trail now makes a gradual descent. On the R at 2.6 mi is the first of many side trails serving primarily as canoe carries to some of the ancillary ponds of the area. This is the carry to St. Regis Pond (trail 131). At 2.8 mi, another trail comes in on the L. This is the carry to Grass Pond (trail 132). At 3.2 mi the canoe carry to Ochre Pond (trail 133) comes in on the R. These three relatively short canoe carry trails are described below.

The trail continues ahead. At 3.5 mi it begins to descend more steeply from the ridge it has been travelling. Large specimens of sugar maple are in evidence for the first time on the well-drained soil of the ridge. At 3.8 mi, two large gravel pits on the L provided the material for the truck trail. This truck trail was originally paved, at least rudimentarily, and remnants of some paving stones can occasionally be noted.

At 4.8 mi, a ridge comes into view on the R. Directly behind the ridge lies the enchanting Mud Pond—from which another canoe carry trail also leads to Fish Pond.

At 5.1 mi, the trail reaches Fish Pond. Fish Pond is set amid gorgeous surroundings, with several campsites nearby. There are two lean-tos on the shores of Fish Pond—one to the L of the trail and the other across the lake on the far shore. There is a beaver dam R at the inlet of the bay on which the trail terminates. All around this shore are large specimens of hemlock, while on the far shore white pines line the pond.

❊ Trail in winter: Well suited, and heavily used, for cross-country skiing. The way is wide and usually well cleared, with a steep, twisting ascent and descents toward the middle.

🚶 Distances: Gate to beaver pond, 1.3 mi; to St. Regis Pond Carry, 2.6 mi; to Grass Pond Carry, 2.8 mi; to Ochre Pond Carry, 3.2 mi; to Fish Pond, 5.1 mi (8.2 km).

131 St. Regis Pond Canoe Carry

Trails Illustrated Map 746: DD17

This canoe carry begins on Fish Pond Truck Trail (trail 130). It proceeds through majestic stands of trees to reach a remote, jewel-like body of water lying in a magnificent scenic setting.

▶Locator: At 2.6 mi on Fish Pond Truck Trail (trail 130).◀

The trail departs from Fish Pond Truck Trail to the R (0.0 mi) and leads through a mixed forest to a quiet bay of St. Regis Pond, which is rimmed mostly by mature spruce and pine. A DEC fish barrier dam is across the outlet at the point where it flows out of this bay. Above this dam the native brook trout has its main habitat, and the dam's primary function is to prevent non-native, so-called "warm water" fish from entering the trout waters and probably out-competing the native fish.

❋ Trail in winter: Suited for cross-country skiing as a brief side trip.

🚶 Distance: Truck trail to St. Regis Pond, 0.2 mi (0.3 km).

132 Grass Pond Canoe Carry

Trails Illustrated Map 746: DD17

Like the trails to St. Regis and Ochre Ponds (trails 131 and 133), this canoe carry begins on Fish Pond Truck Trail (trail 130) and travels through majestic stands of trees. Grass Pond is in a magnificent scenic setting.

▶Locator: At 2.8 mi on Fish Pond Truck Trail (trail 130).◀

The trail proceeds L off Fish Pond Truck Trail (0.0 mi) through a hardwood forest with a heavy undergrowth of hobblebush lining both sides of the trail. It descends slightly to arrive on the shore of Grass Pond at 0.5 mi. Large white pines are on the shore, and a rim of sedges encircles the pond. A large spruce swamp is visible across the pond at its S end.

❋ Trail in winter: Suited for cross-country skiing as a brief side trip.

🚶 Distance: Truck trail to Grass Pond, 0.5 mi (0.8 km).

133 Ochre Pond Canoe Carry

Trails Illustrated Map 746: DD17

Like the two canoe carries above, this trail begins on Fish Pond Truck Trail (trail 130). The pond is in a magnificent, remote setting.

▶Locator: At 3.2 mi on Fish Pond Truck Trail (trail 130).◀

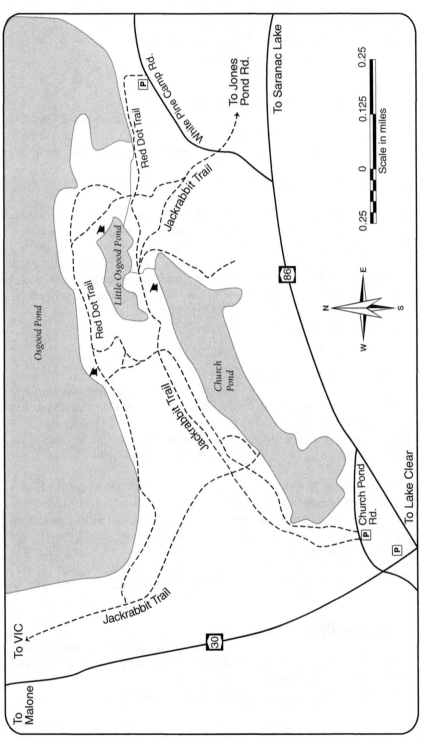

Red Dot Trail map

The trail begins on the R from Fish Pond Truck Trail (trail 130), with monarch specimens of white pine on its R (0.0 mi). At 0.2 mi, a glacial boulder is enveloped by the roots of a large yellow birch (R). This situation probably originated seventy-five or more years ago when a seed germinated on the moss that lay atop the boulder. At 0.3 mi, Ochre Pond, rimmed with large white pine, is framed by St. Regis and Little St. Regis Mts. looming above it.

❋ Trail in winter: Suited for cross-country skiing as a brief side trip.

⚹ Distance: Fish Pond Truck Trail to Ochre Pond, 0.3 mi (0.5 km).

134 Red Dot Trail

Trails Illustrated Map 746: FF18 | P. 190

Red Dot Trail is in fact a group of maze-like trails owned by Paul Smith's College. With three lean-tos (for day use), several small ponds, canals, benches, and bridges, these trails are fun to explore. Surrounded as one is by roads and lakes there is little possibility of becoming lost for long. Students from Paul Smith's College use this area to camp, run, hike, and enjoy nature.

▶Trailhead: Access is possible from two locations. The W trailhead is off Church Pond Rd., a gravel road going NE from NY 30 approximately 0.1mi N of its intersection with NY 86 at the Paul Smith's College entrance. Cars can be parked in front of the church. From the parking area at the church there are two trails leading into the woods. The trail L is plain but unmarked and is the preferred route for skiers. The yellow paint-marked trail (described here) starts 100 yd to the R at a sign on the L.

The E access is on White Pine Camp Rd., which heads L (NE) 1 mi E of the intersection of NY 30 and NY 86. It is approximately 0.4 mi to the Osgood Pond Waterway Access site on the L. Parking is in the lot adjacent to the road. The trail starts at the register S of a boat ramp. There is a DEC sign with a map of the trails here. ◀

Starting at the Church Pond trailhead (0.0 mi), the trail is marked with yellow paint blazes as it enters the forest and descends to a bench on the shore of Church Pond. At 0.2 mi the trail comes to a jct. A sign indicates that the Red Dot Trail lies straight ahead and Cathedral Pines is to the R. (The trail R leads down to another bench on the shore of Church Pond, after which a vaguer trail with red marks continues along the shore to Cathedral Pines before turning L and up to rejoin the main trail. A L turn at the jct. at 0.2 mi takes one in a few hundred feet to a jct. on Jackrabbit Ski Trail.)

Continuing straight through this jct., at 0.3 mi Red Dot Trail comes to a side trail R, which is the other end of the loop through the imposing group of white pines clustered together and known locally as "Cathedral Pines." The yellow paint–marked trail proceeds straight ahead to another jct. at 0.5 mi. This is the start of the Red Dot Loop segment of the trail network. The Jackrabbit Ski Trail joins from the L. (To the L the Jackrabbit Trail parallels Red Dot Trail for 0.3 mi.

to a jct. with the alternate approach from the church parking area and then turns R to reach the VIC in about 1 mi.)   Although the loop can be hiked in either direction, this description assumes a turn R at this jct.

At 0.7 mi, the trail reaches a lean-to on the shore of Church Pond R. The forest here is impressive, with many mature white and red pine, hemlock, and white birch. The trail crosses a small wooden bridge over a canal between Church and Little Osgood Ponds at 0.8 mi. Jackrabbit Ski Trail continues straight, along with another yellow paint–marked spur trail. Jackrabbit Trail (with Jackrabbit Trail markers) reaches White Pine Camp Rd. in 0.2 mi, crosses it, and continues E. The yellow spur branches R along the shore of Church Pond, reaching the Paul Smith's College faculty gardens and soccer fields in 0.2 mi.

Red Dot Trail continues L along the canal and then the shore of Little Osgood Pond to a second canal and then another bridge at 0.9 mi. Locally called "Paul Smith's Canal," the canal was constructed early in the twentieth century to link the waters of Osgood Pond with the St. Regis lakes. There is a four-way jct. at the bridge. (Straight ahead leads in 0.3 mi to the alternate trailhead on White Pine Camp Rd. at the Osgood Pond Waterway Access.) Red Dot Trail turns L, crosses the bridge, and proceeds to a lean-to L on Little Osgood Pond at 1.1 mi.

Past the lean-to, Red Dot Trail continues on an esker overlooking Osgood Pond until at 1.4 mi a branch R leads in several yd to a lean-to on Osgood Pond. (A yellow paint–marked trail continues from this lean-to along the shore and in 0.4 mi reaches a jct. with the Jackrabbit Ski Trail/Old Military Rd.) The L branch leads to a sign at 1.5 mi. This sign, directed at hikers following the loop in the other direction, indicates "Osgood Pond Lean-to" with an arrow pointing straight ahead, and "Red Trail" with an arrow R. Hikers in their haste to reach the lean-to have made a shortcut here, creating a circle.

At 1.6 mi, the trail reaches the yellow spur trail from the start point (see above) and the Jackrabbit Ski Trail. Continuing straight on the yellow spur trail here leads back to the trailhead at 2 mi.

❋ Trail in winter: Suitable for cross-country skiing and snowshoeing, often used by students of the college.

🐾 Distances: Church Pond Rd. to first jct., 0.2 mi; to lean-to on Church Pond, 0.7 mi; to lean-to on Little Osgood Pond, 1.1 mi; to completion of loop, 1.6 mi; to W trailhead, 2 mi (3.2 km).

135 St. Regis Mt.

Trails Illustrated Map 746: EE17

This DEC red-marked trail makes a relatively short, steep climb to the summit of an isolated northern Adirondack peak with magnificent views in nearly all directions. A fire tower, now restored (2016), dominates the top.

▶Trailhead: From the main entrance to Paul Smith's College at the intersection of NY 30 and 86, drive N on NY 30 about 200 yd and then W (L) on Keese Mills Rd. Proceed 2.6 mi to an ample DEC parking lot on the L, just beyond a gravel road leading L to Camp Topridge, the former estate of Marjorie Merriweather Post. Park in the designated parking lot, and not along the private Topridge Rd. ◀

Leaving the parking lot (0.0 mi), walk S down Topridge Rd., which immediately crosses the St. Regis River on a narrow metal bridge. At 0.1 mi the DEC-marked trail diverges to the R and passes a trail register a few yards into the woods. The trail begins an ascent through mature second growth, with brief level sections at 0.2 and 0.4 mi.

The trail switchbacks sharply L at 0.7 mi and reaches a height of land at 1 mi in an impressive stand of large hemlocks. It now begins a gradual descent, reaches a low point at 1.5 mi, and resumes a gradual ascent. At 1.8 mi, a metal pipe and cairn L mark the boundary between the Franklin County towns of Brighton and Santa Clara.

The trail crosses a perennial brook on a sturdy wooden bridge at 2.2 mi. Some 35 yd beyond the bridge, a side trail L leads 35 yd to an open grassy campsite, the site of the former DEC fire tower observer's cabin. The main trail soon begins to rise more steeply. Between here and the summit, note impressive water bars, stepping stones, and rock cribs constructed by Paul Smith's forestry students.

At 3.2 mi, the trail passes enormous boulders. At 3.3 mi, a path R leads 20 yd to open bedrock and views W. The mostly bare summit at 3.4 mi is dominated by the fire tower. The bareness of the summit and the presence of white birch attest to the work of surveyors under Verplanck Colvin, who in the late 1800s cleared several Adirondack summits to facilitate Colvin's survey work. A few stunted spruce and fir are present on the top, along with mountain ash.

The High Peaks, along with Mt. McKenzie and the Seward Range, can be seen to the S. Directly below is a stunning expanse of lakes and ponds in the St. Regis Canoe Area. Eastward is the pointed top of Whiteface Mt., with Esther Mt. to its L. Slightly to the NE the isolated peaks of DeBar and Loon Lake Mountains stand out clearly.

❀ Trail in winter: A fine summit for snowshoers. Steepness in the last mile will discourage all but the most skillful backcountry skiers.

❧ Distances: Parking area to height of land, 1 mi; to bridge, 2.2 mi; to fire tower, 3.4 mi (5.4 km). Ascent, 1266 ft (386 m). Elevation, 2874 ft (876 m).

136 Azure Mt.

Trails Illustrated Map 746: HH14

This is another short, steep climb to one of the isolated northern Adirondack peaks that usually stand in a sea of green forest. The restored fire tower provides long-distance views in all directions.

▶Trailhead: Access to this DEC red-marked trail is from Blue Mountain Rd., which goes S from NY 458 approximately 4 mi S of St. Regis Falls and 3 mi N of the hamlet of Santa Clara. Proceed approximately 7 mi S until a dirt road comes in on the R. It is 0.1 mi down the dirt road to a gate, room to park a few cars on

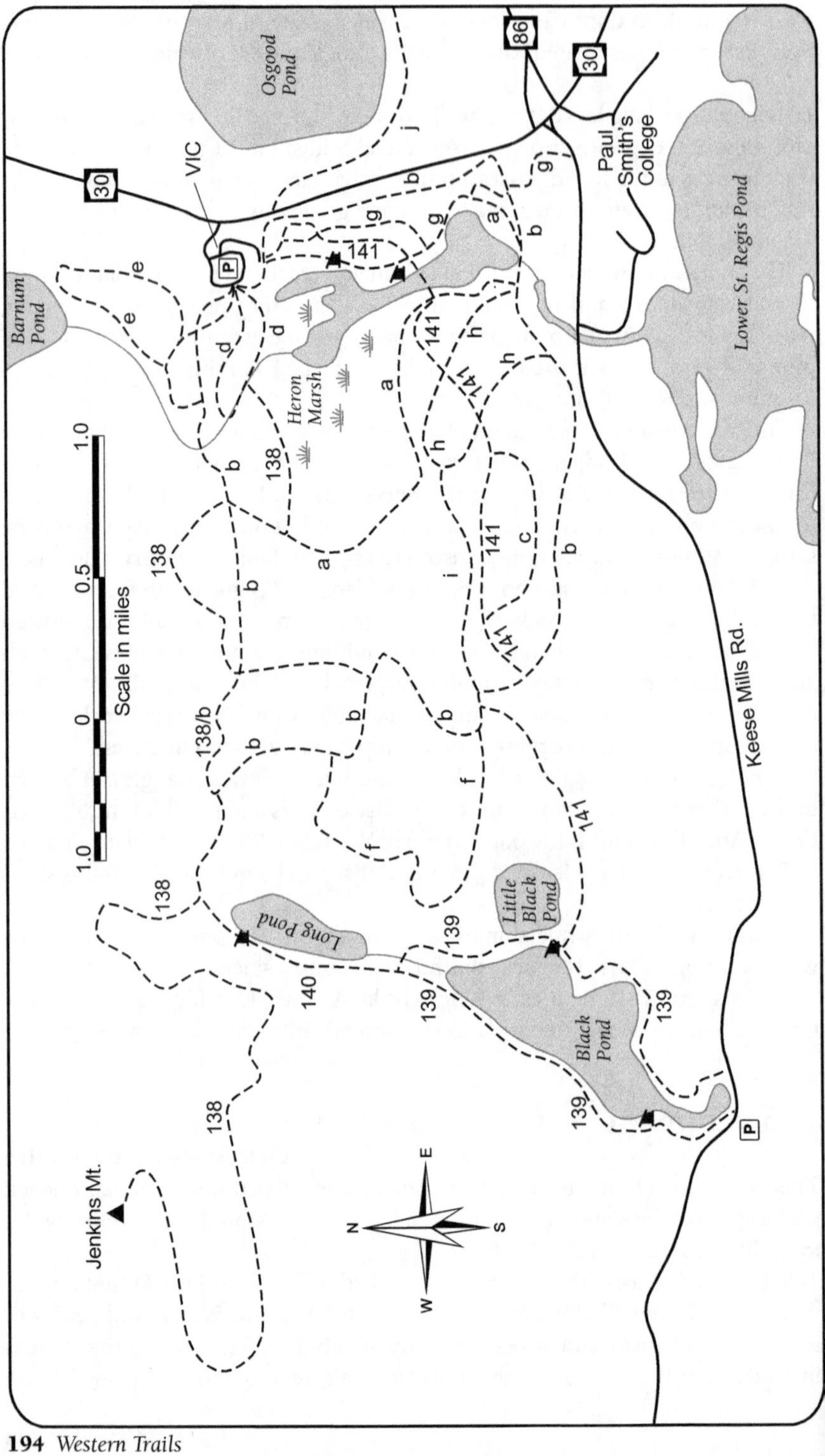

Osgood Pond

86

30

Paul Smith's College

VIC

30

Barnium Pond

e e
e
e
d d
d
Heron Marsh

g
141
g g a
b
b
a
g
j

Lower St. Regis Pond

138

138

138/b

138

b

b

b

a

a

i

h

h

h

h

141

141

141

141

c

b

Scale in miles
1.0   0.5   0   1.0

Jenkins Mt.

N
E
W
S

b

b

f

f

b

f

140

Long Pond

139

39

Little Black Pond

Black Pond

139

139

141

139

Keese Mills Rd.

...Center Paul Smiths

P

the L, and the start of the trail. ◀

The trail begins at the gate (0.0 mi) and rises almost imperceptibly, reaching a shallow stream and the site of the fire observer's cabin at 0.3 mi. The trail now begins to climb more steeply, passing through a pole-sized maple grove with occasional white ash. At 0.5 mi both white and yellow birch begin to appear. This usually indicates a past burn.

The trail now starts to weave in and out of an eroded herd path that proceeds straight up the slope of the mountain at a perpendicular axis to the fall line. The trail crisscrosses the old herd path for the rest of the steep pitch and eventually reaches the crest of the hill at 0.9 mi, with the open summit slightly beyond at 1 mi.

The tower is open thanks to the efforts of the Azure Mt. Friends, who provide volunteer summit interpreters on weekends and holidays from May to October. Whiteface, Mt. Marcy, and the Sewards are clearly seen to the S and SE; DeBar Mt. looms large to the E, while below lie shimmering ponds. To the N the farm lands and settlements of the St. Lawrence Valley can be discerned. A walk W along the top of cliffs on the S side of the summit leads to an impressive glacial erratic perched on the verge of the precipice.

❃ Trail in winter: Unsuitable for skis owing to steepness, but a good snowshoe hike.

🐾 Distance: Blue Mountain Rd. to summit, 1 mi (1.6 km). Ascent, 944 ft (288 m). Elevation, 2518 ft (767 m).

137 Visitor Interpretive Center Trails and Cross-Country Ski Trails

Trails Illustrated Map 746: FF18 | P. 194

The Visitor Interpretive Center (VIC), which portrays and interprets the many facets of the Adirondack Park, was opened at Paul Smiths in 1988. A smaller visitor center was subsequently opened in Newcomb in the central Adirondacks. The VIC at Paul Smiths is L off NY 30 approximately 0.2 mi N of Paul Smith's College and the NY 30/86 intersection.

The center is located in a handsome, spacious building erected as a replica of one of the traditional Great Camps for which the Adirondacks were renowned. A full spectrum of historical and ecological displays pertinent to the Adirondacks is featured at the center, which is open year-round and run by Paul Smith's College.

An interconnecting network of interpretive trails emanates from the main building to make loops of assorted length through the scenic glacial topography that abounds at the center. During the winter months, trails at the VIC are groomed and open for cross-country skiing, skate skiing, and snowshoeing. There is a fee for trail use in the winter.

Brief synopses of the VIC trails' outstanding features are below. Jenkins Mt.,

Black Pond, Long Pond, and Woods and Waters Trails (trails 138–141), which interconnect with several of these trails, are also part of the VIC. Detailed trail information may be obtained from maps and materials at the VIC.

The following trails are reached from the same area behind the VIC main building. Several of the trails intersect.

❊ Trails in winter: Groomed for snowshoeing, classic cross-country skiing, or skate skiing. Generally easy to moderate in difficulty with only a few fairly steep downhill sections.

(a) Heron Marsh Trail—3 mi (4.8 km)
The trail crosses a 900 ft boardwalk over Heron Marsh, a natural wetland whose size was increased by a dam erected mainly for wildlife purposes by Paul Smith's College. The trail passes an enchanting natural waterfall, an abandoned home site, and scenic vistas.

(b) Loggers Loop—6 mi loop (9.6 km)
One of the longer loops, this interconnected series of logging roads and trails may be muddy when wet. The 0.5 mi Fox Run Trail branches off, offering skiers an alternative to steep sections on this trail.

(c) Silvi Trail—1 mi (1.6 km)
Starting at a point on the Woods and Waters Trail (trail 167), this trail traverses the former golf course of the Paul Smith's Hotel. Trees have been planted along the route by students of Paul Smith's College.

(d) Barnum Brook Trail—1 mi (1.6 km)
This wheelchair-accessible loop provides views of a beaver lodge and Heron Marsh.

(e) Boreal Life Trail—1 mi (1.6 km)
The trail passes through a forest of spruce, fir, pine, hemlock, cedar, tamarack, and white pine; crosses a spruce swamp and bog on a 1600 ft boardwalk; and offers glimpses of several kinds of orchids and year-round boreal birding.

(f) Esker Trail—1.5 mi (2.4 km)
A loop off the Logger's Loop (b), the trail climbs quickly up a sequence of switchbacks to a scenic vista. Ski the trail clockwise to best navigate steep terrain.

(g) Bobcat Trail—1.3 mi (2.1 km)
The trail can be accessed from the VIC or from Keese Mills Rd. It connects the main VIC building with the Paul Smith's College campus.

(h) Easy Street Trail—1 mi (1.6 km)
As the name implies, this is an easy walk through mostly open hardwoods.

(i) Skidder Trail—1 mi (1.6 km)
This trail passes through managed hardwood and softwood forest.

(j) Jackrabbit Ski Trail
The VIC is currently the NW terminus of a 9 mi section of the Jackrabbit Ski Trail that starts at Lake Clear Jct.; it may someday be connected to an extension that runs from Saranac Lake to Tupper Lake via Lake Clear Jct.

The trail leaves from the staff parking lot SE of the main building. A sign at this point indicates 1 mi to White Pine Rd., 3.5 mi to NY 86, and 9 mi to Lake Clear Jct. The trail is marked with special red Jackrabbit Ski Trail markers and yellow DEC ski trail markers after NY 86.

Paul Smith's VIC. Gerry Lemmo

The trail reaches and crosses NY 30 in 0.1 mi. It then passes through a small wood and enters a large pasture area surrounding a barn. Crossing the pasture, it comes to a gate at 0.2 mi. The trail follows Old Military Rd. and bears R at a jct. at 0.4 mi. (The trail L leads to Osgood Pond.)

The Jackrabbit Trail reaches a four-way jct. at 0.7 mi. (A short spur to Paul Smith's College goes R.) Turning L the trail parallels Red Dot Trail before meeting Red Dot Trail (trail 134) at 1 mi. Now the same as the Red Dot Trail, the Jackrabbit Trail descends to the lean-to on Church Pond and crosses the canal on a bridge. It soon parts R from Red Dot Trail and crosses White Pine Rd.

Past White Pine Rd. the trail is mostly level for 0.2 mi to a L turn onto a wide road. The road narrows after another 0.2 mi and Jackrabbit Trail follows a rolling course to Jones Pond Rd. at 2.6 mi. Past Jones Pond Rd., the trail eventually climbs to a crossing of NY 86 at 3.3 mi. Past NY 86 the trail follows an old road on the flat to an old clearing, then narrows and follows another rolling profile to a jct. with a wide, fresh lumber road at 4.6 mi.

The mostly flat road reaches a power line at 5.8 mi, where Jackrabbit Trail turns sharp L. The trail follows the power line, which is also the road bed of the long-abandoned Paul Smiths Electric Railway. This mostly straight, flat route crosses the road to the Harrietstown Transfer Station, and a side road leading L to Charlie's Inn. Continuing to follow the power line, the Jackrabbit Trail reaches a trail marker denoting a sharp R turn to the southern trailhead on NY 30 at 8.8 mi. This trailhead is 0.3 mi N of the jct. of NY 30 and NY 186 and across the highway from the currently unused Lake Clear Elementary School.

138 Jenkins Mt.

Trails Illustrated Map 746: FF18 | P. 194

This trail leaves the access road for the Adirondack Park Visitor Interpretive Center (VIC) and, after passing through the Forest Ecosystem Research and Demonstration Area of Paul Smith's College, reaches the top of Jenkins Mt. at 4.3 mi.

▶Trailhead: Access is from the VIC, which is L off NY 30 approximately 0.2 mi N of Paul Smith's College and the NY 30/86 intersection. Parking is in the lot N of the main building. To reach the trailhead from the parking lot, return along the entrance road to the junction with a gated access road to the W. ◀

A trail register is located N of the trail shortly past the gate (0.0 mi). The blue-marked trail starts through mixed hardwoods and pines on an old logging road with gentle grades, reaching the outlet of Blue Heron Marsh at 0.4 mi.

The wide trail now starts a slight climb, reaching the first sign for the Forest Ecosystem and Research Demonstration Area at 0.5 mi. Several of these signs appear before the trail reaches a clear-cut area at 0.7 mi, with a view of Jenkins Mt. to the W.

The trail now descends through mostly pines. The trail continues W, crossing a small creek at 1.4 mi with another view of Jenkins Mt. to the W. At 1.5 mi, the red-marked Long Pond Trail (trail 140) enters from the L (S). This is an alternate route of access to Jenkins Mt., from Keese Mills Rd.

The trail now begins its climbs to the top of an esker. Eskers are made up of sand and gravel deposited by a stream running under a glacier. When the glacier melts, the sand and gravel remain in a pile, much like the pile of dirt that is left from mole activity when winter snows melt. At this point, this esker is braided with many branches.

The trail makes a short jog S and starts a steep climb through mixed hardwoods. Turing N again, the trail continues on a branch of the esker, then turns W, cutting through the esker at 1.8 mi. To the N of the trail is a depression in the esker, called a kettle hole. Kettle holes are caused by blocks of ice trapped in the sand and gravel of the esker that, after melting, leave depressions with no outlet. The trail turns S past an outhouse and passes several kettle lakes, which are kettle holes filled with water. At 1.9 mi, with a kettle lake to the W, the trail leaves the logging road and follows the top of the esker between ponds. At a break in the esker, the trail drops into a small stream and crosses a bridge at 2 mi with a beaver dam to the W (R). The trail climbs back to the top of the esker and continues S through pines and mixed hardwoods. It leaves the esker, turning W and reaching the base of Jenkins Mt. at 2.5 mi.

The trail now climbs and drops, skirting the base of the mountain as it proceeds W. At 3.4 mi, it turns N and starts a steep climb, reaching a ridge at 3.5 mi. The trail climbs the N side of the ridge through glades of hardwoods and pines, passing under the summit to the S and E and then making a switchback toward the NW before reaching the top of Jenkins Mt. at 4.3 mi. Views from the top include Whiteface to the E; the High Peaks to the SE; Spectacle Ponds, Spitfire Lake, Upper and Lower St. Regis Lakes, and Upper Saranac Lake arrayed to the S; St. Regis Mt., distinguishable by its fire tower, to the SW; and Follensby Junior Pond to the NW.

❄ Trail in winter: This is part of the cross-country trail system at the VIC. Until steep stretches at the base of Jenkins Mt., it is well-suited for cross-country skiing.

⋈ Distances: Gate at trailhead to Forest Ecosystem Research and Demonstration Area, 0.5 mi; to jct. with Long Pond Trail, 1.5 mi; to end of logging road, 1.9 mi; to steep climbing, 3.4 mi; to top of Jenkins Mt., 4.3 mi (6.9 km). Ascent, 840 ft (256 m). Elevation, 2513 ft (766 m).

139 Black Pond Trail

Trails Illustrated Map 746: FF18 | P. 194

This trail can be hiked as a loop around Black Pond with two lean-tos for scenic stops. The lean-tos are for day use only. The final 0.1 mi of the loop is on Keese Mills Rd. This trail, when combined with Long Pond Trail (trail 140), connects to the Jenkins Mt. trail (trail 138) for an alternate route to Jenkins Mt. A second connection to the VIC trails can be made using the Woods and Waters Trail (trail 141).

▶Trailhead: Access is from Keese Mills Rd., which goes L (W) just N of the jct. of NY 30 and NY 86 at Paul Smiths. Follow Keese Mills Rd. for 2.5 mi. The parking lot just past the former St. Regis Presbyterian Church on the N (R) side of the road has room for approximately ten cars. ◀

The orange-marked trail starts (0.0 mi) among large pines with a canoe put-in branching to the R (E). The trail follows Black Pond's W shore through mixed hardwoods and pines, reaching the base of a large esker at 0.1 mi. Following the base of the esker with glimpses of a large picturesque rock outcrop on the E shore, the trail reaches a small bridge at 0.2 mi. A view to Black Pond now opens up and the trail passes a lean-to that sits on a point with a nice vista of the pond. Lean-tos in this area are for day use only.

The trail continues N close to the pond's shore and at the base of the esker. At 0.6 mi, a view across the lake opens and a bridge that spans the small passage to Little Black Pond can be seen. The trail crosses a small bridge over an incoming stream at 0.7 mi and reaches a rough dock and take-out for the 0.3 mi carry to Long Pond at 0.9 mi. The trail continues N along the side of the outlet of Long Pond, reaching a jct. with Long Pond Trail (trail 140) at 1 mi.

The orange-marked Black Pond Trail continues E (R) from the jct., crossing a fish barrier dam on the outlet of Long Pond. It then turns S (R), reaching a steep section and a high point with an attractive area of hemlocks and pines at 1.3 mi. The trail now drops to a bridge across a narrows between Black Pond and Little Back Pond at 1.4 mi. A lean-to is located just across the bridge under large pines on a point, giving an enchanting view of Black Pond and Jenkins Mt. At this point Woods and Waters Trail (trail 141) heads inland to the SE, following an old road.

Black Pond Trail continues S, occasionally crossing boardwalks along the E shore of Black Pond. At 1.6 mi, it comes to a point with a bench and then skirts a wet bay and reaches a high point at 2.2 mi. It now drops to a large, smooth outcrop of bedrock reaching down to the water of the narrow outlet. The trail continues to the S and reaches Keese Mills Rd. at 2.4 mi. To the R (W) along the road, the parking lot is at 2.5 mi.

✢ Trail in winter: Black Pond Trail on the W side of Black Pond and Long Pond Trail (trail 140), though narrow in places, could be used as a ski and snowshoe route to connect to the Jenkins Mt. trail (trail 141). The E side of the trail is not suitable for skiing owing to narrowness and steepness in spots. Use of the groomed trail is subject to a trail fee (see Visitor Interpretive Center Trails, trail 137).

🚶 Distances: Keese Mills Rd. parking area to first lean-to, 0.2 mi; to jct. with Long Pond Trail, 1 mi; to bridge and E side lean-to, 1.4 mi; to Keese Mills Rd., 2.4 mi; to parking area, 2.5 mi (4 km).

140 Long Pond Trail

Trails Illustrated Map 746: FF18 | P. 194

This trail connects the N end of Black Pond Trail (trail 139) to the Jenkins Mt. trail (trail 138) along the W shore of Long Pond.

▶Locator: S end of Long Pond Trail starts at the 1 mi mark of Black Pond Trail (trail 139); N end is at the 1.5 mi mark on the Jenkins Mt. trail (trail 138).◀

Long Pond Trail departs from Black Pond Trail (trail 139) at a point where the latter turns R and begins its return to Keese Mills Rd. (0.0 mi). It continues N to Long Pond at 0.1 mi and Beaver Lodge Lean-to at 0.4 mi. This lean-to is located on the NW shore of Long Pond and has a dock that extends into the pond. The lean-to is for day use only. The trail meets the Jenkins Mt. trail (trail 138) at 0.7 mi, providing an alternate access route to the mountain.

✢ Trail in winter: See Black Pond Trail (trail 139).

🚶 Distances: Black Pond Trail to Beaver Lodge Lean-to, 0.4 mi; to Jenkins Mt. trail, 0.7 mi (1.1 km).

141 Woods and Waters Trail

Trails Illustrated Map 746: FF18 | P. 194

This trail passes through hardwood and conifer forests and traverses a floating bridge across a marsh. It connects Black Pond Trail (trail 139) to the network of trails emanating from the Visitor Interpretive Center (VIC; see trail 137) with many loops possible when combined with other VIC trails. The trail passes through an area that was heavily lumbered in 2014 but remains easily passable.

▶Trailheads: The E trailhead is at the VIC (see trail 137). The W trailhead is at Little Black Pond Lean-to on the E side of Black Pond Trail (trail 139). (The former trailhead on Keese Mills Rd. has been closed.) The Black Pond Trail trailhead is on Keese Mills Rd., 2.5 mi W of its jct. with NY 30 just N of the jct. with NY 86. There is a small parking area on the R side of the road. The E side of Black Pond Trail starts 100 yd back to the E from the parking lot. The trail is described here from the W trailhead.◀

From the jct. with Black Pond Trail (0.0 mi), the trail heads SE on an old road, reaching a jct. at 0.1 mi with a now-closed old road. It turns E (L) and continues on a road that soon enters a recently logged area. After crossing two logging roads, the trail passes through old clearings with young pioneering pines and at 0.8 mi reaches a jct. with Loggers Loop of the VIC (trail 137b), a well-used service road.

Turning R on Loggers Loop, Woods and Waters Trail bears R in 50 yd where Skidder Trail (trail 137i) goes straight. In another 0.1 mi Woods and Waters Trail leaves the service road to the L (NW) and starts to climb, reaching a jct. with Silvi Trail (trail 137c) at 1.2 mi.

Continuing straight, Woods and Waters Trail reaches a second jct. with Silvi Trail at 1.8 mi. Continuing straight again, the trail crosses two branches of Easy Street (trail 137h) and reaches a jct. with Heron Marsh Trail (trail 137a) at the floating bridge at 2.3 mi. After crossing the bridge, the trail continues to the VIC's main building at 2.8 mi.

❋ Trail in winter: Suitable for winter travel and may be groomed for skiing as far as Little Black Pond Lean-to. Use of the groomed trail is subject to a trail fee.

❀ Distances: Little Black Pond Lean-to to Loggers Loop, 0.8 mi; to Silvi Trail, 1.2 mi; to VIC main building and E trailhead, 2.8 mi (4.5 km).

Boreal forests. Joanne Kennedy

DeBar Mt. Wild Forest Section

The sprawling DeBar Mt. Wild Forest, which stretches from just N of Paul Smiths to the boundary of the Adirondack Park, is framed in its main section by the twin pinnacles of DeBar and Baldface Mountains. The summits of these wild and aloof peaks—one marked, one a bushwhack—are prominent features of the hikes in this section.

From the base of these two sentinels an almost uninterrupted boreal forest unfurls in all directions as far as the eye can register. Bogs and swamps are common, ponds and lakes less so, especially in contrast to the St. Regis Canoe Area and Saranac Lake Wild Forest to the S. There are some, however, and several of the trails have them as their destination. Meandering streams and pine-clad eskers are also prominent in the terrain traversed by the trails.

Two short trails in the isolated Everton Falls Preserve are also included in this section (see trails 142 and 143).

A popular DEC campground is located at Meacham Lake.

A suggested hike for this section is listed below.

MODERATE HIKE
Sheep Meadow and Hays Brook Truck Trail: 6.6 mi (10.6 km) round-trip. An easy walk ending in a charming clearing surrounded by mountains. See trail 170.

Trail Described		Total Miles (one way)		Page
142	Hardwood Trail	0.6	(1.0 km)	203
143	Balsam Trail	0.2	(0.3 km)	204
144	Sheep Meadow and Hays Brook Truck Trail	3.3	(5.3 km)	204
145	Grass Pond	1.4	(2.2 km)	205
146	Slush Pond Ski Trail	2.5	(4.0 km)	206
147	Kettle Trail	3.2	(5.1 km)	206
148	DeBar Game Mgmt. Area Trail	6.4	(10.2 km)	207
149	DeBar Mt.	2.6	(4.2 km)	209

142 Hardwood Trail

Trails Illustrated Map 746: KK16

This is a short loop through a regenerating forest near Everton Falls, a 530 acre nature preserve that straddles the East Branch of the St. Regis River on the N edge of the Adirondack Park. Acquired by the Adirondack Nature Conservancy in 1974 and maintained by volunteers, including members of ADK's Laurentian Chapter, it takes its name from a nineteenth-century logging hamlet that thrived at that location. The tract also offers canoe access to a scenic 9 mi stretch of still water above the falls, an 18 ft series of plunges over rock ledges, and a 0.8 mi float below the falls before another series of rapids.

▶Trailhead: Hardwood Trail begins on CR 14, approximately 7.6 mi W of its intersection with NY 30 at Duane Corners. The trailhead is also approximately 6.9 mi E of St. Regis Falls; the sign for CR 14 identifies it as Duane Rd. where it heads E from CR 5/North Main St., opposite the abandoned school in St. Regis Falls. Look for a small gravel parking area with a DEC sign on the N side of the road, about 100 yd E of the falls, which can be seen on the S side of the road just W of the parking area. Interpretive brochures are sometimes available at the DEC trail register here, or from the Conservancy at 518-576-2082.◀

The trail is marked with green triangles bearing the Nature Conservancy's oak leaf emblem. It starts at a post at the SE corner of the parking lot (0.0 mi). The trail parallels the road, then at less than 0.1 mi turns L at the head of a beaver pond. The trail skirts the pond, which is in the process of filling with vegetation.

The trail bends back to reach the parking area at 0.6 mi. In this mixed hardwood forest that is regenerating after years of intensive logging, the dominant species are black cherry, yellow birch, red and sugar maple, and American beech, with some balsam fir evident, especially in low areas. Lichens, ferns, shrubs, and ground-cover plants demonstrate forest succession.

❈ Trail in winter: Not advisable for skiing owing to narrowness and short length, although snowshoeing is possible.

🚶 Distance: Loop, 0.6 mi (1 km).

143 Balsam Trail

Trails Illustrated Map 746: KK15

This short loop trail to the East Branch of the St. Regis River downstream from Everton Falls offers a view of the first rapids below the falls.

▶Trailhead: See Hardwood Trail (trail 142); the trail starts on the river side of CR 14 0.55 mi downstream from the parking area. Nature Conservancy trail markers indicate the start, which can be difficult to spot. There is room to park one or two cars on the opposite side of the road here.◀

The trail loops through soothing softwood forest lining the river and follows the riverbank briefly before returning to its point of origin.

❈ Trail in winter: An easy snowshoe, though narrow and very short.

🚶 Distances: To river, 0.1 mi; to start, 0.2 mi (0.3 km).

144 Sheep Meadow and Hays Brook Truck Trail

Trails Illustrated Map 746: GG18

This DEC trail, marked very sporadically with old yellow horse and snowmobile disks, mostly follows the route of an old truck trail to a meadow deep in the DeBar Mt. Wild Forest where sheep were once pastured and two lean-tos and a multi-stall covered horse shelter are now located. This is a good mountain bike trail.

▶Trailhead: Access is from NY 30, 3.7 mi N of the intersection of NY 86 and NY 30 at Paul Smith's College. A DEC sign at a gravel road is on the R. Take this road 0.2 mi to a parking lot. The trailhead, at the gated truck trail, is 0.2 mi E of the parking lot.◀

The Hays Brook Truck Trail starts around the metal gate (0.0 mi), with a DEC register L and a DEC sign displaying incorrect distances. Following the old truck trail through a pine plantation, at 0.4 mi it crosses the Osgood River on a wooden bridge. The Grass Pond trail (trail 145) begins 90 yd ahead on the R as a wide jeep trail. Shortly thereafter, at 0.5 mi, the Sheep Meadow Trail turns sharply L off the Hays Brook Truck Trail and makes a sharp ascent. (The Hays Brook Truck Trail continues straight ahead, ending at Hays Brook; a truck trail at 1.3 links the Hays Brook Truck Trail to the Sheep Meadow Trail)

The Sheep Meadow Trail begins a sharply undulating course through a mature red pine plantation with a luxurious undergrowth of bracken fern. Upon rejoining a truck trail at 1.3 mi, the trail turns L and crosses Hays Brook at 1.5 mi on a wooden bridge. The brook's banks are densely lined with alders. Farther upstream, the headwaters of Hays Brook are an important winter deer yard.

At 1.8 mi, the trail levels off and passes a flat sandy area with large white pine and an understory of balsam and spruce. These are boreal sand flats, quite common elsewhere in this section. At 2.7 mi, old meadows on the R have conifers directly reforesting them.

As the route nears the Sheep Meadow at 3.3 mi, a trail comes in L. Although this trail is easy to discern at its start, it quickly degrades and should not be followed without map and compass. The Sheep Meadow, with its two lean-tos and horse shelters, is in a charming setting entirely encircled by mountains.

❀ Trail in winter: Most suitable for cross-country skiing or snowshoeing.

🐾 Distances: Gate to Osgood River, 0.4 mi; to Hays Brook, 1.5 mi; to Sheep Meadow, 3.3 mi (5.3 km).

145 Grass Pond

Trails Illustrated Map 746: GG18

▶Locator: The unmarked Grass Pond trail starts at 0.5 mi on Sheep Meadow and Hays Brook Truck Trail (trail 144). It leads through some stunning boreal habitat at the edge of the Forest Preserve at Grass Pond. This is a good trail for mountain biking.◀

From the jct. (0.0 mi), the route follows a wide jeep trail between towering white pines on an esker L and the valley of the Osgood River R. It begins a slow descent through spruce and tamarack to a fork, with a lean-to just past the fork, at 1.3

mi. This lean-to, at the S end of Grass Pond, replaces two older lean-tos that have been removed. It overlooks the pond, which is reached at 1.4 mi. Grass Pond is semicircular and mostly lives up to its name, being almost completely encircled by a mat of grass-like sedges with some cattails in places.

❄ Trail in winter: Suitable for cross-country skiing or snowshoeing.

🐾 Distance: Sheep Meadow and Hays Brook Truck Trail to Grass Pond, 1.4 mi (2.2 km).

146 Slush Pond Ski Trail

Trails Illustrated Map 746: FF18

This generally unplowed gravel road leads 2.5 mi through Forest Preserve to the gate of a large private park. It is marked partway as a snowmobile trail and receives moderate cross-country ski use in winter.

▶Trailhead: Access is from a gravel road 3.7 mi N of Paul Smiths on NY 30. The road is on the W side of NY 30, opposite the access road for Sheep Meadow and Hays Brook Truck Trail (trail 144).◀

From NY 30 (0.0 mi), the trail is mostly level as it proceeds through an extensive evergreen plantation. At 0.6 mi the Kettle Trail (trail 147) diverges R. The trail reaches Slush Pond on the R at 2 mi. The pond is typical of many boreal bodies of water in this area—entirely ringed by conifers and marsh. The monolithic pine plantations here were an attempt at reforestation after disastrous forest fires early in the twentieth century almost completely denuded many sections of woodland. Several primitive campsites are located on the L under the pines. The road/trail ends at the gate of the private estate at 2.5 mi.

❄ Trail in winter: This trail's primary use is as a cross-country ski trail.

🐾 Distances: NY 30 to Slush Pond and campsites, 2 mi; to gate, 2.5 mi (4 km).

147 Kettle Trail

Trails Illustrated Map 746: FF18

▶Locator: The start of this trail is at 0.6 mi on Slush Pond Ski Trail (trail 146). Begin on the R following the red snowmobile disks prominently attached to the pine trees.◀

The trail starts (0.0 mi) by entering an extensive plantation of Scotch and red pine, which embraces the trail for almost its entire route. The consequent lack of sunlight has severely limited the undergrowth, although, in places, maple and balsam fir saplings can be observed trying to subsist along with the ever-present bracken fern.

The trail is on an esker at the beginning and then takes an undulating course over several kame-like hills. Along the way, the trail passes numerous kettle holes, additional evidence of glacial topography. These legacies of glacial ice are especially interesting as they are seen here in all stages of succession, from the original ponds that existed after the ice melted.

At 0.3 mi, the trail reaches the first kettle pond off to the R—it still exists as a pond, albeit a very shallow one. At 0.6 mi, the trail passes another kettle on the R. The pond here has progressed to a bog, as the plumes of cotton grass growing on the sphagnum mat attest. The next two kettles have almost achieved the ultimate in progression, as they are now completely dry land. However, because they lie in a frost bracket and have a high water table after snow melt in the spring, they have not been reforested as other dry areas in this region have been. Instead, their bottoms are covered with a thick growth of spirea and blueberry, which play a part in retarding tree growth.

The last kettle pond is a field just before the trail zigzags L around private land at 2.2 mi. The trail proceeds another mile to dead-end at a gravel road at 3.2 mi; this point is generally considered the end of the trail. (A R on the gravel road, which may be driven with care during summer, leads to NY 30 in 1.9 mi. The start of Slush Pond Rd. is 2.4 mi S on NY 30.)

❋ Trail in winter: Generally well-adapted to cross-country skiing. Add 1.2 mi to any total round-trip, as Slush Pond Rd. is rarely plowed.

𝕸 Distances: Slush Pond Rd. to first kettle pond, 0.3 mi; to second kettle pond, 0.6 mi; to last pond, 2.2 mi; to gravel road, 3.2 mi (5.1 km).

148 DeBar Game Management Area Trail

Trails Illustrated Map 746: II18

This lengthy trail, only sporadically marked with both red and yellow disks, starts at Meacham Lake DEC Campground and proceeds through the heart of the old DeBar Game Management Area to a gravel road off CR 26 (formerly NY 99). This area, unique in the Forest Preserve, was once the scene of an initially successful attempt to return elk to the Adirondacks. The elk, the gift of the governor of a western state to the governor of New York, were originally held in pens here before being gradually released to spread through the northern Adirondacks. The elk persisted from the 1930s until approximately 1960 when they finally disappeared, mostly owing to poaching. The Game Management Area was established for agricultural and wildlife propagation purposes.

Meacham Lake, at 1203 acres, is the second largest lake whose borders are entirely within the Forest Preserve. Relatively unaffected by acid rain, it has an excellent fishery of lake trout and northern pike with at least one endangered species, the whitefish, present in some numbers.

▶Trailhead: Access is from Meacham Lake Campground, on the R off NY 30 9.5 mi N of Paul Smiths. There is a small fee for day use. To make a one-way hike possible, a second car can be parked at the N end of the trail. To reach the northern trailhead, return to NY 30 and proceed N 8.2 mi to the intersection with CR 26. Turn R on CR 26 and go 8.9 mi to a gravel road on the R. It is 1.4 mi on this road to the trailhead. ◀

From the campground entrance it is 0.5 mi to the start of DeBar Game Management Area Trail, which is also the access to the DeBar Mt. trail (trail 149). A dirt road leads W at Campsite 48 to the trail's start at the site of an old gravel pit (0.0 mi). Vehicles may be parked here. The gate banning vehicle access is to the R.

The trail begins by rising slightly in a mixed forest with occasional large yellow birch. At 0.3 mi the trail stays R at an intersection. The trail so far is marked sporadically with DEC markers of both red and yellow. At 0.5 mi, a large, mostly open spruce bog is on the L. The typical bog vegetation is prominent here—leatherleaf, cotton grass, etc.

At 0.7 mi, the trail begins to pass through a spruce flat with scattered fir. It crosses the outlet to Winnebago Pond at 1 mi. Winnebago Pond is a small northern Adirondack kettle pond that is in the process of reverting to a bog. At 1.1 mi the trail reaches a jct.; to the L the red trail markers denote the start of the DeBar Mt. trail (trail 149).

The trail continues R from the jct. and passes an old beaver flow L at 1.6 mi. At 2.1 mi it crosses a creek on a wooden bridge and passes through a mixed forest while beginning to rise somewhat for the first time. At 2.6 mi a sign on the R saying "trail not maintained" can be disregarded—it alludes to a side trail long officially abandoned—and the trail continues on an old tote road to a fork at 3.1 mi.

The trail continues L, rising moderately and crossing another wooden bridge at 3.2 mi. At 3.4 mi, it crosses a swamp using a corduroy bridge. The trail rises again through a hardwood forest with only an occasional sign present, to another intersection of two old tote roads. The trail goes L and continues through a mixed forest, crossing several creeks before reaching two yellow gateposts where another trail goes R at 4.6 mi. (This is the start of the Beaver Valley Trail, which leads in 0.7 mi to a human-made pond constructed during the wildlife management era. Although the artificial dam and spillway are readily apparent at the pond, this location is secluded and blissful, framed on two sides by protective hills looming above.)

The main trail passes one of the wildlife ponds constructed in the days of the Game Management Area at 5.2 mi, then splits at 5.9 mi. (The trail R drops to cross a feeder creek to Hatch Brook. A sign warns that the bridge is washed out, but the creek can be crossed below the bridge on rocks and the washed-out culvert pipe. This trail then climbs through pines to rejoin the main trail at a parking area in 0.6 mi.) The main trail continues on L and passes to the N of a wetland. At 6.1 it reaches a gate as it crosses the wetland. After the trail leaves the wetland it climbs through a pine plantation and reaches a three-road jct. at 6.4 mi. This marks the N trailhead; there is space for two vehicles to park.

❀ Trail in winter: Admirably suited as a cross-country ski trail, but must be shared with snowmobiles.

𖠿 Distances: Meacham Lake Campground to DeBar Mt. trail, 1.1 mi; to Beaver Valley Trail, 4.6 mi; to N trailhead, 6.4 mi (10.2 km).

149 DeBar Mt.

The red-marked trail to the top of Debar Mt. starts on the DeBar Game Management Area Trail (trail 148) and ascends the massive hulk of one of the most prominent isolated peaks in the northern Adirondacks. The peak, in a remote setting, looms large on the horizon from all directions. The view on top, while worthwhile, does not quite live up to the promise DeBar gives from the valley floor.

This peak, like many, was scorched by fire early in the twentieth century. The dryness and thin soil of these peaks, combined with their attractiveness to lightning and inaccessibility to firefighting apparatus, make them extremely vulnerable to fire.

▶Locator: At 1.1 mi on the DeBar Game Management Trail (trail 148). The sporadically red-marked trail to the L is the DeBar Mt. trail; the R fork is the continuation of the Game Management Trail.◀

From the jct. (0.0 mi), the trail is mostly flat at the start. It begins to rise moderately at 0.3 mi under a canopy of large yellow birch and continues rising moderately as sugar maple and beech begin to replace yellow birch.

At 0.9 mi, the trail begins to level off and crosses a shoulder between two peaks—Baldface L with DeBar on the R. At 1.8 mi, a DEC lean-to is on the L. Just beyond is a small meadow with the foundation of the fire observer's cabin still noticeable. The rest of the meadow is grown up to pin cherry and perennial herbs (goldenrod, etc.) as it starts its march back to woodland.

At 2 mi, the trail begins to rise steeply. At 2.1 mi, white birch and yellow birch are present amidst piles of talus rock. The angular shape of the rocks shows they are not glacial erratics but rather have been split off from the bedrock of the upper slopes.

At 2.3 mi, black spruce start to appear. The going gets quite steep and is difficult in spots; a good amount of scrambling is necessary. Scattered mountain ash begins to appear.

Finally, after another steep pitch, the trail achieves the 3300 ft high summit of DeBar Mt. at 2.6 mi. The foundation of the old fire tower is all that remains; aerial survey has replaced these towers in the Adirondacks. From the top an excellent view can be had of the northern Adirondacks and the adjacent St. Lawrence Valley. The tops of the forested hills roll on to the horizon. The land all around the mountain is in the DeBar Mt. Wild Forest; the forests surrounding it are the mixture of private timberlands and Forest Preserve that characterize the Adirondack Park. Meacham Lake and Clear Pond are visible below, along with the Deer River Flow. A sense of serenity prevails.

❋ Trail in winter: Not suitable owing to steepness.

𝌭 Distances: DeBar Game Management Trail to Baldface/DeBar shoulder, 0.9 mi; to lean-to, 1.8 mi; to summit, 2.6 mi (4.2 km). From trailhead, 3.7 mi (5.9 km). Ascent from trailhead, 1655 ft (504 m). Elevation, 3300 ft (1006 m). 🦃

Lows Ridge. Chris Murray

Massawepie–Horseshoe Lake Section

 In 1991 New York State completed acquisition of two contiguous tracts of land in St. Lawrence County—the 7500 acre Otterbrook parcel in fee and the 19,500 acre Yorkshire parcel under conservation easement. These two parcels are now known as Cranberry Lake Wild Forest and the Conifer-Emporium Easement, respectively. Together they extend state land from the shores of Cranberry Lake E all the way to the shores of Big Tupper and Horseshoe Lakes, envelop the headwaters of the Grass River, and are part of the proposed Bob Marshall–Greater Oswegatchie Forest. They present excellent opportunities for hiking, cross-country skiing, mountain biking, and showshoeing, utilizing the abandoned and active logging roads that travel their length and breadth.

The Cranberry Lake Wild Forest generally lies SW of the Conifer-Emporium Easement and is open for full public use. Most of the trails in Cranberry Lake Wild Forest are described in Cranberry Lake–Wanakena Section. These trails are connected to those in the Conifer-Emporium Easement by the Dog Pond and Sucker Brook Rd. Trails, which connect both areas to Horseshoe Lake Wild Forest and, subsequently, Eastern Five Ponds Access Primitive Area with Lows Lake.

The parcel known as the Conifer-Emporium Easement was acquired under the innovative conservation easement method, through which the state obtained the development and recreation rights to the property while the original landowner retained timber management rights. Areas undergoing active lumbering may be posted as off-limits for the duration of the logging. The easement lands are otherwise open to full public use in much the same manner as Forest Preserve lands, particularly with regard to camping, numbers in a party, etc. Any additional restriction is pointed out on the posted signs that delineate the area. The rights of any sportsmen's club that may exist should be scrupulously respected for the period they are in effect.

There is a ranger station in Cranberry Lake.

150 Massawepie-Yorkshire Trail

Trails Illustrated Map 745: Z12

This route makes use of Massawepie Rd. (sometimes referred to as Town Line Rd., a gravel road irregularly plowed in winter) and the main haul road of a timber company in coursing through generally rolling terrain to make a 10.2 mi round-trip hike or ski tour. It passes through a Boy Scout reservation and criss-crosses the Emporium Trail (trail 151), a former railroad bed. The route can be extended to Horseshoe Lake via Sucker Brook Rd. Trail (trail 153), a good option if two cars are available.

The road (or ski route in season) through the Scout camp proceeds for several miles on top of a winding esker under a canopy of majestic white pine and hemlock with a number of enchanting lakes and ponds clearly visible on both sides of the ridge. It is, in many respects, as entrancing a route as exists in the entire Adirondack Park. The Boy Scout camp is open for public use, subject to some restrictions, from September 1 through June 14.

▶Trailhead: The trail begins at the intersection of the former Grass River Railroad (now another gravel logging road) and the main haul road of a lumber company at 4.9 mi on Massawepie Rd. from NY 3. If the area is unplowed, the ski route begins at the point where plowing ends. Plowing is usually done to a point where the town road ends and the main haul road begins. After a relatively fresh snowfall, however, the road may be unplowed through the Massawepie Boy Scout section. Massawepie Rd. leaves NY 3 5.4 mi W of the Raquette River bridge in Piercefield and 5.8 mi E of the NY 3/56 intersection at Sevey Corners, at a large sign for the Massawepie Boy Scout Camp on the S side of the road.◀

Beginning at the jct. of the railroad bed and main haul road (0.0 mi), where cars may be carefully parked on the side, the main haul road proceeds on a rolling course. The red-marked Emporium Trail (trail 151) crosses at 0.3 mi. The W leg of the Emporium Trail provides a slight detour away from the road and snowmobile traffic.

At 0.8 mi, a clearing on the E side of the road marks the N end of the yellow-marked spur trail of the Emporium Trail. Just downhill, where a stream crosses, the red-marked Emporium Trail crosses again at a culvert pipe.

The road now climbs, with the Emporium Trail joining from the E shortly after the crest of a hill at 1.3 mi. At 1.6 mi, after the road crosses a small wetland, the Emporium Trail forks E. A gate at 1.7 mi signals yet another merging with the Emporium Trail. Ahead lies the caretaker's cabin; occasionally the road will be plowed to this point.

The route goes over rolling hills covered with hardwoods, with descents in wetland valleys, usually with very obvious beaver activity to the side. Walking here in late summer discloses a bounteous supply of blackberries and red raspberries.

The caretaker's cabin marks the start of an ascent up a rather steep hill with handsome, maturing hardwoods on both sides, along with frequent evidence of deer browsing. Little Mt. comes into view ahead just before a descent at 2.7 mi.

The trail now begins to level out and proceeds through an extensive plantation of Scotch and red pine. This is the old Usher Farm. The plantation was undertaken with private effort.

At 3.2 mi, the trail crosses a wooden bridge and at 3.8 mi it encounters a fork. It turns R here and shortly passes a gravel pit and beaver pond, the latter next to the road on the L. Little Mt. can be seen again. In addition to the gravel pits seen, the other open areas along the road are where cut logs are brought for loading onto trucks going to mills.

At 4 mi, the route goes L on a grassy jeep trail that turns off the main road, which has been washed out ahead. At 4.4 mi, this trail meets the boundary of the former Otterbrook property (now Forest Preserve) and at 4.6 mi it ends at a T intersection with another logging road.

Turn R here to another gate at 5.1 mi. The round-trip can end here. If two cars are available, an additional 4 mi (approximately) via Sucker Brook Rd. Trail (trail 153) to Horseshoe Lake is possible.

❋ Trail in winter: Ideal as a ski or snowshoe route, but it is also used by snowmobiles.

𝄪 Distances: To first Emporium Trail jct., 0.3 mi; to crest of hill, 1.3 mi; to bridge, 3.2 mi; to jeep trail, 4 mi; to logging road, 4.6 mi; to gate at end of trail, 5.1 mi (8.2 km).

151 Emporium Trail

Trails Illustrated Map 745: Z12

This hiking and cross-country ski trail has historical interest. Located on logging spurs of the old Grass River Railroad, it was constructed in conjunction with the DEC under an Adopt-a-Resource agreement. The Emporium Trail intertwines with Massawepie Rd. and can be combined with Massawepie-Yorkshire Trail (trail 150) to make a loop of 4.8 mi or less using various jcts. along Massawepie Rd.

▶ Trailhead: The trail begins 0.6 mi E of the intersection of the old Grass River Railroad (now a gravel logging road) and the main haul road of a lumber company at 4.9 mi on Massawepie Rd. from NY 3. ◀

The red-marked trail starts on the S side of the road across from a hunting camp on the N (0.0 mi). The trail proceeds for a short way perpendicular to the road (S), then makes an abrupt R turn (W) onto the railroad grade and passes through some dense pines before coming into an open meadow area.

The trail continues through an area of young mixed hardwoods intersecting several old skid trails. At 0.3 mi a yellow-marked spur branches S while the red-marked Emporium Trail continues W across a marsh at 0.4 mi. Beavers have used the railroad bed to create a dam, and it can be wet through this stretch.

The trail crosses the Massawepie-Yorkshire Trail (trail 150) at 0.6 mi. (This first part of the trail can be skipped by using trail 150; refer to trail 150 or map.) After crossing a small creek at 0.8 mi, the trail enters a beautiful section. Tall middle-aged hardwoods have suppressed the undergrowth to provide a wonderful cathedral effect. Old cuts made for the railroad grade can be seen through this section, with some ties still visible and what appears to be part of a small collapsed trestle bridge.

The route again crosses the Massawepie-Yorkshire Trail (trail 150) at 1.3 mi. Look carefully for red trail markers. The trail now passes through widely spaced trees into an open area, then starts to climb as it passes out of the meadow. The trail passes another cut, then crosses and recrosses a small creek at 1.6 mi. At 1.7 mi and beyond, talus slopes appear at intervals to the E on the slopes of Wheeler Mt. Interesting boulders and outcrops with some talus caves can be observed. A steep skid trail branches up Wheeler Mt. to the E at 2.1 mi, just before the trail drops to join the Massawepie-Yorkshire Trail. Two red trail markers appear at this point on the trail. The trail now follows trail 150 S until the old railroad grade (trail 151) diverges E. The grade passes through a marshy area; remaining on the Massawepie-Yorkshire Trail will assure dry feet.

At 2.3 mi, double red trail markers indicate the trail leaving the road to the L. It continues through a meadow, where it can be difficult to follow. The trail leaves the meadow at a small cut in the hill. At 2.6 mi, a skid trail crosses, indicated with double red markers. The railroad grade has been cleared beyond this point, but the trail turns W here. If you miss the turn and the trail ends, backtrack to the double markers. Continue W through a log staging area to a gate on the Massawepie-Yorkshire Trail (trail 150) at 2.7 mi. A loop can be made by returning N on trail 176 to the parking area for a total distance of 4.8 mi.

❉ Trail in winter: Potentially an ideal cross-country ski trail, if cleared of undergrowth. The yellow spur tail can be challenging in its upper elevations.

❦ Distances: Parking area to yellow-marked spur, 0.3 mi; to first jct. with Massawepie Rd., 0.6 mi; to second jct. with Massawepie Rd., 1.3 mi; to merger with Massawepie Rd., 2.1 mi; to departure from Massawepie Rd., to the E, 2.3 mi; to gate, 2.7 mi (4.3 km).

152 Center Pond

Trails Illustrated Map 745: AA12

This route proceeds over a logging road to Center Pond, generally considered to be the headwaters of the South Branch of the Grass River.

▶Trailhead: The trail begins at the jct. of the roadbed of the Grass River Railroad and a main haul road at a point 4.9 mi from NY 3. (See Massawepie-Yorkshire Trail, trail 150.)◀

From the jct. (0.0 mi), the trail goes R, crossing the Grass River in 0.3 mi on a small wooden bridge. The river is narrow here but the floodplain of alders is wide. At 0.8 mi the trail turns L just before the road straight ahead intersects with a road to the R.

The path is wide now with a slight gradual ascent until 2 mi, where it begins to undulate. On the way Berkley Mt. is visible across a flooded valley off to the R. The topography of the area is quite obvious in winter—a pattern of wetland valleys and fairly steep mountains looming above them. The road and ski route, however, are generally level to rolling in terrain, a function of the care exercised in laying out the logging roads.

After undulating for a while, the road resumes its slow ascent before leveling at 3 mi. The predominant hardwood forest has fairly good-sized specimens of black cherry and maple with an occasional hemlock. The valley of the Grass River with Little Mt. rising above it is off to the L.

The road begins a descent, turning R at 3.9 mi (there is a side road L). At 4.2 mi, the road ends with Center Pond off to the L. Center Pond, with its marshy shoreline and some flooded timber, is quite representative of the many small Adirondack lakes slowly evolving into wetlands.

❋ Trail in winter: Used primarily as a cross-country ski trail.

🐾 Distances: To bridge over Grass River, 0.3 mi; to level stretch, 3 mi; to Center Pond, 4.2 mi (6.7 km).

153 Sucker Brook Rd.

Trails Illustrated Map 745: Y13

An enjoyable round-trip cross-country ski is possible on the logging roads of the Cranberry Lake Wild Forest. These roads, until recently used for logging, are still in relatively good condition. The segment of trail between Horseshoe Lake and the South Branch of the Grass River receives moderate to heavy snowmobile use in winter, discouraging muscle-powered travel.

▶Trailhead: Access is from NY 30, 6.8 mi S of the NY 3/30 intersection in Tupper Lake and 13.4 mi N of the NY 30/28N intersection in Long Lake. Going W on NY 421 here, pavement ends at approximately 6 mi. This is generally the spot where plowing ceases in the winter although, on occasion, plowing may be extended another 1.5 mi.◀

From the end of pavement (0.0 mi), the trail in the first 1.5 mi hugs the shore of Horseshoe Lake and takes a sharp L over the tracks of the old Remsen–Lake Placid Railroad. A number of primitive campsites are available at Horseshoe Lake, a large, deep, conifer-clad body of water shaped like its name.

At 1.8 mi, the route goes R at a fork. (The gated trail L is Lows Ridge–Upper Dam Trail, trail 154). At 2.2 mi, the route bears L at another fork. (The gated road R leads to Pine Pond.) The next fork is at 2.6 mi, where the route goes R. (The road L leads to a private inholding.) The trail, which has been generally flat, now begins to rise slightly as it passes clumps of regenerating aspen.

At 3.9 mi, there is a jct. with the gated Pine Pond Rd. coming from the R at the site of a huge gravel pit. The trail turns L here, passing a logging road on the R which is the terminus of the Massawepie-Yorkshire Trail (trail 150). A steep cliff lined with spruce stands out sharply to the R.

The terrain now becomes moderately rolling and the trail descends to cross the outlet of Sardine Pond on a bridge at 5 mi. This is considered another source pond of the South Branch of the Grass River. Tamarack and alder line the creek. During the summer and autumn months, the gate just before this creek is the limit to which vehicles can be driven.

The trail rises sharply up a long hill after crossing the creek, and then begins a rather steep descent to cross another small creek with an old beaver vlei L at 6.2 mi. Long Tom Mt., from whose slope the creek flows, is in the background. At 6.6 mi, two of the remaining hunting camps look out over an expansive marsh on the L, with Long Tom Mt. majestically framing the outlook.

The terrain starts to become rolling again until 7.2 mi, where the trail to Dog Pond (trail 155) takes off R just past a piped spring on the L. To the L is the Otter Brook Trail (trail 203). Otter Brook and Dog Pond Trails are both part of the CL50 (see Cranberry Lake 50 Section and Cranberry Lake–Wanakena Section).

❊ Trail in winter: The area between Horseshoe Lake and the South Branch of the Grass River receives moderate to heavy snowmobile traffic.

❦ Distances: End of paved road to railroad tracks, 1.5 mi; to Lows Ridge–Upper Dam Trail (trail 154), 1.8 mi; to gravel pit site, 3.9 mi; to Sardine Pond outlet, 5 mi; to vlei, 6.2 mi; to Dog Pond Trail (trail 155), 7.2 mi (11.5 km).

154 Lows Ridge–Upper Dam Trail

Trails Illustrated Map 745: X12

This hike or ski trip leads to the Upper Dam on the Bog River at the inlet to Hitchins Pond. Looming over the dam and lake and all the early Adirondack history associated with this spot is a steep ridge with open rock ledges on top, from which wonderful views of the region can be obtained.

▶Locator: The trail starts 1.8 mi from the Horseshoe Lake start of the Sucker Brook Rd. (trail 153), where a fork to the L (S) is blocked by a gate.◀

The trail begins past the gate (0.0 mi). Generally flat for the whole distance, it first parallels a vast open peatland on the L for almost a mile. Later it passes a well-drained wetland on the R with a fair-sized creek providing the drainage. The contrast is easily discernible—the peatland with its sphagnum moss, cotton grass, and pitcher plants as opposed to the bluejoint grass, alders, and pickerel weed of the marsh.

At 1.6 mi, the trail proceeds through the remnants of a Scotch pine plantation with several large talus boulders from the cliff to the R. At 2.3 mi it reaches the entrance to an old Boy Scout camp with the Upper Dam straight ahead and Hitchins Pond 400 ft down the road to the L, past the foundation of the former main lodge of the camp.

Just before the gate, on the R between two of the old cabins, a ravine can be located. This is the route to the top of the steep ridge that overlooks the entire area. It is 0.2 mi to the top of the ridge, veering L from the ravine and following

Bog River, stereoscopic photograph by Seneca Ray Stoddard
Courtesy of Daniel Way collection

a moderately distinct herd path over open rock ledges to the summit. There is now also a signed, nicely graded trail of just over 1 mi to Lows Ridge.

An iron bolt and plaque in the rock commemorate the memory of A. Augustus Low, who at the turn of the twentieth century was the lord of all the fiefdom displayed beneath. Visualize, if you can, a huge lumbering operation employing several hundred loggers who were housed in what was later to become the main lodge of the Boy Scout complex that in time followed it. Consider also the thriving maple syrup operation, along with the mineral waters bottled from the cool springs and marketed in the large cities of the Northeast. These were a result of the dynamism and ambition of the man commemorated. Ponder, too, the scenery unfurling below—the entire wilderness that is the Bog River drainage is clearly visible, along with the shimmering waters of Horseshoe Lake and, in the distance to the NW on a clear day, one of the Adirondack monarchs, Whiteface Mt.

❅ Trail in winter: Excellent skiing to dam and foot of ridge.

🐾 Distances: To Scotch pine plantation, 1.6 mi; to dam and foot of ridge, 2.3 mi (4 km); with scramble to top of ridge, 2.5 mi; via trail to ridgetop, 3.3 mi (5.3 km).

155 Dog Pond Trail

Trails Illustrated Map 745: Y11

This short trail leads past an attractive, medium-sized glacial pond where the brook trout fishing can be, on occasion, superb. It connects the network of trails emanating from Cranberry Lake with those in the Conifer-Emporium Easement to the E. It is part of the CL50 (see Cranberry Lake 50 Section).

▶Locator: The trail begins at Proulx Clearing, which is on Dog Pond Loop

South Branch of the Grass River. Mark Bowie

(trail 175), 7.2 mi SE of the first jct. of the Dog Pond Loop and the Burntbridge Pond trail (trail 171). ◀

From Proulx Clearing (0.0 mi), this red-marked trail immediately drops, then climbs. At 0.2 mi it passes the outlet of Dog Pond. Dog Pond, to the S, is a medium-sized glacial pond where brook trout can be found. The pond has an inviting outcrop of boulders on a point on the E shore, and a number of attractive marked campsites dot the shore area. The trail crosses the pond's inlet as it comes cascading down a charming small waterfall R at 0.5 mi and reaches the old Forest Preserve boundary shortly thereafter at 0.7 mi.

The trail follows the boundary. The difference between Forest Preserve of long standing and of recent addition is very dramatic here. The original Forest Preserve has not been subject to logging since early in the twentieth century, and majestic hemlocks, red spruces, and yellow birches follow the entire way until the trail leaves the boundary. The more recently acquired land has begun its long path to reaching this climax.

At 0.9 mi the trail leaves the boundary. It joins an old logging road at 1 mi and rises to a tract of cutover second-growth hardwood. It then drops to cross a creek at 1.4 mi, before climbing again to meet Sucker Brook Rd. Trail (trail 153) at 1.5 mi.

❋ Trail in winter: Not advisable for skiing.

🐾 Distances: Dog Pond Loop (trail 175) to Dog Pond inlet, 0.5 mi; to Forest Preserve boundary, 0.7 mi; to Sucker Brook Rd. (trail 153), 1.5 mi (2.4 km). 🐾

Grass River–White Hill Wild Forest Section

With the 1999 purchase by New York State of land and easements from Champion International Corporation and Forestland Group in the Tooley Pond Tract, several miles of the Grass River became available for public access. Many of the trails described here lead in some manner to waterfalls, most of them on the South Branch of the Grass in the Tooley Pond Tract or the Grass River Wild Forest above or below the hamlet of Degrasse in St. Lawrence County. This attractive wild river remains little known to the general public, primarily because of its remote location and because it flows through very little of the Forest Preserve on its north-flowing course to the St. Lawrence. Several of these trails are accessed from Tooley Rd.; a mileage chart of the road is provided below.

Four isolated trails in the Raquette River drainage basin, the next system to the E, are included in this section. Two of these are in the White Hill Wild Forest, a large, remote Forest Preserve tract in the far northern reaches of the Adirondack Park. The other two are in a section of the Grass River Wild Forest and lead to waterfalls.

A few suggested hikes for this section are listed below.

SHORT HIKES
Lampson Falls: 1 mi (1.6 km) round-trip. A walk on a flat woods road terminates at a wide, lovely falls on the Grass River. See trail 163.

Copper Rock Falls: 1 mi (1.6 km) round-trip. Follows the bank of the Grass River with a view of three falls and multiple cascades. See trail 157.

Rainbow Falls: 0.6 mi (1 km) round-trip. A walk on a gentle sloped trail to one of the most beautiful falls of the Grass River. Not to be missed. See trail 159.

MODERATE HIKES
Harper Falls/North Branch Grass River Trails: 5.8 mi (9.3 km) round-trip. This up-and-down walk is an exemplary tour of northern Adirondack mixed forest and riverbanks. See trails 165 and 166.

Tooley Pond Mt. Loop: 2 mi (3.2 km) loop. This pleasant loop to the top of one of the few summits in this section provides a varied trail and decent view. See trail 156.

Waterfall along Tooley Pond Road. Dick Mooers

Mileage Chart, Tooley Pond Rd. (measured in miles)

Distance from NY 3	Location	Distance from CR 27
0.0 (0.0 km)	Tooley Pond Rd. and NY 3 intersection	16.9 (27.0 km)
2.7 (4.3 km)	River Rd. intersection (Cook Corners) (to Newton Falls)	14.2 (22.7 km)
5.8 (9.3 km)	Tooley Pond	11.1 (17.8 km)
5.9 (9.4 km)	Tooley Pond parking area	11.0 (17.6 km)
6.0 (9.6 km)	Tooley Pond Mt. trailhead, E (trail 156)	10.9 (17.4 km)
6.4 (10.3 km)	Tooley Pond Mt. trailhead, W (trail 156)	10.5 (16.8 km)
8.2 (13.1 km)	Copper Rock Falls (trail 157)	8.7 (13.9 km)
9.0 (14.4 km)	Bridge crossing the Grass River	7.9 (12.6 km)
10.7 (17.1 km)	Grass River Canoe Access (trail 158) parking area	6.2 (9.9 km)
10.9 (17.4 km)	Rainbow Falls (trail 159)	6.0 (9.6 km)
12.1 (19.7 km)	Twin Falls Club Rd.	4.8 (7.7 km)
13.5 (21.6 km)	Bulkhead (Adrenaline) Falls (trail 160)	3.4 (5.4 km)
13.7 (21.9 km)	Stewart Rapids, visible from road	3.2 (5.1 km)
13.9 (22.2 km)	Twin Falls	3.0 (4.8 km)
14.0 (22.4 km)	Private road (posted) to view of Twin Falls and canoe launch	2.9 (4.6 km)
14.9 (23.8 km)	Lake George Rd. intersection	2.0 (3.2 km)
14.9 (23.8 km)	Sinclair Falls (trail 161)	2.0 (3.2 km)
15.5 (24.8 km)	Basford Falls (trail 162)	1.4 (2.2 km)
16.9 (27.0 km)	Tooley Pond Rd. and CR 27 intersection in Degrasse	0.0 (0.0 km)

156 Tooley Pond Mt. Loop

Trails Illustrated Map 745: BB8

This route was created by utilizing jeep trails, skid roads, and some new trail. The trail can be hiked as a loop from the parking area across from Tooley Pond climbing the E route to the summit, descending the W route, and using Tooley Pond Rd. to return to the parking area. The trail is described in this direction, although the shortest route to the summit is via the W trail. An interesting variation would be to park at the small lot on Tooley Pond and canoe to a short spur of the E trail (see below) to combine hiking with canoeing.

▶Trailhead: E access is from NY 3 via Tooley Pond Rd. Turning W from NY 3, travel 2.7 mi to the intersection with River Rd. to Newton Falls. Continue straight here to Tooley Pond at 5.8 mi. A parking lot is located on the N side of the road at 5.9 mi, with the E trailhead 0.1 mi to the W (ahead). From the W, take CR 27 to Degrasse and turn E onto Tooley Pond Rd. At 10.5 mi the W trailhead has limited parking. Continuing E, the E trailhead is at 10.9 mi and the parking area at 11 mi. ◀

Leaving the parking area (0.0 mi), walk W on Tooley Pond Rd. for 0.1 mi and turn L (S) into the woods at the E trailhead. The red-marked trail begins on an old jeep road through mostly hardwoods, climbing a small hill and then descending into a small valley before climbing again. At 0.2 mi, after a short climb, the trail leaves the jeep trail to the E. Be sure to look for markers; failure to turn here will lead one into a maze of old jeep trails and intersecting skid trails.

The trail immediately crosses a small stream and follows a rise through young pines toward Tooley Pond. The pond can be seen through the trees to the E. At 0.3 mi, a branch leads L (E) to an overlook on Tooley Pond and continues down to the shore of the pond in a few hundred feet. This branch provides canoe access to the trail; see above.

Continuing R from this jct., the trail leaves Tooley Pond, dropping to a small stream at 0.4 mi and then climbing through a predominantly birch woods. The trail intersects and joins a jeep trail from the N at 0.5 mi, then diverges from the jeep trail to the W in a few hundred feet.

The trail continues to climb and at 0.8 mi comes to a jct. with the W trail. A L turn and a short climb lead to the summit of Tooley Pond Mt. at 0.9 mi. The view is to the E; after the leaves have fallen, Tooley Pond can be seen. Exploration among the pines on the top reveals the remains of the base of a fire tower with an inscription and a partly visible date. Bench marks—large brass inserts—used for surveying can also be found in the exposed bedrock, along with a vein of quartz.

Leaving the summit on the same trail, the E trail is again encountered. To complete the loop, continue straight on the jeep trail that the W trail follows to Tooley Pond Rd. The trail starts a steady drop, reaching a jct. with an old skid trail at 1.2 mi. Turn R (E) across the slope here. The route crosses a stream at 1.3 mi and intersects another skid trail; again, turn R (E). Tooley Pond Rd. is at 1.6 mi. Turn R (E) here and follow the paved road to the E trailhead at 2 mi and the parking area at 2.1 mi.

❀ Trail in winter: E trail is not advisable for skiing owing to narrowness, but because it has only one short downhill could be used for climbing the mountain. W trail, which follows an old jeep trail, could be used for a challenging ski in either direction.

⚹ Distances: Parking lot to E trailhead, 0.1 mi; to jct. overlooking Tooley Pond, 0.3 mi; to W trail jct., 0.8 mi; to summit, 0.9 mi (1.4 km); to W trailhead on Tooley Pond Rd., 1.6 mi; to E trailhead, 2 mi; to parking area, 2.1 mi (3.4 km). Ascent from E trailhead, 271 ft (83 m); ascent from W trailhead, 248 ft (76 m). Elevation, 1790 ft (546 m).

157 Copper Rock Falls

Trails Illustrated Map 745: BB7

This short trail, partially marked with orange paint blazes, leads along the S bank of the South Branch of the Grass River to a falls.

▶Trailhead: From the E, access is on Tooley Pond Rd., 8.2 mi from NY 3 at the base of a hill. From the W, follow Tooley Pond Rd. from Degrasse, crossing the Grass River at 7.9 mi. The trailhead is at 8.7 mi. There is parking space for approximately six vehicles on the S side of the road, which has wide shoulders.◀

The trailhead (0.0 mi) is marked with a sign on the N side of the road. Orange paint blazes lead one along the base of a hill to the E as the trail heads N to the Grass River.

At 0.1 mi, the well-worn trail reaches the river and turns upstream. Following the river, it reaches the base of three falls, various drops, and cascades, all called Copper Rock Falls at 0.2 mi. Here, a large tongue of rock extends into the river and the river reunites after splitting around an island. This is beautiful spot for a picnic. By standing on the very tip of this rock tongue, one is tempted and sometimes rewarded—depending on water levels—with a view of the falls on the far side of the island.

Continuing up, the trail reaches the top of the most downstream falls at 0.3 mi. The trail skirts the falls, first climbing and then dropping in a scramble, providing exciting glimpses of the rushing river until the top of the second falls at 0.4 mi. The trail reaches the uppermost falls at 0.5 mi. This is not the head of the rapids, but the trail ends here. It is possible to continue upstream above this point, since the vegetation is not thick, but the rapids above will disappoint in comparison to the more spectacular falls below.

❊ Trail in winter: Not advisable for skiing owing to narrowness and short length.

🚶 Distances: To Grass River, 0.1 mi; to base of Copper Rock Falls, 0.2 mi; to top of uppermost falls, 0.5 mi (0.8 km).

158 Grass River Canoe Access

Trails Illustrated Map 745: CC7 | Trails Illustrated Map 746: BB7

This is a short trail (canoe carry) to the Grass River. The spot is designed as a canoe and kayak take-out point before the dangerous Rainbow Falls.

▶Trailhead: From the E, access is on Tooley Pond Rd. at a long parking area parallel to the S side of the road at 10.7 mi from NY 3. From the W, follow Tooley Pond Rd. from Degrasse to the trailhead at 6.2 mi. The parking lot has room for more than eleven vehicles.◀

The trail is marked by a very small canoe carry sign at the W end of the parking lot. From the parking lot (0.0 mi), it follows an old road through an open forest of pines and hardwoods. At 0.1 mi, the trail leaves the road and turns R (W), dropping down to a large lazy bend in the river. The river here is calm and wide with little indication of the upcoming dangerous drop at Rainbow Falls.

❊ Trail in winter: Not advisable for skiing owing to short length.

🚶 Distance: To Grass River, 0.1 mi (0.2 km).

159 Rainbow Falls

Trails Illustrated Map 746: CC7

This is perhaps the most beautiful of all the waterfalls described in this section. The South Branch of the Grass River drops 25 ft into a box canyon, sending spray and creating rainbows in low-angle sun, which gives the falls its name. The trail is only a short walk for such great beauty and is not to be missed.

▶Trailhead: From the E, access is on Tooley Pond Rd., at a large timber landing area blocked by large boulders, 10.9 mi from NY 3. From the W, follow Tooley Pond Rd. from Degrasse to the trailhead at 6 mi. Look for large boulders on the S side of the road. There is no parking area. The road has somewhat narrow shoulders here, providing limited parking.◀

A sign attached to a tree marks the beginning of a well-worn but unmarked trail that starts (0.0) just past several large boulders blocking vehicular access in a large cleared area. This appears to have been a staging area for loading logs. The route crosses the clearing to the SW and the trail starts its descent to the river through a mostly open mature hardwood forest. The trail enters a small meadow and then denser woods, dropping steeply to a short footbridge. A few orange paint blazes can be seen on the trees here.

The footbridge crosses a small side channel of the river to the falls island. On the island, several side trails L access the brink of the falls. The main trail continues, reaching a cliff overlooking the falls at 0.2 mi. This viewing point can be quite wet and muddy, turning icy in cold weather. Appropriate care should be taken; parents will want to warn children against running as they approach the falls. The trail skirts the brink of the small canyon, providing additional views with a final view at 0.3 mi.

❀ Trail in winter: Not advisable for skiing owing to short length.

🐾 Distances: To first overlook, 0.2 mi; to downstream view of falls, 0.3 mi (0.5 km).

160 Bulkhead (Adrenaline) Falls

Trails Illustrated Map 746: CC6

A short hike through a beautiful grove of pines leads to a large pool at the base of this approximately 10 ft drop.

▶Trailhead: From the E, access is on Tooley Pond Rd. after a sharp R turn 13.5 mi from NY 3. From the W, follow Tooley Pond Rd. from Degrasse to the trailhead at 3.4 mi. Look for two large boulders blocking a road on the S side of Tooley Pond Rd. The trail is marked with a "No Motor Vehicles beyond This Point" sign. There is no parking area; parking is limited to the shoulders of the road.◀

From Tooley Pond Rd. (0.0 mi), the trail follows an old road, dropping immediately toward the river and passing through a beautiful forest of large pines. The trail reaches the river at a large pool at 0.1 mi and continues upstream, providing a view of the river funneled through a flume that drops approximately 10 ft. The historical name for this is Bulkhead Falls, but local kayakers have named it Adrenaline Falls, reflecting their physical reaction before and while paddling over this drop.

❄ Trail in winter: Not advisable owing to short length.

⛰ Distances: To Grass River and falls, 0.1 mi (0.2 km).

Stewart Rapids (bushwhack)

Trails Illustrated Map 746: CC6

Stewart Rapids is located at a large turn in the river and can be seen from Tooley Pond Rd. There is no trail, but a short bushwhack to the river will provide a better view of the rapids.

▶Access: From the E, access is on Tooley Pond Rd. at 13.7 mi from NY 3. From the W, follow Tooley Pond Rd. from Degrasse 3.2 mi. Look for a large turn in the river below, with rapids. There is no parking area. Parking is limited to the shoulders of the road.◀

❄ Access in winter: Not advisable.

⛰ Distance: To Grass River and rapid, approximately 0.1 mi (0.2 km).

Twin Falls and Bony Falls (bushwhack)

Trails Illustrated Map 746: CC6

Twin Falls is the former location of Clarksboro, a community founded in 1866 after iron was discovered in the area in the 1860s. Clarksboro had a blast furnace, water-powered hammer mill, and saw mill. The R channel of Twin Falls can be viewed from Tooley Pond Rd.; the upper part of the channel is lined with laid stone and was part of the mill works. The steep drop below the pool at the base of Twin Falls is called Bony Falls, named by local kayakers in honor of the many boulders that punctuate the serpentine channel.

▶Trailhead: From the E, access is on Tooley Pond Rd. The R channel of the falls is at 13.9 mi from NY 3. From the W, follow Tooley Pond Rd. from Degrasse 3 mi. There is limited parking on the shoulders of the road.◀

There is no trail to the falls from Tooley Pond Rd. The R channel can be viewed from the road; the rockwork is interesting to study in light of its place in the history of the working mill. Often along this channel, a tree has fallen or a log has been placed, making access to the island possible, if potentially wet. The best plan would be to use a vessel of some type to cross the R channel above the falls, or put in at the base of this channel. Any crossing above the falls should be attempted only by experienced paddlers.

Once on the island, it is a joy to explore. Most of the underbrush has been shaded and much of the island is covered with pine needles. The explorer will discover a mound of iron ore on the upper point of the island. These rocks are easily twice the weight of the average rock. Next to the smaller R channel are foundations and a round brick structure, perhaps once part of the blast furnace. Slag with intriguing patterns, left from smelting the ore, makes up the beach between the two channels.

The L channel falls should not be missed. The water of this channel of Twin Falls makes a straightforward frothy plunge over the smooth bedrock in a drop of approximately 35 ft. The bank provides ample space to sit and contemplate the beauty.

At 0.1 mi below the falls, there is a dirt road to state land that has been used as canoe access and for viewing Twin Falls. This road crosses private property and those utilizing it for access are trespassing.

❀ Trail in winter: Not advisable.

🚶 Distance: To Twin Falls island, approximately 0.1 mi (0.2 km).

161 Sinclair Falls

Trails Illustrated Map 746: CC6

There is a short trail here. The falls can be viewed from the bridge on Lake George Rd. or one may follow the paths along the R shore around the first bend.

▶Trailhead: From the E, take Tooley Pond Rd. 14.9 mi and turn L on Lake George Rd. From Degrasse, Lake George Rd. is on the R at 2 mi. There is a kiosk and parking area on Tooley Pond Rd. or one may park beside the bridge a short way down Lake George Rd.◀

First, take in the view from the bridge (there is a small parking area here), then follow herd paths along the R (N) side of the river. The L (S) side is private and posted. The falls is a 20 ft drop where the river makes a sharp turn S (L). There is another excellent view of the falls from its base. It is approximately 0.1 mi to the bend in the river.

❀ Trail in winter: Not suitable.

🚶 Distance: To bend, approximately 0.1 mi.

162 Basford Falls

Trails Illustrated Map 746: CC6

This is a short hike to a 20 ft cascade in a majestic grove of pines.

▶Trailhead: From the E, access is on Tooley Pond Rd. 15.5 mi from NY 3. From the W, follow Tooley Pond Rd. from Degrasse 1.4 mi. The trailhead is located at a large boulder between two steel gateposts. There is no parking area. Parking is limited to the shoulders of the road.◀

From Tooley Pond Rd. (0.0 mi), the unmarked trail follows an old logging road on a ridge toward the W, passing through hardwoods underlain with a lush growth of ferns. At 0.1 mi, the trail turns S, dropping into a small valley before climbing back onto the ridge, only to start a final drop to the river at approximately 0.2 mi. The trail descends to the river through a glade of hemlock and white pines, with the floor of the forest covered with pine needles. It comes to the falls at a little over 0.3 mi. This is indeed a beautiful spot and perfect place for a picnic. Basford Falls is a 20 ft cascade. As you start to return, note the ridge to NE; the trail follows this nose of the ridge as you return up the hill to the starting point.

❋ Trail in winter: Suitable for skiing, though short, and the final slope will be a challenge to all but the best skiers.

🦌 Distances: To turn from ridge, 0.1 mi; to Basford Falls, approximately 0.3 mi (0.5 km).

163 Lampson Falls

Trails Illustrated Map 746: EE5

Marked with red DEC markers, this trail extends W from Clare Rd. (CR 27) to the head of Lampson Falls along the main branch of the Grass River. This falls is an imposing 60 ft cascade with a width almost matching its total descent.

▶Trailhead: The trailhead is on Clare Rd. (CR 27) 4.5 mi N of its intersection with CR 17 in the hamlet of Degrasse. A DEC sign L indicates the Grass River Wild Forest. There is ample parking.◀

The route passes around a gate on a former jeep trail (0.0 mi). The first part of the trail is a level right-of-way through private land, until tall white pines mark the Forest Preserve at 0.2 mi. These and hemlocks fringe the path to an obvious fork at 0.4 mi. On the L, a short spur leads to an open area and large rock just upstream of the head of Lampson Falls. The jeep road swings R, and in a few yards a path diverges L, descending and then climbing onto a rocky peninsula from which there are marvelous views of the falls and its pool at 0.5 mi.

The first sight of this falls, particularly after a rain or in spring, is truly breathtaking. Many lesser falls have been heavily commercialized. Fortunately, this will not occur here with the inclusion of Lampson Falls in the Forest Preserve.

❋ Trail in winter: Ideally suited for skiing, although descent to the base of the falls is challenging.

🦌 Distances: To state land, 0.2 mi; to foot of Lampson Falls, 0.5 mi (0.8 km).

164 Grass River Trail

Trails Illustrated Map 746: EE5

The trail, which is in essence an extension of the Lampson Falls trail (trail 163), follows along the R bank of the Grass River downstream. Trails ambling along river banks like this one are relatively rare in today's Forest Preserve.

▶Locator: This trail, marked with red DEC markers, starts at the foot of Lampson Falls (see trail 163).◀

Spring paddlers near Lampson Falls. James Bullard

At the start (0.0 mi), the trail winds around a low promontory with rock out-croppings. At 0.2 mi, the way is impeded by beaver-induced flooding at a spot where a small inlet stream flows into the river. This may require a bypass of approximately 50 yd. The trail resumes following the river under a canopy of towering hemlocks on the slope to the R.

At 1 mi the trail reaches the abutment of a bridge that formerly crossed the river. It was destroyed during the great ice storm of 1998 and DEC has no plans to replace it. The trail now ends here. A return to the Lampson Falls trail (trail 163) can be made via the old road to the R, the same road that the Lampson Falls Trail follows. It is not marked but is wide and can be easily followed through attractive forest.

❋ Trail in winter: Not suitable, but the old road from the terminus of the trail, returning to the Lampson Falls trail, is an ideal ski or snowshoe route and is used locally for that purpose.

❋ Distances: Lampson Falls to bridge, 1 mi (1.6 km).

165 Harper Falls

Trails Illustrated Map 746: FF5

This unmarked but distinct trail proceeds from a partially abandoned town road and eventually reaches the foot of an attractive, little-known waterfall.

▶Trailhead: Access is from Clare Rd. (CR 27), 7.2 mi from its intersection with CR 17 in the hamlet of Degrasse. This is 2.7 mi N of the trailhead to Lampson Falls on Clare Rd. At 7.2 mi, Donnerville Rd. comes in on the L. Take Donnerville Rd. 0.6 mi to the parking area. A trailhead sign identifying this as the Grass River Wild Forest and a small, rough parking area have been installed here.◀

Past the gate (0.0 mi), the trail passes through some large aspens at the beginning. These are probably holdovers from a fire. The trail is undulating at first and then begins a long, gradual descent to the North Branch of the Grass River, on which Harper Falls is located. The heavy growth of hemlock beneath the hardwood canopy that lines the cool slopes here points the way to the forest to come. Noticeable, too, are the scattered remnants of the subsistence agriculture that was once practiced here. These manifest themselves mostly in the form of old stone walls and barbed wire fences. These agricultural remnants are a rarity in the Forest Preserve of today.

At 0.9 mi the trail reaches the foot of the waterfall. It veers R another 0.1 mi where an even better glimpse of the falls can be obtained. Harper Falls descends to the floor of the valley in two distinct cascades. The total descent almost equals that of nearby Lampson Falls (trail 163), but the falls, although impressive, lacks some of the grandeur of the much wider waterfall on the main branch of the Grass River.

❋ Trail in winter: Mostly downhill, twisting. Parking in winter will likely have to be on CR 27, adding 0.5 mi to the one-way distance.

🚶 Distances: Trailhead to Harper Falls, 0.9 mi; to end of trail, 1 mi (1.6 km).

166 North Branch Grass River Trail

Trails Illustrated Map 746: FF5

▶Locator: This river ramble begins at the end of the unmarked Harper Falls trail, 0.9 mi from the trailhead on Donnerville Rd. (see trail 165).◀

Red disks on the R define the trail (0.0 mi), which proceeds along the river bank until it reaches the Donnerville State Forest at 0.4 mi. The trail swings away from the river for a while after entering the State Forest. The difference between Forest Preserve lands and those of the State Forest soon becomes apparent as the trail enters a fairly extensive logged-over area.

The trail rejoins the river's bank after a wide circuit of a floodplain wetland and follows the river for its duration. In several places it ascends and descends rather steep bluffs above the river as it travels under an attractive canopy of hemlock. Striking specimens of big-tooth aspen, close to the maximum size for this early successional species, are a feature of the route. An occasional basswood, a relative rarity in the Forest Preserve, can also be seen.

At 1.9 mi, the Donnerville State Forest truck trail marks the end of the trail. The river, which the trail has been paralleling is attractive, displaying one series of gentle rapids after another. This makes it pleasing visually, but not canoeable.

Although vehicles may legally be driven to the trail's terminus on the State Forest truck trail, the truck trail is better suited to 4WD vehicles. Because of this and because of the relative remoteness of the terminus, North Branch Trail is best considered a round-trip hike.

❄ Trail in winter: Owing to narrowness and steepness in places, generally not suitable for cross-country skiing.

🚶 Distances: Harper Falls to Donnerville State Forest, 0.4 mi; to truck trail, 1.9 mi (3 km).

167 Moody Falls

Trails Illustrated Map 746: CC11

This short trail passes through a pine forest to a campsite on the Raquette River below Moody Falls. Continuing on a short unmarked trail takes one to the falls.

▶Trailhead: Access is on NY 56 approximately 1.6 mi N of its jct. with NY 3 at Sevey Corners. This is approximately 1.5 mi S of Ham's Inn. Look for a red paint blaze on a tree on the E side of the road at a road cut. There is no parking area, so care is required in parking.◀

Marked with yellow canoe carry disks, the trail leaves NY 56 (0.0 mi) and passes through a mature pine forest as it drops toward the river. It enters a marsh and crosses a boggy area as the Raquette River comes into view. A well-used camping area with a fire ring is at 0.1 mi. The pool and boulder garden at the base of Moody Falls are visible from this location.

An unmarked trail continues S, reaching a steep slope on the W side of the falls and dropping to a point with a beautiful view of the falls at 0.3 mi. This is a nice place for a picnic. There is a canoe carry trail on the other side of the river.

❀ Trail in winter: Not suitable for skiing in the winter owing to steepness, but snowshoes would allow a short scenic trip.

🐾 Distances: NY 56 to campsite, 0.1 mi; to view of Moody Falls, 0.3 mi (0.5 km).

168 Jamestown Falls

Trails Illustrated Map 746: CC11

The trail to Jamestown Falls begins at the end of a short dirt road to the Raquette River. This unmarked trail follows the L (W) shore to the falls.

▶Trailhead: Access is on NY 56 approximately 2.6 mi N of its jct. with NY 3 at Sevey Corners. This is approximately 0.5 mi S of Ham's Inn. The dirt road to the river can be rough at times. There is a small area suitable for parking on the L side of the road immediately after the NY 56 turnoff.◀

From this parking area (0.0 mi) the road proceeds to the Raquette River at 0.3 mi. Go to the end of the boat launching area to obtain a clear view of Jamestown Falls. Return up the road and look for a game path that branches to the S and upstream.

The path immediately crosses a small stream joining the Raquette River from the W. This crossing may present a challenge during high water. The path continues along the shore to the boundary of state land at 0.4 mi. The Jamestown Club owns this land and its lodge can be seen on the opposite bank. Paul Jamieson in his book, *Adirondack Canoe Waters: North Flow*, now out of print, stated that, "The club's lands include also a narrow strip along the L bank, W of which is Forest Preserve. Though most of the carry trail is in private land, it is not posted (except perhaps in hunting season), and I am told that the club does not object to its use as a carry trail so long as no litter is left." The base of the falls is at 0.5 mi. Jamestown Falls has a double drop as the river makes a L turn in the process. There are many beautiful rocks on which to picnic and enjoy the view. The trail reaches the top of the falls at 0.7 mi.

❀ Trail in winter: Not suitable for skiing owing to its length and narrowness.

🐾 Distances: NY 56 to Raquette River, 0.3 mi; to base of Jamestown Falls, 0.5 mi; to top of falls, 0.7 mi (1.1 km).

169 Rainbow Falls Ski Trail

Trails Illustrated Map 746: HH10

This abandoned road in the remote White Hill Wild Forest runs from a former Boy Scout camp to the Raquette River just below Rainbow Falls Reservoir.

▶Trailhead: From the N, take George St./Whites Hill Rd. S from the town of Parishville 5.2 mi to Clear Pond Rd. on the R with a stone pillar pointing the way. Access from the S is via Stark Rd. (also known as Joe Indian Rd.), which turns sharply to the R off NY 56 at a sign indicating Joe Indian Pond, 13 mi N of the intersection of NY 56 and NY 3 at Sevey Corners.

Follow Stark Rd. (which changes to White Hill Rd.) 12.1 mi to Clear Pond Rd. on the L. Drive down the gravel road 1.9 mi to the shore of Clear Pond where a Boy Scout camp complex stood until the inholding was acquired by New York State in the mid-1980s. A number of foundations are still apparent. ◀

The trail goes R around Clear Pond (0.0 mi) and follows snowmobile disks. At a jct. at 0.3 mi, Lilypad Pond Trail (trail 170) goes L. The trail crosses a series of knolls covered with mostly pole-sized hardwoods with an occasional conifer. At 2 mi it reaches the outlet of Big Rock Pond. The pond lies 150 yd upstream and is clearly delineated in autumn by a fringe of golden tamarack encircling the sedge mat around it.

The trail crosses the outlet on a beaver dam and proceeds to a jct. with a 4WD gravel road at 4.8 mi. This is the site of the old village of Picketville. Several of the old building foundations are still in the vicinity. There is often a snowmobile base to this point, and a base is even more likely after a L turn on Picketville Rd. The old Picketville Rd. goes through mostly Forest Preserve to the shore of Rainbow Falls Reservoir just below the dam. The path is generally fairly wide and the grades moderate. A state acquisition has provided access to the reservoir itself at 7.6 mi.

❋ Trail in winter: Primarily a ski route, with some snowmobile use.

🐾 Distances: Clear Pond to Lilypad Pond Trail, 0.3 mi; to Big Rock Pond, 2 mi; to Picketville Rd., 4.8 mi; to Rainbow Falls Reservoir, 7.6 mi (12.2 km).

170 Lilypad Pond

Trails Illustrated Map 746: HH10

This trail connects four of the White Hill Wild Forest's glacial gems, whose waters lie neatly folded under the brows of a series of fairly steep beech ridges.

▶Locator: This trail begins at 0.3 mi on Rainbow Falls Ski Trail (trail 169). ◀

The trail bears L from Rainbow Falls Ski Trail (0.0 mi) and follows small red trail disks. The initial ridge is only moderately steep and has more beech trees still alive than the other ridges. At 1.6 mi, the trail crosses the outlet of Little Rock Pond. This small pond is quite marshy; the process of eutrophication, to which all bodies of water eventually succumb, has progressed further here than on the other ponds.

The trail now begins a moderately steep ascent and proceeds to cross two ridges clothed mostly with dead and infected beech trees. The culprit here is beech scale disease—a combination of a fungus and an insect. An occasional majestic live sugar maple is also evident on the ridge.

Long Pond is at 2.6 mi. The trail circles one end of the pond, passing several nice campsites. Long Pond and Clear Pond are the largest of the area's bodies of water; both have many handsome specimens of hemlock and white pine lining their shores. The trail ascends yet another beech ridge as it makes its way to Lilypad Pond. From the claw marks on the trees it appears that every bear in creation has partaken of the bounteous beech nut crop here at one time or another.

The trail ends at Lilypad Pond at 3.3 mi. Flooded trees are more apparent here than at the other ponds. Marked trees abound in several directions—a legacy of the time the Boy Scouts blazed trails to their own destinations.

✼ Trail in winter: Not suitable for cross-country skiing owing to steepness, and more particularly narrowness.

🚶 Distances: Clear Pond to Little Rock Pond, 1.6 mi; to Long Pond, 2.6 mi; to Lilypad Pond, 3.3 mi (5.3 km). ➤

Oswegatchie River. Chris Murray

Cranberry Lake–Wanakena Section

 The hamlets of Cranberry Lake and Wanakena are at the hub of the hiking trails in this section of the Adirondacks. Cranberry Lake Hamlet is at the foot of Cranberry Lake, a widening of the Oswegatchie River made wider by the erection of a dam. Wanakena, the site of the New York State Ranger School, is on the Oswegatchie where it begins its flow into Cranberry Lake. South of these two hamlets an unbroken forest stretches to distant Stillwater Reservoir on the Beaver River. Despite damage from the derecho in 1995, it still contains the largest area of virgin forest remaining in the entire Northeast and the largest trailless area in the state. Both of these are S of High Falls on the Oswegatchie River.

The trail network extends S of the two hamlets and penetrates the Five Ponds Wilderness Area and the adjacent Cranberry Lake Wild Forest. A 50-mi loop trail around Cranberry Lake, known as the Cranberry Lake 50 (CL50), has been created from several existing and new trails in this area (see Cranberry Lake 50 Section). As is the situation with the northern Adirondacks as a whole, beaver flooding is occasionally a problem and a few of the interior trails are somewhat indistinct in their markings. The forest is comprised mostly of maturing hardwoods, with conifers in the numerous wetlands and also on top of the many eskers. The area of virgin timber is pierced only peripherally by these trails, most notably the Sand Lake Trail.

The trails are generally moderate in grade and most lead to small- to medium-sized conifer-ringed ponds and lakes. The northernmost of these ponds have been relatively unaffected by acid rain and still reflect in a general way the excellent brook trout fishing for which the area is famous. Among these bodies of water are Wolf Pond, Sand Lake, Cage Lake, Big Deer Pond, Cowhorn Pond, Cat Mt. Pond, Glasby Pond, Burntbridge Pond, and, at the center of the woods, the entrancing Five Ponds themselves. There are several prominent ascents: Bear Mt., overlooking Cranberry Lake; Cat Mt., once the site of a fire tower; and the short trail to the overlook on Dog Pond Mt.

There is a state campground just outside the hamlet of Cranberry Lake.

A few suggested hikes for this section are listed below.

SHORT HIKE
Moore Trail: 4 mi (6.4 km) round-trip. An easy walk along a scenic, tumbling section of the Oswegatchie River. See trail 201.

MODERATE HIKE
Bear Mt. from state campground: 3.4 mi (5.4 km) round-trip. The top offers excellent views of Cranberry Lake, one of the largest lakes in the Adirondacks, and

of the expansive Five Ponds Wilderness Area. See trail 179.

HARDER HIKE
High Falls Loop: 16.9 mi (27 km). This long woods walk incorporates two former logging railroad beds and two foot trails, the highlight being the pleasant setting and lean-tos at High Falls on the Oswegatchie River. See trail 186.

171 Burntbridge Pond

The trail to Burntbridge Pond uses the grade of an old railroad bed, as do many of the trails in this region. This one, a spur line of the Grass River Railroad constructed by the Emporium Lumber Company in 1911, was last used to haul logs to the company's sawmill in Cranberry Lake just before the state purchased the land in 1933. Part of this trail has been incorporated into the CL50 (see Cranberry Lake 50 Section).

▶Trailhead: This orange-marked snowmobile trail goes from NY 3 in a SE direction to Burntbridge Pond deep in the heart of the Cranberry Lake Wild Forest. The DEC-marked trailhead is at a parking lot on the S side of NY 3 approximately 2 mi E of the hamlet of Cranberry Lake.◀

From NY 3 (0.0 mi), the trail (a dual-track four-wheeler trail currently marked as a snowmobile trail) climbs and winds to the railroad grade at 0.2 mi. The trail then follows a gentle grade and crosses numerous streams and wet spots on wide snowmobile bridges. Four-wheeler use of the trail is evident. The trail continues S through an area of cutover hardwoods to arrive at a trail register and the jct. with Burntbridge Pond–Bear Mt. Trail (trail 172), R, at 1.5 mi.

(A R at the jct. leads to Bear Mt. and Cranberry Lake Campground. This is an alternate route for those hiking the Cranberry Lake 50 and wanting to avoid some of the walking on NY 3. See Cranberry Lake 50 Section.)

Burntbridge Pond Trail continues straight ahead. An old, open meadow, once a logging camp, is reached at 1.6 mi. The creeks along this stretch of the trail drain into a large spruce swamp to the W and eventually into Cranberry Lake. At 2.3 mi the trail turns R and leaves the grade of the old railroad to join a logging road. It makes several turns back and forth, losing elevation while passing through muddy areas until crossing Brandy Brook on a bridge at 2.9 mi.

The trail turns R and follows the brook under a canopy of hemlocks, then veers L, passing a trail R to designated Campsite 6 at the point where Brandy Brook joins the flow. This flow is one of the flooded inlets of Cranberry Lake. The trail enters a dark area of dense small pines as it curves gently to the R into an open area with young trees growing on the margins. Barney Burns, a famous nineteenth century Adirondack guide, had a sportsmen's camp nearby.

The trail arrives at an open glade on the shores of Brandy Brook Flow at 3.1 mi. In the middle of this open glade, a DEC sign points the way L to Burntbridge Pond and the E end of Dog Pond Loop (trail 175). (The W segment of Dog Pond Loop and the Cranberry Lake 50 go straight, marked with orange and blue disks.) A trail R goes to designated Campsite 7 on Brandy Brook Flow.

Going L at this jct., the trail, which has been generally flat so far, begins to rise moderately. It crosses several more creeks on rocks as it ascends a ravine. The forest becomes more mature hardwood, mostly maple and black cherry with some beech. At 5.5 mi the E segment of the blue-marked Dog Pond Loop comes in on the R. Burntbridge Trail continues straight on a mostly even grade to a fork at 6.1 mi, where it veers sharply R. The trail straight ahead, which is similarly marked with red disks as a snowmobile trail, goes on to end shortly at the edge of the Conifer-Emporium Easement lands.

At 6.5 mi, the trail makes another R turn away from a similar dead-end snowmobile trail coming in on the L. At 6.7 mi, the trail reaches Burntbridge Pond, circular, marsh-fringed, and lined with an attractive mixed forest. A lean-to situated under the conifers adds considerably to the charm of this remote spot.

❄ Trail in winter: An excellent cross-country ski trip, with moderate grades the entire distance.

🐾 Distances: NY 3 to Burntbridge Pond–Bear Mt. Trail, 1.5 mi; to Brandy Brook Flow and Dog Pond Loop (W end), 3.1 mi; to Dog Pond Loop (E end), 5.5 mi; to Burntbridge Pond, 6.7 mi (10.7 km).

172 Burntbridge Pond–Bear Mt. Trail
Trails Illustrated Map 745: AA10

This trail connects Burntbridge Pond Trail to Cranberry Lake Public Campground near the northern approach to Bear Mt. (trail 179).

Two vehicles allow for an easy hike from the Burntbridge Pond trailhead (trail 171) to the campground. The trail is also part of the CL50 (see Cranberry Lake 50 Section).

▶Locator: This trail begins at the 1.5 mi mark on the Burntbridge Pond trail (trail 171). There is a trail register at this jct.◀

This yellow-marked trail begins at the trail register on the Burntbridge Pond trail (0.0 mi). The trail starts down a slope, turning R then L through a second growth of black cherry, red maple and occasional aspen, and reaching a bridge at 0.3 mi. There is a marshy area to the L created by beaver activity. The trail now climbs to a pleasant, rather level valley between two hills with little undergrowth. As the trail drops from this valley it makes a turn to the R (N) and climbs.

After reaching a high point, the trail (now on an old logging road or four-wheeler trail) turns abruptly L (W) and descends to Bear Mt. Creek at 1 mi. The trail crosses the creek on a plank boardwalk to reach a sliver of dry land; wetlands are visible on both sides of the trail. The trail crosses a second plank boardwalk at 1.2 mi. The large, attractive natural boreal wetland that existed here has been reinforced and increased in size with the construction of the dam at Cranberry Lake Hamlet. Tamarack, white cedar, and white pine make a pleasing spectacle as they drape over the alders and sedges that line the course of the creek. Lady slippers have been seen here in the spring.

After leaving the second boardwalk, the trail climbs out of the wetlands and enters a logged area following old roads and skid trails. The forest is mostly young hardwoods here with some areas reseeding to pine. There is a jct. at 1.4 mi, where the East Connector (trail 173) meets the trail from the N. (The East Connector is part of the CL50; it reaches NY 3 in 1 mi.) The trail leaves the logging road and reaches the top of a small hill at 1.8 mi, then drops slightly into a marshy fern meadow just before reaching the base of a large cliff. The trail skirts the base of the mountain with a marshy area to the L. The forest here is older and mostly beech. At 2.2 mi the trail passes a large gneissic erratic on the R. Under a large hemlock tree at 2.3 mi, the trail reaches the jct. with the Bear Mt. trail coming from Cranberry Lake Campground (trail 179). A L turn here leads to the summit overlook on Bear Mt. in 1.5 mi; a R turn leads to the trail 179 trailhead in the campground in 0.2 mi.

✿ Trail in winter: Generally not suited for cross-country skiing owing to narrowness combined with wetlands and plank boardwalks.

⚲ Distances: To first plank boardwalk, 1 mi; to Bear Mt. trail (trail 179), 2.3 mi (3.7 km); to Cranberry Lake campground, 2.5 mi (4 km).

173 East Connector

Trails Illustrated Map 745: AA 9

This trail is part of the CL50 (see Cranberry Lake 50 Section). It is located on state land and provides a connection between NY 3 and the Burntbridge Pond–Bear Mt. Trail (trail 172). For those completing the CL50, this trail cuts 2 mi of hiking along NY 3 and shortens the loop by 1.1 mi.

▶Trailhead: Access is from a parking lot S of NY 3, 0.1 mi E of the "Hamlet of Cranberry Lake" sign. From the E, this is approximately 7.5 mi W of the jct. of NY 3 and NY 56 at Sevey Corners. The parking lot can hold approximately twelve cars; it is shared with the Gilbert Tract Loop (trail 174).◀

The blue-marked trail (0.0 mi) begins at the SW corner of the parking lot and follows old logging roads through rolling hills its entire length. The trail immediately encounters a wet area with a boardwalk passing through mixed hardwoods, mostly composed of yellow birch. A small stream has washed out the road, which at 0.1 mi reaches a small beaver pond and a clearing. The trail turns to the R, leaving the clearing and proceeding up a gentle grade.

At 0.3 mi, on top of a gentle rise, a road branches R; continue straight (on the L branch). A well-marked second branch is reached at 0.4 mi; again keep to the L. The trail crosses a second beaver dam at 0.5 mi, and meets Burntbridge Pond–Bear Mt. Trail (trail 172) at 1 mi. (To the L [E], the Burntbridge Pond–Bear Mt. Trail arrives at the the Burntbridge Pond trail [trail 171] in 1.4 mi. To the R [W], the trail arrives at the Cranberry Lake Campground trailhead in 1.1 mi.)

✿ Trail in winter: Gentle rolling terrain, suitable for cross-country skiing and snowshoeing.

⚲ Distances: NY 3 to jct. with Burntbridge Pond–Bear Mt. Trail (trail 172), 1 mi (1.6 km). Ascent, 50 ft (15.2 m) to highest point, then drops 26 ft (7.9 m) to the jct. with the Bear Mt. trail.

David Hough

174 Gilbert Tract Loop

Trails Illustrated Map 745: AA 9

Marked for skiing, but suitable also for hiking, this loop trail mostly follows old logging roads through rolling hills its entire length.

▶Trailhead: Access is from a parking lot S of NY 3, 0.1 mi E of the "Hamlet of Cranberry Lake" sign. From the E, this is approximately 7.5 mi W of the jct. of NY 3 and NY 56 at Sevey Corners. The parking lot can hold approximately twelve cars; it is shared with the East Connector (trail 173).◀

The yellow-marked ski trail (0.0 mi) begins at the SE corner of the parking lot. It climbs on a wide logging road through mixed hardwoods mostly composed of yellow birch. In 300 ft the trail passes a trailhead sign. The trail now makes a gentle turn L (E), ascending. At 0.1 mi the trail forks L off the logging road, with the returning loop to the R.

The trail is rougher now and drops as it follows NY 3, which can be heard and occasionally glimpsed through the trees to the L. At 0.3 mi a low-lying logging road joins L from NY 3. The trail follows logging roads for the reminder of its length. The trail is now generally level, leaving NY 3 and trending E along the S side of a marshy area until it makes a gentle R turn at 0.7 mi and then starts to climb. At 1.1 mi the trail reaches its halfway point on a gently curving boardwalk in a marshy area. The trail continues through marsh until 1.3 mi where it turns R and climbs to dryer ground. The trail now climbs and drops along the NW flank of a small hill until it reaches a jct. with itself at 2 mi. The trail returns to its start at 2.1 mi.

❊ Trail in winter: Gentle rolling terrain, suitable for cross-country skiing and snowshoeing.

❧ Distances: NY 3 to jct. with branch to loop, 0.1 mi; start of climb, 0.7 mi; lowest point, 1.3 mi; highest point, 1.7 mi; return to start, 2.1 mi (3.4 km). Ascent, 77 ft (23 m) to highest point.

175 Dog Pond Loop

Trails Illustrated Map 745: Z10

Some of the nearly hidden joys of Cranberry Lake Wild Forest can be found on this loop off the Burntbridge Pond trail (trail 171). The trail provides a glimpse of majestic old-growth hardwood stands, secluded glacial ponds, and even an historic cave, all of which were previously inaccessible. Part of this trail has been incorporated into the CL50 (see Cranberry Lake 50 Section).

This loop trail is marked with blue disks for its entire distance. It also has orange disks for its first 0.3 mi as it parallels the shores of Brandy Brook Flow. These disappear as the trail jogs L and continues to follow the shore of the flow.

▶Locator: This trail begins at 3.1 mi on the Burntbridge Pond trail (trail 171); it loops around to end at 5.5 mi on the Burntbridge Pond trail.◀

From the jct. (0.0 mi), Dog Pond Loop continues straight ahead (S) as the Burntbridge Pond trail (trail 171) goes L (E). The Dog Pond Loop trail immediately dips to a wet stream crossing then climbs a small incline and turns R. The trail continues to parallel the flow, following a fairly straight path among hardwoods. A jct. is reached at 0.4 mi. A snowmobile trail to the R leads to Brandy Brook Flow, where snowmobiles can travel on the lake during the winter and canoes can land in summer. Dog Pond Loop continues straight.

The trail crosses a bridge at 0.8 mi. There are three designated campsites along the shore in this section of trail. All are attractive, under fringes of conifers with headland settings that feature insect-dispelling breezes. The connector trails to these sites are not marked and can be difficult to find. Views of Cranberry Lake and some of its island are visible at times.

The loop trail continues to parallel the flow, climbing and dropping to avoid wet shoreline as it crosses the heads of several small bays under a canopy of hardwoods. The trail follows the shore to a turn R to designated Campsite 10 at 1.4 mi. This is a beautiful campsite with a view of Bear Mt. and a tumbled stone chimney, which once graced the premises of the historic Indian Mt. Club. The trail turns to follow the bay behind the campsite.

Turning R, the trail leaves the shore at 1.7 mi and starts climbing as it passes through a particularly beautiful garden-like area of rocks, hardwoods, ferns, and pines to a high point with old-growth hardwoods. Imposing beech and sugar maple highlight the route; some of the beeches have succumbed to the fungus now ravishing the species. This is red tail hawk nesting territory.

The trail drops and crosses two more streams before reaching the outlet of Hedgehog Pond. Climbing again, the trail levels off before intersecting the trail to Hedgehog Pond (trail 176) at 2.4 mi. The trail L leads to the pond in 0.2 mi. Some call this Clear Pond, but one hopes Hedgehog Pond sticks. The name is unique. This is the first of the glacial ponds along this route. Low mountains frame the pond on one side, and striking glacial erratics lie strewn on its shore. The trail R leads to Cranberry Lake in 0.3 mi.

The Dog Pond Loop continues straight, leveling off, then climbing to a high point, before descending to a bay on the East Inlet of Cranberry Lake. The trail now follows the shore of the bay to the E and crosses the bay's inlet to Campsite 13 at 4 mi. The trail makes a sharp turn L (E), soon passing Campsite 14. (A short trail R leads to Campsite 15.)

The trail leaves Cranberry Lake following an old logging road that parallels East Creek to a R turn, then crosses East Creek on a bridge at 3.6 mi. It immediately begins a steep climb to a high point at 3.7 mi, then crosses a slope graced by a boulder garden and impressive old-growth northern hardwoods. The trail continues its slow climb through scattered glacial boulders.

As the trail drops, boulders appear which seem to be arranged in a straight line. It is interesting to speculate what type of glacial motion may have created such a pattern. At 4.3 mi the trail reaches an amazing group of erratic boulders. Many of the tumbled-together boulders are topped with ferns, creating the feel of a Japanese garden. There is a courtyard-like area called Willys Cave within one group of boulders; it can be accessed by crawling through a tunnel.

The trail starts to climb again. Cranberry Lake can be glimpsed when the trees have dropped their leaves. At 4.5 mi the trail reaches a high point and starts a slight descent, then follows a ridge toward the S along the W flank of East Mt. generally holding its elevation. At 5 mi the trail meets the red-marked East Inlet Trail (trail 177), which leads to Cranberry Lake in 1.1 mi. The loop trail continues straight, quickly climbing to a high point, then descending with nice views of Curtis Pond (L).

Before the trail crosses the pond's outlet, a group of boulders a few hundred feet to the R make an interesting side trip. These glacial erratics create a natural rock shelter where Adirondack trapper and backwoodsman Nat Foster reputedly hid from a hostile hunting party of Indians in the early nineteenth century. Shortly beyond the boulders the trail crosses the outlet. Curtis Pond, to the L, is framed by handsome white pines and spruce trees on ledges; it is known for its hungry brook trout. A side trail L at 5.3 mi leads to a designated campsite on Curtis Pond.

The trail now leaves Curtis Pond on a small ridge, climbs, and enters a fault valley, reaching a high point at 5.6 mi. It then drops. Large talus boulders litter the cliffs and their bases to the R. Willy's Pond appears to the L; the trail follows the pond's SW shore. Dead trees guard the shore on one side, giving the pond a somewhat haunting appearance. The trail reaches the outlet of Willys Pond at 6 mi then leaves the pond and climbs up along a ridge, turning R with rock and cliffs on the L.

The trail follows the S shore of Irish Pond, which, like Willys Pond, was previously reached only by bushwhacking, then leaves the pond, crosses its outlet, and, at 6.6 mi, reaches a jct. with a little used yellow-marked trail (L) that leads to a designated campsite on the pond's E shore. The trail now passes through an area with large majestic hemlocks. It dips and rises, then skirts a hill at its high point and reaches a ridge at 6.9 mi before dropping to a creek.

The trail climbs to a large clearing known as Proulx Clearing. This was once the site of one of the region's early traditional lumber camps. During his stay at the Cranberry Lake Biological Center in the 1920s, the youthful Bob Marshall was fond of hiking to this spot. Today the clearing is reverting to forest, led by some rapidly growing red spruce; a beaver flow adjacent to the clearing makes it look larger than it is. Here the trail meets a jct. with Dog Pond Trail (trail 155), at 7.2 mi. (From Proulx Clearing, the red-marked Dog Pond Trail goes R 1.5 mi to end at the jct. of the Otter Brook Trail [trail 203], R, and Sucker Brook Rd. [trail 153], L. The latter provides a short link to the trails of the Massawepie–Horseshoe Lake area; the former is part of the CL50.)

The loop turns L (N) at the clearing and begins a mild ascent until it levels off in a magnificent forest. It then begins to climb to a draw between Bear Mt. (L) and Dog Pond Mt. (R). It passes a designated campsite at 8.9 mi. Going straight ahead, the blue-marked loop continues to undulate moderately through a mostly hardwood forest with occasional glimpses of the wild Berkley range of mountains off to the R.

It passes a stand of large hemlock just before crossing a creek on a wooden bridge at 10.4 mi. The loop ends at a jct. with the Burntbridge Pond trail (trail 171) at 11.2 mi. To the R, the Burntbridge Pond trail leads 1.2 mi to the lean-to on Burntbridge Pond. To the L, it leads 5.5 mi back to the trailhead on NY 3.

❋ Trail in winter: Generally not suitable owing to steepness of terrain.

𝕸 Distances: the Burntbridge Pond trail to Hedgehog Pond trail (trail 176), 2.4 mi; to East Creek bridge, 3.6 mi; to East Inlet Trail (trail 177), 5 mi; to Curtis Pond, 5.3 mi; to Irish Pond, 6.6 mi; to Proulx Clearing, 7.2 mi; to the Burntbridge Pond trail, 11.2 mi (17.9 km).

176 Hedgehog Pond

Trails Illustrated Map 745: Z10

▶Locator: The trail to Hedgehog Pond (also known as Clear Pond) starts at Dog Pond Loop (trail 175), 2.4 mi from the W end of the loop.◀

From the jct. (0.0 mi), the trail follows yellow disks the short distance to Hedgehog Pond. Hedgehog Mt. broods protectively over the pond as if to guard the wily Adirondack brook trout that dwell in the depths from the avid anglers who constantly seek them out.

❋ Trail in winter: Not skiable owing to steepness and narrowness of access trail.

𝕸 Distance: Dog Pond Loop Trail to Hedgehog Pond, 0.2 mi (0.3 km).

177 East Inlet Trail

Trails Illustrated Map 745: Y10

▶Locator: This short red-marked trail to the shore of an inlet on Cranberry Lake begins at Dog Pond Loop (trail 175), 5 mi from the W end of the loop.◀

From the jct. (0.0 mi), the trail proceeds downhill for almost its entire length before reaching the East Flow, or inlet, of Cranberry Lake at 1.1 mi. East Flow is one of the bays created by construction of a dam at the lake's outlet in the nineteenth century.

The trail parallels East Inlet Creek and passes under a canopy of towering hemlocks for part of its route. Occasional large hardwoods can also be seen along the way.

❈ Trail in winter: Not suitable owing to steepness.

🏃 Distance: Dog Pond Loop to East Flow, 1.1 mi (1.8 km).

178 Dog Pond Mt.

This trail once began N of Proulx Clearing on the Dog Pond Loop (trail 175). DEC confirms it is now obsolete (2018).

179 Bear Mt.

Trails Illustrated Map 745: Z9

This moderately steep red-marked trail climbs from Cranberry Lake Campground on the shores of Cranberry Lake to the summit of Bear Mt., where unfurls a broad vista of the lake below and of the wild forested hills rolling into the distance.

▶Trailhead: Access is from Bear Mt. Campground Rd. just E of the hamlet of Cranberry Lake. Take this road S for 1.3 mi to the campground. The marked trailhead lies another 0.4 mi inside the campground.◀

From the trailhead (0.0 mi), the trail navigates a growth of mature hardwoods, passing through a jct. with Burntbridge Pond–Bear Mt. Trail (trail 172) at 0.2 mi. It starts a gradual ascent before reaching a DEC lean-to at 0.8 mi. At 1.2 mi, it reaches a crest of the mountain at an overlook with a limited view of Cranberry Lake. The trail proceeds along the crest under a canopy of trees significantly smaller than those on the slopes. White ash is common.

The trail begins a slight descent before reaching a scenic rock overlook R at 1.7 mi. State-owned Joe Indian Island is clear, along with privately owned Buck Island off to the L. At the foot of the mountain, the marshes of Bear Mt. Swamp are visible. In the distance, many of the rolling forested hills appear to be of approximately the same height. Bear Mt., at 2160 ft elevation, is, however, one of the highest. Cat Mt., lying due W with its perpendicular cliffs quite noticeable, is 101 ft higher than Bear Mt.

The trail descends sharply to reach a back road of the campground after a mile; since this entails walking almost another mile over macadam road to reach the trailhead, most hikers retrace their steps from the scenic overlook.

❈ Trail in winter: Not suitable owing to steepness.

Joanne Kennedy

⚑ Distances: DEC campground to lean-to, 0.8 mi; to first overlook, 1.2 mi; to summit overlook, 1.7 mi (2.7 km). Ascent, 660 ft (201 m). Elevation, 2160 ft (658 m).

180 Peavine Swamp Trail

Trails Illustrated Map 745: Y8

This trail skirts Peavine Swamp—an extensive conifer-clad peatland—on its way to the Inlet Flow of the Oswegatchie River, and upstream from its confluence with Dead Creek Flow, the SW tentacle of Cranberry Lake. It surmounts a series of hills and ridges under a canopy of mixed forest with individual trees occasionally attaining heroic proportions. It connects NY 3 to Ranger School Rd. in Wanakena and forms part of the CL50 (see Cranberry Lake 50 Section).

▶Trailhead: Located on NY 3, approximately 1.8 mi S of the bridge spanning the Oswegatchie River on the western outskirts of the hamlet of Cranberry Lake. From the S it is 5 mi from the Wanakena turnoff. A small DEC sign pointing to a rough parking area on the S side of the road can be seen approximately 0.2 mi W of a state DOT parking lot on the N side of NY 3.

As of this writing (2016), the trail can also be accessed from the S, at the SUNY-EFS Ranger School in Wanakena. The Ranger School plans to relocate parking for this trail; those planning this approach should check the college website for updates at www.esf.edu. Coming from Wanakena, follow Ranger School Rd. along the river to a parking area on the R in front of the main administration building. Note that no overnight parking is allowed here or anywhere else on the college campus. The trail starts just where the road bears L away from the lake.◀

Leaving the trailhead parking area on NY 3 (0.0 mi), the trail immediately spans one of the area's many small streams. At 0.3 mi, Balancing Rock Loop (trail 183) branches L. At 0.5 mi, a small wooden bridge carries the trail across another stream, just before a sharp rise to the top of a hill. The forest here is mostly red spruce and balsam fir on the knolls, with tamarack and black spruce joining them in the peatland to the R (W). Near the top of the hill the forest's composition begins to change to second-growth northern hardwoods with occasional conifers.

The trail undulates through the forest, passing the edge of an old log clearing at 0.9 mi. A small campsite is available at the back of the clearing. At 1 mi, the S end of Balancing Rock Loop comes in on the L (E). At 1.2 mi, Christmas Tree Loop (trail 184) departs L (E).

At 1.6 mi, the trail begins to ascend a steep ridge. Partway up it passes two impressive red spruces; at one point, DEC foresters measured their diameter at breast height (DBH) at 25 inches, quite imposing for this normally slender species. At 2 mi, just after another small creek, the trail passes a hemlock of 40 inches DBH and, at 2.1 mi, one of 42 inches DBH. These hemlocks and the large red spruce may be considered "old-growth" or "virgin" timber, and give some indication of what this area's forest looked like to the early hunters and trappers who penetrated it in the last century.

At 2.6 mi the trail reaches the top of its steepest hill and begins a gradual descent until it meets the S end of the Christmas Tree Loop coming in from the L (E) at 2.9 mi. (A L turn here leads also to the N end of Peavine Swamp Lean-to Loop, trail 185). At 3.2 mi the trail crosses a creek, and at 3.6 mi it comes to a jct. with the S end of Peavine Swamp Lean-to Loop. The trail bears R (W). Peavine Swamp Lean-to Loop, L (E), leads to a side trail to the lean-to and the shore of Inlet Flow in 0.3 mi.

Continuing, the trail (a logging road) generally drops in elevation until a bay on Cranberry Lake comes into view at a large erratic at 4 mi. The trail now generally follows the shore, leaving state land at 4.2 mi. The trail ends at Ranger School Rd. at 4.4 mi. (This road serves as part of the CL50, connecting the Peavine Swamp and High Falls Trails; see Cranberry Lake 50 Section.)

A pleasant alternative to retracing the Peavine Swamp Trail all the way back to the trailhead on NY 3 is to turn onto the Peavine Swamp Lean-to Loop (trail 185) and follow that to its jct. with the Christmas Tree Loop. (A L at that jct. will lead back to Peavine Swamp Trail in 0.2 mi; a R will lead back to Peavine Swamp Trail in approximately 2.3 mi.) Total round-trip ski distances combining parts of Peavine Swamp Trail, Peavine Swamp Lean-to Loop, and Christmas Tree Loop range from approximately 8 to 10 mi.

❄ Trail in winter: Constructed primarily as a ski trail. There are several difficult downhill glides along the route, which is also somewhat narrow in places.

❧ Distances: NY 3 to first leg of Balancing Rock Loop (trail 183), 0.3 mi; to second leg of Balancing Rock Loop, 1 mi; to first leg of Christmas Tree Loop (trail 184) , 1.2 mi; to second leg of Christmas Tree Loop, 2.9 mi; to Peavine Swamp Lean-to Loop (trail 185), 3.6 mi; to Ranger School Rd., 4.4 (7 km).

181 West Connector

This trail is part of the CL50 (see Cranberry Lake 50). Located on state land and Conifer Emporium Easement, the trail provides a connection from the Cranberry Lake State Boat Launch parking lot on Columbian Rd. to Balancing Rock Loop (Loop 1, trail 183) and the Peavine Swamp Trail (trail 180).

▶Trailhead: Access is from a parking lot across from the Cranberry Lake State Boat Launch approximately 0.4 mi E of the jct. of NY 3 and Columbian Rd. on the S (R) side of the road. The parking lot is large and has space for approximately fifty-five cars, trucks, and boat trailers. ◀

Both the blue-marked CL50 West Connector and the yellow-marked Lost Pond Nature Trail (trail 182) start out from the trailhead (0.0 mi) on the S side of the parking lot. The wide trail starts with a moderate grade to the SW through mixed hardwoods. It then turns R (W) and follows a ridge paralleling the parking lot. At 0.2 mi the trail turns L. It soon reaches an impressive high cliff with overhangs and caves on the L (E) side of the trail. At 0.4 mi, the West Connector trail turns L. (Lost Pond Nature Trail, trail 182, continues straight.) The trail becomes rougher as it climbs, entering a recently logged section and following, leaving, and crossing skid trails.

This strange mix of hiking trail and skid trail continues until yellow paint blazes indicate state land at 1.3 mi. The trees are a more mature here. The trail reaches a steep downhill, then crosses a wide bridge at 1.6 mi. The trail now starts to climb, then turns W following the contours. The trail passes a large erratic boulder on the L before the jct. with Balancing Rock Loop (Loop 1, trail 183) at 2.2 mi. (To the R [W], Balancing Rock Loop leads to Peavine Swamp Trail, trail 180, in approximately 1 mi.)

❋ Trail in winter: First section and the end are suitable for cross-country skiing. The drop to and climb from the bridge are less suitable owing to steep terrain, but possible.

𝕸 Distances: Parking lot on Columbian Rd. to split with Lost Pond Nature Trail (trail 182), 0.4 mi; to boundary between state land and Conifer Emporium Easement, 1.3 mi; to bridge, 1.6 mi; to jct. with Balancing Rock Loop (Loop 1, trail 183), 2.2 mi (3.5 km). Ascent, 150 ft (45.7 m). Elevation at jct. with Balancing Rock Loop (Loop 1, trail 183), 1650 ft (502.9 m).

182 Lost Pond Nature Trail

Located on Conifer Emporium Easement land, this trail provides access to Lost Pond.

▶Trailhead: Access is from a parking lot across from the Cranberry Lake State Boat Launch, approximately 0.4 mi E of the jct. of NY 3 and Columbian Rd. on the S (R) side of the road. The parking lot is large, with space for approximately fifty-five cars, trucks, and boat trailers. ◀

Both the yellow-marked Nature Trail and the blue-marked CL50 West Connector (trail 181) start out from the trailhead (0.0 mi) on the S side of the parking lot. The wide trail starts with a moderate grade to the SW through mixed hardwoods. It then turns R (W) and follows a ridge paralleling the parking lot. At 0.2 mi the trail turns L. It soon reaches an impressive high cliff with overhangs and caves on the L (E) side of the trail.

At 0.4 mi, CL50 West Connector turns L and Lost Pond Trail continues straight. The trail now turns L and descends to the loop jct. at 0.6 mi. Turning L (E) going in a clockwise direction, the trail passes through hardwoods then pines in a low marshy area NE of Lost Pond. The trail continues around the pond with views of the water at 0.8 mi. The trail begins to climb the hill to the SE of the pond with views through the trees down to the pond and its several islands.

At 0.9 mi the trail begins to drop as it passes a large erratic composed of gneiss, a metamorphic rock, on the R. As the trail levels out at 1 mi, it passes a very interesting second large erratic on the L that has a yellow birch growing directly on its top. Shortly after this the trail crosses one of the two outlets caused by the beaver dam on the pond. The trail now turns R, follows the outlet, then turns L. It reaches the second outlet at 1.1 mi. Now turning R, the trails follows the NW shore, returning to the jct. of the loop at 1.5 mi. Turning L, the trail continues to the start at 2 mi.

❁ Trail in winter: Suitable for cross-country skiing and snowshoeing.

𝕄 Distances: Parking lot to split with CL50 West Connector (trail 181), 0.4 mi; to jct. with loop, 0.6 mi; to second outlet of pond, 1.1 mi; to return to loop jct., 1.5 mi; to return to start, 2 mi (3.2 km).

183 Balancing Rock Loop

Trails Illustrated Map 745: Z9

The first 0.9 mi of this trail has been incorporated into the CL50 (see Cranberry Lake 50 Section).

▶Locator: This moderate loop veers E off Peavine Swamp Trail (trail 180) 0.3 mi S of the Peavine Swamp trailhead on NY 3. It rejoins the trail 1 mi S of the trailhead. This describes the loop in a clockwise direction.◀

From the Peavine Swamp Trail (0.0 mi), the trail heads NE. Immediately down-slope to the L (N) is one of the area's hidden jewels: a tiny, dark, limpid pond and encircling peat bog, barely 75 yd away.

The trail slowly ascends and descends several moderate ridges. At 0.9 mi, the CL50 turns L on the West Connector (trail 181). (The West Connector trail, cut in 2015, leads in 2.2 mi to the Cranberry Lake Boat Launch parking lot on Columbian Rd.) At 1.3 mi, a sharp turn R (S) and loop occur, and a slow steady descent begins. Second-growth hardwoods are the order of the day here, with an occasional large beech. Some of the beech are succumbing to the beech scale insect and fungus, but still sporadically produce beechnuts to the delight of local bears.

The trail now starts to climb again, reaching the balancing rock that gives the trail its name at 1.7 mi. The trail passes several cliffs and outcrops, creating interesting terrain.

The trail now starts to drop, crossing a wooden bridge at 2.4 mi. At 2.8 mi it rejoins the Peavine Swamp Trail (trail 180). It is 1 mi R (N) to the trailhead on NY 3. To the L (S) lies the lean-to on Inlet Flow (via trail 185) in a little over 3 mi.

❄ Trail in winter: Constructed primarily as a ski route; grades are generally fair to moderate, serving snowshoers as well.

🐾 Distances: Peavine Swamp Trail to balancing rock, 1.7 mi; to return to Peavine Swamp Trail, 2.8 mi (4.5 km).

184 Christmas Tree Loop

Trails Illustrated Map 745: Z9

▶Locator: This moderate loop veers E off Peavine Swamp Trail (trail 180) 1.2 mi S of the Peavine Swamp trailhead on NY 3. It rejoins the trail 2.9 mi S of the trailhead. This describes the loop in a clockwise direction.◀

From Peavine Swamp Trail (0.0 mi), the trail heads SE and starts to ascend, reaching a large split boulder at 0.5 mi. The trail then reaches height of land with gentle rolling. At 1.1 mi, it passes a small cliff on the R (W). The trail starts to drop and at 1.4 mi passes through an area with large yellow birches.

At 2 mi the trail enters a primeval valley with beautiful boulders, huge old-growth trees, and little undergrowth. The area has the feeling of a cathedral. There is one large boulder with a yellow birch growing on the stony top. It's not hard to imagine this as one of the areas cleared by Hagrid in the Forbidden Forest of the Harry Potter stories. At any minute one might see centaurs or unicorns.

The loop reaches a jct. with the Peavine Swamp Lean-to Loop (trail 185) at 2.3 mi. (A L turn here leads to the lean-to on Inlet Flow.) Christmas Tree Loop continues straight (W) through the jct. and starts a steep descent. It turns R (N) after the descent and meets Peavine Swamp Trail (trail 180) at 2.5 mi. A turn to the L leads to Ranger School Rd.; R is the direct route to the trailhead on NY 3.

❄ Trail in winter: Constructed primarily as a ski route; grades are generally fair to moderate with some steeper sections.

🐾 Distances: Peavine Swamp Trail to split boulder, 0.5 mi; to cliff, 1.1 mi; to Peavine Swamp Lean-to Loop (trail 185), 2.3 mi; to return to Peavine Swamp Trail, 2.5 mi (4 km).

185 Peavine Swamp Lean-to Loop

Trails Illustrated Map 745: Z9

This trail leads to a lean-to on Inlet Flow and offers an alternate route back to the Peavine Swamp Trail from the lean-to.

▶Locator: The loop can be accessed from the N via the Christmas Tree Loop (trail 184) or from the S via the Peavine Swamp Trail (trail 180). This description starts on the Peavine Swamp Trail 3.6 mi S of the Peavine Swamp trailhead on NY 3 and proceeds counterclockwise.◄

From the jct. with Peavine Swamp Trail (0.0 mi), the Lean-to Loop passes through mature pines until it reaches a jct. at 0.3 mi. The side trail R leads in 0.2 mi to the lean-to and the shore at Inlet Flow. The lean-to is in sound condition, though it shows damage from initials carved into the wood and improper use of nails. It is in a splendid setting. A handsome grove of white pines and hemlocks protectively envelops the lean-to, and the waters of the flow—placid in summer, ice-clad in winter—draw one's attention.

Beyond this jct., the trail continues E on an old logging road that parallels the shore of Inlet Flow. At 0.7 mi a large burl on a yellow birch tree can be observed N of the trail. The trail crosses a bridge and starts to climb to the N. At 0.8 mi it turns W, leaving the logging road. The trail continues to climb and at 1.1 mi turns sharply L. It ends at a jct. with the Christmas Tree Loop (trail 184) at 1.4 mi. The Christmas Tree Loop leads back to the Peavine Swamp Trail in 2.3 mi (to the R) or 0.2 mi down a steep descent (to the L).

❄ Trail in winter: Constructed primarily as a ski route; grades are generally fair to moderate with some steeper sections.

🐾 Distances: To side trail for lean-to, 0.3 mi; to jct. with Christmas Tree Loop (trail 184), 1.4 mi (2.2 km).

186 High Falls Loop

Trails Illustrated Map 745: Y8

High Falls, a scenic cataract nestled deep in the Five Ponds Wilderness Area, has long been a focal point of hikers in this area. The High Falls Loop is a combination of the trails known locally as the High Falls Trail, the Plains Trail, and the Dead Creek Flow Trail. Much of the High Falls Loop has been incorporated into the CL50 (see Cranberry Lake 50 Section).

Hikers traditionally start at the High Falls Trail trailhead and conclude at the Dead Creek Flow Trail trailhead (traveling in a counterclockwise direction). From the Dead Creek trailhead, a walk of 0.5 mi W is necessary to reach the High Falls trailhead. Since the parking area has been enlarged and improved at the Dead Creek Flow terminus, the hiker has an option to begin here. However, for the purposes of this guide, tradition will be adhered to and the loop begun at the High Falls Trail.

▶Trailhead: Access to the trailhead is from NY 3 at the Wanakena turnoff (CR 61) approximately 8 mi SW of Cranberry Lake and 6 mi E of Star Lake. Proceed S approximately 1 mi, staying to the R at two forks and crossing a metal bridge that spans the Oswegatchie River. Shortly after, a driveway with a DEC trailhead sign (R) leads to a parking area for approximately a dozen vehicles. The trailhead is a 50 yd walk on the driveway, near a metal gate that bars vehicular traffic. The

Hiker bridge, Wanakena. Jamie Savage

DEC trail register is just past this point on the L. ◀

From the register (0.0 mi), the red-marked route follows an old truck trail that was once a railroad logging line, built during the heydays of logging in the region. The trail passes an old mill pond on the L. One of the few artificial ponds in this area of abundant natural water bodies, it was created in connection with lumbering activities around the turn of the twentieth century. The first mile of this trail is used to access a water reservoir that supplies the hamlet of Wanakena, creating a strange mix of civilization and wilderness.

At 0.5 mi, the trail crosses Skate Creek on a culvert, then curves R to join a drier path at the base of a hill. At 0.8 mi, the trail passes a cast iron water cutoff protector (R), a reminder of the multiple uses of this trail section. The trail passes another creek at 0.9 mi. Just beyond this creek, the unmarked Dobson Trail once branched L. This unofficial trail, once used by the owner of a sportsmen's hotel formerly located at High Falls, was a shortcut through the Plains to High Falls. It is almost impossible to follow and is not recommended.

At 1 mi the trail passes a spring coming from a pipe, L. These pipe springs were built by early woodsmen and are quite common in this region. Shortly thereafter a large cut in the forest diverges L. This is the buried waterline from the reservoir and where vehicular use of the trail ends. The trail now turns R and starts a gentle climb, leaving a little more of civilization behind.

The trail crosses Skate Creek again on a bridge at 1.2 mi then joins a small ridge as it continues to climb. It reaches the start of the Leary Trail (trail 187) at 1.7 mi, L. The truck trail straight ahead is the way to High Falls.

The trail now passes through a rock cut and reaches the high point of the trail in a gentle pass at 1.9 mi before beginning its descent to the Oswegatchie River. It passes a large open wetland on the R shortly thereafter. The trail, now rather flat, follows a tributary of the Oswegatchie and finally joins the base of the hills to the L. At 3.8 mi, a distinct three-way jct. is encountered. A path R proceeds 0.1 mi to the river at a landing called High Rock, named for the huge glacially rounded outcrop overlooking the river here. This site makes a pleasant destination for a winter ski or a day hike.

The trail continues straight ahead through the forest, encountering a stone bridge and cascade at 4.3 mi. It now skirts the marsh along the base of the hills to the E, turns due W, then continues S. At some points the trail passes through low areas of balsam, tamarack, and spruce; at others it climbs to the base of the hills to areas with yellow birch and species that like drier ground. At 5.4 mi, the trail crosses a stream. Depending on beaver activity, this and other streams may be difficult to cross.

The trail continues generally level, as befits the route of a logging railroad. At 6.1 mi the trail passes another creek with a beaver pond. As the trail nears the Oswegatchie, open areas of water are visible. The trail passes through a designated campsite located adjacent to the river at 6.7 mi. Shortly, a side trail R leads to designated Campsite 28, which overlooks the river. This stretch of the Oswegatchie River is known as Ross Rapids.

The trail now bears L through a rock cut and onto the fill area, with marsh and river to the R. The trail soon meets the river again with a view of an oxbow at the end of Straight Rapids, then leaves the river and follows the course of a small stream. The trail crosses a low area that has at times has been flooded by beaver activity; there is a rough makeshift trail to the L.

At 7.4 mi, the Sand Lake trail (trail 188), which leads to Five Ponds, goes R (S). Just beyond this jct. is the second terminus of the Leary Trail (trail 187) on the L. At 7.5 mi, beaver flooding may be a problem at a creek crossing. A marshy area soon appears R, and the Oswegatchie comes into view L at 7.8 mi. This is Carters Landing, once a timber-staging location. Shortly after, a trail L leads to Campsite 21, which provides a pleasant view of the river floodplain.

The trail now is often flooded by beaver dams on Glasby Creek to the R, making it wet in places. At 8 mi, the trail crosses Glasby Creek on a wooden bridge. The route is now in the western edge of the famous "Oswegatchie Plains," which can be seen L after the bridge. The blueberry and meadow-sweet shrubs of this unique area, classified as a boreal heath by DEC, are being infringed upon by sporadic black spruce, black cherry, and tamarack trees, which are starting to establish themselves.

The trail reaches a jct. at 8.5 mi. The High Falls Loop continues L on a section of the loop also known as the Plains Trail. The trail straight ahead (R) leads to High Falls in 0.5 mi. High Falls seems almost a mandatory visit after coming this far, and the mileage to and from the falls is included in the loop total. (For those hiking the CL50, the round-trip to High Falls adds 1 mi.)

Continuing straight to High Falls, at 8.7 mi the trail passes a tracked vehicle that looks as if it once had a cable wench on it for pulling logs out of the woods. It's another interesting remnant of civilization in the wilderness. Past this, a trail entering from the L is a shortcut over the hill; the main trail continues R, skirting the base of the hill and passing through Campsite 16.

At 9 mi, the trail reaches High Falls. A popular destination for both hikers and canoeists, the falls present a charming vista as they tumble 20 ft over granitic gneiss bedrock under a partial canopy of white pine. There are two lean-tos, one on each side of the river, but a bridge that formerly spanned the river has been removed to conform to the State Land Master Plan.

The trail returns to meet the section of trail locally known as the Plains Trail at 9.5 mi from the trailhead, and turns R. The trail leaves the truck trail and takes on a rougher character. It starts to climb, following a ridge through rocky ground with large amounts of blowdown. The trail reaches a high point on a bare rock ridge at 9.9 mi then begins to zigzag. It drops to cross a stream at 10.2 mi on a bridge cleverly constructed from a large, downed white pine. Though roughened by an ax, the pine may be slippery when wet and care should be exercised in crossing. The trail turns L now and follows the stream downhill briefly before continuing NE.

At 10.3 mi the first of a surviving group of extremely large white pines is encountered. The trail then navigates around a beaver pond. Farther L, marshy Glasby Creek is visible. The trail crosses the beaver dam at 10.6 mi, passes through more large white pines, and reaches the base of Threemile Mt. at 10.7 mi. The trail follows along the base of the mountain for quite a distance. It crosses several creeks cascading down ravines from the spruce-covered mountain, and passes a number of large talus boulders. Frost has been recorded in the Plains every month of the year. This is due to its location, tucked between Roundtop and Threemile Mts. The location also probably contributes, with other factors, to the area's generally treeless condition.

The trail swings L away from the base of the mountain and crosses a gentle swale at 11.7 mi. Glasby Creek comes into view on the L just before the trail passes the old Plains Trail on the L at 11.8 mi. At 12.1 mi, the trail crosses Glasby Creek, now considerably smaller nearer its headwaters, and at 12.2 mi it ascends a ridge and meets the Cowhorn Jct. trail (trail 191) coming in sharply on the R. This is Sand Hill Jct.

The loop climbs slightly and veers L to the top of the pass, then begins a long descent down a wooded draw hemmed in by a cliff and a ridge. In summer, owing to the presence of leafy vegetation, these are generally not noticeable. Just before the route crosses a stream at 13.4 mi there are springs on either side of the trail. The trail continues to drop following an old logging road through mostly hardwoods. At 14 mi, the short Janacks Landing trail (trail 190) comes in on the R. A trail register is located here.

The loop veers L and circumvents the end of Dead Creek Flow, crossing bridges over four small creeks draining off the slopes of Roundtop Mt. Dead Creek Flow is the largest of the "arms" of Cranberry Lake created by construction of the dam in the nineteenth century. The trail crosses Dead Creek itself at 14.5 mi. The trail continues with rolling ups and downs through some muddy areas until it reaches an old railroad grade at 14.9 mi. A short trail L leads to a designated lakeside campsite popular with boaters.

The loop makes a sharp L and follows close to the shore of the E end of the flow. This loop segment is known locally as Dead Creek Flow Trail. It follows a truck trail constructed by the Civilian Conservation Corps during the Depression and has a level route. At 15 mi on the L is lakeside Campsite 28. The trail continues to follow the shore of Cranberry Lake, then starts to climb, leaving the lake at 15.4 mi, then passing an old beaver pond on the L. Some of the beaver ponds on this part of the trail have caused flooding, but the DEC has placed pipes to keep the ponds drained and the trail dry.

The trail now follows a gentle grade through an area heavily affected by the 1995 derecho. Along the trail young hardwoods grow among their fallen predecessors. The trail crosses a small marshy creek and follows it to the trail register at 16.9 mi. From here it is 0.5 mi L along a paved town road to reach the start of the loop at the High Falls trail register at 17.4 mi. This can be shortened 0.5 mi by placing vehicles at the parking areas for both trailheads.

❀ Trail in winter: A ski loop can be accomplished but has some severe constraints upon it. Narrowness, occasional beaver flooding, blowdown, rough trail SE of the Plains, and a few sharp downward twists all combine to create challenges.

ᛗ Distances: High Falls trailhead to pipe spring, 1 mi; to spur to High Rock, 3.8 mi; to Sand Lake trail (trail 188), 7.4 mi; to High Falls, 9 mi; to Sand Hill Jct., 12.2 mi; to spur to Janacks Landing (trail 190), 14 mi; to railroad grade on Dead Creek Flow, 14.9 mi; to Dead Creek Flow trailhead, 16.9 mi (27 km); to High Falls trailhead, 17.4 mi (27.8 km).

187 Leary Trail (unmaintained)

Trails Illustrated Map 745: X8

The DEC closed the Leary Trail in 1995 owing to extensive blowdown after a derecho passed through this area. Recently, volunteers have cleared the blowdown and have been maintaining the trail (2016). It is relatively easy to follow, though it is not marked or maintained by the DEC. Please check with the local ranger for more information.

Prior to 1995 the Leary Trail was often used for cross-country skiing to High Falls. Though still skiable, the trail is now rougher and progress is slowed by the need to bypass uprooted trees.

►Locator: This interior trail joins the High Falls trail (trail 186) on both ends. The northern jct. is 1.7 mi from the High Falls trail trailhead; the southern jct. is approximately 7.5 mi from the trailhead, or about 75 ft E of the jct. of the High Falls Trail and the Sand Lake trail (trail 188).◄

From the jct. (0.0 mi), the trail, marked with old blue DEC markers and can tops painted blue, rises moderately to a pass in the ridge that ends to the W at High Rock. It then dips down slightly to climb again, dropping to High Rock Creek at 0.7 mi. There was once a large logging camp here. The small clearing that is here now was once known as the Swanson Johnson Clearing.

At 1.3 mi the trail crosses a southern branch of High Rock Creek. Just before the creek, the trail turns slightly L where the Old Albany Road intersected the Leary Trail. The trail now follows the route of the Old Albany Road as it climbs the W flank of Roundtop Mt. and then descends to a swampy area, leaving the Old Albany Road as it crosses the creek at 2.4 mi. Just before the creek, the trail splits. Both branches are blue-marked and both cross the creek on beaver dams. The two branches rejoin shortly beyond the creek.

The trail now follows the W side of the creek, rising and dropping over several small steep hills; it was moved from its original route to avoid flooding caused by beaver activity. The trail rejoins the High Falls Loop at 2.9 mi.

❋ Trail in winter: Suitable for skiing and snowshoeing.

🐾 Distances: High Falls Loop jct. to High Falls Loop jct., 2.9 mi (4.7 km).

188 Sand Lake

Trails Illustrated Map 745: V7

This trail passes through the enchanting Five Ponds to Wolf Pond Jct. on its way to haunting and remote Sand Lake in the heart of the wilderness.

▶Locator: The trail begins on the High Falls Loop (trail 186) 7.4 mi from the High Falls trailhead in Wanakena.◀

This blue-marked trail leaves the High Falls Loop (0.0 mi) in a sandy area with pines and tamarack growing in abundance. Tamarack probably prosper in this sterile, sandy soil for the same reason they are able to survive in the area's bogs— lack of competition from the usually more successful hardwoods.

At 0.3 mi, after traversing a conifer swamp, the trail crosses the Oswegatchie River on a wooden bridge. Beaver activity is continual here, so care should be exercised in crossing the wet area just before the bridge. The conifer swamp of spruce and fir continues across the river and the rare Canada jay can sometimes be seen here. At 0.7 mi, the blue-marked trail makes a sharp turn L at a point where an unmarked hunters' trail goes R to an informal campsite on Wolf Creek. The trail crosses creeks at 1 mi and 1.2 mi, the latter on a corduroy plank. The trail then proceeds across a modified esker with the floodplain wetland of Five Ponds Creek on the R.

The trail enters a glen lined with mature hemlock and yellow birch and with a babbling brook on the R. The trail turns to cross the creek at 1.9 mi. Caution should be exercised here; there is no bridge for the crossing and it is easily missed. The trail now crosses the side of a steep esker, crowned with occasional large white pines on top. Generally, these eskers are considered to be either part of the Cranberry Lake Esker or one of its "tributaries."

At 2.8 mi, the trail reaches Big Shallow Pond; a DEC lean-to is on the W shore. This extremely shallow pond is lined with large white pines and its waters have an attractive greenish coloring, unique in this area. Informal herd paths lead over the top of the esker to Big Five Pond and beyond that to Little Five Pond.

The trail crosses the outlet of the pond and ascends the esker once again, encountering some large red spruce on the top at 2.9 mi. There has been some blowdown damage here. The stands of virgin red spruce are not as thick as those of white pine, but they still make an impressive sight. Unfortunately, many of the red spruce here seem to be dying; there has been speculation that acid rain could be the cause of this.

At 3.2 mi, Washbowl Pond is visible L and at 3.4 mi the trail reaches Little Shallow Pond, where another lean-to is located. Little Shallow, like all five enchanting ponds that have given this Wilderness Area its name, is a shallow kettle hole lying amidst some of the most magnificent eskers in the Adirondacks.

Beyond the lean-to, the trail ascends a ridge and begins to undulate as it proceeds through several small wetlands on short corduroys. Both flooding and occasional blowdown are common in this section. The trail enters a draw with mature hardwoods lining the adjacent ridges, replacing the red spruce and hemlock of the past mile. At 4.2 mi, blowdown is fairly easily crossed after a short distance. An area of small second-growth spruce announces Wolf Pond Jct. at 4.7 mi. The trail R goes to Cage Lake (trail 189); the way to Sand Lake is straight ahead.

The trail ascends a ridge crowned with majestic conifers and occasional hardwoods on its way to Sand Lake. On the descent from the ridge, the trail passes a medium-sized waterfall and, soon after, Wolf Pond is visible R at 5.7 mi. Beaver flooding may also be encountered in this section, along with some blowdown of the old-growth conifers.

The trail continues under an impressive canopy of mature conifers to Sand Lake at 7.2 mi. Sand Lake is truly worth the long hike. Encircled by a ring of majestic white pines, its sandy shores beckon the hiker for a refreshing swim. An attractive lean-to is located R of the lake. An unmarked trail leads over the NW side of the esker a very short distance to Rock Lake. Equally beautiful, Rock Lake lacks only the magnificent brook trout present in Sand Lake.

❊ Trail in winter: An extremely challenging although scenic ski trip. Occasional flooding, blowdown, and bridge crossings put it out of reach for most skiers. If attempted as part of a backcountry camping trip, careful preparation and caution should be exercised.

❧ Distances: High Falls Loop to Oswegatchie River, 0.3 mi; to Big Shallow Pond Lean-to, 2.8 mi, to Little Shallow Pond Lean-to, 3.4 mi; to Wolf Pond Jct., 4.7 mi; to Sand Lake, 7.2 mi (11.5 km).

189 Wolf Pond–Cage Lake Trail

Trails Illustrated Map 745: W7

This trail passes Wolf Pond on its way to Cage Lake through some of the wildest terrain in New York State.

▶Locator: The trail goes R from the Sand Lake trail (trail 188) at Wolf Pond Jct. at 4.7 mi.◀

Leaving Sand Lake Trail (0.0 mi), this yellow-marked trail reaches the lean-to at Wolf Pond in 0.5 mi. Nestled on the NW shore of this large wilderness lake with towering white pines gracing the shore, the lean-to seems the essence of what a wilderness lean-to should be. Just before the lean-to, the trail veers R to continue toward Cage Lake. At 0.8 mi, an expansive wetland, the outlet of Wolf Pond, can be difficult to cross owing to flooding; the beaver dams usually present are an aid.

The trail continues to cross the outlet of Muir Pond at 1.4 mi and then at 2.1 mi it crosses the outlet of Deer Marsh. It crosses several other small creeks and wet areas on the way to Cage Lake, but in general this section has more dry areas than wet ones. Care should still be exercised in following the disks because blowdown in this remote section often is not removed for a considerable length of time.

Finally the trail ascends a ridge to arrive in 3.3 mi at the Cage Lake Lean-to just before the outlet of Cage Lake cascades across the trail. The trail ahead (Cage Lake, trail 205), leads to Buck Pond and eventually Youngs Rd. S of the hamlet of Star Lake.

❄ Trail in winter: Generally not recommended for winter use owing to the remoteness of the trailhead, combined with frequent flooding and blowdown.

🚶 Distances: Wolf Pond Jct. to Wolf Pond Lean-to, 0.5 mi; to Muir Pond outlet, 1.4 mi; to Deer Marsh outlet, 2.1 mi; to Cage Lake Lean-to, 3.3 mi (5.3 km).

190 Janacks Landing

Trails Illustrated Map 745: X8

This is a short, frequently used trail to a lean-to on Dead Creek Flow.

▶Locator: The trail goes to the R off the High Falls Loop (trail 186) at 14 mi from the High Falls trailhead in Wanakena. A DEC trail register is located at this jct., which is also 2.9 mi from the Dead Creek Flow trailhead.◀

From the High Falls Loop (0.0 mi), the yellow-marked trail enters a wet marshy area, crossing it and a creek on planks. The trail turns L once higher ground is reached and passes through large white pines. It crosses another bridge before climbing to a charming spot on Dead Creek Flow where a DEC lean-to is located at 0.2 mi.

The trail continues in front of the lean-to to a sandy beach. Small-boat traffic from Cranberry Lake is heavy here in summer. Near this site, John Janack, the first fire observer at the nearby Cat Mt. fire tower, had his abode and raised his children in the early years of the twentieth century.

❄ Trail in winter: Can be skied as a brief side-trip of the High Falls Loop.

🚶 Distance: High Falls Loop to Janacks Landing, 0.2 mi (0.3 km).

191 Cowhorn Jct.

Trails Illustrated Map 745: X8

This trail connects High Falls Loop with Cowhorn Pond at a remote spot known as Cowhorn Jct. The trail is part of the CL50 (see Cranberry Lake 50 Section).

▶Locator: This trail begins at Sand Hill Jct. on High Falls Loop (trail 186), 12.2 mi from the High Falls trailhead or 4.7 mi from the Dead Creek Flow trailhead.◀

As the yellow-marked Cowhorn Jct. trail leaves High Falls Loop (0.0 mi), it gradually proceeds up a hemlock glen where it overlooks the High Falls Loop. The trail turns L abruptly when it encounters Glasby Creek. Soon the trail passes an entrancing little waterfall (R) formed as Glasby Creek cascades down from Glasby Pond over bedrock that is softer than the bedrock surrounding it. The trail climbs away from the creek and crosses an open glade at 0.2 mi.

The trail now climbs a slight rise to reach Glasby Pond and its outlet at 0.3 mi. It passes a designated campsite shortly after and skirts the shore of the pond for a short distance through blowdown from the 1995 derecho. The trail here is rough and wet at times. The trail climbs away from the pond, quickly drops back to the pond, and then begins another gradual rise to reach the jct. with the Cat Mt. trail (trail 192) at 0.8 mi. Cat Mt. Trail goes straight (L) here; Cowhorn Jct. Trail turns R.

The trail again climbs slowly then begins its descent into the cleft under Cat Mt. The trail passes over two small bedrock outcrops and through a boulder-strewn landscape under a canopy of beech and maple. Resurrected after the 1995 derecho, the trail now cuts back and forth to avoid downed trees. Cat Pond comes into view on the L at 1.6 mi. The trail for the most part passes above the pond with spectacular views of Cat Mt. in the background. It dips to pond level only once, at a bay on the SW side of the pond.

The trail crosses a beaver dam. At 1.8 mi a side trail L leads to a designated campsite on a point near the outlet of the pond. The trail crosses Sixmile Creek at 2 mi and then crosses a smaller stream as it begins a gentle climb before a final short, sharp rise to reach Cowhorn Jct. at 2.3 mi. (The trails S from Cowhorn Jct. to Big Deer Pond and Clear Pond, which had been closed owing to blowdown, are now open. See trails 199 and 200.) The yellow-marked trail turns L sharply to become the blue-marked Sixmile Creek Trail (trail 193) to Cranberry Lake. Cowhorn Pond can be seen through the trees ahead and L.

❅ Trail in winter: Generally not suitable owing to roughness of terrain.

🚶 Distances: Sand Hill Jct. to Glasby Pond, 0.3 mi; to Cat Mt. trail (trail 192), 0.8 mi; to Cowhorn Jct., 2.3 mi (3.7 km).

192 Cat Mt.

Trails Illustrated Map 745: X9

This short trail leads to the summit of Cat Mt., elevation 2261 ft, from which a seemingly endless panorama of forested hills rolls on to the horizon in all directions.

▶Locator: This red-marked trail is accessed from the Cowhorn Jct. trail (trail 191), 0.8 mi E of its jct. with High Falls Loop (trail 186) or 1.5 mi W of its jct. with Sixmile Creek Trail (trail 193).◀

Leaving the jct. (0.0 mi), the trail continues straight then takes a R turn and begins a moderate climb, sometimes on bedrock, through mature hardwoods. The trail stays to the N of the ridge. The trail reaches a low spot in the ridge to the R at 0.5 mi, follows a cleft in the rock, then begins to rise again. It reaches a meadow just before reaching a very steep area at 0.6 m. There is a somewhat poorly marked switchback to the R at the top of the climb where the trail has been relocated owing to blowdown. The trail attains the summit of Cat Mt. at 0.7 mi.

From the top of Cat Mt., there is no sign of civilization, if one discounts the DEC's Emergency Fire Control Radio Equipment and the cement base of a former fire tower present on the summit. Threemile Mt. is the only ridge distinctive enough to be instantly recognizable in the endless wave of

Cat Mt summit, fire control radio equipment. David Hough

green forest. Cat Mt. Pond lies nestled in the valley below and a partial glimpse of Bassout Pond and its marshy inlet can be seen.

Total distance to the top of the mountain from the Dead Creek Flow trailhead is 5.2 mi one way.

❄ Trail in winter: Not suitable owing to steepness of terrain.

🏃 Distance: Cowhorn Jct. trail to Cat Mt., 0.7 mi (1.1 km). Ascent from Cowhorn Jct. trail to top of Cat Mt., 388 ft (118 m). Elevation Cat Mt., 2261 ft (689 m).

193 Sixmile Creek Trail

Trails Illustrated Map 745: X9

This trail connects Cowhorn Jct. with Cranberry Lake. Part of the trail has been incorporated into the CL50 (see Cranberry Lake 50 Section).

▶Locator: This trail begins at Cowhorn Jct. at the E end of the Cowhorn Jct. trail (trail 191). It can also be accessed from Cranberry Lake's West Flow, approximately 6 mi by boat from the DEC boat-launching site outside the hamlet of Cranberry Lake.◀

Leaving Cowhorn Jct. (0.0 mi), the trail heads S. (Big Deer Pond trail, trail 199, goes R. Closed because of blowdown after the 1995 derecho, this trail is now open. Clear Pond Trail, trail 200, is also open.)

The trail follows blue markers along the top of an esker through blowdown and under tunnels of tree trunks. It is interesting to see forest succession taking place, with young trees growing up amongst the fallen pines that once dominated the ridge. Some large white pines still survive; they give a hint of what the ridge looked like before the derecho. Occasionally Cat Mt. can be seen to the L (W) and Cowhorn Pond to the R (E).

At 0.4 mi a yellow-marked side trail comes in R. (The side trail descends moderately to an attractive lean-to on a point of Cowhorn Pond, which is hardwood-fringed and shaped like a cowhorn. The lean-to is often occupied in the summer months.) The trail continues on top of the esker until it reaches a second esker branching off L.

The esker is almost breathtaking in this section with its tall, steep slopes. A 2 mi thick ice sheet once covered this area. Meltwater carved huge caves under the ice, where icy torrents deposited sand and gravel, creating these eskers, which look like upside-down streambeds. There are hundreds of miles of eskers in the Adirondacks; this one is called the Cranberry Lake Esker.

The trail mostly follows the top of the esker, climbing and dropping with a general drop in elevation. Wetlands can be seen at times on both sides and ponds appear R. The outlet of Cowhorn Pond is on the R while Sixmile Creek, the outlet of Bassout Pond, and Cat Mt. Pond, are on the L.

At 1.7 mi the trail slips to the L of the top of the esker ridge and starts a gradual descent toward Tamarack Bog. At 2 mi the bog comes into view on the L. Pitcher plants are particularly abundant here. The trail continues between the bog and the esker, then bears R and follows a gap in the esker. It makes a quick steep climb at 2.3 mi, then drops again. The trail now bears L and goes through yellow birch and hemlock forest while climbing back to the top of the now broader, gentler sloped esker.

At 2.9 mi, the trail reaches a jct. with Olmstead Pond Loop (trail 195), L. (There is no sign for Olmstead Pond.) Sixmile Creek Trail continues straight, dips to pass a beaver flow on the R at 3.2 mi, then follows the creek, passing a huge glacial erratic with young birch and polypod fern growing on it. The trail now climbs away from the creek, passing Sliding Rock Falls on Sixmile Creek on the L at 3.5 mi. This falls is as high as High Falls (see High Fall Loop, trail 186), but has considerably less water volume.

The trail climbs back to the top of the esker, then drops along the W side of the esker until the jct. with South Bay Trail (trail 194) at 3.9 mi. Sixmile Creek Trail continues straight and in approximately 400 ft arrives at the trail register and a second jct. with Olmstead Pond Loop (trail 195) to the L. Continuing straight, the trail leaves the creek, joining a small pleasant parallel valley. It rejoins the creek and reaches the West Flow on Cranberry Lake at 4.2 mi. It is approximately 6 mi by boat from here to the DEC launching site in the hamlet of Cranberry Lake.

❄ Trail in winter: Can be skied, but it is twisting and narrow in places as well as quite remote.

ℜ Distances: Cowhorn Jct. Trail to Cowhorn Pond Lean-to spur, 0.4 mi; to Olmstead Pond Loop (trail 195) S end, 2.9 mi; to Sliding Rock Falls, 3.5 mi; to Olmstead Pond Loop N end, 3.9 mi; to Cranberry Lake, 4.2 mi (6.7 km).

194 South Bay Trail

Trails Illustrated Map 745: Y10

South Bay Trail was constructed using modern trail-building and conservation methods to bridge a gap between Sixmile Creek Trail and Otter Brook Trail in the CL50 (see Cranberry Lake 50 Section). Many of the original Adirondack trails were scouted and blazed by early guides and follow the shortest distance between the base of a mountain and the peak, only avoiding major obstacles in between. Modern trail building takes into account many aspects of terrain, including steepness, vegetation, and the hiker. This trail has gentle switchbacks that slow erosion and help the hiker make the grade, much like a truck shifting to a lower gear. The trail was laid out with great care, and it shows.

▶Locator: W access is from Sixmile Creek Trail (trail 193) 0.3 mi S of its end point on Cranberry Lake's West Flow. E access is at the W end of Otter Brook Trail (trail 203). The trail is described W to E.◀

From its jct. with Sixmile Creek Trail (0.0 mi), the trail heads E and crosses a low section of the Sixmile Creek Esker. It then turns NE, losing elevation until it crosses Sixmile Creek at 0.3 mi. This is a picturesque location as the creek flows on bedrock before joining South Flow, framed by outcrops and trees. The trail now leaves the creek following a small valley. At 0.4 mi, at a sign indicating private property, South Bay Trail starts to climb upward to the R.

The trail passes through a forest of large yellow birch and hemlocks perched on cliffs of gneissic rock. These rocks are part of the Grenville formation and are connected to the ancient rocks in Canada that make up the core of North America. The layers are contorted and twisted because the rocks have been under intense heat and pressure. The lenticular mineral grains shaped like eyes that are visible upon close inspection are called "augen," from the German word for eyes.

The trail climbs gently with several switchbacks before reaching its high point at approximately 1 mi. It starts to drop toward Chair Rock Flow, crosses the outlet stream from Indian Mt. Pond, and, at 1.7 mi, turns sharply R onto a trail that comes from private property on Chair Rock Flow. The trail crosses a creek then gently climbs and drops following the shore of Chair Rock Flow. At 2.3 mi the trail crosses Chair Rock Creek at a beautiful spot where the creek flows into the lake.

After crossing the bridge, South Bay Trail and CL50 continue R. (The L trail leads to water access and designated Campsite 17 on Chair Rock Flow.) The trail comes to another jct. at 2.4 mi. The CL50 continues straight on Otter Brook Trail; to the R are Darning Needle Pond (trail 196) and Cranberry Lake–Grass Pond Trail (trail 197). The trail L returns to the campsite and canoe landing.

❋ Trail in winter: Generally not suitable for skiing owing to steepness of terrain.

👣 Distances: Sixmile Creek Trail to Sixmile Creek, 0.3 mi; to Chair Rock Flow, 2.4 mi (3.8 km).

195 Olmstead Pond Loop

Trails Illustrated Map 745: Y9

This loop trail passes three ponds: Olmstead, Simmons, and Spectacle. Simmons Pond is one of relatively few water bodies in the area characterized by a greenish-blue coloring. The minerals in the water give it this attractive look, in contrast to the usual brownish-gray of the typical Five Ponds Wilderness bodies of water. This trail is part of the CL50 (see Cranberry Lake 50 Section).

▶Locator: This loop leaves Sixmile Creek Trail (trail 193) at two points: at 2.9 mi and at 3.9 mi from Cowhorn Jct. (from the S); and at 0.3 mi and 1.3 mi from Cranberry Lake (from the N). It is described from the 2.9 mi point.◀

From its jct. with Sixmile Creek Trail, this yellow-marked trail starts a descent off an esker to meet the stream that drains Tamarack Bog at 0.1 mi. The trail crosses Sixmile Creek at 0.2 mi. There is no bridge and Sixmile Creek has some size here. The forest is of mixed hemlock and hardwoods. The trail begins to climb and soon joins the outlet of Olmstead Pond, L, cascading down to join Sixmile Creek. The trail follows the creek and at 0.5 mi reaches Olmstead Pond. The outlet waters here have been dammed by beavers.

The trail works its way along the S shore between the pond and a hill to reach the lean-to at the pond's head at 1.1 mi. The lean-to receives frequent use, especially in fishing season. There is a wet trail to the pond ending on a small outcrop of bedrock.

The trail continues skirting the shore of Olmstead Pond until at 1.4 mi it crosses the outlet from Simmons Pond. (An unmarked side trail, L, soon crosses the outlet to a small thin pond that runs N and S. This may be an extension of Simmons Pond, depending on water levels and beaver activity.) The trail then climbs slightly to reach the main body of Simmons Pond.

The trail loops around Olmstead Pond and at 1.5 mi reaches a turnoff for a designated campsite. Behind the campsite, which is situated on a point, is a large area of blowdown. The trail continues along the shore and through a second campsite at 1.8 mi, then leaves the pond and begins a steady ascent to join a ridge. It drops off the ridge and crosses a low point at 2.1 mi, then climbs steeply to the top of the ridge that bounds the SE shore of Spectacle Pond. At 2.2 mi a view down the length of Spectacle Pond opens up to the L.

The trail leaves the pond at 2.3 mi and quickly reaches a beaver pond. The trail crosses the outlet of the pond between the beaver dam (L) and a marshy area (R) at 2.4 mi. It continues to the end of the marshy area, turns R, crosses the inlet to the marsh, and follows the marsh on the opposite side. The trail leaves the marsh and tops a small rise, then starts its descent through a generally mixed forest.

The trail is muddy in places and generally follows a series of low disconnected outcrops. The trail crosses a small creek at 3.2 mi and follows the creek briefly before leaving it to ascend to meet Sixmile Creek Trail at 3.3 mi, 1 mi N of the loop's starting point.

❅ Trail in winter: Generally not suitable for skiing owing to steepness of terrain.

ᛦᛦ Distances: Sixmile Creek Trail to Olmstead Pond Lean-to, 1.1 mi; to side trail to Simmons Pond, 1.4 mi; to Spectacle Pond, 2.2 mi; to return to Sixmile Creek Trail, 3.3 mi (5.3 km).

196 Darning Needle Pond

Trails Illustrated Map 745: Y10

This trail makes its way from one of Cranberry Lake's inlets, or "flows," to a remote backcountry pond.

▶Locator: Recommended access to this yellow-marked trail is by boat to the point on South Bay where Chair Rock Creek empties into Chair Rock Flow. Chair Rock Creek is the outlet of Darning Needle Pond and the trail generally runs parallel with the creek until it reaches the pond.◀

Leaving the lake (0.0 mi), the trail begins to rise steadily through pole-sized hardwoods as it parallels the creek. This trail is remote, thus regular maintenance is difficult and beaver flooding can occasionally be a problem.

At 0.5 mi, the blue-marked Cranberry Lake–Grass Pond Trail (trail 197) diverges R. At 0.8 mi, the trail passes rapids along the creek with a small attractive waterfall in one spot. The valley of this short creek is relatively wide and has wetlands created by beaver in quite a few places along its course.

At 1.9 mi, the trail crosses the creek on a beaver dam and proceeds along a bluff overlooking fairly extensive wetlands until it reaches the shores of Darning Needle Pond at 2.6 mi. Darning Needle Pond, long and narrow, is ringed with a mixture of conifers and hardwoods, with several low hills on the S side of the pond.

❅ Trail in winter: Not suitable owing to remoteness, wetness, and numerous creek crossings that could prove difficult and dangerous.

ᛦᛦ Distances: Cranberry Lake to Cranberry Lake–Grass Pond Trail, 0.5 mi; to Darning Needle Pond, 2.6 mi (4.2 km).

197 Cranberry Lake–Grass Pond Trail

Trails Illustrated Map 745: X10

This trail is best reached by boat from either its S end on Grass Pond (an extension of Lows Lake) or its N end on Cranberry Lake, where it begins as part of Darning Needle Pond Trail (trail 196). The trail connects the Bog River drainage with Cranberry Lake on the Oswegatchie River drainage.

▶Locator: N access from Cranberry Lake is at 0.5 mi on the Darning Needle Pond trail (trail 196), which is accessed from the southernmost tip of Chair Rock

Flow. S access is via a paddle almost the entire length of Lows Lake and into Grass Pond, which is in actuality a N-reaching bay of Lows Lake; the trailhead is in a small bay on the NE part of Grass Pond. The trail is described here from the N. ◀

Leaving the yellow-marked Darning Needle Pond trail (0.0 mi), this blue-marked trail branches to the W and crosses Chair Rock Creek at 0.1 mi. The trail begins a steady ascent toward Indian Mt., then turns S, following the mountain's flank through mostly mixed hardwoods until it descends to the outlet of Fishpole Pond at 1.7 mi.

The trail continues on, crossing a small creek at 2 mi and passing E of Fishpole Pond, which can be viewed through the trees. The route then follows along a boggy area to the E. It makes a sharp turn E at 2.8 mi and follows a creek. The trail then turns S again, crosses two creeks, and starts to climb the flank of Wolf Mt. At 3.4 mi the trail reaches a high point of land and begins its descent, joining an old logging road at 3.8 mi. It reaches a landing on Grass Pond at 3.9 mi.

❀ Trail in winter: Not suitable for cross-country skiing owing to remoteness of setting.

🀰 Distances: Darning Needle Pond trail to outlet of Fishpole Pond, 1.7 mi; to Grass Pond, 3.9 mi (6.2 km). From Cranberry Lake to Grass Pond, 4.4 mi (7.1 km).

198 Headwaters Canoe Carry

Trails Illustrated Map 745: W9

This remote canoe carry, linking the headwaters of the Bog and Oswegatchie Rivers, is the ultimate in a wilderness trail. The carry is in two stages: from Lows Lake to Big Deer Pond (see the Big Deer Pond trail, trail 199), then from Big Deer Pond to the upper reaches of the Oswegatchie River.

▶Locator: The trail starts on the W bay of Lows Lake, which is the extension of the Bog River, at a canoe carry sign on a peninsula on the S (L) side of the bay. This point is reached after a paddle of approximately 15 mi from the put-in at the Bog River lower dam. ◀

From the shore (0.0 mi), the trail follows yellow canoe carry disks to an intersection with an old logging road at 0.4 mi. The route veers R on the wider logging road and follows the yellow disks through second-growth hardwoods to arrive at the canoe put-in on the N shore of Big Deer Pond at 0.9 mi.

The canoe carry trail resumes on the W shore of Big Deer Pond, where the yellow disks start again. A paddle can be made across the pond, or a bushwhack of approximately 0.5 mi can be made R around the pond until the disks reappear on the SW shore of the pond.

The carry crosses the outlet of Deer Pond at 2 mi. Planks help in this flooded area, but occasionally the crossing will have to be made using a beaver dam. The trail rises and crosses over the top of a steep hill, one of the area's numerous es-

Bog River lower dam and put-in. Daniel Way

kers, at 2.9 mi. This esker, according to DEC measurements, is 180 ft high from base to top.

The trail descends and begins a long, steady course to the bank of the Oswegatchie River reaching it at 3.5 mi, at a point below the area referred to as Beaver Dam. Large white pine line this last section and a DEC campsite is on the bank of the river.

❋Trail in winter: Not recommended for winter travel, mainly owing to exceptional remoteness.

𝕸 Distances: Lows Lake to Big Deer Pond, 0.9 mi; Big Deer Pond SW shore via bushwhack, 1.4 mi; to Oswegatchie River, 3.5 mi (5.6 km).

199 Big Deer Pond

Trails Illustrated Map 745: X9

DEC closed the Big Deer Pond trail in 1995 owing to extensive blowdown after a derecho passed through this area. Blowdown has since been cleared and the trail is in use, however DEC does not maintain it. Please check with the local ranger for more information.

►Locator: This trail begins at Cowhorn Jct., which is 6 mi from the Dead Creek Flow trailhead and the hamlet of Wanakena via High Falls Loop (trail 186) and Cowhorn Jct. Trail (trail 191). It is at the end of Sixmile Creek Trail (trail 193), 4.1 mi from its start at the West Flow of South Bay.◄

From the jct. (0.0 mi), the trail descends slightly, proceeding through a forest of mostly medium-sized hardwoods and arriving at an open glade at 0.6 mi. Passing tiny Grassy Pond L at 0.8 mi, the trail begins to climb to the top of an esker at 1 mi. The trail descends past Slender Pond, seen on the L at 1.3 mi. This small pond lying in a glacial depression is narrow at the waist and widens out at the head. It is almost completely encircled by a bog mat of heath and sphagnum.

At 2.1 mi a jct. is reached. Big Deer Pond lies straight ahead. It is a large, shallow lake with emergent grassy vegetation protruding in many areas. Owing to the abundance of deer, this was a favorite spot for hunters to be flown in before the area was classified as Wilderness.

A L turn at the jct. leads to Lows Lake. Continuing on straight, in about 400 ft an unmaintained trail R leads to the tri-county marker. Beyond this, the trail leads in about one-third of a mile to the canoe carry from Big Deer Pond to the Oswegatchie River (trail 198).

❋ Trail in winter: A lengthy ski. Attempt only with extreme caution and detailed preparation and planning.

𝕸 Distances: Cowhorn Jct. to Grassy Pond, 0.5 mi; to Slender Pond, 1.3 mi; to Big Deer Pond, 2.1 mi (3.4 km).

200 Clear Pond Trail

Trails Illustrated Map 745: X9

DEC closed Clear Pond Trail in 1995 owing to extensive blowdown after a dere-cho passed through this area. Blowdown has since been cleared and the trail is in use, however DEC does not maintain this trail. Please check with the local ranger for more information.

▶Locator: From the W, the trail begins on the R on the Cowhorn Jct. trail (trail 191), about 300 ft before Cowhorn Jct.◀

From its jct. with the Cowhorn Jct. trail (trail 191), this short trail heads S. The trail is roughly cut about 0.5 mi. It comes close to, but does not reach Clear Pond. Fringed with sedges and grass, this shallow pond is slowly turning into a wetland. Once the trail continued to Nicks Pond, but that portion of trail has been officially abandoned.

❋ Trail in winter: Can be skied with caution, but is hampered by lengthy dis-tances from the trailhead.

201 Moore Trail

Trails Illustrated Map 745: Y7

This trail follows the banks of the Oswegatchie River. The rapids along this stretch of river make it unsuitable for canoeing but contribute to a splendid view from the trail, as the many cataracts and pools are almost continually in sight. In early spring, the painted trillium in bloom under the tall hemlock, spruce, and balsam fir also present a pretty picture. Each end of the trail crosses private property on easements; please keep to the trail.

▶Trailhead: Access to this yellow-marked trail is from Wanakena Rd. (CR 61), approximately 1 mi from NY 3 just before the metal bridge crossing the Oswe-gatchie River. A DEC trail sign can be seen on the R. This is less than 0.1 mi be-fore the trailhead for the High Falls Loop (trail 186).◀

Leaving the sign (0.0 mi), the trail goes behind a private residence to proceed along the banks of the Oswegatchie River. The start of the trail presents a view of many large boulders in the riverbed. At 1 mi, the trail passes a series of small waterfalls. At 1.3 mi, a charming beaver pond can be seen R. Shortly thereafter, the trail passes a number of white cedars on the riverbank. Trailing arbutus or mayflower also blooms here in the spring.

At 2 mi, the trail reaches Inlet Rd. after crossing a parcel of private land. (Please keep to the trail while crossing private property.) A short walk on Inlet Rd. to the L leads to Inlet Landing. From here, the river is passable by canoe to its upper reaches. The landing was once the site of a sportsmen's hotel, and the trail is named after one of the early hotel proprietors.

❋ Trail in winter: Can be skied as a round-trip of 4 mi. Narrow in places.

🚶 Distances: Wanakena to series of falls, 1 mi; to Inlet Rd., 2 mi (3.2 km).

202 Cathedral Rock

Trail Illustrated Map 745: Y8 | P. 272

This trail is on land owned by the Ranger School of the State University of New York College of Environmental Science and Forestry at Wanakena. The school is relocating the current trail for this peak with a parking area planned at the Hays Brook access gates off of NY 3. As of this writing (2016), the Ranger School allows access by the public, requesting that hikers park in the parking lot described below. (See the college website at www.esf.edu for parking updates.)

The materials for the fire tower on the summit were salvaged in 1971, with DEC permission, by the school's students and faculty from an abandoned tower that once stood atop Tooley Pond Mt., 5 mi NW of Cranberry Lake. Reconstruction of the tower on Cathedral Rock began in the 1980s; the cab was essentially finished by volunteer labor in 1999 and final restoration measures were completed in 2000.

Cathedral Rock and Mount Arab sport the only two fire towers left in St. Lawrence County, both built by the Aermotor Company of Chicago in 1918.

▶Trailhead: See first paragraph above for information about plans to relocate parking. From NY 3 between the villages of Star Lake and Cranberry Lake, turn S on CR 61, the short side road shown on most highway maps as leading toward the village of Wanakena. After 0.8 mi, bear L at the first jct. Turn L again in 0.2 mi on Ranger School Rd., bypassing Wanakena's central hamlet area. Proceed 1.2 mi along this road to a L turn into the campus at the first sign marking one's arrival at the Ranger School. At a T jct. 0.1 mi farther, turn L. Drive 0.1 mi into a large student parking lot beside the sports fields with a gated gravel road on the R. The trail begins at this gate. ◀

From the gate (0.0 mi), the route begins on a gravel road. About 60 yd down the road, the route turns R onto the Latham Trail, marked as trail #10 on trail markers of black and white diamonds with a ranger's badge background. This well-marked and maintained foot trail crosses four times over gravel roads before reaching a mixed conifer plantation and the base of Cathedral Rock.

About 70 yd from the last road intersection, where a side trail goes R, the trail continues straight ahead and then turns L at 0.8 mi, starting a steeper climb up Cathedral Rock on a switchback. The trail switchbacks R at 0.9 mi, reaches a wooden staircase, then turns L along rocky ledges to a picnic pavilion and scenic view at 1 mi.

Continue past the pavilion and follow the trail WNW 90 yd to the fire tower at the top of the hill at 1.1 mi. Please sign the tower notebook to help the school monitor use. The tower provides otherwise unobtainable views of nearby Cranberry Lake and the glacial hills in this region of the Adirondack Park. Algonquin Peak and the Seward Range can be discerned to the E on a very clear day. NY 3 is visible to the W.

❊ Trail in winter: Most of trail #10 to Cathedral Rock is passable on skis or snowshoes, however, the final switchback section should be avoided. At the fourth road intersection, follow the unplowed road L, uphill, for about 0.2 mi. Turn R onto Tower Rd. and follow this to the fire tower.

⚭ Distances: To firetower, 1.1 mi (1.8 km). Ascent, 185 ft (56 m). Summit elevation, 1725 ft (526 m).

203 Otter Brook Trail

Trails Illustrated Map 745: Y10

This trail connects several trails in the Five Ponds Wilderness Area and is part of the CL50 (see Cranberry Lake 50 Section). The trail highlights the downside of using logging roads as hiking trails: the growth of new trees adjacent to the trail can block the view, leaving one with the impression of hiking in a monotonous green tunnel.

▶Locator: Recommended access to the W end of this trail is by boat to Cranberry Lake's South Bay, where Chair Rock Creek empties into Chair Rock Flow. Access to the E end is by Sucker Brook Rd. Trail (trail 153) or N by Dog Pond Trail (trail 155). ◀

As the blue-marked trail leaves the jct. (0.0 mi), it starts a gentle climb through mixed hardwoods. A view of Chair Rock Creek can be seen R. At 1 mi the trail leaves the Five Ponds Wilderness Area and enters Cranberry Lake Wild Forest. The trail crosses a creek at 1.1 mi and turns into a logging road that has been used as a four-wheeler trail. To the R is an open area of marsh and beaver flows as the trail follows higher ground.

At 1.6 mi the trail reaches the site of an abandoned hunting camp. Collapsed buildings, stoves, and other debris litter the site. The trail continues to follow a ridge, passing through mostly young-growth mixed hardwoods. After a drop and a cut in a stream bank, the trail crosses a creek at 2.1 mi. The trail now follows the contours of a hill with relatively gentle grades, first climbing, then turning L and dropping in a steep plunge to a bridge on Sucker Brook at 3.4 mi.

The trail now starts a series of R and L turns as it climbs to a gentle R turn to cross a creek at 3.9 mi. Be careful to look for blue trail markers and the trail at turns, as there are many branching roads and skid trails in this area. The blue markers may be few and far between. The trail continues to climb until there is a final drop in grade to a trail jct. at 5 mi. Sucker Brook Rd. Trail (trail 153) continues straight here; the trail to Dog Pond (trail 155) and the CL50 turn L.

❊ Trail in winter: Can be skied from the W by crossing Cranberry Lake and from the E from Sucker Brook Rd. Trail. Remoteness is a factor.

⚭ Distances: Chair Rock Flow to border of Five Ponds Wilderness Area, 1 mi; to bridge on Sucker Brook, 3.4 mi; to Sucker Brook Rd. Trail (trail 153) and Dog Pond Trail (trail 155), 5 mi (8 km). ⬤

Cranberry Lake 50 Section

One of the original challenges of the Adirondacks was climbing its forty-six major peaks. There is now a new Adirondack challenge: the Cranberry Lake 50 (CL50), a 50-mile trail loop around Cranberry Lake. Most of the trails that comprise the CL50 were already in place. With the construction of a few connector trails and the use of existing roads, the CL50 was born.

Cranberry Lake gets its name from the cranberry bogs that surrounded it before the lake was dammed in 1867 and the water level increased. This area is unlike the Adirondack High Peaks region, with its large changes in relief. This is because Cranberry Lake lies in an area of Precambrian rocks, which encircle the harder anorthositic rock at the core of the Adirondacks. These old, weathered rocks, mostly gneisses, marbles, and quartzites, form the low rolling hills of the Cranberry Lake region. They are connected to similar rocks, which make the core of the North American continent, in Canada by a narrow band called the Frontenac Arch. This is why the Thousand Islands, part of the Frontenac Arch, have the same topographic feel as this part of the Adirondacks. The region has low-lying land features, and the trails of the CL50 are much gentler than those of the High Peaks.

The Cranberry Lake area has a rich and interesting history. Well known to hunters and anglers in the nineteenth century, the region was nonetheless difficult to access. The Rich Lumber Company opened it up with logging when it moved here from Pennsylvania in 1902. Railroads and roads came, and tourists soon followed. There was mining, too. After the logging companies left, much of the land was sold to New York State. The forest started to regrow, and signs of civilization began to fade.

Many have made the case that the Five Ponds Wilderness is the wildest place east of the Mississippi River. In its present state, the area could be described as "civilized wilderness." Here you can find great areas of virgin forest, yet hike on old railroad grades or logging roads. You can come around the bend on a trail and find abandoned logging equipment or the remains of a logging camp. Places like Carters Landing and Janacks Landing are named after log staging areas, and wild places were once home to sportsmen's camps, lodges, and even hotels. It is one of the wildest places in New York state, but it is a civilized wilderness. Even in the heart of Five Ponds Wilderness one is never that far from civilization.

The Cranberry Lake 50 can be divided into fourteen parts with two alternate routes. These are listed below sequentially, starting from the Peavine Swamp Trail trailhead and proceeding around Cranberry Lake in a counterclockwise direction. All of these trails, except the Ranger School Rd. and NY 3 connectors, are described in their entirety elsewhere in this guide.

Hikers who have finished the CL50 loop can register on the Cranberry Lake 50 website and buy a patch. The website is www.cranberrylake50.org.

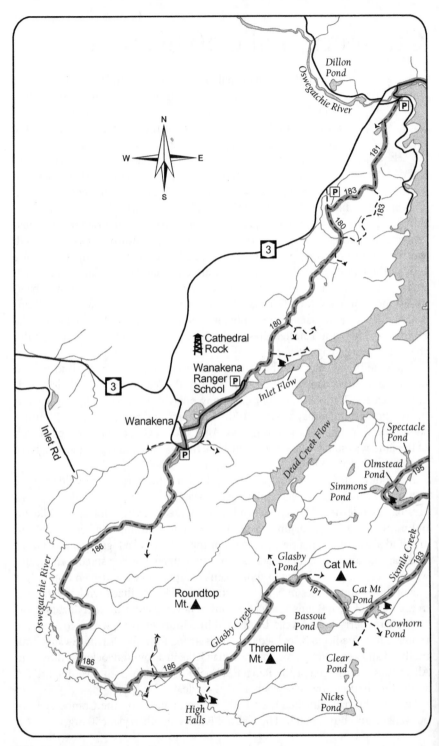

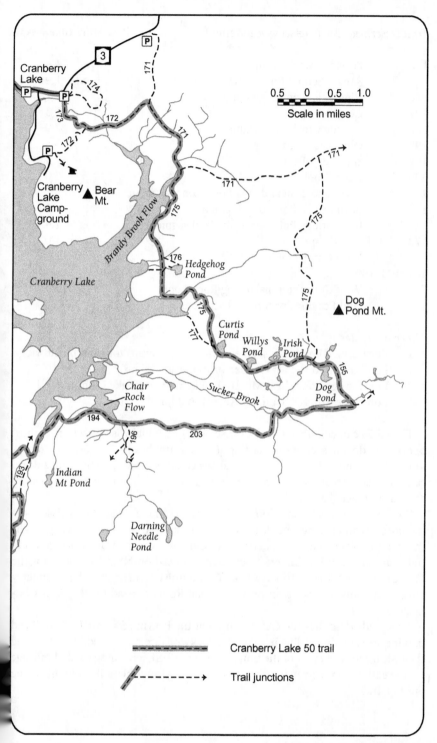

Cranberry Lake

Cranberry Lake Campground

Bear Mt.

Brandy Brook Flow

Cranberry Lake

Hedgehog Pond

Dog Pond Mt.

Curtis Pond

Willys Pond

Irish Pond

Dog Pond

Chair Rock Flow

Sucker Brook

Indian Mt Pond

Darning Needle Pond

0.5   0   0.5   1.0
Scale in miles

▬▬▬▬▬   Cranberry Lake 50 trail

╱ ------→   Trail junctions

Trail Described (counterclockwise direction)		CL50 Miles (one way)
180	Peavine Swamp Trail	4.4
	Ranger School Rd. Connector	1.9
186	High Falls Loop segment	11.2
191	Cowhorn Jct.	2.3
193	Sixmile Creek Trail segment	2.9
195	Olmstead Pond Loop	3.3
194	South Bay Trail	2.4
203	Otter Brook Trail	5.0
155, 175	Dog Pond Trail and Dog Pond Loop segment	8.7
171	Burntbridge Pond trail segment	1.6
172	Burntbridge Pond–Bear Mt. Trail segment	1.4
173	East Connector	1.0
	NY 3 Connector	1.7
181, 183, 180		
	West Connector, Balancing Rock Loop, and Peavine Swamp Trail segment	3.5

Alternate Routes

171 Burntbridge Pond trail segment with NY 3 Connector from Burntbridge Pond trailhead to East Connector trailhead, 3.6 mi

172 Burntbridge Pond–Bear Mt. Trail and Cranberry Lake Campground, Lone Pine Rd., NY 3 alternative, 4.1–6.2 mi

The CL50 can be hiked in a clockwise or counterclockwise direction. A third option is to do it in sections by starting at various trailheads. To shorten distances to trailheads and reduce backtracks, canoes could be used. Groups with several canoes could start at different trailheads, meet somewhere in the middle to swap canoes, and meet back at the canoe put-in.

For a complete continuous loop without canoes, there are seven possible starting points with parking: the Peavine Swamp trailhead on NY 3; the High Falls trailhead in Wanakena; Cranberry Lake Campground; the Burntbridge Pond trailhead on NY 3; the Gilbert Tract Loop trailhead on NY 3 (trailhead for the East Connector); the Cranberry Lake Community Center; and the Cranberry Lake Boat Launch parking lot on Columbian Rd. (trailhead for the West Connector).

This guide describes the CL50 starting at the Peavine Swamp Trail trailhead parking area and proceeding in a counterclockwise direction. In addition to citing the mileage for each part of the trail as it is described, a running total of mileage for the entire loop is given in parentheses, starting from the trailhead for Peavine Swamp Trail.

180 Peavine Swamp Trail

Trails Illustrated Map 745: Y8 | P. 272

►Trailhead: Located on NY 3, approximately 1.8 mi S of the bridge spanning the Oswegatchie River on the western outskirts of the hamlet of Cranberry Lake. From the S it is 5 mi from the Wanakena turnoff. A small DEC sign pointing to a rough parking area on the S side of the road can be seen approximately 0.2 mi W of a state DOT parking lot on the N side of NY 3.

The trail can also be accessed from the S at the SUNY-EFS Ranger School in Wanakena. Coming from Wanakena, follow Ranger School Rd. along the river. There is a parking area on the R in front of the main administration building, however no overnight parking is allowed here or anywhere else on the college campus. The trail starts just where the road bears L away from the lake.◄

Leaving the trailhead parking area on NY 3 (0.0 mi), the trail immediately spans one of the area's many small streams. At 0.3 mi, Balancing Rock Loop (trail 183) branches L. At 0.5 mi, a small wooden bridge carries the trail across another stream, just before a sharp rise to the top of a hill. The forest here is mostly red spruce and balsam fir on the knolls, with tamarack and black spruce joining them in the peatland to the R (W). Near the top of the hill the forest's composition begins to change to second-growth northern hardwoods with occasional conifers.

The trail undulates through the forest, passing the edge of an old log clearing at 0.9 with a marked campsite off the trail to the L. At 1 mi, the S end of Balancing Rock Loop comes in on the L (E). At 1.2 mi, Christmas Tree Loop (trail 184) departs L (E).

At 1.6 mi, the trail begins to ascend a steep ridge. Partway up it passes two impressive red spruces; at one point, DEC foresters measured their diameter at breast height (DBH) at 25 inches, quite imposing for this normally slender species. At 2 mi, just after another small creek, the trail passes a hemlock of 40 inches DBH and, at 2.1 mi, one of 42 inches DBH. These hemlocks and the large red spruce may be considered "old-growth" or "virgin" timber, and give some indication of what this area's forest looked like to the early hunters and trappers who penetrated it in the last century.

At 2.6 mi the trail reaches the top of its steepest hill and begins a gradual descent until it meets the S end of the Christmas Tree Loop coming in from the L (E) at 2.9 mi. At 3.2 mi the trail crosses a creek, and at 3.6 mi it comes to a jct. The Peavine Swamp Trail and CL50 continue to the R (W). (The trail L [E] leads to the lean-to and shore of Inlet Flow, in approximately 0.5 mi. See Peavine Swamp Lean-to Loop, trail 185, in Cranberry Lake–Wanakena Section.)

The Peavine Swamp Trail and CL50 continue on a logging road. The trail generally drops in elevation until a bay on Cranberry Lake comes into view at a large erratic at 4 mi. The trail now generally follows the shore, leaving state land at 4.2 mi. The trail ends at the paved Ranger School Rd. at 4.4 mi.

Ranger School Rd. Connector

Trails Illustrated Map 745: Y8 | P. 272

At the jct. with the road (0.0 mi; 4.4 mi) the route mapped out for the CL50 turns L (W), passing the main administration building of SUNY College of Environmental Science and Forestry Ranger School (R) and a boat launch and parking area (L). After climbing a small hill, the road leaves the Ranger School at 0.2 mi (4.6 mi) and starts downhill with views of Cranberry Lake through the camps to the S. Eddy St. branches off to the L at 0.6 mi (5 mi). (This is a small loop drive that rejoins Ranger School Rd. in 0.2 mi.)

At 0.9 mi (5.3 mi) a pond is visible to the R. Called the Set Back, the pond was created many years ago when bridges here were replaced with culverts and a bay of Cranberry Lake was cut off from the lake. The road now curves L; there is a boat launch on the narrow causeway between pond and lake. The road passes the Pine Cone Restaurant at 1.2 mi (5.6 mi).

The road curves back to the R and continues beside the pond, leaving Cranberry Lake behind. At 1.4 mi (5.8 mi) a sign on the L recounts the damage caused on July 15, 1995, when winds from a derecho resulted in some of the most extensive blowdown ever observed in the Adirondacks. At 1.5 mi (5.9 mi) the road intersects with Second St. (CR 61). Turn L at this jct.

The road now enters the hamlet of Wanakena. The road rises, passes First St., and descends to the Oswegatchie River. The town square with a gazebo, public restroom, and historical kiosk is R, as is the Wanakena Post Office and a small store that sells basics. Continuing on through the jct. with Front St., the picturesque Wanakena Footbridge is reached at 1.7 mi (6.1 mi). This suspension bridge was constructed to connect the sawmills, residences, and businesses of Wanakena. A scenic view down the lake and up the Oswegatchie River, which enters Cranberry Lake at this point, can be had from the bridge. This bridge was heavily damaged by ice in 2014. Prior to its restoration, begun in 2016, the bridge had been on the National Registry of Historic Places. Until restoration is complete, it will be necessary to detour using the road bridge to South Shore Rd., which will add slightly to the mileage cited here.

Once across the footbridge, the trail passes through the yards of camps and residences. It crosses another small bridge over a bay and at 1.8 mi (6.2 mi) joins South Shore Rd. Directly across the road beside the tennis courts is the trailhead parking area, for those wanting to start the trip from this location. A second Wanakena history kiosk is a few hundred feet E. Turn R at this point past the tennis courts and the Wanakena pump station to a jct. on the L at 1.9 mi (6.3 mi). At the corner is a DEC sign for High Falls. Turn L and continue down the road to a yellow gate and the trail register.

186 High Falls Loop segment

High Falls Loop trailhead is an alternate CL50 trailhead. See trailhead information for High Falls Loop, trail 186, in Cranberry Lake–Wanakena Section.

From the trail register (0.0 mi; 6.3 mi), the red-marked High Falls Loop follows an old truck trail. This was once a logging railroad line built by the Rich Lumber Company during the heyday of logging in the region. The trail passes an old mill pond on the L. One of the few artificial ponds in this area of abundant natural water bodies, it was created in connection with lumbering activities around the turn of the twentieth century. The first mile of this trail is used to access a water reservoir that supplies the hamlet of Wanakena, creating a strange mix of civilization and wilderness.

At 0.5 mi (6.8 mi), the trail crosses Skate Creek on a culvert, then curves R to join a drier path at the base of the hill. At 0.8 mi (7.1 mi) the trail passes a cast iron water cutoff protector, R, a reminder of the multiple uses of this trail section. The trail passes another creek at 0.9 mi (7.2 mi). Just beyond this creek, the unmarked Dobson Trail once branched L. This unofficial trail was used by the owner of a sportsmen's hotel formerly located at High Falls as a shortcut through the Plains. It is almost impossible to follow and is not recommended.

At 1 mi (7.3 mi) the trail passes an improved spring coming from a pipe on the L. These pipe springs were built by early woodsmen and are quite common in this region. Shortly thereafter a large cut in the forest diverges L. This is the buried waterline from the reservoir; vehicular use of the trail ends here. The trail now turns R and starts a gentle ascent, leaving a little more of civilization behind. It crosses Skate Creek again on a bridge at 1.2 mi (7.5 mi) then joins a small ridge as it continues to climb.

The trail reaches the start of the Leary Trail (trail 187) L at 1.7 mi (8 mi). (This trail had been officially abandoned owing to the effects of the 1995 derecho. It has been reopened, but is unmaintained. See Cranberry Lake–Wanakena Section for trail description.) The High Falls Trail and CL50 continue on the truck trail straight ahead.

The trail now passes through a rock cut and reaches the high point of the trail in a gentle pass at 1.9 mi (8.2 mi) before descending to the Oswegatchie River. It passes a large open wetland (R) shortly thereafter.

Now rather flat, the trail follows a tributary of the Oswegatchie, finally joining the base of the hills to the L. At 3.8 mi (10.1 mi), a distinct three-way jct. is encountered. (The path R proceeds 0.1 mi to a landing called High Rock, named for the huge glacially rounded outcrop overlooking the river here. This site makes a pleasant destination for a winter ski or a day hike.)

The trail continues straight ahead through the forest, encountering a stone bridge and cascade at 4.3 mi (10.6 mi). It now skirts the marsh along the base of the hills to the E, turns due W, then continues S. At some points the trail passes through low areas of balsam, tamarack, and spruce, then climbs to the base of the hills to areas with beautiful yellow birch and species that like drier ground. At 5.4 mi (11.7 mi) the trail crosses a stream. Depending on beaver activity, this and other streams may be difficult to cross because of flooding. The trail continues generally level, as befits the route of a logging railroad.

At 6.1 mi (12.4 mi) the trail passes another creek with a beaver pond. As the trail nears the Oswegatchie, open areas of water are visible. The trail passes through a designated campsite adjacent to the river at 6.7 mi (13 mi) and shortly thereafter a side trail R leads to Campsite 28, which overlooks the river as it squeezes between two rocks. This stretch of the Oswegatchie River is known as Ross Rapids.

The trail now bears L through a rock cut and onto the fill area, with marsh and river to the R. The trail meets the river again with a view of an oxbow at the end of Straight Rapids, and then leaves the river to follow a small stream. The trail crosses a low area that may be flooded; there is a rough makeshift trail to the L.

At 7.4 mi (13.7 mi) the Sand Lake trail (trail 188) goes R (S, leading to Five Ponds). The second terminus of the Leary Trail (trail 187) may be discernible just beyond this jct. on the L. It may be impossible to locate as, just before the 1995 derecho, a new trail end had been constructed to avoid beaver flooding.

At 7.5 mi (13.8 mi), beaver flooding may be a problem at a creek crossing. The trail then passes a marshy area, and the Oswegatchie comes into view on the L at 7.8 mi (14.1 mi). This is Carters Landing, once a timber staging location. Shortly after, a trail L leads to Campsite 21, which provides a pleasant view of the river floodplain.

The trail here is often flooded by beaver dams on Glasby Creek to the R, making it wet in places. At 8 mi (14.3 mi), the trail crosses Glasby Creek on a wooden bridge. The trail is now in the western edge of the famous "Oswegatchie Plains," which can be seen L after the bridge on Glasby Creek. The blueberry and meadow-sweet shrubs of this unique area, classified as a boreal heath by DEC, are being infringed upon by sporadic black spruce, black cherry, and tamarack trees, which are starting to establish themselves.

The trail reaches a jct. at 8.5 mi (14.8 mi). The High Falls Loop and CL50 continue L on a rerouted segment of what is locally known as the Plains Trail. (The trail straight ahead [R] leads to High Falls in 0.5 mi, adding 1 mi to the CL50; see High Falls Loop, trail 186, in Cranberry Lake–Wanakena Section for more about High Falls and a description of this side trail. It is a worthy side trip.)

The trail leaves the truck trail and takes on a rougher character. It starts to climb, following a ridge through rocky ground with large amounts of blowdown. The trail reaches a high point on a bare rock ridge at 8.9 mi (15.2 mi), then begins to zigzag and drops to cross a stream at 9.2 mi (15.5 mi) on a bridge cleverly constructed using a large, downed white pine. Though roughened by an ax, the pine may be slippery when wet and caution should be exercised in crossing.

The trail turns L now and follows the stream downhill briefly before continuing NE. At 9.3 mi (15.6 mi) the first of several extremely large white pines is

Meadow near Cranberry Lake. Joanne Kennedy

encountered. The trail then navigates around a beaver pond. Farther L, marshy Glasby Creek is visible. The trail crosses the beaver dam at 9.6 mi (15.9 mi), passes through more large white pines, and proceeds to the base of Threemile Mt. at 9.7 mi (16 mi). The trail follows along the base of the mountain for quite a distance. It crosses several creeks cascading down ravines from the spruce-covered mountain, and passes a number of large talus boulders. Frost has been recorded in the Plains every month of the year. This is due to its location, tucked between Roundtop and Threemile Mts. The location also probably contributes, with other factors, to the area's generally treeless condition.

The trail swings L away from the base of the mountain and crosses a gentle swale at 10.7 mi (17 mi). Glasby Creek comes into view on the L just before the trail passes the old Plains Trail on the L at 10.8 mi (17.1 mi). At 11.1 mi (17.4 mi), the trail crosses Glasby Creek, now considerably smaller nearer its headwaters, and at 11.2 mi (17.5 mi) it ascends a ridge and meets the Cowhorn Jct. trail (trail 191) coming in sharply on the R. This is Sand Hill Jct. The CL50 turns R on the Cowhorn Jct. trail.

(High Falls Trail turns L. It descends to Janacks Landing on Cranberry Lake in 1 mi and proceeds on to the Dead Creek Trail trailhead in Wanakena in 3.7 mi. An additional 0.5 mi is required to return to the register for the High Falls loop. See complete trail description in Cranberry Lake–Wanakena Section.)

191 Cowhorn Jct. Trail

Trails Illustrated Map 745: X8 | P. 272

The yellow-marked Cowhorn Jct. trail leaves the High Falls Loop at Sand Hill Jct. (0.0 mi; 17.5 mi). It gradually proceeds up a hemlock glen to overlook the High Falls Loop. The trail turns L abruptly when it encounters Glasby Creek. Soon the trail passes an entrancing little waterfall (R) formed as Glasby Creek cascades down from Glasby Pond over bedrock that is softer than the bedrock on either side of it. The trail climbs away from the creek and rolls along until it crosses an open glade at 0.2 mi (17.7 mi).

The trail now climbs a slight rise to reach Glasby Pond and its outlet at 0.3 mi (17.8 mi). The trail passes a designated campsite shortly after and skirts the shore of the pond for a short distance through blowdown from the 1995 derecho. The trail here is rough and wet at times. It climbs away from the pond, quickly drops back to the pond, then finally begins to rise again gradually, reaching the jct. with the Cat Mt. trail (trail 192) at 0.8 mi (18.3 mi). The Cat Mt. trail goes straight (L) here; Cowhorn Jct. Trail turns R.

The trail again climbs slowly, then begins to descend into the cleft under Cat Mt. It passes over two small bedrock outcrops and through a boulder-strewn landscape under a canopy of beech and maple. Resurrected after the derecho, the trail now cuts back and forth to avoid downed trees. Cat Pond comes into view on the L at 1.6 mi (19.1 mi). The trail for the most part passes above the pond with spectacular views of Cat Mt. in the background. It dips to pond level only once, at a bay on the SW side of the pond.

The trail crosses a beaver dam. At 1.8 mi (19.3 mi), a side trail (L) leads to a designated campsite on a point near the outlet of the pond. The trail crosses Sixmile Creek at 2 mi (19.5 mi), and crosses a smaller stream as it begins a gentle climb before a final short, sharp rise to reach Cowhorn Jct. at 2.3 mi (19.8 mi).

193 Sixmile Creek Trail segment

Trails Illustrated Map 745: X9 | Pp. 272–273

The CL50 turns S at Cowhorn Jct., leaving the Cowhorn Jct. trail (trail 191) (0.0 mi; 19.8 mi) and following Sixmile Creek Trail. The red-marked Big Deer Pond trail (trail 199) goes R. This trail was closed after the derecho of 1995 but has been reopened. The nearby anglers' path to Clear Pond (trail 200) is passable, but does not extend to Nicks Pond (2016).

The trail follows blue markers along the top of an esker through blowdown and under tunnels of tree trunks. It is interesting to see forest succession taking place, with saplings growing up amongst the fallen pines that once dominated the ridge. Some large white pines still survive and give a hint of what the ridge looked like before the 1995 storm. Cat Mt. can occasionally be seen L (W) and Cowhorn Pond R (E).

At 0.4 mi (20.2 mi) a yellow-marked side trail comes in R. (This trail leads in 0.2 mi to a lean-to at Cowhorn Pond.) The trail continues on top of the esker until it reaches a second esker branching off L. The esker is almost breathtaking in this section with its tall, steep slopes. It is an excellent place to think about the two-mile-thick ice sheet that once covered this area. Meltwater carved huge caves under the ice, where icy torrents then deposited sand and gravel, creating these eskers, which look like upside-down streambeds. There are hundreds of miles of eskers in the Adirondacks; this one is called the Cranberry Lake Esker.

The trail mostly follows the top of the esker, climbing and descending with a general drop in elevation. Wetlands can be seen at times on both sides and ponds appear R. The outlet of Cowhorn Pond is on the R while Sixmile Creek, the outlet of Bassout and Cat Mt. Ponds, is on the L. At 1.7 mi (21.5 mi) the trail slips L of the top of the esker ridge and starts a gradual descent toward Tamarack Bog, which comes into view on the L at 2 mi (21.8 mi). Pitcher plants are particularly abundant here. The trail continues between the bog and esker, then bears R and follows a gap in the esker. It makes a quick steep climb at 2.3 mi (22.1 mi), then drops again. The trail now bears L and goes through yellow birch and hemlock forest while climbing back to the top of the now broader, gentler sloped esker.

At 2.9 mi (22.7 mi), the trail reaches a jct. with Olmstead Pond Loop (trail 195), L. The CL50 continues on the Olmstead Pond Loop. There is no sign for Olmstead Pond so be careful to turn here. (Sixmile Creek Trail continues straight. The Olmstead Pond trail and CL50 rejoin Sixmile Creek Trail at 3.9 mi, just before the CL50 turns onto the South Bay Trail, trail 194. See complete description of Sixmile Creek Trail in Cranberry Lake–Wanakena Section.)

195 Olmstead Pond Loop

Trails Illustrated Map 745: Y9 |Pp. 272–273

From its jct. with Sixmile Creek Trail (trail 193) (0.0 mi; 22.7 mi), the yellow-marked Olmstead Pond Loop starts a descent off the esker to meet the stream that drains Tamarack Bog at 0.1 mi (22.8 mi). The trail crosses Sixmile Creek at 0.2 mi (22.9 mi). There is no bridge and Sixmile Creek has some size here. The forest is of mixed hemlock and hardwoods. The trail begins to climb and soon meets the outlet of Olmstead Pond, cascading down to join Sixmile Creek below. The trail follows the creek and at 0.5 mi (23.2 mi) reaches Olmstead Pond. The outlet waters here have been dammed by beavers.

The trail works its way along the S shore between the pond and a hill to reach the lean-to at the pond's head at 1.1 mi (23.8 mi). The lean-to receives frequent usage, especially in fishing season. There is a wet trail to the pond ending on a small outcrop of bedrock.

The trail continues skirting the shore of Olmstead Pond until at 1.4 mi (24.1 mi) it crosses the outlet from Simmons Pond. An unmarked side trail L crosses the outlet to a small thin pond that runs N and S and that may be part of Simmons Pond, depending on water levels and beaver activity. The trail then climbs slightly to reach the main body of Simmons Pond, with hardwoods and occasional white pine on the shore. This is one of the relatively few water bodies in the area characterized by a greenish-blue coloring. The minerals in the water give it this attractive look.

The trail now loops around Olmstead Pond and at 1.5 mi (24.2 mi) reaches a turnoff for a designated campsite. Behind the campsite, which is situated on a point, is a large area of blowdown. The trail continues along the shore and through a second campsite at 1.8 mi (24.5 mi). The trail now leaves the pond and begins a steady ascent to join a ridge. It drops off the ridge and crosses a low point, then climbs steeply to the top of the ridge that bounds the SE shore of Spectacle Pond. At 2.2 mi (24.9 mi), a view down the length of Spectacle Pond opens up to the L.

The trail leaves the pond at 2.3 mi (25 mi) and crosses its outlet between a beaver dam (L) and a marshy area (R) at 2.4 mi (25.1 mi). The trail continues to the end of the marshy area, turns R, crosses the inlet to the marsh, and follows the marsh on the opposite side. It then leaves the marsh, tops a small rise, and starts to descend through a generally mixed forest.

The trail is muddy in places and generally follows a series of low, disconnected outcrops. It crosses a small creek at 3.2 mi (25.9 mi), follows the creek briefly, then climbs to meet Sixmile Creek Trail at 3.3 mi (26 mi). (The West Flow of Cranberry Lake is 0.3 mi N [L] of this jct. See complete description of Sixmile Creek Trail, trail 216, in Cranberry Lake–Wanakena Section.) From this jct., the CL50 continues to the R (S) on Sixmile Creek Trail for approximately 400 ft., until it reaches a jct. with South Bay Trail (trail 194).

194 South Bay Trail

Trails Illustrated Map 745: Y10 | P. 273

At the jct. of Sixmile Creek and South Bay Trails, the CL50 turns E (0.0 mi; 26 mi). South Bay Trail is a new trail constructed to bridge a gap between the Sixmile Creek and Otter Brook Trails in the CL50. The beginning of the trail originally went to the private holdings on South Flow.

The trail heads E and crosses a low section of the Sixmile Creek Esker, then turns NE, losing elevation until it crosses Sixmile Creek at 0.3 mi (26.3 mi), just before the creek flows into South Flow. The trail leaves the creek following a small valley. At 0.4 mi (26.4 mi), at a sign indicating private property, South Bay Trail starts to climb upward to the R. The trail now passes through a forest of large yellow birch and hemlocks perched on cliffs of gneissic rock. These rocks are part of the Grenville formation and are connected to the ancient rocks in Canada that make up the core of North America. The layers are contorted and twisted because the rocks have been under intense heat and pressure. The lenticular mineral grains shaped like eyes that are visible upon close inspection are called "augen," from the German name for eyes.

The trail climbs gently with several switchbacks before reaching its high point at approximately 1 mi (27 mi). It now starts to drop toward Chair Rock Flow, crosses the outlet stream from Indian Mt. Pond, and, at 1.7 mi (27.7 mi), turns sharply R onto a trail that comes from private property on Chair Rock Flow. The trail crosses a creek then gently climbs and drops following the shore of Chair Rock Flow. At 2.3 mi (28.3 mi) the trail crosses Chair Rock Creek at a beautiful spot.

After crossing the bridge, the CL50 continues to the R. (The trail L leads to water access and Campsite 17 on Chair Rock Flow.) The trail comes to another jct. at 2.4 mi (28.4 mi), where the CL50 continues straight on the Otter Brook Trail (trail 203). (Darning Needle Pond and Cranberry Lake–Grass Pond Trail, trails 196 and 197, respectively, are R. The trail L returns to the campsite and canoe landing.)

203 Otter Brook Trail

Trails Illustrated Map 745: Y10 | P. 273

As the blue-marked Otter Brook Trail leaves the jct. (0.0 mi; 28.4 mi), it starts a gentle climb through mixed hardwoods. Chair Rock Creek can be seen to the R. At 1 mi (29.4 mi) the trail leaves the Five Ponds Wilderness Area and enters the Cranberry Lake Wild Forest. The route crosses a creek at 1.1 mi (29.5 mi) and turns into a logging road that has been used as a four-wheeler trail. To the R is an open area of marsh and beaver flows as the trail follows higher ground.

At 1.6 mi (30 mi) the trail reaches the site of an abandoned hunting camp, littered with collapsed buildings, stoves, and other debris. The trail continues following a ridge, passing through mostly young growth mixed hardwoods. After a drop and a cut in a stream bank, the trail crosses a creek at 2.1 mi (30.5 mi).

The trail now follows the contours of a hill with relatively gentle grades, first climbing, then turning L and dropping in a steep plunge to a bridge on Sucker Brook at 3.4 mi (31.8 mi).

The trail now starts a series of R and L turns as it climbs to a gentle R turn to cross a creek at 3.9 mi (32.3 mi). Be careful to look for blue trail markers and the trail at turns, as there are many branching roads and skid trails in this area. This is a relatively new trail and the blue markers can be few and far between. The trail continues to climb until there is a final drop in grade to a trail jct. at 5 mi (33.4 mi). Otter Brook Trail becomes Sucker Brook Rd. Trail (trail 153) and continues straight here. The CL50 and Dog Pond Trail (trail 155) turn L.

155 Dog Pond Trail
175 Dog Pond Loop segment

Trails Illustrated Map 745: Y11 | P. 273

As the red-marked Dog Pond Trail (a logging road) leaves the jct. with Otter Brook Trail (trail 203) (0.0 mi; 33.4 mi), it drops and crosses a creek at 0.1 mi (33.5 mi). The trail climbs into a tract of cutover second-growth hardwood then drops again until it leaves the logging road at 0.5 mi (33.9 mi). The trail reaches the old Forest Preserve boundary shortly thereafter, at 0.6 mi (34 mi), and follows the boundary. The difference between Forest Preserve of long standing and of recent addition is dramatic here. The original Forest Preserve has not been subject to logging since early in the twentieth century, and majestic hemlocks, red spruces, and yellow birches follow the entire way to Dog Pond. The more recently acquired land has begun its long path to reaching this climax.

The trail leaves the boundary at 0.8 mi (34.2 mi) and soon Dog Pond comes into view between the trees. At 1 mi (34.4 mi) the trail crosses the inlet as it comes cascading down a charming small waterfall R. Dog Pond is a medium-sized glacial pond in which brook trout can be found. A number of attractive marked campsites dot the shore area. The trail passes N of the pond and leaves it behind as it passes the outlet at 1.3 mi (34.7 mi). The trail now begins to lose elevation and arrives at the jct. with Dog Pond Loop (trail 175) at Proulx Clearing at 1.5 mi (34.9 mi). The CL50 turns L on Dog Pond Loop. (Dog Pond Loop also continues straight ahead N to Burntbridge Pond.)

The large clearing at this jct. was once the site of Proulx Camp, one of the early traditional lumber camps of the region. During his stay at the Cranberry Lake Biological Center during the 1920s, the youthful Bob Marshall was fond of hiking to this spot. Today the clearing is reverting to forest, led by some rapidly growing red spruce; a beaver flow adjacent to the clearing makes it look larger than it is.

The blue-marked Dog Pond Loop drops to a creek flowing from the beaver flow and begins to climb through mixed hardwoods, reaching a ridge at 1.8 mi (35.2 mi). The trail skirts a hill at its high point, then dips and rises before passing through an area with large majestic hemlocks. At 2.1 mi (35.5 mi) a little-used yellow-marked trail branches R, leading to a designated campsite on the E shore of Irish Pond. The trail crosses the pond's outlet shortly thereafter; Irish Pond is now visible.

The trail continues along the S shore of Irish Pond, then leaves the pond and climbs up along a ridge, turning L with rock and cliffs R. The trail reaches the outlet of Willys Pond at 2.7 mi (36.1 mi). It follows the SW shore of the pond before beginning a climb through what appears to be a fault valley. Large talus boulders litter the cliffs and their bases (L).

At 3.1 mi (36.5 mi) the trail reaches a high point and then drops toward Curtis Pond, leaving the valley and approaching the pond on a small ridge. A side trail R at 3.4 mi (36.8 mi) leads to a designated campsite on Curtis Pond. The pond is known for its brook trout. The trail crosses the pond's outlet then begins to climb. A group of boulders can be observed a few hundred feet to the L. These glacial erratics form a natural shelter where Adirondack trapper and backwoods-man Nat Foster reputedly hid from a hostile hunting party of Indians in the early nineteenth century.

The trail continues to climb with nice views of Curtis Pond (R). It reaches a high point at 3.7 mi (37.1 mi) then drops quickly to the jct. with the red-marked East Inlet Trail (trail 203), which leads to Cranberry Lake in 1.1 mi. The Dog Pond Loop and CL50 continue straight (R). The trail now follows a ridge toward the N along the W flank of East Mt., generally holding its elevation. At 4.2 mi (37.6 mi) the trail reaches a high point then starts a general drop to Cranberry Lake. When the trees have dropped their leaves, views of the lake can be seen. At 4.4 mi (37.8 mi) the trail reaches a group of erratic boulders. There is a court-yard-like area called Willys Cave within one group of boulders; it can be accessed by crawling through a tunnel.

The trail continues to descend through several less dramatic boulder gardens, graced by old-growth northern hardwoods, with yellow birch, sugar maples, and birches. At 5 mi (38.4 mi) the trail starts a final steep grade that ends at a bridge on East Creek in 0.1 mi. The trail intersects an old logging road, where the trail turns R. The trail follows the logging road downgrade, paralleling East Creek. Shortly after, Cranberry Lake comes into view. At 5.4 mi (38.8 mi) a short trail L leads to Campsite 15. The trail continues, following the shore of the lake and soon passing Campsite 14. It arrives at the turn for Campsite 13 (located on the point) at 5.7 mi (39.1 mi).

The trail now turns to follow the bay behind the campsite. It crosses an inlet, follows the shore, then leaves the bay and starts to climb to a high point. It de-scends and levels off before intersecting the trail to Hedgehog Pond (trail 176) at 6.3 mi (39.7 mi). The trail R leads to the pond in 0.2 mi and the trail L leads to Cranberry Lake in 0.3 mi.

The CL50 and Dog Pond Loop continue straight, dropping to and crossing the outlet of Hedgehog Pond, then rising and dropping to two more streams be-fore finally descending through old-growth hardwoods. The trail passes through a garden-like area of rocks, hardwoods, ferns, and pines at the base of the descent at 7 mi (40.4 mi), where the trail turns R to follow the shore.

At 7.3 mi (40.7 mi), a trail L leads to Campsite 10. The trail continues to parallel the flow, climbing and dropping to avoid wet shoreline as it crosses the heads of several small bays under a canopy of hardwoods that gradually decrease in size. Cranberry Lake and some of its island are sometimes visible. There are three more designated campsites along the shore to the L in this section of the trail. All are attractive, though the connector trails to these sites are not marked and can be difficult to find.

The trail crosses a bridge at 7.9 mi (41.3 mi) and reaches a jct. with a snowmobile trail at 8.3 mi (41.7 mi). (The trail L leads to Brandy Brook Flow, where snowmobiles can travel on the lake during the winter or canoes can land in summer.) The Dog Pond Loop and CL50 continue straight at this point; the trail is now mostly marked with orange disk markers. This final stretch of trail is fairly straight until at 8.6 mi (42 mi), the trail turns L and drops to a wet stream crossing. It reaches the jct. with the Burntbridge Pond trail (trail 171) at 8.7 mi (42.1 mi). The CL50 goes straight on the Burntbridge Pond trail. (To the R, the Burntbridge Pond trail leads to Burntbridge Pond and the other end of Dog Pond Loop. For a complete description of Dog Pond Loop or the Burntbridge Pond trail, see Cranberry Lake–Wanakena Section.)

171 Burntbridge Pond Trail segment

Trails Illustrated Map 745: AA10 | P. 273

The N trailhead of the Burntbridge Pond trail is an alternate CL50 trailhead, good for hiking the CL50 in a clockwise direction. See the "alternate routes" at the end of this section and find trailhead information for the Burntbridge Pond trail (trail 171) in the Cranberry Lake–Wanakena Section.

At the jct. of Dog Pond Loop (trail 175) and the Burntbridge Pond trail near Brandy Brook Flow (0.0 mi; 42.1 mi), the CL50 follows the Burntbridge Pond trail N. The trail passes through an open area with young trees growing on the margins, curves gently to the L, and enters a dark area of dense small pines. An unmarked trail to Campsite 6 joins from the L just before the trail takes a hard R at 0.1 mi (42.2 mi).

The route now follows Brandy Brook under a canopy of hemlocks, turning L and crossing the brook on a bridge at 0.2 mi (42.3 mi). The trail joins a logging road, making several turns back and forth and climbing while passing through muddy areas. At 0.8 mi (42.9 mi) the trail turns L and joins the grade of an old railroad spur. The going is easier now, with a gentle grade and wide snowmobile bridges crossing most streams. Four-wheeler use of the trail is evident.

At 1.6 mi (43.7 mi), just after an open meadow, the trail reaches a trail register and the jct. with Burntbridge Pond–Bear Mt. Trail (trail 172), L. CL50 turns L onto the yellow-marked Burntbridge Pond–Bear Mt. Trail. (The Burntbridge

Cranberry Lake Campground. Joanne Kennedy

Pond trail continues straight ahead, providing an alternate route to NY 3. For a description of the segment of trail from this jct. N to NY 3, see the alternate routes listed at the end of this section.)

172 Burntbridge Pond–Bear Mt. Trail segment

Trails Illustrated Map 745: AA10 | P. 273

From its jct. with the Burntbridge Pond trail (0.0 mi; 43.7 mi), Burntbridge Pond–Bear Mt. Trail starts down a slope. It turns R then L through second-growth black cherry, red maple, and occasional aspen, and reaches a bridge at 0.3 mi (44 mi). There is a marshy area to the L created by beaver activity. The trail now climbs to a rather level valley between two hills with somewhat widely spaced trees and little undergrowth. As the trail drops from this valley it makes a turn to the N (R) and ascends.

After reaching a high point, the trail (now following an old logging road or four-wheeler trail) turns abruptly L (W) and descends to Bear Mt. Creek at 1 mi (44.7 mi). It crosses the creek on planks to reach a sliver of dry land, then crosses on planks again at 1.2 mi (44.9 mi). The large natural boreal wetland that existed here increased in size with the construction of the dam in the hamlet of Cranberry Lake. Lady slippers may be seen here in the spring.

After leaving the second planked section, the trail climbs out of the wetlands and at 1.4 mi (45.1 mi) joins a logging road at the jct. with the East Connector (trail 173). The CL50 proceeds to the R (N). (The Burntbridge Pond–Bear Mt.

Trail continues L [W] at this jct., leading in 1.1 mi to the Cranberry Lake Campground, an alternate CL50 route described under "alternate routes" later in this section. The Burntbridge Pond–Bear Mt. Trail is described in full in the Cranberry Lake–Wanakena Section.)

173 East Connector

Trails Illustrated Map 745: AA10 | P. 273

The parking area for the Gilbert Tract Loop (trail 174), at the N end of the East Connector, is an alternate place to begin the CL50. For trailhead information, see the East Connector description in the Cranberry Lake–Wanakena Section.

At the jct. of Burntbridge Pond–Bear Mt. Trail (trail 172) and East Connector (0.0 mi; 45.1 mi), the CL50 East Connector climbs, reaching a beaver pond dam (and crossing it) at 0.5 mi (45.6 mi). There is a well-marked branch at 0.6 mi (45.7 mi); CL50 proceeds to the R. The trail reaches a second branch at 0.7 mi (45.8 mi); the CL50 continues straight (R). The trail now drops to a second small beaver pond and a clearing. The trail turns L, following a washed-out section of the road and crossing a wet area on planks. It reaches the Gilbert Tract Loop parking area at 1 mi (46.1 mi).

NY 3 Connector

Trails Illustrated Map 745: AA9 | P. 272

This section of CL50 follows NY 3 SW. NY 3 can be a busy highway, however this is a state designated bike route and the shoulders are wide.

The Cranberry Lake Community Center, in Cranberry Lake, is an alternate place to begin the CL50.

From the East Connector (trail 200A) trailhead at the Gilbert Tract Loop (trail 174) parking area (0.0 mi; 46.1 mi), the CL50 turns L (W) on NY 3. The road enters the hamlet of Cranberry Lake, passing a sign on the R, at 0.1 mi (46.2 mi). In the right season, Thompson Bay of Cranberry Lake can be seen through the woods L. At 0.3 mi (46.4 mi) Lone Pine Rd. meets NY 3 from the S. This is the turnoff for Cranberry Lake Campground, an alternate start and route for the CL50. (See the alternate routes at the end of this section for a description of the route combining Burntbridge Pond–Bear Mt. Trail, the Cranberry Lake Campground, and Lone Pine Rd.) Silver Lake can be seen to the R behind the residences.

At 0.5 mi (46.6 mi), NY 3 passes First St. on the L and then continues on to the Cranberry Lake beach, with tables, a pavilion, grills, and a view S to the lake. On the R is the Cranberry Lake Community Center, another alternate starting point for the CL50. There are a few businesses in Cranberry Lake, including a diner and ice cream stand, a marina, a pub, and a general store. Most of these are seasonal and may be closed during the late fall, winter, and early spring.

The road passes the general store at 1 mi (47.1 mi) and then starts to climb. At 1.3 mi (47.4 mi) there is a "Cranberry Lake" sign on the L side of the road, marking the W entrance to the hamlet. The trail turns L here onto a grassy mowed area under power lines, offering an escape from the busy NY 3, to River Side Dr. Cranberry Lake Dam is passed at 1.5 mi (47.6 mi). Just past the dam is a panel with information about the dam and a park bench.

Continuing on River Side Dr., the trail turns L (S), then crosses the Park Bridge on the Oswegatchie River Walk at 1.6 mi (47.7 mi). It then follows the road and climbs the hill to reach Columbian Rd. at 1.7 mi (47.8 mi). The trail now crosses the Cranberry Lake Boat Launch site parking lot to the start of the West Connector (trail 181).

181 West Connector, with Balancing Rock Loop (trail 183) and Peavine Swamp Trail (trail 180)

Trails Illustrated Map 745: AA9 | P. 272

The Cranberry Lake Boat Launch site parking lot is an alternate place to begin the CL50. The parking lot is large, with space for approximately fifty-five cars, trucks, and boat trailers.

The trailhead (0.0 mi; 47.8 mi) is on the S side of the Cranberry Lake Boat Launch parking lot. The wide blue-marked trail starts with a moderate grade to the SW through mixed hardwoods before turning R (W) and following a ridge paralleling the parking lot. At 0.2 mi (48 mi) the trail turns L. It soon reaches an impressive high cliff with overhangs and caves on the L (E) side of the trail. The trail reaches a jct. with the Lost Pond Nature Trail (trail 182) at 0.4 mi (48.2 mi). The CL50 West Connector Trail turns L. The trail becomes rougher as it climbs, entering a recently logged section and following, leaving, and crossing skid trails.

This strange mix of hiking trail and skid trail continues until yellow paint blazes indicate state land at 1.3 mi (49.1 mi). The trees are more mature here. The trail reaches a steep downhill, then crosses a wide bridge at 1.6 mi (49.4 mi). It starts to climb, then turns W following the contours. The trail passes a large erratic boulder on the L before the jct. with the Balancing Rock Loop (Loop 1, trail 183) at 2.2 mi (50 mi).

The CL50 continues R (W) on the Balancing Rock Loop, reaching the Peavine Swamp Trail (trail 180) in approximately 1 mi (51 mi). At the jct. of the Balancing Rock Loop and Peavine Swamp Trail, the CL50 turns R, following the Peavine Swamp Trail to its trailhead and NY 3 in 0.3 mi (51.3 mi).

Alternate Routes

171 Burntbridge Pond Trail segment (from jct. with Burntbridge Pond–Bear Mt. Trail to NY 3) with NY 3 Connector (from Burntbridge Pond trailhead parking lot to East Connector parking lot) alternative

Trails Illustrated Map 745: AA10 | P. 273

From its intersection with the yellow-marked Burntbridge Pond–Bear Mt. Trail (trail 172), the Burntbridge Pond trail continues 1.5 mi N to NY 3. This route can be combined with a walk of 2.1 mi on NY 3 to the Gilbert Tract Loop (trail 174) parking area (and East Connector trailhead) to provide an alternate route for the CL50. Note that NY 3 can be a busy highway, however, it is a state designated bike route and the shoulders are wide.

From the trail register and the jct. with the yellow-marked Burntbridge Pond–Bear Mt. Trail (trail 172) (0.0 mi), the Burntbridge Pond trail continues straight (N) with gentle grades, crossing numerous bridges. At 1.3 mi the trail leaves the railroad grade and winds its way to NY 3 over a dual-track four-wheeler trail. It ends at the Burntbridge Pond trailhead parking lot at 1.5 mi, approximately 2 mi E of the hamlet of Cranberry Lake. The alternate CL50 proceeds to the L (SW) on NY 3.

From the parking lot, the road starts a gentle climb. At 1.8 mi the road enters the town of Clifton, as indicated by a sign. At 2.3 mi, the road passes through dark green gneissic rock; this is a metamorphic rock that had been under great heat and pressure deep within the Earth. This is the high point of the route; the road now starts a rolling descent into the hamlet of Cranberry Lake.

At 2.4 mi the road to Bear Mt. Club is on the L. An engraved stone marker reads, "Bear Mt. Club, King, Paul Larocque, 2004." At 3.4 mi a snowplow turnaround is on the L side of the road. At a round, broad turn at 3.6 mi, the road reaches the Gilbert Tract Loop parking area and the N end of the East Connector (trail 173), an alternate starting point for the CL50. See NY 3 Connector description above for continuation of the CL50 route.

172 Burntbridge Pond–Bear Mt. Trail and Cranberry Lake Campground, Lone Pine Rd., NY 3 alternative

Trails Illustrated Map 745: AA10-Z9 | P. 273

A segment of Burntbridge Pond–Bear Mt. Trail, when combined with 0.2 mi of Bear Mt. trail (trail 179) and approximately 1.5 mi on Cranberry Lake Campground and Lone Pine Rds., offers a variation on part of the CL50 for those wishing to start at the Cranberry Lake Campground. The campground also provides an alternate trailhead for the CL50. Note that the Burntbridge Pond–Bear Mt. Trail is described here from the Burntbridge Pond trail to the campground (E to W). This trail begins at the jct. of the yellow-marked Burntbridge Pond–Bear Mt. Trail (trail 172) and the East Connector (trail 173).

Note that NY 3 can be a busy highway, however, it is a state designated bike route and the shoulders are wide.

From its jct. with the East Connector (0.0 mi), Burntbridge Pond–Bear Mt. Trail leaves the logging road and reaches the top of a small hill at 0.4 mi. It then drops slightly into a marshy fern meadow just before reaching the base of a large cliff. The trail skirts the base of the mountain, with a marshy area to the L. The forest here is older and mostly beech. At 0.8 mi the trail passes a large gneissic erratic on the R. This area has some large mature yellow birches, maples, and hemlocks.

Under a large hemlock at 0.9 mi, the trail reaches the jct. with the Bear Mt. trail (trail 179) coming from the campground. The CL50 alternative continues R along the Bear Mt. trail, marked with red, and drops toward Cranberry Lake Campground. The trail here is rough. It reaches the trail register and parking lot at 1.1 mi. The hike continues to the R along the campground road, passing campsites with views of Cranberry Lake and the beach area, and reaches the gate at 1.6 mi.

The route now follows Lone Pine Rd. R, with views of the lake and camps to the L. The road reaches a high point at 1.9 mi then trends downward to cross Thompson Bay on a causeway. It climbs to meet NY 3 at 2.7 mi. A L here on NY 3 leads to the Peavine Swamp Trail trailhead in 3.5 mi, for a total of 6.2 mi.

A shorter alternative is to turn L and leave NY 3 at 3.7 mi, where a "Cranberry Lake" sign marks the W entrance to the hamlet on the L side of the road. The trail turns L here onto a grassy mowed area under power lines, offering an escape from the busy NY 3 to River Side Dr. Following this route, the trail passes Cranberry Lake Dam at 3.9 mi. Just past the dam is a park bench and a panel with information about the dam. Continuing on River Side Dr., the trail turns L (S), then crosses the Park Bridge on the Oswegatchie River Walk at 4 mi. It then follows the road and climbs the hill to Columbian Rd. at 4.1 mi. The trail now crosses the parking lot of the Cranberry Lake Boat Launch parking lot to the start of the West Connector (trail 181). 🖜

Beaver. Joanne Kennedy

Star Lake–Streeter Lake Section

The regional center of Star Lake together with outlying Streeter Lake forms the nucleus of the hiking trails in this section of the Adirondack Park. The trails travel in a generally S direction from the hamlet of Star Lake and then form a network running E and W. In many cases the trails connect with others, offering a series of circuits in addition to the basic round-trips.

These trails go mainly through the Aldrich Pond Wild Forest, and in a few instances penetrate deeply into the Forest Preserve, allowing the additional option of extended round-trips. Grades are mostly moderate and trails usually lead through second-growth hardwood forests with dense conifer swamps and beaver flows present more often than not in low-lying areas. As in the adjoining Cranberry Lake area, these beaver-flooded areas along the trail fluctuate widely in their presence, contingent on food supply, predation, and fur harvesting.

The destinations of these trails are often the myriad small jewel-like ponds that lie scattered in enchanted, remote hollows throughout the region: Round Lake, Long Lake, Scuttle Hole Pond, Streeter Lake, Crystal Lake, Buck Pond, Little Otter Pond, Cage Lake, and others. On the E these trails connect with the trail system emanating from the area covered in the Cranberry Lake–Wanakena Section. This gives ultimate access to the virgin timber of the remote sections of the Five Ponds Wilderness Area. There are no ascents of mountains with views, although trails do cross the wooded shoulders of a few moderate-sized hills.

Suggested hikes for this section are listed below.

MODERATE HIKE
Streeter Lake from Youngs Rd.: 7 mi (11.2 km) round-trip. A hike on a snowmobile trail ends at historic and mysterious Streeter Lake. See trail 204.

HARDER HIKE
Cage Lake: 16.8 mi (26.9 km) round-trip. Deep in the Five Ponds Wilderness Area, Cage Lake has a true wilderness feeling. See trail 205.

Trail Described		Total Miles (one way)	Page
204	Streeter Lake	3.5 (5.6 km)	294
205	Cage Lake	8.4 (13.4 km)	294
206	Round Lake	5.0 (8.0 km)	296
207	Aldrich–Streeter Lake Trail	4.7 (7.5 km)	297
208	Totten-Crossfield Trail	5.6 (9.0 km)	298

204 Streeter Lake

Trails Illustrated Map 745: X6

This DEC red-marked snowmobile trail connects the hamlet of Star Lake and Streeter Lake, with its unusual history.

▶Trailhead: Proceed S on Youngs Rd. from its intersection with NY 3 in the center of the hamlet of Star Lake. The trailhead is on the R at 1.4 mi from NY 3, just after a metal bridge across the Little River. This route begins at a gated jeep trail.◀

From the gate (0.0 mi), the trail proceeds through pole-sized black cherry to a wooden bridge across Tamarack Creek at 0.3 mi. Just before the crossing an old logging road comes in on the L and joins the snowmobile trail. This is a marked horse trail that leads back in 0.4 mi to a trailhead on Youngs Rd. approximately 0.2 mi S of the snowmobile trailhead.

The trail now goes through medium-sized spruce and fir that have seeded in on hayfields. These hayfields were once used to raise feed for the horses that were employed in connection with the logging industry. The trail goes R at a fork and shortly thereafter, at 0.7 mi, goes L at another fork. At 0.8 mi a small field of spirea is a holdover from the old hayfields; apparently the thick growth of the spirea plus the fact that the field is in what appears to be a low-lying frost pocket, has hindered the regrowth of forest in this one small section.

At 1 mi, a red-marked snowmobile trail veers in sharply from the R to join this trail. Snowmobile trail markers indicate the route from here to the Potato Patch (see below). At 1.1 mi, the trail passes a hunting camp on a private in-holding (L) and at 1.2 mi it enters a Scotch pine plantation. At 1.3 mi, the trail goes R at a jct. Shortly thereafter it passes a logging road on the R. A few of the metal posts for the underground telephone wires that once serviced a large private estate on Streeter Lake can still be seen standing here.

The trail now becomes moderately steep; the wooded top of Streeter Mt. can be seen clearly outlined ahead at 2.3 mi. The trail crosses the outlet of Streeter Lake on a bridge at 2.7 mi, and shortly thereafter climbs over the shoulder of Streeter Mt. At 2.9 mi, old yellow state boundary markers can be seen; the rest of the trail is within what was originally the Schuler Estate. The trail continues to the Potato Patch at 3.3 mi. Here, potato chip magnate Andrew Schuler experimented with different strains of potatoes. Directly W across the Potato Patch, the trail reaches Streeter Lake and its lean-to at 3.5 mi.

❄ Trail in winter: Suitable for skiing.

🐾 Distances: Youngs Rd. to outlet of Streeter Lake, 2.7 mi; to Amo Rd. Trail, 3.1 mi; to Potato Patch, 3.3 mi; to Streeter Lake, 3.5 mi (5.6 km).

205 Cage Lake

Trails Illustrated Map 745: X6

This trail, marked with both yellow and red markers, proceeds through remote forest, sometimes following the bed of a one-time logging railroad, to Buck Pond and on to Cage Lake, deep in the Five Ponds Wilderness Area.

▶Trailhead: Proceed S on Youngs Rd. from its intersection with NY 3 in the center of the hamlet of Star Lake. The trailhead is on the L at a small parking area 1.9 mi from NY 3.◀

The trail, marked with yellow disks at first, begins at the parking area (0.0 mi). It slowly begins an ascent as it undulates through a mature forest featuring splendid specimens of hemlock, yellow birch, and black cherry and interspersed with occasional large glacial erratics. The yellow paint on the trees along the trail indicates what was formerly the boundary between Forest Preserve and private land.

At 0.6 mi the trail goes L as it starts to follow a jeep trail marked with red disks; the yellow disks are no longer in evidence. At 1.1 mi an old, abandoned trail comes in on the L and, shortly thereafter, the route mounts the bed of the old logging railroad, to follow it almost the entire distance to Buck Pond.

The trail proceeds through a pole-sized hardwood forest, arriving at Little Otter Pond at 2.1 mi. Little Otter, hardwood-fringed and with a number of beaver lodges on its banks, is one of the typically shallow ponds of this region. The trail crosses the pond's outlet at 2.3 mi and a balsam-lined beaver vlei at 3.1 mi. The beaver have long gone from here and the vlei that succeeded the open water is in turn being replaced by the encroaching forest.

At 3.4 mi, the trail crosses the outlet of Little Otter Pond again and continues to a difficult crossing of beaver flooding at 4.9 mi. At this point it may be necessary to bushwhack to the R around the flow. At 5.3 mi, the old railroad bed turns R while the trail keeps to the L. A gate barring further ATV travel has been placed across the railroad bed here.

The trail now begins to rise again rather sharply, crossing a hill crowned with tall hemlocks at 6.1 mi. The trail then begins a slow, gradual descent until it reaches the shore of Buck Pond at 7.3 mi. Buck Pond, approximately the same size as Little Otter Pond, is rimmed with both hardwoods and conifers. There is an interesting glacial erratic just before the shore; this large boulder is composed of reddish granitic gneiss, the same composition as the underlying bedrock. Two small camps of a private inholding are located at the head of the lake.

The trail to Cage Lake makes a sharp R turn just before Buck Pond. Markers change back to yellow. The trail passes a jct. with the abandoned Cage Lake Springhole trail at 7.6 mi on the L. The trail now begins a slow trek across a ridge adorned with extremely large red spruce, hemlock, and yellow birch. The forest here could be an extension of the old-growth northern hardwood parcel W of the Oswegatchie River from near Griffin Rapids to the vicinity of Big Otter Pond.

The trail descends into an extensive wooded swamp, partially the result of beaver flooding along Hammer Creek. The trail and yellow disks may be obscure here in several places, depending on beaver activity and trail maintenance. Finally, at 8.2 mi the trail crosses the side of an esker with large conifers crowning its top. At 8.4 mi it crosses the outlet of Cage Lake as it cascades down from a beaver dam to a large marshy vlei beneath it. From the dam a view can be had down the length of the lake. A wooded peninsula (actually another esker) splits the lake into two sections. Loons and brook trout inhabit both. The Cage Lake Lean-to is located just beyond this point. Here the trail meets Wolf Pond–Cage Lake Trail (trail 189), which provides access to High Falls on the Oswegatchie and Wanakena.

❄ Trail in winter: Generally suitable for skiing until Buck Pond, then twisting and wetness make it less suitable. The portion past Buck Pond is very remote and skiers should be adequately prepared.

🚶 Distances: Youngs Rd. to jeep trail with red disks, 0.6 mi; to Little Otter Pond, 2.1 mi; to vlei, 3.1 mi; to gate, 5.3 mi; to Buck Pond, 7.3 mi; to Cage Lake outlet and lean-to, 8.4 mi (13.4 km).

206 Round Lake

Trails Illustrated Map 745: X3

This DEC red-marked snowmobile trail begins in the vicinity of the abandoned hamlets of Jayville and Kalurah and travels S toward the St. Lawrence–Lewis county line, then turns E to Round Lake. Kalurah and Jayville were formerly thriving hamlets borne of the lumbering and mining industries, respectively. When the timber and iron ore deposits depleted at the turn of the twentieth century, the population left the area. Today only rustic hunting camps are present where once the school bell rang.

▶Trailhead: Access is from NY 3 in the hamlet of Pitcairn via Jayville Rd. Pitcairn is approximately 2 mi E of the village of Harrisville. Jayville Rd. is on the E edge of Pitcairn; it goes S from NY 3 at a sharp angle, climbing steadily uphill and crossing railroad tracks three times before reaching its final crossing and jct. with Powell Rd., 4.4 mi from NY 3. This is the site of Kalurah.

Shortly after crossing the railroad tracks, the road forks. Jayville Rd. continues L to the abandoned mines of Jayville, now mostly on private land. Take the R fork—Powell Rd.—and proceed to the jct. with Dobbs Rd. at 4.5 mi from NY 3. Again take the R fork, crossing a metal bridge over Gulf Stream at 5 mi. At 5.8 mi from NY 3, a gate marks the start of the trail as it enters the Forest Preserve. There is a parking area on the W (R) side of the road with space for approximately six vehicles. ◀

From the gate (0.0 mi), the trail follows a logging railroad bed through maturing hardwoods with a number of large poplar. At 0.2 mi, a large open beaver vlei on the R is a good spot for wildlife viewing. At 1 mi, the trail comes to a fork. R is a dead-end snowmobile trail. The Round Lake route continues L to South Creek Lake at 1.6 mi. This lake is noted for its excellent bass fishing. The far shores are private.

The trail continues on a mostly level grade through pole-sized hardwoods until Scuttle Hole, R, at 2.3 mi. This is an extremely narrow, marshy lake that probably had its origin as a string of beaver ponds.

The trail leaves the old logging railroad bed behind and makes a turn. It proceeds to an old open spirea-studded glade at 2.8 mi. A sign in the middle of the glade points the way R, where the trail crosses several open beaver flows before reentering the forest at 3.4 mi. The trail ascends a steep ridge with large sugar maples and beech and follows it for the next mile until a rather sharp descent to the shore of Round Lake at 4.3 mi.

❋ Trail in winter: Suitable, especially for skiing, but must be shared with snowmobiles.

🐾 Distances: To South Creek Lake, 1.6 mi; to Scuttle Hole, 2.3 mi; to end of beaver flows, 3.4 mi; to Round Lake, 4.3 mi (6.9 km).

207 Aldrich–Streeter Lake Trail

Trails Illustrated Map 745: Y5

The trail follows the bed of an old logging railroad that is open to vehicular traffic because of an inholding at Streeter Lake—a small private cemetery—from May through November. For the remainder of the year, it can be used as either a hiking or ski trail that is also used by snowmobiles. It proceeds entirely through the Forest Preserve and links the rustic hamlet of Aldrich to Streeter Lake.

▶Trailhead: To reach Aldrich, take NY 3 to a blinking traffic signal 2 mi W of Star Lake. Go L at the light and proceed approximately 200 yd to a T intersection and take another L. Take this road uphill 0.2 mi until Coffin Mills Rd. comes in on the R. It is 3.2 mi, mostly on gravel, until a woods road comes in on the L in the hamlet of Aldrich. Park carefully at the side of the road.◀

From the road jct. (0.0 mi), the trail follows the woods road with both red and blue disks indicating its dual use as a snowmobile and horse route. The Little River valley floodplain is on the L as the trail goes on a mostly level grade past the Round Lake snowmobile trail R at 1.5 mi. Shortly thereafter, it crosses Mud Creek on a wooden bridge at 1.8 mi.

After Mud Creek, the trail begins to rise steadily as it crosses several creeks cascading in ravines. It crosses an open marsh at 4.4 mi, just before turning L between two stone pillars that marked the beginning of what was the Schuler estate before the state acquired the land in the 1970s. The trail descends to a steel gate just beyond Streeter Lake outlet at 4.7 mi.

One may return to Aldrich for a round-trip of 9.4 mi, or proceed around the gate and cross the Potato Patch to join the Streeter Lake trail (trail 204). If a car is parked at the Streeter Lake trailhead on Youngs Rd., this makes for a through trip of 8.5 mi.

❋ Trail in winter: Primary use is as a ski route.

🐾 Distances: Aldrich to Mud Creek, 1.8 mi; to Streeter Lake, 4.7 mi (7.5 km).

208 Totten-Crossfield Trail

This trail proceeds S from the outlet of Streeter Lake, passing a loop of the Middle Branch of the Oswegatchie River on its way to the St. Lawrence–Herkimer county line. Near this line lies a famous Totten-Crossfield boundary marker. This identified a corner of the Totten-Crossfield Purchase of the Revolutionary War era, and, when located by the legendary surveyor Verplanck Colvin in 1878, fixed the boundaries of most of the land in northern New York.

Grades are generally flat and the walking easy until the final segment. The jeep road this trail follows is also for a period the boundary between the Five Ponds Wilderness Area and the Aldrich Pond Wild Forest.

▶Locator: This trail begins at the gated end of Aldrich–Streeter Lake Trail (trail 207). It can also be reached via the Streeter Lake trail (trail 204).◀

Following an old jeep road, the trail, marked with both red snowmobile disks and blue horse trail disks, goes around the metal barrier (0.0 mi) and proceeds under a canopy of tall hardwoods to the old Potato Patch (see Streeter Lake, trail 204) at 0.1 mi. The trail leaves the jeep road, turns sharply R, and follows an old rutted track across this open area. (The old jeep road follows the edge of the Potato Patch and could be followed as a longer alternative to walking the rutted path through the sandy field.) The old potato ridges, festooned with a thick carpet of moss, are still readily noticeable in this sandy clearing. With a little luck a woodchuck might be seen. They are the only wildlife likely to be seen for miles around in a solid panorama of unbroken forest.

At 0.3 mi, the trail crosses the old jeep road. The road R leads, after a R turn, to Streeter Lake. The trail continues straight ahead, joining the road at 0.4 mi at a clearing with the Streeter Lake Lean-to; the trail will follow this road for all but the last mile or so before the St. Lawrence–Herkimer county line.

Passing the Streeter Lake Lean-to on the R, the trail goes by a road R. The road leads shortly to the foundation of a boathouse and continues along the shore of Streeter Lake to the N, rejoining the road and trail to complete a loop. The trail then passes by the foundations of buildings that once stood on the private Schuler estate at 0.5 mi. The setting here is park-like, pastoral rather than wild, with large specimens of exotic Norway spruce common.

The trail now drops steeply to a four-way intersection just beyond the foundations. (The road R goes to the boathouse foundation; the L road goes back to the Potato Patch.) The trail heads straight, affording a view of Streeter Lake to the R at 0.6 mi, and comes to a jct. at 0.7 mi, where it turns L.

The R road leads to the privately owned Schuler family plot in 0.3 mi. It is well maintained with a gate and split rail fence. A monument on the wooded point reads:

THE ANDREW SCHULER MEMORIAL PARK
4000 ACRES
DEDICATED TO EVERYONE TO ENJOY FOREVER

THE SCHULER FAMILY ENJOYED THIS LAND FOR 27 YEARS. WE NOW
WISH THE PEOPLE OF NEW YORK STATE TO HAVE THIS SAME PRIVILEGE
AND PLEASURE. ACQUIRED BY THE SCHULER FAMILY APRIL 15, 1947
PURCHASED BY THE PEOPLE OF NEW YORK STATE APRIL 12, 1975

There are benches and a steep path to the lake. The Schuler mausoleum stands in the center of the well-manicured clearing. It is constructed of Adirondack granitic gneiss and has a copper roof. Andrew M. Schuler, his wife, Emma O. Schuler, and his father, Andrew S. Schuler, are interred there.

Continuing L at the jct., at 0.8 mi the main trail reaches an unmarked trail R that leads 0.1 mi to the shore of Crystal Lake. This small, circular conifer- and heath-lined lake was used for swimming by the Schulers. A dip in the water will show why: the minerals in the water give a feeling of buoyancy. The same minerals probably account for the clarity of the water and for the fact that the lake was reputed to be without fish long before the era of acid rain.

The trail continues through pole-size hemlocks and red spruce until another side trail enters L at 1.2 mi. (This trail dead-ends in 0.3 mi at the shore of Tamarack Creek, which can be followed for 0.2 mi downstream to a beautiful gneiss dam.) At 1.4 mi, the trail crosses the outlet of Pansy Pond. Like many small streams in this locale, this is often dammed by beaver, sometimes causing flooding of the trail. At these locations hikers can often cross on the beaver dams.

At 2.1 mi, the trail heads R while a trail L goes over Francis Hill and rejoins the main trail at 3.9 mi. The Francis Hill Trail can be used for variety on the return trip; though less scenic than the "river trail," it is less prone to flooding by beavers and it is 0.1 mi shorter than the main trail. It begins a gentle but steady climb, passes through a flat wet area, and reaches a high point after 1 mi, on the W shoulder of Francis Hill; it then drops steadily over slightly rolling terrain until it rejoins the "river trail."

The R trail is no longer maintained by the DEC, but hunters have continued to maintain it and though some blowdown is encountered the trail is easy to follow. At 2.6 mi, it turns E, reaching a wide loop on the Middle Branch of the Oswegatchie River on the R. This spot makes a pleasant informal campsite. The trail continues E as it passes through a classic spruce-fir swamp with occasional glimpses of the river and its balsam-lined corridor on the R.

At 3.2 mi, the trail has been flooded; crossing can be made on the beaver dams. The trail then turns S and at 3.9 bears R at the jct. with the Francis Hill Trail (see above). At 4.1 mi, it crosses Bassett Creek on a wooden bridge. The beaver here often try to dam the area under the bridge, flooding the trail. Local DEC personnel are often quick to respond, and the bridge is usually passable.

At 4.2 mi, the jeep road disappears at an old, roughly circular log landing.

Joanne Kennedy

Timber was previously taken to this spot to be hauled out via the jeep road. Three old logging roads radiate from here; follow the markers straight ahead. The route passes through a mostly hardwood forest that was subject to heavy logging before state acquisition in the 1970s.

At 5 mi, the trail enters a spruce swamp. It continues through it for a short distance, soon passing the remnants of old logging and hunting camps, including a stone fireplace. The granite Totten-Crossfield marker, set in place in 1903 over the spot where Verplanck Colvin placed his monument in 1878, now lies hidden in the forest close to 200 yd from the trail. It can be reached by taking a compass reading of 135° from the remnants of the last demolished outbuilding. The going is rough, as conifer growth is thick, so caution must be exercised in any attempts to locate the marker and monument.

At 5.2 mi, the trail crosses into Herkimer County and Watsons East Triangle Wild Forest. The forest here was not logged as heavily before state acquisition, and the trail now passes large beech and maple. At 5.6 mi, the trail ends as it meets the Middle Branch of the Oswegatchie River for a second time. Balsam and spruce line the river here. Across its waters lies a maze of interconnecting logging roads that eventually lead to the end of Forest Preserve lands in Lewis County.

❄ Trail in winter: Makes an excellent round-trip ski jaunt, but the remoteness of the setting and the distance (approximately 20 mi, depending upon which access trail is used) demand adequate preparation.

🐾 Distances: Streeter Lake to spur to Crystal Lake, 0.8 mi; to Pansy Pond outlet, 1.4 mi; to Francis Hill Trail jct., 2.1 mi; to Middle Branch of Oswegatchie River, 2.6 mi; to log landing, 4.2 mi; to county line, 5.2 mi; to Middle Branch of Oswegatchie, 5.6 mi (9 km). 🐾

Watsons East Triangle Wild Forest Section

State purchase in 1986 of the 16,288-acre Watsons East Triangle Tract consolidated the Pepperbox Wilderness Area on the S with the Aldrich Pond Wild Forest on the N and was a pivotal acquisition of a key inholding in the projected Bob Marshall–Oswegatchie Great Forest. Hunting club leases expired in September 1991, and the remaining hunting camps were destroyed or removed at that time.

The main logging road in the area extends 10.8 mi as a gravel, twisting thoroughfare that ends where a DEC barrier gate bars further vehicular progress. This road was improved in 2003. The road inside the gate can be walked another 4.3 mi to the posted signs of a private inholding.

This main haul road, unplowed in winter but usually with a firm snowmobile base, provides a lengthy cross-country ski trek. At other times of year, it is ideally suited to a bicycle tour. Traffic is scarce, generally only a few vehicles per day. Ancillary logging roads that are barred to vehicular traffic lead to a number of the area's abundant ponds.

A suggested hike in this section is listed below.

MODERATE HIKE
Jakes Pond: 8.6 mi (13.8 km) round-trip. This remote hike features a crossing of the West Branch of the Oswegatchie River and an isolated, attractive glacial pond. See trail 209.

Trail Described		Total Miles (one way)	Page
209	Jakes Pond	4.3 (6.9 km)	301
210	Watsons East Main Haul Rd.	10.8 (17.3 km)	302
211	Wolf Pond	0.6 (1.0 km)	303
212	Buck Pond	0.3 (0.5 km)	304
213	Hog Pond–Tied Lake Trail	1.2 (1.9 km)	304
214	Upper South Pond	1.8 (2.9 km)	304

209 Jakes Pond

Trails Illustrated Map 745: U4

This outlying snowmobile trail starts in a remote area of eastern Lewis County and provides the best access to Watsons East Triangle Wild Forest. The trail proceeds in a SE direction, following mostly moderate grades to the Forest Preserve parcel. Beaver flooding can impede the way in a few areas, but this is more than offset by the views of the little-known West Branch of the Oswegatchie River afforded along the way.

▶Trailhead: The trail starts in an area of hunting camps known as Bergrens. Access to Bergrens is from NY 812 in the hamlet of Indian River, 6 mi N of the village of Croghan. Coming from the S, turn R off NY 812 onto Erie Canal Rd. Proceed E 4 mi to the hamlet of Belfort, which appears just after a L turn onto Old State Rd. Past Belfort, this is called Long Pond Rd. Proceed 3.2 mi from Belfort to a fork. Go L and continue about 8 mi to a jeep trail R, 0.7 mi past the last bridge crossing over the West Branch of the Oswegatchie River. A parking lot 0.1 mi down the jeep trail is no longer accessible; instead, proceed about 200 ft ahead and park off the road just before a gate that marks the start of the Watsons East main haul road, then return on foot to the parking lot. The trail register lies a little beyond the parking lot on the S side of the road.◀

From the register (0.0 mi), this red-marked trail follows an easement over private land and climbs a large outcrop of pink granitic gneiss to the head of a waterfall at 0.2 mi. Mostly pole-sized aspen and cherry line this initial stretch of the trail, which gives excellent views of the West Branch of the Oswegatchie River on the L.

At 1 mi, the trail crosses the river on a long wooden bridge. Extensive tamarack- and spruce-lined wetlands fringe the river on both sides. Pink-blooming wild azalea can be seen here. At 1.2 mi, the trail crosses a flooded area on a beaver dam then ascends an esker. Red spruce and balsam fir become more prevalent. At 1.6 mi, the trail enters the Forest Preserve and at 1.8 mi proceeds over exposed bedrock, passing through cutover hardwoods with patches of poverty grass still remaining under them.

At a jct. at 2 mi the trail goes R. At 2.2 mi, the way is often impeded by beaver flooding. At 2.6 mi, the trail negotiates a handsome stand of tamarack. Shortly thereafter hardwoods predominate again. At 3.4 mi, passage may again be impeded by beaver flooding. The trail then ascends another esker. At 4.1 mi Jakes Pond, entirely rimmed by eskers, is visible below. Its banks are lined with mature hardwoods and occasional conifers.

The trail proceeds around Jakes Pond and ends at 4.3 mi at the end of Forest Preserve land. A short distance ahead, the trail is barred by a gate indicating private land.

❋Trail in winter: Generally not advisable for skiing owing to wetlands and bridge crossings. Can be undertaken with caution.

🐾 Distances: Bergrens to Oswegatchie bridge, 1 mi; to jct., 2 mi; to Jakes Pond, 4.1 mi; to end of Forest Preserve land, 4.3 mi (6.9 km).

210 Watsons East Main Haul Rd.

Trails Illustrated Map 745: V4

This is the main trail access for the area and a good route for a round-trip ski or bicycle tour. Other trails in the area branch off it.

▶Trailhead: The trail starts in an area of hunting camps known as Bergrens; for directions, see Jakes Pond, trail 209. The gate marks the start of the Watsons East Main Haul Rd.◀

From the gate (0.0 mi), the haul road almost immediately begins a slow ascent of a rather steep hill. The road is quite rocky and winding. At 0.8 mi the road reaches the boundary of conservation easement lands; until this point the road is a public right-of-way through private lands.

Still rising, the road reaches the boundary of Forest Preserve lands at 1.6 mi. The land was lumbered fairly intensively before being acquired by New York State, and as a result a second-growth forest of red maple and some white ash is common. These species have fall foliage coloring of blazing red contrasted with amber-purple, which usually appears early in September. This is an added incentive to a trip at this time.

At 3.5 mi, a snowmobile trail goes N (L). A road fork L at 4.7 mi leads to Wolf Pond (trail 211). Beyond this jct., the road begins to ascend another steep hill slowly. At 5.8 mi it reaches the top of the hill and starts a slow descent. The road now becomes generally undulating and winding with several rough areas.

The trail crosses the outlet of Massawepie Pond at 6.4 mi; a grassy path just before this goes to the pond in 100 yd. This marshy pond is a good place to see ducks. The road starts to ascend again and, at 9.8 mi, arrives at a locale L known as High Landing. Below this point, at the bottom of a steep cliff, the Middle Branch of the Oswegatchie River can be seen for the first time.

At 10.5 mi, a short spur R leads to Buck Pond (trail 212). At 10.6 mi, the road leading to Hog Pond and Tied Lake (trail 213) forks R, and at 10.8 mi, the route ends at a gate. The trail to Upper South Pond (trail 214) continues beyond the gate.

❋Trail in winter: Primary use, aside from access, is as a long round-trip cross-country ski (possibly combined with backpacking) or as a bicycle path. The way is wide and winding with several steep hills. Snowmobile traffic, except on weekends, is generally light.

🐾 Distances: To Forest Preserve, 1.6 mi; to Wolf Pond trail (trail 211), 4.7 mi; to Massawepie Pond outlet, 6.4 mi; to High Landing, 9.8 mi; to gate, 10.8 mi (17.3 km).

211 Wolf Pond

Trails Illustrated Map 745: W5

▶Locator: This trail begins at 4.7 mi on Watsons East Main Haul Rd. (trail 210).◀

From the main haul road (0.0 mi), a logging road L leads to the pond in 0.2 mi. The pond is rather long and narrow with a mixed forest on its shore, including conifers that are dead as a result of beaver flooding. Several knolls on the shore make good camping sites, especially where one hunting camp stood. The road continues to the outlet of Wolf Pond at 0.6 mi.

❋Trail in winter: Suitable as a side excursion off the main haul road.

🏃 Distances: Main haul road to Wolf Pond, 0.2 mi; to Wolf Pond outlet, 0.6 mi (1 km).

212 Buck Pond

Trails Illustrated Map 745: V5

▶Locator: This trail begins at 10.5 mi on Watsons East Main Haul Rd. (trail 210).◀

From the main haul road (0.0 mi), a side road leads in 0.3 mi to Buck Pond, considered the source of the West Branch of the Oswegatchie. A very attractive private camp stood on the pond's shore until 1991.

❋Trail in winter: Suitable as a side excursion off the main haul road.

🏃 Distance: Main haul road to Buck Pond, 0.3 mi (0.5 km).

213 Hog Pond–Tied Lake Trail

Trails Illustrated Map 745: U5

▶Locator: This short trail to two of the area's many modest-sized ponds begins at 10.6 mi on Watsons East Main Haul Rd. (trail 210).◀

Leaving the main haul road (0.0 mi), the trail, following an old jeep road, starts a slow rise to top an esker at 0.5 mi. Linear-shaped Hog Pond is below R. The somewhat marshy shores of the pond are surrounded by a typical mixed Adirondack forest of conifers and hardwoods.

The trail continues to Tied Lake, L at 1 mi. Tied Lake is more circular in shape, with waters of a dark brown hue from tannic acids. Until 1991, it was the site of one of the area's many hunting camps. Its outlet, Alder Brook, flows generally SW to the Beaver River. At 1.2 mi, a gate bars further access. The road continues to a private inholding.

❋Trail in winter: Admirably suited to a side trip off the main haul road, with generally moderate grades.

🏃 Distances: Main haul road to Hog Pond, 0.5 mi; to Tied Lake, 1 mi; to gate, 1.2 mi (1.9 km).

214 Upper South Pond

Trails Illustrated Map 745: V6

This path dates back over one hundred years, when it was built as the primary logging road in the region.

►Locator: The beginning of this unmarked trail is at the gate at mi 10.8 of Watsons East Main Haul Rd. (trail 210).◄

The trail follows the logging road beyond the gate (0.0 mi). At 0.6 mi, the trail turns L to take an ancillary logging road to a crossing of the Middle Branch of the Oswegatchie River at 1 mi. The bridge here was reconstructed to handle the weight of vehicles heading to private inholdings.

At 1.4 mi at a fork, the Upper South Pond trail goes L, then slowly descends to reach the shores of Upper South Pond at 1.8 mi. An occasional large hemlock and an abundance of marshy shoreline prevail at this point. Farther upstream on the inlet of Upper South Pond lie Middle South and Lower South Ponds, both reached only by bushwhacking.

Past the turnoff for the Upper South Pond trail, the main haul road leads in 0.2 mi to a parcel of original Forest Preserve that has remained essentially old growth. The tract, consisting of majestic yellow birch and red spruce, was severely affected by blowdowns in the storm of 1950.

❊Trail in winter: Generally suitable for cross-country skiing if the bridge over the Middle Branch of the Oswegatchie River is passable.

❧ Distances: Main haul road to L fork, 0.6 mi; to river, 1 mi; to Upper South Pond, 1.8 mi (2.9 km). ➤

View from Rocky Mountain. Stephanie Graudons

Western-Central Overlap Section

 Several of the trails located on the eastern edge of the area covered in this guidebook are close to or cross into the area covered in *Adirondack Mountain Club Central Trails*. These trails are described in this section as well as in *Central Trails*. The numbers for these trails correspond to the numbering used in *Central Trails*. On the south side of *Trails Illustrated Map 745: Old Forge/Oswegatchie*, where these trails are located, *Central* trail numbers are in brown to distinguish them from trails in *Western Trails*.

72	Constable Pond–West Mt. Trail	8.1	(13.0 km)	307
73	Rocky Mt.	0.5	(0.8 km)	309
74	Fourth Lake–Black Bear Mt. Trail	2.3	(3.7 km)	310
76	Black Bear Mt. Ski Trail	3.0	(4.8 km)	312
77	Old Black Bear Mt. Trail	1.4	(2.2 km)	312
85	East Shore Path and Snowmobile Trail	2.7	(4.3 km)	313
95	Indian River Trail	6.3	(10.1 km)	315
95A	Horn Lake	3.0	(4.8 km)	317

72 Constable Pond–West Mt. Trail (*Central Trails* number)

Trails Illustrated Map 745: R9 | Trails Illustrated Map 744: R10

This long wilderness trail extends from Higby Rd. just S of Big Moose Lake NE past Constable Pond, Pigeon Lake, and Otter Pond to the summit of West Mt., W of the northern part of Raquette Lake. There it meets the end of Raquette Lake–West Mt. Trail (*Central Trails* trail 71). The eastern portion of the trail is found on *Trails Illustrated Map 744*. The part of the trail beyond Constable Pond is remote. It has wet areas, blowdowns, and wet stream crossings, passes several magnificent specimens of white pine between Constable Pond and the end of Pigeon Lake, and makes an 800 ft ascent of West Mt., the last 600 ft of which are steep or moderately steep. Once a fire tower peak, today's view from the summit is mostly over Raquette Lake.

Branching SE off the trail are Hermitage Trail, Mays Pond Trail, and Queer Lake Trail (*Western Trails* trails 33, 34, and 35), permitting various circuit and through hikes. A round-trip hike of the network involves backpacking, but the lack of lean-tos or informal campsites along the way is a limiting factor. Because this trail is in a designated Wilderness Area (Pigeon Lake), bicycles are not allowed.

▶Trailhead: From NY 28 in Eagle Bay, drive 3.7 mi on Big Moose Rd. Turn R on Higby Rd. for 1.3 mi to Judson Rd. (R), and park along the road (without blocking Judson Rd.). If necessary, park along the boat landing road on the R, a little farther down Higby Rd. The trail starts on Judson Rd., a private unpaved road with a barrier (on the E). There are state symbols on a sign, but it may not be evident that that is the trail, and there are no markers along Judson Rd. The rest of the trail is marked with DEC blue markers, with additional red markers near West Mt. ◀

From Higby Rd. (0.0 mi), the route follows Judson Rd. for the first 0.2 mi, then turns R just before the road turns L to cross Constable Brook. After about 20 yd there is a vehicle barrier, a large map sign, and a trail register. The blue trail follows an old road along the S side of broad, rocky Constable Brook.

At 0.5 mi the red-marked Hermitage Trail (*Western Trails* trail 33) goes R (SSE) toward Queer Lake. Some 25 yd beyond this jct. the path turns L, crosses Constable Brook on a bridge, and goes E, now on a footpath, on the N side of the brook, reentering private land.

The trail meets another old road at 0.9 mi and follows it R. In 100 yd, the trail recrosses Constable Brook on a logging bridge and within 20 yd turns L on the other side, leaving the old road. This footpath soon enters the state Forest Preserve and Pigeon Lake Wilderness Area. Another jct. on the R at 1.3 mi is for the yellow-marked Mays Pond Trail (*Western Trails* trail 34), which goes to that pond and on to the Queer Lake area.

The trail parallels Constable Brook and its open wetland L. At 2.2 mi the path nears Constable Pond, visible through tall spruce and hemlock, and goes parallel to its S shore. Just before 2.6 mi a spur path goes L a few yards to the edge of the pond. Fifty-five yd beyond, the yellow-marked Queer Lake Trail (*Western Trails* trail 35) goes R (SE) 0.6 mi to Chub Lake and the Queer Lake region. Seventy yd beyond the jct., with a brook on the L, an informal campsite is on the R, the only one to be found along this trail.

Some streams and wet spots alternate with sections of nice woodland path. Pigeon Lake's outlet stream crosses the trail at 3.9 mi. The trail then turns R, going through messy undergrowth and across a bog. The water of Pigeon Lake becomes visible through the trees on the R by a sign at 4.9 mi. In less than 100 yd the trail comes closer to the lake at its narrow N section and another sign.

This lake is about the size of Constable Pond, 0.7 mi long, with a boggy shoreline fringed by white pine and spruce. Some red markers start to appear near the lake. Both blue and red markers are found on the rest of the trail.

At 5.4 mi, about opposite the end of the lake, the trail passes a magnificent white pine on the L as Pigeon Lake passes from the scene. At 5.6 and 5.8 mi, in a spruce forest, there are two crossings of the outlet of Otter Pond. For the rest of the way the trail is on higher, drier ground in a forest of hardwoods and scattered spruce and fir.

After paralleling Otter Pond's outlet for a considerable distance, the route crosses it a third time and then a small pond appears on the R just below Otter Pond. Otter Pond may be detected through the trees R after the trail passes the small pond, at 6.7 mi.

At 7.6 mi, having already gradually ascended 1280 ft, the trail begins the final, steeper 620 ft ascent of West Mt. At 8 mi the trail levels near the summit, crosses a saddle between the N peak and summit, and then turns R (S) to climb slightly before reaching a jct. with Raquette Lake–West Mt. Trail (*Central Trails* trail 71) at 8.1 mi. Turn R on that trail and reach the open summit of West Mt. in 50 yd. A fair section of Raquette Lake can be seen, but trees fringing the top limit views in other directions.

One may continue the trip down Raquette Lake–West Mt. Trail to Brown's Tract Rd., but the two trailheads are far apart and there are no trails to complete a loop. Thus two cars are required.

❄Trail in winter: Suitable for snowshoeing. West Mt. would require excellent skiing ability. Only groups with good winter experience should attempt the full distance on unbroken trail.

Distances: Higby Rd. to Hermitage Trail (*Western Trails* trail 33), 0.5 mi; to Mays Pond Trail (*Western Trails* trail 34), 1.3 mi; to Constable Pond and Queer Lake Trail (*Western Trails* trail 35), 2.6 mi; to Pigeon Lake outlet crossing, 3.9 mi; to Pigeon Lake, 4.9 mi; to Otter Pond, 6.7 mi; to summit of West Mt., 8.1 mi (13 km). Continuation to Brown's Tract Rd., via *Central Trails* trail 71, 13 mi (20.8 km). West Mt. ascent (from Higby Rd.), 1073 ft (327 m). Summit elevation, 2902 ft (885 m).

73 Rocky Mt. (*Central Trails* number)

Trails Illustrated Map 745: Q10

This short, popular trail ascends 445 ft from NY 28 to the ledges atop Rocky Mt. near the head of Fourth Lake, offering a splendid view of the lake. It is a round-trip hike of 1 mi.

▶Trailhead: From the jct. of NY 28 and Big Moose Rd. in Eagle Bay, drive 1.2 mi E on NY 28. Turn L onto the old road, now a parking area off the highway. From the opposite direction drive 0.9 mi toward Eagle Bay on NY 28 from the public parking area in the center of Inlet. Turn R into the trailhead parking area.◀

Near the center of the parking area, the yellow-marked trail (markers are sparse) starts (0.0 mi) in a NNE direction, then soon turns L. It is wide, eroded from much use, and steep in several places.

Ascending through a hardwood forest, the trail turns NW and finally W along bedrock to the summit (elevation 2225 ft) at 0.5 mi. In another 60 yd along the open cliff top with a SW drop-off, there is a wide, open view over most of Fourth Lake lying 500 ft below. To the L on the wide E end of this large lake, one can see the village of Inlet.

❄Trail in winter: Suitable only for snowshoes. The route is steep. Care must be taken at the cliffs, where the rock can be windswept and icy.

🐾 Distances: Trailhead to summit, 0.5 mi (0.8 km). Ascent, 445 ft (136 m). Summit elevation, 2225 ft (678 m).

Eagle Bay.   Laurie Grover Humbolt

74 Fourth Lake–Black Bear Mt. Trail

(*Central Trails* number)

Trails Illustrated Map 744 and 745: Q10

Scenic Black Bear Mt., at 2448 ft elevation, stands 1.7 mi E of Fourth Lake and over 1 mi N of the W part of Seventh Lake. This mountain affords excellent views, especially from the long expanse of open rock at the SE side of the crest. The mountain may be ascended from Fourth Lake on the W or from Uncas Rd. on the N (*Central Trails* trail 75). The more traditional and popular route is from Fourth Lake, although the top part is steeper than the Uncas Rd. approach. The trails in this area lend themselves to round-trip, circuit, and through hikes. Parts of the mountain hold beautiful stands of larger trees, with open woods beneath.

The Fourth Lake–Black Bear Mt. Trail route has yellow ski trail markers and occasional yellow hiking trail markers. At the base of Black Bear Mt., the trail divides into two routes: the skiable yellow route L and the steep but shorter blue route R. In winter, the last part of the yellow trail to the summit (the Old Black Bear Mt. Trail, *Central Trails* trail 77) should be undertaken by advanced skiers only. In springtime and in wet weather, the blue route can be difficult, and hikers' boots can cause a lot of erosion damage. Both routes are described below.

▶Trailhead: From the jct. of NY 28 and Big Moose Rd. in Eagle Bay, drive 1.2

mi E on NY 28 and turn L into an extensive parking area (part of the old highway) off the main highway. From the opposite direction, drive 0.9 mi toward Eagle Bay on NY 28 from the public parking area in the center of Inlet and turn R into the trailhead parking area. ◀

From the end of the pavement at the SE end of the parking area (toward Inlet) (0.0 mi), walk 50 yd to the trail sign. The trail is marked with DEC yellow markers, with blue markers on an alternate route.

Turn L onto the beginning of a woods road, and pass a barrier across it in another 30 yd. The yellow-marked route proceeds E on the woods road in a pleasant hardwood forest with a stream on the L. It ascends a rather wet grassy section.

At 0.7 mi, in a clearing, the route forks. Uphill R, first with yellow markers and later with blue, is the Old Black Bear Mt. Trail (*Central Trails* trail 77). Continuing on the level straight across the clearing, the yellow trail follows a grassy old woods road through a partly wet area for 0.3 mi. In wet season, a pleasant 10 ft cascade can be heard on the L, just below the trail.

Beyond 1.2 mi, the trail becomes a narrow footpath with tall hardwoods and spruce trees along the way. The route passes on the N side of Black Bear Mt., and at 2.3 mi it ends at Uncas Rd.–Black Bear Mt. Trail (*Central Trails* trail 75), from Uncas Rd. This jct. does not have a sign and could be missed easily. Users should take a good look at the trail if they plan to return this way. Follow Uncas Rd.–Black Bear Mt. Trail R the rest of the way to the top for a total distance of 3.1 mi.

The most direct route from the summit back to the starting point is to follow the mostly blue-blazed trail W over the summit, and to the jct. with Old Black Bear Mt. Trail (*Central Trails* trail 77),turning R and following Old Black Bear Mt. Trail back to the jct. with Fourth Lake–Black Bear Trail, making a 5.2 mi roundtrip. Retracing your steps on the return trip will avoid the steep and slippery descent on Old Black Bear Mt. Trail, for a round-trip of 6.2 mi.

The cross-country skier, whether ascending Black Bear Mt. or not, may return to NY 28 either over the same route, or by Black Bear Mt. Ski Trail (*Central Trails* trail 76). To reach this latter trail, not open in hiking season, turn L down Uncas Rd.–Black Bear Mt. Trail (*Central Trails* trail 75) for 0.3 mi NE. The yellow-marked Black Bear Mt. Ski Trail (*Central Trails*, trail 76) goes R (S) then W for about 3 mi to reach NY 28 on the N edge of Inlet, just N of the telephone building (about 0.6 mi from the Fourth Lake–Black Bear Mt. trailhead).

❋ Trail in winter: Suitable for snowshoes. Also skiable, but those who continue on Uncas Rd.–Black Bear Mt. Trail (*Central Trails* trail 75) to the top would need to be expert skiers owing to steeper slopes.

🐾 Distances: NY 28 to jct. with Old Black Bear Mt. Trail (*Central Trails* trail 77), 0.7 mi; to jct. with Uncas Rd.–Black Bear Mt. Trail (*Central Trails* trail 75), 2.3 mi (3.7 km). To summit via trail 75, 3.1 mi (5 km). Ascent, 728 ft (222 m). Summit elevation, 2448 ft (746 m).

76 Black Bear Mt. Ski Trail (*Central Trails* number)

Trails Illustrated Map 744: Q10 | Trails Illustrated Map 745: P10

This route is open only in winter, owing to wet trail conditions.

▶Trailhead: The trailhead is on NY 28 on the N side of Inlet, just N of a telephone building near Black Bear Trading Post, a quilt shop, and across the street from Stiefvaters Motel. Look carefully in the trees about 20 ft up the road from the building for the trailhead. Parking depends on snow conditions. For a loop trip, one may return to NY 28 via Fourth Lake–Black Bear Mt. Trail (*Central Trails* trail 74) without having to go over the summit of Black Bear Mt. ◀

Passing through the trees at the road's edge (0.0 mi), this yellow-marked trail has a nondescript start. It follows nearly level terrain through an area that is very wet in summer.

At 0.2 mi, the route meets a woods road and turns L onto the road. In another 500 ft, the route curves R and continues on easy ground until crossing Cedar Creek at 1 mi. The climbing leads to a jct. with the abandoned and impassable Seventh Lake–Black Bear Mt. trail at 2.3 mi, with the ski trail terminating at another jct., this one with Uncas Rd.–Black Bear Mt. Trail (*Central Trails* trail 75), at 3 mi.

To continue to the summit of Black Bear Mt., turn L on Uncas Rd.–Black Bear Mt. Trail (*Central Trails* trail 75) and ascend more steeply. This route to the summit, totaling 3.7 mi, is suitable for expert skiers only.

To continue on a loop of Black Bear Mt., turn L and follow Uncas Rd.–Black Bear Mt. Trail (*Central Trails* trail 75) up (SW) for 0.3 mi and turn R onto Fourth Lake–Black Bear Mt. Trail (*Central Trails* trail 74). This jct. is not well marked. Keep a careful watch for the yellow ski trail markers. It is an additional 2.3 mi of easy skiing down to the highway.

❋Trail in winter: For cross-country skiers only. It is a generally easy trail, except for the summit of Black Bear Mt; that part is for experts only.

⚕ Distances: Telephone building to Cedar Creek, 1 mi; to Uncas Rd.–Black Bear Mt. Trail (*Central Trails* trail 75), 3 mi (4.8 km). To summit, 3.7 mi (5.9 km). Loop to NY 28 via Fourth Lake–Black Bear Mt. Trail (*Central Trails* trail 74), 5.3 mi (8.5 km). Ascent to highest point on ski loop, 335 ft (102 m).

77 Old Black Bear Mt. Trail (*Central Trails* number)

Trails Illustrated Map 744 and 745: Q10

This older, steeper section of trail, combined with the first part of Fourth Lake–Black Bear Mt. Trail (*Central Trails* trail 74), is the shortest route up Black Bear Mt.

▶Locator: Interior trail starting at 0.7 mi from the NY 28 trailhead on Fourth Lake–Black Bear Mt. Trail (*Central Trails* trail 74). ◀

From the jct. with Fourth Lake–Black Bear Mt. Trail (0.0 mi), Old Black Mt. Trail

Black Bear Mountain. Stephanie Graudons

heads R, uphill, following yellow and then blue markers. The trail climbs E on an old logging road to a nearly level clearing at 0.2 mi. Beyond the clearing, the old road curves L and continues on level ground as an open, grassy, but often wet route to about 0.4 mi.

After a gradual ascent on an eroding, rocky, and root-filled trail to the base of the final slope—where careful watch must be kept for markers—a steep ascent starts at 1 mi with the forest partly changing from hardwoods to conifers. The rest of the ascent is mostly on rock, with several pitches requiring some scrambling. Ledges provide fine S lookouts over Sixth and Seventh Lakes, and at 1.3 mi one has a beautiful view W and SW of Fourth Lake, the only view of that lake to be had from the trails on this mountain. This trail reaches the summit at 1.4 mi (2.1 mi from NY 28).

❄Trail in winter: Too steep to ski; also not suitable for snowshoeing owing to steep sections.

𝄞 Distances: Fourth Lake–Black Bear Mt. Trail (*Central Trails* trail 74) to clearing, 0.2 mi; to steep ascent, 1 mi; to summit, 1.4 mi (2.2 km). Ascent, 728 ft (222 m). Summit elevation, 2448 ft (746 m).

85 East Shore Path and Snowmobile Trail

(*Central Trails* number)

Trails Illustrated Map 744 and 745: O10

The East Shore Path gives access to the shores of Limekiln Lake below Fawn Lake Mt. Public access to this beautiful shoreline is via a snowmobile trail from

Moose River Rd. The other end of the trail connects with Limekiln Rd. on the N, but as a private path going right through the front yards of many cottages along the E bay. Hikers who have not obtained permission should not use that route.

▶Trailhead: From the W entrance to Moose River Plains Wild Forest (MRPWF), go E on Moose River Rd. for 3 mi. As the road takes a sharp turn to the L, an almost unnoticed snowmobile trail goes straight off the road, headed downhill. There is a slight clear spot for parking one or two cars 30 ft down the road at the bend. ◀

The trail passes across the lower rear of the small clearing (0.0 mi), headed downhill L. This is a very pleasant old road, somewhat overgrown, with a green soft-carpeted surface. It passes a wetland on the L, then goes over a slight hill before descending to cross Limekiln Lake inlet at 0.6 mi. From here on, the almost level trail follows the side of the inlet, which bubbles along rock ledges and under large boulders, until it reaches quiet meadowlands.

Continuing W, the width of the meadow grows, while the trail keeps on solid ground at its edge. The forest on the uphill side is of well-established open hardwoods. Soon after first glimpses of the lake appear, the wide old road ends abruptly at the lake's edge at 1.8 mi. There is heavy brush on either side of the trail, seeming to block all further travel. The view over Limekiln Lake is quite nice, with the prominent W peninsula dominating the scene.

About 30 ft back from the end of the snowmobile trail, there is an unmarked but maintained path on the R (N) side of the trail which continues on around the lake. This is the East Shore Path. Continuing on this path, there is an unofficial campsite above the lake shore at 1.9 mi. The path continues near the shore until it turns abruptly R at 2.1 mi and passes behind a slight hill at the tip of the E shore peninsula. This inland passage doesn't last long, and the lake shore is soon close on the L. Thereafter, the route stays close to the shore and its beautiful views.

State land ends at 2.7 mi, where a house is visible uphill, R. From this point on, the path crosses right through the tiny front yards of side-by-side private cottages and is clearly not a public trail. The hiker should return by the snowmobile trail.

❄Trail in winter: Easy snowshoeing; easy and pleasant skiing, although the beginner may find the first 0.5 mi a bit steep. Parking is no closer than the W entrance to MRPWF, 3 mi from the trailhead. Note that much of this route is a snowmobile trail.

🚶 Distances: Moose River Rd. to level ground at creek crossing, 0.6 mi; to end of snowmobile trail, 1.8 mi; to informal campsite, 1.9 mi; to end of state land, 2.7 mi (4.3 km).

94 Indian River Trail

The trail cited in *Western Trails* as trail 72 is included in the *Central Trails* description below (trail 95).

95 Indian River Trail (*Central Trails* number)

Trails Illustrated Map 745: N9 | Trails Illustrated Map 744: M10

Indian River Rd. formerly continued past Indian Lake as a private road extending to Canachagala Brook near the Moose River (now on private land). The old road is now an access route into a remote section of the West Canada Lake Wilderness Area. After it crosses the Indian River, marked trails lead to Balsam, Stink, and Horn Lakes (see *Central Trails* trail 95A).

▶Trailhead: The trailhead is shown on *Trails Illustrated Map 744*. Start at the jct. of Moose River Rd. and Otter Brook Rd. in the Moose River Plains Wild Forest (8.3 mi from the W entrance and 12.9 mi from the E entrance). Drive S on Otter Brook Rd. for 3.3 mi to the crossing of Otter Brook. Turn R at the next jct. Continue past several ponds and trails and park at a barrier and trailhead next to Indian Lake, 5.2 mi from Otter Brook. ◀

Starting at the barrier at the Indian River trailhead (0.0 mi), the route goes SW through a gentle notch below Indian Lake Mt., passing beaver meadows first L and then R. At 1.9 mi, the road reaches the Indian River and turns R to follow along it. To the L at the turn, a clearing leads down to the banks of the river. This is a possible crossover spot for wilderness travel by experienced bushwhackers to the group of lakes near Mountain Lake; however, if the water is high, do not attempt the crossing as it's likely to be dangerous.

Continuing on around the tip of Indian Lake Mt., the route turns N across swampy low ground, and at 2.6 mi enters the first of several "hallways" along this route—a trail with conifers packed tightly along each side with visibility sharply limited. The trail climbs slightly along a shoulder of the mountain and descends again to the Indian River at 3.8 mi. An old bridge is long gone, and the river must be waded, if conditions permit. The hiker can choose water that is ankle deep over slippery rocks, or nearly waist-deep water with firmer footing under a cable upstream. It can be dangerously high after heavy rains. A rock for changing back into boots about 50 yd beyond the river has a benchmark showing an elevation of 1899 ft. From here on, the main route is generally W.

Horn Lake Trail (*Central Trails* trail 95A; see below) provides the first side trail at 4.4 mi. Continuing on the main trail past the Horn Lake turnoff, it is a short way to the Balsam Lake spur trail R (N) at 4.6 mi. This trail goes N on yellow markers to the shore of boggy, pond-size Balsam Lake (4.7 mi from the trailhead) with a round-trip distance from the main trail of less than a 0.3 mi.

Past the Balsam Lake turnoff, the main trail parallels the Balsam Lake outlet R, now a beaver pond nearly 0.3 mi long, and then crosses the end of another

Moose River. Chris Murray

beaver pond L, making travel wet. It reaches a clearing with a trail jct. at 5.9 mi. The trail proceeds 0.4 mi N on level ground to the SW end of pond-sized Stink Lake at 6.3 mi.

Straight ahead beyond the jct. to Stink Lake, the old road continues but eventually crosses into posted private land of the Adirondack League Club. Do not proceed beyond the jct.

❄Trail in winter: Extremely remote, accessible only by snowmobiles, which can legally go as far as the wilderness boundary at the trailhead. Otherwise, it is suitable for backcountry skiing and snowshoeing, taking into consideration the river crossing. Any group attempting this trip should be well prepared for winter wilderness conditions.

🏃 Distances: Indian Lake trailhead to Indian River crossing, 3.8 mi; to Balsam Lake via spur, 4.7 mi (7.5 km); to Stink Lake, 6.3 mi (10.1 km).

95A Horn Lake Trail

Trails Illustrated Map 745: M9

This trail is cited in *Central Trails* as trail 95.

▶Locator: This interior trail begins at 4.4 mi on Indian River Trail (*Central Trails* trail 95, above).◀

From Indian River Trail (0.0), turn L (S) onto an old road. The yellow-marked trail climbs continuously, but not too steeply, to a jct. at 1.9 mi. The Horn Lake Trail goes L while another road goes R. After turning L at the jct., the trail crosses a creek and climbs again to reach an informal campsite on Horn Lake at 3 mi (7.4 mi from the Indian River Trail trailhead).

There is a jct. in the old road not far from Horn Lake. When going up, the branch to the R is an old logging road which leads W along the lower edge of Ice Cave Mt. This would give experienced bushwhackers a path to continue on to North Lake in the North Lake Tract. Refer to North Branch Trail (*Western Trails* trail 87E). That route is among suggestions for the North Country Trail from North Dakota to Lake Champlain.

❄ Trail in winter: See Indian River Trail (*Central Trails* trail 95).

🏃 Distances: To first jct., 1.9 mi; to Horn Lake, 3 mi (4.8 km). 🐾

Glossary of Terms

Azimuth   A clockwise compass bearing swung from north

Bivouac   Camping in the open with improvised shelter or no
                      shelter

Bushwhacking   Off-trail hiking, often with compass and map essential
                      for direction

Col   A pass between high points of a ridgeline

Corduroy   Logs laid side by side across a trail to assist travel in wet areas

Fire ring   A rough circle of stones used as a site in which to
                      build small fires

Lean-to   A three-sided shelter with an overhanging roof and
                      one open side

Logging road   A road used to haul logs after lumbering; often found in
                      marshy areas that would be frozen in winter

Summit   The top of a mountain

Tote road   A woods road used year-round for hauling supplies;
                      found on dry ground slopes

Vlei   A low marshy area (pronounced "vly")

State Campgrounds
Western Trails Region

Campgrounds have been established by DEC at many attractive locations throughout the state. Listed below are public campgrounds that might be useful as bases of operations for hiking in the *Western Trails* region of the Adirondacks.

Information on state campgrounds and procedures for making reservations can be found online at www.dec.ny.gov/outdoor/camping.html and in a booklet titled *New York State Camping Guide*. The latter is available at DEC regional offices; by telephoning the DEC Bureau of Recreation at 518-457-2500; online; or by writing DEC at 625 Broadway, Albany, NY 12233-5253.

Campgrounds in the Region

Alger Island. *Boat access only* from Fourth Lake Day Use Area, 303 Petrie Rd., off South Shore Rd. N of Old Forge

Cranberry Lake. Lone Pine Rd, 1 mi S of NY 3

Eighth Lake, 1353 NY 28, 6 mi E of Inlet, 5 mi S of Raquette Lake

Fish Creek Pond/Rollins Pond. NY 30, 12 mi N of Tupper Lake

Forked Lake. NY 30, 3 mi S of Long Lake. Take Deerland Rd. 2.8 mi. to fork, turn R to end of road

Lake Eaton. NY 30, 2 mi N of Long Lake

Limekiln Lake. Off NY 28, 3 mi SE of Inlet on Limekiln Lake Rd.

Meacham Lake. NY 30, 19 mi N of Lake Clear Jct.

Moss Lake campsites. CR 1 (Big Moose Rd.), 2.2 mi W of Eagle Bay

Nicks Lake, 278 Bisby Road, 1.5 mi E of Old Forge post office

Stillwater Reservoir campsites. *Boat access only* from DEC station, 2600 Stillwater Rd., 28 mi E of Lowville, 18 NW of Eagle Bay

Campgrounds near the region

Brown Tract Pond. Uncas Road, off NY 28; 7 mi NE of Eagle Bay, 2 mi W of Raquette Lake village. E of region

Buck Pond. Between NY 30 and NY 3, on Rainbow Lake near Onchiota. E of region

Golden Beach, NY 28, about 4 mi E of Raquette Lake village. E of region

Lake Durant. NY 28, 3 mi E of Blue Mt. Lake. E of region

Lewey Lake. 4155 NY 30, Lake Pleasant; 14 mi N of Speculator. E of region

Moose River Plains campsites. Off NY 28 from Inlet or NY 30 from Indian Lake. E of region

Otter Creek Horse Trail Assembly Area. 6498 Chases Lake Rd., Lewis County; primitive camping. W of region

Note
For NYS accessible destinations, including campsites,
see http://www.dec.ny.gov/outdoor/34038.html

Acknowledgments

Many people assisted in the completion of ADK's original Northern Region guidebook, on which many trail descriptions in this book are based. Peter O'Shea wrote the first edition, with the help of DEC Foresters John Kramer and James Papero and Forest Ranger Terry Perkins. He also edited the second edition. ADK Laurentian Chapter member Duncan Cutter also updated information for the second edition, and assisted with updates in this book as well, as did Gary Koch and Fred Wilhelm, surveyor. Jamie Savage helped with the Cranberry Lake 50 material. Many thanks, too, to Tony Goodwin, Sam Eddy, Dave Birchenough, Sherman Craig, and Brian McDonnell, who all helped with updates to trails in the northern reaches for this edition.

DEC personnel whose help was invaluable include John Gibbs, Supervising Forester, Region 6, Potsdam office; Peter D'Luhosch, Conservation Easement Coordinator, Region 6, Potsdam office; Joel Nowalk, Forest Ranger, Region 6, Croghan office; Joseph Rupp, St. Regis Canoe Area Forest Ranger, Region 5; Jamie Smith, Forest Ranger, Region 5, Chateaugay office; and Bob Zurek, Forest Ranger, Region 5, Little Tupper Lake.

When patience, perseverance, and support were needed, they were given by two editors, Neal S. Burdick and Lisa Crosby Metzger, who questioned both book and map, making sure distances added up and descriptions were correct and clear. Thanks also to Andrea Masters and staff at ADK headquarters along with the Publications Committee in the production of this book.

Others assisted in ADK's former West-Central Region guidebook, on which many of the trails in the southern area covered in this book are based. The first edition was by Robert J. Redington, the second and third by Arthur W. Haberl, and the fourth by Norm Landis. Many DEC personnel answered questions and verified information. Significant help was obtained from foresters Scott Healy (Herkimer) and Keith Rivers (Lowville) and Ranger John Scanlon (Stillwater Reservoir–area trails).

Last, but definitely not least, Bradly offers thanks to Laurie Pendergraft, his wife, and his boys, Kyle, Evan, and Jake Pendergraft. They all hiked with him, canoed with him, and dropped him off where and when necessary, but most importantly they gave him space and encouragement when writing. Norm expresses gratitude for those who accompanied him on research hikes and who were sometimes distracted by his talking to his (note-taking, tape-recording) self, thinking he was pointing out something to them.

—*Bradly A. Pendergraft and Norm Landis*

About the Editors

Norm Landis has been an ADK member for more than thirty years. He served as trips chair for ADK's Iroquois Chapter and as chapter chair for five years. He has participated in Adopt a Lean-to projects for the chapter in the Ha-De-Ron-Dah Wilderness and has done trail work there and elsewhere. He's a long-time Johns Brook Lodge volunteer.

A state-licensed outdoor guide, Landis is also DEC certified in Basic Wildlands Search and as a Basic Wildlands Search Crew Boss, and has assisted state forest rangers as a searcher and search crew boss.

Landis edited and updated ADK's *Adirondack Trails: West-Central Region* (fourth edition) and contributed to a book about the journalism program at Morrisville State (formerly SUNY Morrisville). He has had articles published in *Adirondack Life, Adirondac,* and *Adirondack Explorer.* His photos have appeared in the ADK calendar and in ADK's *Classic Adirondack Ski Tours.*

Landis was in the first class of journalism graduates at SUNY at Morrisville (associate degree) and has two bachelor's degrees from SUNY Institute of Technology at Utica/Rome, which has honored him as a Distinguished Alumnus. He is semi-retired, working part-time with thirty-seven years as a writer and editor at the *Daily Sentinel,* of Rome, New York, after countless articles and photos. Originally from Albion, New York, he started work in Oneida after graduating from Morrisville and took the job at the Rome paper nearly ten years later.

Bradly Pendergraft was born in the panhandle of Texas. Camping trips to New Mexico and Colorado were his first experiences with mountains. He moved to the Rocky Mountains (Gunnison, Colorado) and graduated fifth in his class at Gunnison High School. He graduated *cum laude* with a B.A. in geology and art from Western State College of Colorado in Gunnison in 1977. Pendergraft worked in Alaska for four years as a geologist, staking over 10,000 mining claims; helping to discover the  largest lead-zinc mine in the world; living 130 miles above the Arctic Circle for a year; flying mile-square grids on much of Seward Peninsula, the Brooks Range, and central Alaska; and surviving a helicopter crash into Kotzebue Bay.

Pendergraft moved to St. Lawrence County in 1979, where he built a stone house and raised Black Angus beef cattle and honeybees on a 183-acre farm. He resisted the siren call of the Adirondacks until the fall of 1980, when he took his first canoe trip through the Saranac Lakes. Canoeing soon became his passion in his exploration of what he calls "the civilized wilderness."

In 1988 Pendergraft returned to geology as an environmental consultant. Two years later he co-founded TerraTech Inc. for investigating and cleaning up petroleum spills. In 1997 he sold his share of the company and entered SUNY Potsdam's Master of Science in Teaching (MST) program to become an Earth science teacher. Pendergraft completed his M. Ed. in 1999, with distinction. He taught at Salmon River Central School in Fort Covington, New York, until 2015, when he retired. Pendergraft continues to work at SUNY Potsdam in the Geology Department. He resides two miles outside the Blue Line on the West Branch of the St. Regis River near Parishville, New York.

Join us!

30,000 members count on us, and so can you:
• We produce the most-trusted, comprehensive trail maps and books
• Our outdoor activities take you all around the world
• Our advocacy team concentrates on issues that affect the wild lands and waters important to our members and chapters throughout the state
• Our professional and volunteer crews construct and maintain trails
• Our wilderness lodges and information centers give you shelter and direction

Benefits of membership include:
• Fun outdoor recreation opportunities for all levels
• *Adirondac* magazine (bimonthly)
• Special rates for ADK education and skill-building programs, lodging, parking, publications, and logo merchandise
• Rewarding volunteer opportunities
• Supporting ADK's mission and thereby ensuring protection of the wild lands and waters of New York State

Lodges and campground
• Adirondak Loj, on the shores of Heart Lake, near Lake Placid, offers year-round accommodations in private and family rooms, a coed loft, and cabins. It is accessible by car, and parking is available.
• The Adirondak Loj Wilderness Campground, located on ADK's Heart Lake property, offers thirty-two campsites and sixteen Adirondack lean-tos.
• Johns Brook Lodge (JBL), located near Keene Valley, is a backcountry facility accessible only on foot and open on a seasonal basis. Facilities include coed bunkrooms or small family rooms. Cabins near JBL are available year-round.

Both lodges offer home-cooked meals and trail lunches. Member discounts are available at all lodges and the campground.

Visit us!
ADK centers in Lake George and on our Heart Lake property near Lake Placid offer ADK publications and other merchandise for sale, as well as backcountry and general Adirondack information, educational displays, outdoor equipment, and snacks.

ADK Publications

FOREST PRESERVE SERIES
1 Adirondack Mountain Club High Peaks Trails
2 Adirondack Mountain Club Eastern Trails
3 Adirondack Mountain Club Central Trails
4 Adirondack Mountain Club Western Trails
5 Adirondack Mountain Club Northville–Placid Trail
6 Adirondack Mountain Club Catskill Trails

OTHER TITLES
Adirondack Alpine Summits: An Ecological Field Guide
Adirondack Birding: 60 Great Places to Find Birds
Adirondack Paddling: 60 Great Flatwater Adventures
An Adirondack Sampler I: Day Hikes for All Seasons
Catskill Day Hikes for All Seasons
Forests and Trees of the Adirondack High Peaks Region
Kids on the Trail! Hiking with Children in the Adirondacks
No Place I'd Rather Be: Wit and Wisdom from Adirondack Lean-to Journals
Ski and Snowshoe Trails in the Adirondacks
The Adirondack Reader
The Catskill 67: A Hiker's Guide to the Catskill 100 Highest Peaks Under 3500'
Views from on High: Fire Tower Trails in the Adirondacks and Catskills
Winterwise: A Backpacker's Guide

MAPS
Trails of the Adirondack High Peaks topographic map
Trails Illustrated Map 736: Northville-Placid Trail
Trails Illustrated Map 742: Lake Placid/High Peaks
Trails Illustrated Map 743: Lake George/Great Sacandaga
Trails Illustrated Map 744: Northville/Raquette Lake
Trails Illustrated Map 745: Old Forge/Oswegatchie
Trails Illustrated Map 746: Saranac/Paul Smiths
Trails Illustrated Map 755: Catskill Park

ADIRONDACK MOUNTAIN CLUB CALENDAR
Price list available upon request, or see www.adk.org.

Contact Us

ADK Member Services Center (Exit 21 off I-87, the Northway)
814 Goggins Road
Lake George, NY 12845-4117
Website: www. adk.org   Information: 518-668-4447
Membership, donations, publications, and merchandise: 800-395-8080

ADK Heart Lake Program Center (at Adirondak Loj on Heart Lake)
PO Box 867
1002 Adirondack Loj Road
Lake Placid, NY 12946-0867
Educational programs and facility reservations: 518-523-3441

ADK Public Affairs Office
301 Hamilton Street
Albany, NY 12210-1738
Public Affairs: 518-449-3870

The Adirondack Mountain Club (ADK) is dedicated to the conservation, preservation, and responsible recreational use of the New York State Forest Preserve and other parks, wild lands, and waters vital to our members and chapters.

The Adirondack Mountain Club is a charitable organization, 501(c)(3). Contributions are tax deductible to the extent the law allows.

Index

Locations are indexed by proper name with Lake, Mount, or Mt. following.